THE CASE FOR ASTROLOGY

John Anthony West is a writer, scholar and Pythagorean, born in New York City in 1932. He is the author of *The Traveler's Key to Ancient Egypt* and consulting editor for the *Traveler's Key* series. His previous book, *Serpent in the Sky: High Wisdom of Ancient Egypt*, is an exhaustive study of the revolutionary Egyptological work of the French mathematician and Orientalist, the late R. A. Schwaller de Lubicz. Mr West has published a novel and many short stories; his plays have been produced on stage, television and radio, and he writes articles, essays and criticism for *The New York Times Book Review*, the *New Yorker*, Condé Nast's *Traveler* and other general-interest and specialized newspapers and magazines in America and abroad.

He lectures extensively on Egypt and personally leads several in-depth study tours to Egypt every year. At present, with the support of a number of eminent geologists and geophysicists, he is working on a theory proving that the Great Sphinx of Giza is many thousands of years older than egyptologists believe. Once established and recognized, this will force a drastic revision of ancient history and of all currently accepted ideas about the evolution of advanced human civilization on earth.

JOHN ANTHONY WEST

THE CASE FOR ASTROLOGY

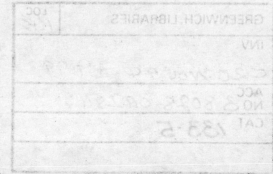
ARKANA

ARKANA

Published by the Penguin Group
Penguin Books Ltd, 27 Wrights Lane, London W8 5TZ, England
Penguin Books USA Inc., 375 Hudson Street, New York, New York 10014, USA
Penguin Books Australia Ltd, Ringwood, Victoria, Australia
Penguin Books Canada Ltd, 10 Alcorn Avenue, Toronto, Ontario, Canada M4V 3B2
Penguin Books (NZ) Ltd, 182–190 Wairau Road, Auckland 10, New Zealand

Penguin Books Ltd, Registered Offices: Harmondsworth, Middlesex, England

First published by Viking 1991
Published in Arkana Books 1992
10 9 8 7 6 5 4 3 2 1

Printed in England by Clays Ltd, St Ives plc

Contents

Corrupts Rome. Foolish Daughter Carries on: Islam and the Early Middle Ages. Astrology in the Renaissance. Copernicus, Galileo, Brahe, Kepler and Newton. Foolish Daughter: In Disgrace. The Eighteenth Century and the Triumph of Reason. Sleeping Beauty Awakes: Astrology in the Nineteenth Century. Enter Mme Blavatsky. World War I to World War II. Re-enter the Corner Soothsayer ... Hitler's Astrologer. Astrology Moves into the Age of Aquarius.

II. OBJECTIONS TO ASTROLOGY

III. THE EVIDENCE

Acknowledgements

I should like to express my gratitude to the following sources for permission to reprint copyrighted materials:

The New Scientist. 'The pull of the planets on the lives of men', by Nigel Henbest, 12 May 1988, and excerpts from the editorial, 'The spiv decade', 23/30 December 1989.

Fate magazine. Excerpts from sTARBABY by Dennis Rawlins originally appeared in *Fate* magazine, October 1981, St Paul, MN.

Time magazine. Excerpts from articles on astrology in issues dated 21 March 1969 and 16 May 1988, copyright 1969, 1988 Time Inc. Reprinted by permission.

Prometheus Books. Excerpts reprinted from *Objections to Astrology* by Lawrence E. Jerome and Bart J. Bok and from *The Gemini Syndrome* by R. B. Culver and P. A. Ianna, with permission of Prometheus Books, Buffalo, New York.

Dr Percy Seymour. Excerpts from *Astrology: The Evidence of Science*, Lennard Publishing, 1987, and his reply to Nigel Henbest's *New Scientist* review (private correspondence).

Martin Gardner for his review, 'Eysenck's Folly', in his column, 'Skeptical Eye', in *Discover* magazine, October 1982.

Introduction

The disclosure that astrology determined the timing of major American political moves during the Reagan era sparked public recognition of one of the more astounding movements of modern times: the renaissance of astrology. This has taken place over the course of a century, in the teeth of the massed opposition of science, education and the media. Since these institutions, together, dictate and guide public opinion in virtually every other arena of modern life, the resurgence of astrology, and its infiltration into the highest echelons of government and business may be seen as more than a sociological curiosity.

Opponents insist astrology is no more than outworn superstition, an early bungled attempt to come to grips with the mysterious physical universe. They claim astrology has been disproved by science, and that its appeal today is purely to human gullibility, the unwillingness of the unevolved to face 'the harsh facts of reality'.

But astrology most emphatically has *not* been disproved by science. On the contrary, there is a body of evidence, much of it apparently unchallengeable, that proves astrology has a scientific basis according to accepted modern ground rules. Nor is astrology superstition. Rather it is a key element in the corpus of ancient wisdom that once prevailed over the civilized world. It will become clear, over the course of this book, that ancient civilizations practiced astrology, not because they were taking the first tentative steps toward those truths that would culminate in the hydrogen bomb, worldwide pollution and striped toothpaste, but because they had gained access (in a manner that no doubt must remain mysterious) to much greater truths. This was their sacred (as opposed to our secular) science. It infused their lives and their civilizations with the order that is intrinsic to the universe, and the meaning that is specific to humanity within the grand cosmic scheme. Despite the obvious nonsense of astrology at its modern pop level, we believe its millennial appeal is to something profound and innate within us: a recognition of order, and a longing for meaning. Both are written into astrology. They are basic spiritual human needs our modern science cannot measure and therefore does not recognize, and cannot address. But to legitimize astrology within its modern context it is essential to distinguish between the astrological premise and the *practice* of astrology.

Premise vs. Practice

Astrology is based upon a simple, two-part premise.
1. CORRELATIONS EXIST BETWEEN CELESTIAL AND TERRESTRIAL EVENTS.
2. CORRESPONDENCES EXIST BETWEEN THE POSITION OF THE PLANETS AT BIRTH AND THE HUMAN PERSONALITY.

The evidence supporting both aspects of that premise is now incontrovertible. It is safe to say that if evidence of this caliber existed in support of any other 'borderline' field of science, it would have become academically respectable long ago. The unwillingness and/or inability of astrology's opponents (mainly scientists or people who look to science for authority) to acknowledge this evidence stands as an intriguing psychological and philosophical phenomenon in its own right, one we will be devoting some time to.

But the soundness of the astrological premise is one thing, and the validity of current (or ancient) astrological practice quite another. The latter does not necessarily follow from the former. This point must be made at the onset. Moreover, the practice of astrology is *not* a science in the accepted, modern, rationalist sense, nor can it be reduced to a modern science since it inescapably involves *interpretation* – usually of the horoscope. The practice of astrology is an art (involving personal subjective elements) but based upon a number of proven scientific foundations. Generally speaking, in defending the validity of astrology, its own proponents have not made clear the crucial distinction between astrology's scientifically demonstrable premises and its inescapably qualitative practice. The case for astrology is intelligible only when that distinction is maintained.

It was the marshaling and interpreting the evidence for astrology, rebutting objections to it, and analyzing the intense hostility astrology provokes among its critics that gave impetus to this book. But in the writing it became clear that the evidence alone could not be understood unless placed in its correct metaphysical and historical context.

The Question of Level

Astrology is a complex subject. It exists upon many levels simultaneously – from the silly to the sublime. Deliberately or otherwise, astrology's opponents refuse to acknowledge this question of 'level'. They insist upon regarding astrology in its popular dress as the only astrology there is or has ever been – which is like condemning all of drama as a meretricious art form on the basis of *Dallas*, or all of cinema on the basis of *Rambo*.

> How could this absurd doctrine arise, develop, spread and force itself upon *superior intellects* [italics ours] for century after century? . . . this hallucination . . . the most persistent that ever haunted the human brain . . .?
>
> Franz Cumont, *Astrology and Religion Among the Greeks and Romans*, p. 30

How indeed? A good and fair question. Unfortunately, Franz Cumont, the celebrated and erudite historian of ancient civilization who posed it early in this century, never tried seriously to answer it; nor have any of astrology's other critics since that time. Yet is is not all that difficult to answer. The question of 'level' must be addressed. In astrology there is a better and a worse, a higher and a lower; in science there is only a right and wrong, with degrees of rightness and wrongness in between.

Franz Cumont, and his contemporary spiritual bloodbrothers, could not or would not make the distinction between the daily horoscope in the newspaper and the grand metaphysical concept of the harmony of the spheres. But to Plato, Plotinus, St Thomas Aquinas, Johann Kepler, Goethe, Ralph Waldo Emerson and Carl Jung (to name just a few) that distinction was clear.

Now in modern rationalist circles, metaphysics is not taken seriously either.* Even so, the great minds of the past are generally conceded a foible or two without seriously undermining their stature. Modern believers are treated less generously. They are invariably portrayed as unevolved, irrational types, incapable of facing up to life's harsh realities, unaware of the immutable truths discovered by science, and therefore taking refuge in fantasy and the supernatural.

The Question of Experience

Certainly, in astrological circles there is no shortage of credulity. At the same time, surveys in Europe and in America reveal that serious, practicing astrologers have a higher-than-average level of education. A significant percentage are professionals in other fields. Many are not unaware of the existence and prerequisites (and shortcomings) of science. A few are scientists themselves. And both these last groups know that there is absolutely nothing in modern science that precludes the *possibility* of a valid astrology.

This, of course, is not evidence in itself. Nevertheless, it may to some extent counter the common charge that astrologers are

---

* Rationalism is itself an unacknowledged metaphysics, neither justified nor supported by the science that supposedly does both. We shall be returning to this subject periodically.

necessarily intellectually inferior souls, preying financially upon the gullible masses while themselves reading the *National Enquirer* or the *News of the World* (see pp. 142–7).

Moreover, most serious modern astrologers began life as skeptics. (This is most emphatically true of the author of this book.) 'A most unfailing *experience* (as far as can be expected in nature) of the excitement of sublunary natures by the conjunctions and aspects of the planets *has instructed and compelled my unwilling belief* [italics ours],' declared Johannes Kepler in *De Stella Nova*.

'A most unfailing *experience* . . . has instructed and compelled my unwilling belief.' So it was for Kepler and so it remains for the majority of practicing astrologers today. The metaphysics may be appealing; the scientific evidence these days may even be compelling; but as a general rule what makes astrological believers out of skeptics is experience; actually working with astrology. We cannot think of a single critic of astrology who has deigned to put the matter to the kind of personal test required.*

Objection! Your Honor . . .

But here the prosecution may well object: Since when does personal experience itself count as evidence? Especially as scientific evidence? And that objection has to be sustained.

It is possible that astrologers, the keen-minded and self-critical Kepler among them, have simply been deluding themselves all these thousands of years. Moreover, the prosecution may be correct from another, quite unintentional angle.

Who is to say that modern critics, putting astrology to the test, would share Kepler's experience? Give a dozen tone-deaf

---

* Culver and Ianna in *The Gemini Syndrome* have at least studied the subject in depth. While they avoid or misrepresent the physical evidence and ignore the metaphysical argument, their objections take place on a more mature level than those of Jerome, Bok and other critics. See our Part II: Objections to Astrology.

children violins and they will soon prove scientifically that music cannot be wrung from such a device. They may even prove to their own satisfaction that music does not exist at all. Still, given the millennial experience of astrologers and the eminence of so many of astrology's adherents, experience is a factor any impartial jury ought not to dismiss out of hand, especially when verdict time draws near.

It is this combination of metaphysical elegance, direct and indirect scientific evidence and belief bred of experience that allows astrologers to maintain their convictions with so few misgivings.

It is not so much that astrologers are gullible or dishonest; rather it is that astrology's critics (for profound psychological reasons to be discussed in Part IV, Heresy in the Church of Progress) are incapable of responding emotionally to the great metaphysical verities astrology is based upon, and that commended it to so many of the great minds of the past. It is this emotional incapacity that, on the one hand, incites such irrational hostility, and on the other, that forbids these critics from acknowledging the body of physical evidence – set out according to standards erected by themselves – that proves the point.

> First there is still some confusion between the science of astronomy on the one hand and the medieval hocus-pocus of astrology on the other ... Astronomy is the study of the universe; astrology, which purports to foretell human characteristics and destinies by observing the positions of the planets, is without any scientific foundation and may be aptly summed up by the word, 'rubbish' ...
>
> I cannot resist making a slight digression here in order to dispose of astrology, the so-called science according to which the positions of the planets affect the lives and characters of human beings. Suppose, for instance, the planet Mars is in the constellation of Scorpio ... Astrologers claim this will have profound effects upon the child (born under this configuration). Yet, what precisely is meant by saying that a planet is 'in' a constellation? Planets are very near to us in comparison with the stars ... Taxed with

arguments of this kind, astrologers usually retire baffled, muttering in their beards about Ancient Teachings and Esoteric Influences. No more need be said.

Patrick Moore, *Naked Eye Astronomy*
(Lutterworth, 1966), pp. 2, 17–18

This passage is typical of the level of criticism directed at astrology (see Part II, Objections to Astrology, for more examples). But contrary to Mr Moore's assertion, astrologers – bearded or otherwise – find his arguments supremely untaxing. They have not the slightest bit of trouble countering them. And, disagreeing further, they staunchly maintain that there is considerably more that needs to be said on the subject.

But before it is said, a few pages of explanation may be in order concerning the precursor to this book, its initial reception, and the decision to rewrite it completely, apart from a few historical sections, rather than merely revise and update.

Astrology: The Last Two Decades

The Case for Astrology first appeared in 1970. Not surprisingly, the astrological press welcomed it. Neutral reviewers were impressed by the marshaled evidence. But hostile mainstream critics slated the book for 'bias' – as though anything could be clearer than its title: *The Case for Astrology*. The London *Times Literary Supplement*, for example, assured 'open-minded readers' they would find the book contained nothing that might induce them to change their open minds. Yet not one dissenter challenged the evidence, or tried to provide alternative explanations for data we claimed supported astrology. Since much of this evidence, in particular the indirect evidence, came from rigorously scientific sources, such disdain did little to further the quest for objective truth.

* * *

Over the intervening years, attitudes have been gradually changing, at least in certain areas. Astrology has certainly *not* been incorporated into the educational system, as enthusiastic Aquarians were prophesying it would be not so long ago. It remains taboo in most scientific and academic circles.*

On the other hand, the opposition front is no longer wholly united. At least a few scientists, otherwise respected in their fields, have admitted to an int_rest in astrology, and acknowledged the validity of much of the evidence we shall be discussing. Several major universities have accepted serious studies of astrology as Ph.D. theses. Popular books such as Fritjof Capra's *The Tao of Physics*, Gary Zukav's *The Dancing Wu-Li Masters* and *The Implicate Order* by physicist, David Bohm, have begun to accustom the literate lay public to a cosmology that is on the one hand consonant with the latest developments in physics and on the other curiously reminiscent of ancient metaphysical doctrines – in which astrology always played a major role. A few highly regarded but ordinarily hard-nosed scientists have admitted there is nothing in modern science that rules out the possibility of a valid astrology. A tacit acceptance of astrology has also percolated down into social and business spheres – many businessmen will now openly acknowledge using astrological advice before making business decisions. This suggests they find the advice useful. Businessmen are notoriously pragmatic about such matters. An article in the Business Section of the *New York Times* discussed the connection between business and the 'paranormal' without a hint of the customary derision.†

The attributes of the astrological archetypes have become common knowledge and have filtered into everyday language to such an extent that psychology tests designed to test the validity of sun-sign archetypes were abandoned once it was found that apparently positive results were due to people knowing their

---

* See R. B. Culver and P. A. Ianna, *The Gemini Syndrome: Star Wars of the Oldest Kind* and Lawrence Jerome and Bart J. Bok, *Objections to Astrology*. Both these works will be discussed in detail in Part II.

† 'What's New in Parapsychology', Joanne Kaufman, *New York Times*, 3 November 1983.

archetype and identifying with it. It appears to be nearly impossible to get together a group of adults today who do *not* know their sun-sign archetypes. And of course, the *coup de grâce* was the disclosure that astrologers were being consulted by the White House, that astrology had determined the timing of major American political moves during the Reagan era (and coincidentally that astrology was even flourishing in materialistic Russia). Coverage of the story, though largely superficial and predictable, was much less contemptuous than it would have been twenty years earlier. The relationship between Establishment science and the media is not quite what it used to be, a significant and promising development.

Astrology's opponents have been spectacularly powerless to impede or contain its growing popularity.*

In 1976, 186 scientists, 19 of them Nobel Prize-winners, endorsed a manifesto called 'Objections to Astrology'. The signers recommended a united front and a concerted effort to stamp out the insidious, ancient superstition once and for all; 'otherwise reputable' publishers were exhorted to stop publishing books by 'astrological charlatans'.

Not only was this ineffective, but to astrologers, and to everyone else with a sense of history, it could mean but one thing: a growing fear of heresy. A hundred years ago, such a gesture would have been unthinkable. Astrology was scarcely worth attacking. It was simply dismissed with a grand wave of the heavy Victorian hand. 'Astrology is already dead. It has been dead so long that it no longer stinks,' declared one Dr Charles Arthur Mercier in 1913.

Meanwhile, as astrology was working its way into the public consciousness, the data upon which our original case was built

---

* 'Even in the midst of the greatest resurgence astrology has ever known since the scientific revolution, the response of science to the astrological phoenix has, to date, been largely disjointed and ineffective. Only two book-length works and a few scattered chapters in elementary astronomical texts currently offer any alternative to the plethora of astrological publications which sing astrology's praises.'

Culver and Ianna, *The Gemini Syndrome*, p. v.

was steadily accumulating, albeit with minor setbacks and complications.

Our 'Exhibit A' twenty years ago was the pioneer statistical work of French statistician/psychologist, Michel Gauquelin. In massive statistical surveys Gauquelin was able to demonstrate powerful correlations between positions of planets at birth and specific personality types, and also planetary hereditary links between parents and children. Over the past two decades, the Gauquelin work has been enlarged, refined and violently attacked by scientists determined to debunk it. They have been unable to find anything amiss beyond a few minute procedural discrepancies. It is the Gauquelin work that has convinced a number of scientists, former skeptics all, that the astrological premise at least (the correspondence between positions of planets at birth and the human personality) could no longer be ignored or dismissed by science. Our case for astrology could be argued effectively on the basis of the Gauquelin work alone were that necessary.

Meanwhile, to the astrologers' chagrin and the scientists' delight, experiments designed to test astrology in action, the *practice* of astrology, have fared less well. Some tests, cited as positive evidence in our first edition, have not proven infallibly repeatable; others could be open to alternative explanations. Many new tests have been negative. But even in this delicate area, there is positive evidence.

The combination of new evidence, important new historical scholarship and new concerted attacks by astrology's opponents necessitated this completely rewritten version of our original book.*

*   *   *

* The original edition of *The Case for Astrology* was written in collaboration with my colleague, the Dutch novelist, Jan Gerhard Toonder. Due to other commitments, Toonder was unable to share the work involved in this total rewrite. Though it is my name alone that appears on the jacket, Toonder contributed invaluable advice throughout the long writing and editing process and I have therefore retained the first person plural for our editorial voice.

Will the Prosecution Please Identify Itself?

But given the response to that original, it also seems worth repeating and re-emphasizing: this is *The Case for Astrology*. We are advocates. Our acknowledged aim is to present positive evidence. At the same time, we find ourselves in a peculiar position *vis-à-vis* our opponents – who decline to follow the rules of their own devising.

To begin with, they refuse to own up to their identity as Prosecution. Instead they present themselves as a body of objective, impartial scientists and scholars charged with weighing both sides of the argument – in other words, the Judge. But in their well publicized attacks upon astrology the volume of positive scientific evidence is systematically ignored, downplayed or worse (no one watching television or reading the papers following the Reagan brouhaha would suspect positive evidence existed). Cogent philosophical and metaphysical arguments are dismissed out of hand or distorted. No attempt is made to distinguish between pop and serious astrology. The crucial distinction is never made between the present inability of astrologers to scientifically validate their astrological *practice* and the commanding scientific evidence validating the astrological *premise*. Finally, playing Judge, the prosecution resorts to outdated, exploded science to support its position; science that would be laughed out of any late-twentieth-century scientific conference. The overall result is that it is impossible for the jury to clearly understand what is at stake.

Accordingly, we have unscrambled the Prosecution's argument and presented it along with our defense, whenever possible quoting sources directly, and most importantly, in context. We specifically encourage the jury to acquaint themselves with the opposition literature, particularly in those instances (which we point out) when for reasons of space we are obliged to simplify a complex argument or position. The jury is assured there is no major objection to the astrological premise or practice that goes unanswered or unaddressed.

But to understand astrology's potential importance as well as

its demonstrable validity, it is first essential to set the historical/
metaphysical record straight. To this end we must begin at the
beginning, or as close to the beginning as scholarship and
informed speculation will allow.

I.

ORIGINS

A. Dreams the Chaldeans Never Dreamed

The birth and development of astrology took place in the distant past under unknown conditions. The earliest evidence for its existence reveals it at an already developed stage. There are absolutely no records or observations made by astrology's founders or its early practitioners disclosing the premises their astrology was based upon.

Therefore, modern accounts that pretend to authority on the subject – and most do – are speculative in their entirety. Here is a representative entry – from *Chambers Encyclopedia*, 1966.

> Astrology is one of the oldest and most widespread of superstitions, prevailing in very early times among the Egyptians and Etruscans and especially among the Babylonians through whom it came to Greece in the fourth century BC, spreading to Rome a few centuries later. The rise of astrology may be regarded as produced by man's impatient curiosity and desire for harmony. [1]*
>
> Regularly operating laws were discerned in the more marked changes of material nature, among which the motions and influences of the heavenly bodies were conspicuous. The movements of the sun ruled and vivified the earth. The rains, the storms and the floods also came from the heavens. It was natural

---

* NB, numbers in parentheses here, and in passages quoted from other sources throughout this book, identify points we will be referring back to in the discussion that follows.

then, to suppose that the overruling powers which ordered the apparent chances of human life resided in the heavens and that their decrees might be read there, the motions of the heavenly bodies proving on trial to be predictable. The sun, the moon and the planets were regarded as divine powers and given the names of gods and goddesses. If one could read and interpret aright the activity of these powers, it would be known what the gods were aiming to bring about. So along with the growth of a system of interpretation based largely upon the relative positions of the planetary bodies and, later, the fixed stars, there developed the study of the position and movement of these bodies. Thus there grew up a strange mixture of science and fantastic imagery . . .

The fundamental flaw in the whole system of astrology is the arbitrary character of the presumptions made. In part they were derived from recollections or written records of past happenings accompanying certain phenomena, with the assumption that the same phenomena occurring again would be associated with a similar event; in part they depended upon the association of ideas, a phenomena being regarded as favourable or unfavourable according to whether it had been associated with something good, such as a victory over the enemy, or something bad, such as a famine or a flood; in part they were mythical based on the supposed transference of the character of a deity or planet. The spell with which astrology bound men's minds was due to its apparently scientific basis . . . [2]

This passage summarizes the prevailing Establishment account of astrology's origins.

Despite its factual façade and tone of assurance, it contains but two facts: 1) astrology was widespread over the whole of the ancient world and 2) astrology spread from Babylon to Greece to Rome.

Every other assertion is pure speculation. In every instance, alternative, more convincing speculations can be put forward. This is a matter of some importance. In the accepted view, astrology appears as a sort of running glitch in the evolution of human consciousness (remember Cumont? 'this absurd doctrine ... this hallucination ... the most persistent that ever haunted the human brain'). But if this were the case it would mean of course that Plato, Plotinus and their spiritual brothers throughout history were taken in by a fraud. We are convinced they were not. So let us analyze this passage in some detail.

'Man's impatient curiosity' (1) is put forward as one of the motivating factors for early astrology. But in the study of early (pre-Greek) civilization, there is not a shred of evidence for anything resembling 'impatient curiosity'.

On the contrary, careful examination of Babylon, Egypt, Sumeria and the Orient reveals civilizations conspicuously devoid of curiosity. What we actually see are mighty, long-lived empires devoted to the serene perpetuation of the status quo. (Actually, this is the tip of the great and mysterious iceberg that is ancient history. Most of the major civilizations seem to appear out of the blue; with their languages, religions, architectural, artistic and scientific knowledge fully developed, and, as a general rule, at their height, in the very beginning. This applies especially to Egypt where the physical evidence is so massively to hand, but it may legitimately be extended to the others as well.)

There is compelling evidence proving that astrology played a part in all of these civilizations from the onset. But 'man's impatient curiosity' will not suffice to explain its origins, nor will the equally unsubstantiated 'desire for harmony'.

The ziggurats, pyramids and temples of the ancient world reveal a preoccupation with harmony, geometry and proportion that borders on the obsessional. But there is nothing tentative about any of this. We do not, in a single instance, see early man fumbling through the dark attempting to satisfy some dark unconscious urge for order ... and cooking up astrology along the way.

We see exactly the opposite: an unarguable total command of the principles governing harmony, made manifest in art and architecture. In other words, nowhere is there evidence of experiment; everywhere there is overwhelming evidence of knowledge of a highly developed order. And astrology, as we shall shortly prove, was part of that knowledge.

Unfortunately, attempting to account for astrology's origins,

astrologers often fall into the same trap as their opponents.
'Astrology unquestionably arose, in the beginning, as a wholly
empirical science,' declared Marc Edmund Jones, a 'renowned
American astrologer, in *Astrology: How and Why It Works*
(Shambhala, 1969, p. 37). Astronomers, Culver and Ianna
(*Gemini Syndrome*, p. 12), rightly reject this unfounded assertion:
'It would be quite reassuring if it were so, but this viewpoint has
little support', they comment.

But they then go on to put forward a viewpoint that has even
less support: 'In the beginning, astrology was neither "wholly
empirical" nor "science"; it arose from a blend of imagination,
fear, and religious superstition.'

The truth is that Culver and Ianna do not know how astrology
arose, and neither does anyone else. But as scientists, by their
own admission, interested in *only* that which can be supported by
physical evidence, unfounded allegations such as these are particularly suspect, and cast doubt upon other conclusions these
authors put forward with equal conviction and a comparable
lack of evidence.*

The assertion that astrology arose out of a 'blend of fear,
imagination and religious superstition' is a hypothesis perfectly
immune to testing. We do not know how early man thought,
and we have no real scientific way of knowing. Modern scholars,
for a variety of reasons (see Part IV: Heresy in the Church of
Progress) have reconstructed the thought-processes of early
man to suit their preconceptions, and put forward these pure
fabrications as facts.

---

* 'After all, it is very difficult at times to know what the facts are and to make the
right decision. It is a very complicated world out there – lots of shades of grey,
vested interests, incomplete information, calculated risks. You have to be very, very
careful. Right? Right . . .

Though this may be an unhappy situation, it is not a hopeless one. For we believe
there is very definitely a *best* way to go about finding out what is most likely to be
right . . . it is the approach to knowledge gathering that has been called the *scientific
method* or the *method of hypothesis testing*.'

Gemini Syndrome, p. 28

But the *only* fact we have in this instance is that the ancients regarded the sun, moon, planets and fixed stars as gods (or, to be more accurate, as Divine Principles, which puts the matter in rather a different light). Given the quality and magnitude of the art and architecture of these vanished civilizations (in which astrology always played a demonstrably important role), it is an impertinence – in the face of a conspicuous absence of factual data – to attribute the development of any single aspect of their knowledge to 'impatient curiosity', 'the desire for harmony' or 'a blend of imagination, fear, and religious superstition'. It is also fraudulent and shoddy scholarship . . . You do not have to be a good Christian or even religious to recognize the validity of: 'By their fruits ye shall know them'.

If the standard account of astrology's origins will not stand, neither will the standard account of its persistence. According to the author of the *Chambers Encyclopedia* entry, astrology cast its spell over the long centuries due to its 'apparently scientific basis' (2).

But the allure of science is recent, confined to the West, and even there limited. Science magazines designed to attract the general public are notoriously short-lived and unsuccessful. Throughout history, astrology has generally been allied to religion, not science. The astrologers of Babylon were always priests. That link persists today. There are few modern astrologers who call themselves atheists.

And throughout history, it has been religion, not science, that cast its spell over men's hearts and minds. There is nothing very scientific (in the modern sense) about religion. So if astrology cast its spell by 'appearing scientific', what accounts for the spell cast by religion? The author, who speaks for the entire scholarly and scientific community in this case, has not begun to think the matter through. To account for the hold astrology has exercised upon men's minds, we shall have to look elsewhere. This is not the simple process it appears (in astrology nothing is simple!). It involves knowing both how and where to look. And this in turn involves recognizing the astonishing extent to which our looking has been conditioned by our education.*

At the risk of over-proving certain of the points made above, let us examine one further opinion on the subject.

> When I try to see the Universe as a Babylonian saw it around 3000 BC, I must grope my way back to my own childhood. At the age of four I had what I felt to be a satisfactory understanding of God and the world. I remember an occasion when my father pointed his finger at the white ceiling, which was decorated with a frieze of dancing figures, and explained that God was up there, watching me. I immediately became convinced that the dancers were God ... Much in the same manner, I like to imagine, (1) did the luminous figures on the dark ceiling of the world appear as living divinities to Babylonians and Egyptians ...
>
> Some six thousand years ago, when the human mind was still half asleep, Chaldean priests were standing on watch towers, scanning the stars ...
>
> Arthur Koestler, *The Sleepwalkers*, pp. 19–20

This passage has one merit the Culver and Ianna and *Chambers Encyclopedia* entries lacked: it is honest. It does not presume to authority on a subject that is by definition speculative. (1) Koestler 'likes to imagine' this is how it began.

But perhaps the most interesting aspect of this passage is its source. Arthur Koestler was a bold, independent thinker. Much

---

* See L. Johnson Abercrombie, *The Anatomy of Judgement*. The author, a psychologist, shows how science students, learning to read X-ray plates, were incapable of distinguishing between what was actually shown and what they believed was shown. Interestingly, the initial reactions of the students, confronted by proof of the extent to which preconception coloured their judgement, were surprise and anger. Only after long training were they able to achieve a degree of objectivity. And this, remember, concerned the ability to read X-ray plates, which must rank as one of humanity's least emotionally fraught activities. Since scientists and academics normally go through no more specific objectivity training than astrologers or anyone else, the level of objectivity they achieve is no greater, and probably less – for it is precisely this quality they imagine they possess by virtue of being scientists.

of his life was spent challenging party lines across a number of disciplines. He was capable of defending the reality of extra-sensory perception when, in his view, the evidence demanded defense; and he was no less capable of challenging that most pervasive of twentieth-century superstitions, the Darwinian (now Neo-Darwinian) theory of evolution when the inadequacy of the evidence and the meretriciousness of the argument demanded opposition.

But in the quoted passage, even the normally wary Koestler has been caught off guard. He has swallowed the anthropological and historical party line. And he therefore tries to draw parallels between his own four-year-old consciousness and the thought-processes of Chaldean priests. He has forgotten that the watchtowers built by these dreaming Chaldeans were hundreds of feet long, hundreds of feet wide and a hundred feet high, lined with glazed brick, their topmost chambers richly finished in mosaics of gold and precious stones. Meanwhile, over in Egypt, the drowsy Pharaohs had already built the greatest of their pyramids and temples, structures of such magnitude, involving such prodigious architectural and logistic problems that even wide-awake modern man cannot figure out how it was done.

Something is wrong.

If astrology is superstition produced by man's impatient curiosity, what happened to the same impatient curiosity after the development of astrology? Why was it inadequate to the task of unmasking the error for some six thousand years? Can men patient and tenacious enough to calculate the motions of the planets have been so dim-witted as to neglect to put to a similar trial the predictions based upon those motions? And how did the motion of the sun, moon and planets produce astrology in the first place?

In view of the astrology that has actually come down to us, it is worth trying to re-create astrology as it might be put together by dreaming Chaldeans on watchtowers – impatiently curious as they were, longing for harmony, but at the same time fearful, imaginative, and superstitious.

The dreaming Chaldeans would be bound to notice the rising and setting of the sun; the fact that the sun gives light and warmth, and that its strength appears to regulate the seasons. Since nature herself obeys the sun, it would be a logical step for our protoastrologer to attempt to calculate the influence of the sun in advance; and we should expect this influence to bear a direct relationship to the actual season of the year. We might also expect to find special provision made for cloudy days, since, obviously, the influence of the sun cannot be operating at full force under such conditions.

The second most important planet is the moon. Our Chaldean would not fail to be impressed by its fickle changes of phase. A proto male chauvinist, he might well observe (or imagine he observed) that his own wife shared in this inconstancy of behavior and, by analogy, conclude that the moon was feminine.

He would, if he could see the sea from the top of his watchtower, notice that the tides were in some way controlled by the moon. He would not fail to observe that, despite the swift changes of mood, if observed long enough, the moon, like his wife, was predictable. And he would attempt to add observations made on the moon to those he was making simultaneously on the sun.

Though infinitesimal and one-dimensional compared to the sun and moon, the planets are the next most striking objects in the sky. They move in very erratic courses indeed. So much so that the ancients called them 'goats' or 'wanderers'. The planets exert no visible or detectable influence upon the events of the earth. Nevertheless, having deified the sun and moon, it might perhaps seem right to our Chaldean to apply the same logic to the planets. And while it is difficult to see why there should be any agreement between any two Chaldeans over the characters of these deities, to say nothing of agreement from nation to nation throughout the world, still let us say that at some point definite characters would be ascribed to the planets, and their alleged influence incorporated into the canon.

Meanwhile, efforts would be made to systematize the knowledge gained. Knowledge of the motions of the sun and moon would serve the immediate, practical purposes of making calendars, arranging planting schedules and so on; while observations of the planets, serving no immediate practical purpose, and far more complicated a procedure than observing the sun and moon, would in the end serve to provide employment for an increasing and greedy priesthood, bent upon hoodwinking the public.

Having nothing else to do, the Chaldeans would also fancy they saw strange beasts – bulls, crabs, lions, centaurs – in the patterns of the fixed stars. And when the sun, moon or any of the 'goats' happened to be in that portion of the sky presided over by one or the other of these star-figures, they might like to think that its influence was modified by the nature of the particular constellation.

Apart from all this, we might expect our Chaldeans to be duly impressed by abnormal phenomena of all kinds: earthquakes, floods, comets, eclipses; perhaps even striking events on a purely human scale: famines, wars, pestilences and so on, which would be incorporated into an increasingly unwieldy and top-heavy doctrine.

But it is self-evident there would be no way to impose order upon such an *ad hoc* accumulation of associations, analogies and omens. Yet astrology, whatever else it may be, is *ordered*. In no way does it resemble this hypothetical astrology – though we have cooked it up by faithfully following the official recipe. It follows then that the origins of astrology lie elsewhere, a subject we shall be returning to. Here, let us look briefly at the actual astrology that has come down to us.

In one sense, this astrology is much more illogical than the one developed above. For instance, what kind of mind could it have been that would maintain that a child born 18 March under Pisces would be 'watery', mystical, reclusive, artistic, while the child born a week later, under Aries, would be hotheaded, 'fiery', rambunctious, militant? Why should the Cancerian, born 18 July, come under the influence of the moon and tend to poetry and introspection, while the Leonian, born a week later, comes under the influence of the sun, and takes after his Leonine prototype?

Either the ancients were even sillier and sleepier than modern scholars believe, or there was some method to their madness which the same scholars are unwilling or unable to countenance.

The Principles of the Zodiac and Astrological Technique

Let us look at this actual astrological picture of the universe. In its purest, symbolic sense, far removed from the astrology of the market-place, the astrological doctrine may be seen as an expression or affirmation of the coherence of the universe, and as a guide to the understanding of its laws.

Apart from the fact that it obviously never existed, the astrology accumulated from the observations of dreaming Chaldeans was ugly – though logical. The real astrology is illogical, but elegant; the representation or choreography of a cosmic dance.

The Sun Sign

The zodiac, or circle of the heavens (Fig. 1), is divided into twelve equal sectors.* These are the signs – Aries, Taurus, Gemini, Cancer, etc. – with which everyone is familiar.

These sectors are supposed to represent, or to embody, cosmic functions, and the animal or character applied to the

---

* At different times, and in different places, zodiacs have been divided into eight, sixteen or twenty sectors. The twelve-sector zodiac has long prevailed in the West. These differences do not necessarily mean that one system is right and the others wrong, or that all are wrong since all are different (a common stance taken by critics). The validity of the differing systems may depend upon the *meanings* assigned to the divisions. But there can be no doubt that the different zodiacs present problems not easily explained away.

Planets:

Sun ——— ☉
Moon ——— ☽
Mercury — ☿
Venus —— ♀
Mars ——— ♂
Jupiter —— ♃
Saturn —— ♄
Uranus —— ♅
Neptune — ♆
Pluto ——— ♇

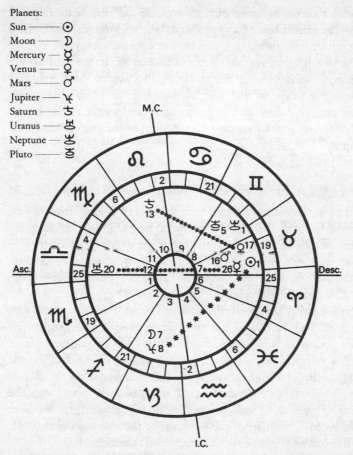

Figure 1. Horoscope for child born 20 April 1889, 6.22 p.m., Braunau (Austria). The individual to whom this horoscope belongs was born with the sun in 1° Taurus. His Ascendant (marked Asc.) is in 25° Libra, however. An astrologer interpreting this horoscope would expect its owner to be psychologically 'Taurean'. ('Taurus is a sign of great fixity of purpose and willpower. As a Taurean you are apt to decide early in life what you want. You may be a slow starter, but you have determination and persistence, and once you have set your goal there is almost nothing that can stop you.' Caroll Righter, in *The Astrological Guide to Marriage and Family Relations*.) In this case, the generalization seems particularly apt – the horoscope is Hitler's. Other Taureans may decline to conform to the standard in quite so striking a fashion.

particular sector is more of a mnemonic aid than a description of the characteristics of a given sign; it is a kind of shorthand to what would otherwise be a cumbersome terminology.

The earth revolves about the sun but it is the sun which appears to move about the circle of the zodiac, and it is this apparent position of the sun at the time of birth that determines the so-called sun sign in the horoscope. This is the familiar 'Are you a Gemini? I'm Aquarius' of cocktail conversations.

The Rising Sign, Houses and Angles

Meanwhile, the earth turns on its axis every twenty-four hours. It therefore goes through the same circle of 'influence' in a day as the sun does in a year, making logical the division of the zodiac into a corresponding further twelve. These divisions are the 'houses' of astrology; and this further but crucial complication rarely enters into cocktail conversations.

Thus a child may be born in April, with the sun in the first degree of Taurus, but at his moment of birth the degree of the zodiac rising at the eastern horizon may be 25 degrees Libra. Libra is then the 'Rising sign', and the degree rising is called the 'Ascendant'. The highest point the sun will reach on the day of birth – which will depend upon the place of birth and the season of the year – will determine the Midheaven, or Medium Coeli, or MC. And from the position of the Ascendant and MC the division of the 'houses' is ascertained (see Fig. 1).

The point opposite the Ascendant is called the Descendant. The point opposite the Midheaven is called the Nadir. These four apparently arbitrary points are the 'angles' which have had imputed to them astrological importance. In a general way it may be said that the position of sun, moon and planets in the sun signs determines the 'character' of the individual while the position of sun, moon and planets in relationship to the angles and in the houses determines 'destiny', circumstances and relationships; the uses to which he or she will put the given character.

Precession of the Equinoxes and the Astrological Ages

The day of birth and moment of birth, providing sun sign and Rising sign respectively, are the two most decisive factors of the individual horoscope. But there is one greater cycle against which all horoscopes are played out, which determines the character or 'personality' of entire civilizations. This is the so-called Platonic or Great Year, a cycle of approximately 25,920 years.

Due to the nutation or wobble of the earth about its own axis, the sun at the vernal (spring) equinox shifts in relation to the backdrop of constellations, gradually moving backwards, or precessing through the signs. It is this phenomenon (for which there is to date no convincing astronomical explanation) that gives rise to the astrological 'ages', each of which lasts approximately 2,160 years.

The Christian era commenced at the time of the ingress into Pisces, the Fishes, and the secret symbol of early Christians was a fish. We will shortly be entering the much heralded Age of Aquarius (there are several different methods for calculating the exact moment of change-over and no agreement among astrologers, or astronomers, which is decisive). To astronomers, of course, the phenomenon of the precession is devoid of significance. But to astrologers, the intrinsic nature of a sign puts its stamp upon the entire two thousand years of its reign. Applying the traditional attributes of the signs to the major civilizations flourishing under them makes for an intriguing historical exercise. We will be discussing matters related to the precession in some detail later on.

The Planets

The planets, according to astrology, differ in nature; they are held to represent or symbolize specific cosmic functions. Individual planets are supposed to 'rule' over the signs corresponding to their functions, which in turn correspond roughly to their distances from the sun. The table below gives, in much abbreviated form, the astrological nature of the planets and the signs they rule (see Fig. 2).

Planet	Rules	Principles symbolized
Saturn	Aquarius/Capricorn	Contraction/Crystallization
Jupiter	Pisces/Sagittarius	Expansiveness/Prodigality
Mars	Aries/Scorpio	Passion/Energy/Vitality
Venus	Taurus/Libra	Harmony/Artistry/Sympathy
Mercury	Gemini/Virgo	Intellect/Mobility
Moon	Cancer	Receptivity/the Subconscious
Sun	Leo	Creativity/Consciousness

The 'new' planets, Uranus, Neptune and Pluto present an obvious challenge to the ancient allocation of planets to signs. We shall be discussing this in due course (pp. 188–91).

The Aspects

In interpreting a horoscope, the astrologer must take all these factors into account. The planets in the signs allegedly give the key to character. Thus, a child born with Mars in Taurus will be, because of this, significantly and predictably stamped. Similarly, his character will manifest itself differently – claim astrologers – if Mars is found in the seventh house than it would if he had been born an hour later and Mars had been instead in the sixth house.

But above and beyond these complexities, both character and its manifestation are modified by the relationships formed by the planets to each other. When planets stand in certain specific angles to each other, which correspond to the laws of harmony, they are held to be in 'aspect'.

Thus when two planets are separated by a distance of 180 degrees they are said to be in 'opposition', when separated by a distance of 90 degrees they are in 'square' aspect, by 120 degrees they are in 'trine', etc.; and these aspects are held to be different in nature, some tending to be 'harmonious', others 'disharmonious'. The principal aspects are opposite:

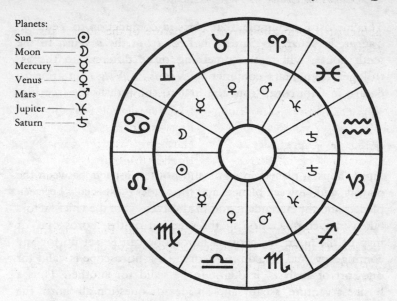

Planets:

Sun ——— ☉
Moon ——— ☽
Mercury ——— ☿
Venus ——— ♀
Mars ——— ♂
Jupiter ——— ♃
Saturn ——— ♄

Figure 2. The signs of the zodiac, and the planets that are held to 'rule' them. This drawing illustrates the traditional rulerships before the discovery of the new planets. These rulerships are not arbitrary but are made upon the basis of complex numerological considerations. Modern astrologers wonder whether or not the new planets should be incorporated, and if this can be done without destroying the rich, inter-related symmetry of the traditional scheme. It is thought possible that Uranus is co-ruler of Aquarius, and Neptune co-ruler of Pisces.

Angle	Name of Aspect	Nature
0	Conjunction	Neutral, depending upon other relevant factors
60	Sextile	Harmonious
90	Square	Disharmonious
120	Trine	Harmonious
180	Opposition	Disharmonious

This means, for example, that Mars in conjunction to Venus in Taurus, in square to Saturn in Leo, from the seventh to the tenth house, will mean something quite different to the astrologer from Mars conjunction Venus in Virgo, in trine to Saturn in Capricorn, from the first to the fifth house (see Fig. 3).

Types of Astrology

Signs, houses, planets in signs and houses, aspects between the planets, and between planets and the angles – especially between planets and the Ascendant and Midheaven – are the chief factors taken into consideration in the erection of the 'horoscope' or map of the hour. In theory a horoscope can be set up for any contingency, and – again in theory – if a horoscope is valid for one sort of analysis, it ought to be valid for another. Thus a business venture, a baby and an idea or question all 'born' the same instant share an identical horoscope.

In theory, the same cosmic 'influences' or correspondences attend their birth. Astrologers believe – with widely divergent degrees of confidence – that the 'character' of a business, a baby and an idea can be determined upon the basis of the horoscope; and – with still more widely varying degrees of confidence – that the future of the business, baby or idea can be determined by studying the positions on the root or 'radix' horoscope. To determine propitious times for setting up an enterprise, or putting an idea into manifestation, or signing a treaty, the radix horoscopes of the idea or business themselves (if they already exist) would be compared to the radix horoscopes of the people involved. These in turn would be examined in the light of the 'progressed' horoscope, which shows the positions of planets at the given moment. When the Reagans' astrologer was giving 'good' and 'bad' times for making speeches and signing treaties, these would have been some of her methods.

Though the method employed for the casting and interpretation of horoscopes is much the same no matter what the nature of the subject under consideration, astrologers make a distinction

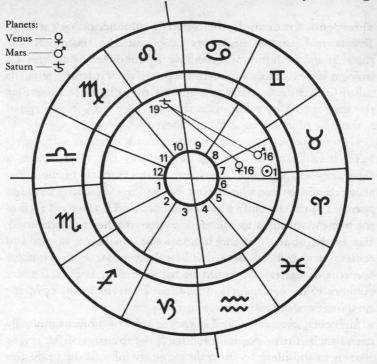

Planets:
Venus —— ♀
Mars —— ♂
Saturn —— ♄

Figure 3. Aspects. Venus and Mars in a double 'square' (90° distance) to Saturn. Venus is the 'ruler' of Hitler's horoscope both by sign and by house, since both Taurus, Hitler's 'sun sign' and Libra, Hitler's Ascendant, are held to be 'ruled' by Venus. The power of Venus is even further enhanced by its position in the seventh house, held by analogy to have affinities with the seventh sign – which is Libra.

Here Venus could scarcely be more seriously 'afflicted' than it is. The conjunction to Mars, by itself capable of blending 'the charm of Venus with the energy of Mars', is turned both sour and violent by their mutual square to Saturn. The Venus–Saturn square is held to bring out the worst and most selfish aspects of any given nature, while the Mars–Saturn square is traditionally conceded to generate the most violent qualities of which human nature is capable. Needless to say, not all people born with such a configuration turn out to be Hitler, but an astrologer would expect something 'Hitlerian' from anyone with such a Venus–Mars–Saturn configuration.

in nomenclature between the different types. Astrology used to analyze and predict the future of businesses, states, nations, races, political parties, etc., is called Mundane Astrology; astrology used to analyze and predict the future of individuals is called Genethliacal Astrology; and astrology used to determine the answer to a question upon the basis of a horoscope erected at the time of its asking is called Horary Astrology.

Generally speaking, the more cautious modern astrologers have limited faith in astrological prophecy but rather more in the ability to determine 'character' upon the basis of the horoscope. Since the popular interest in astrology is, and always has been, its putative ability to prophesy, we find a situation such as the present in which astrology is widely and flagrantly misused. But leaving open for the moment the problems of use and misuse, it should be clear that astrology is far more complex than the casual reader would be led to expect from star-gazer columns in the newspapers, or, indeed, from the media coverage on those occasions when astrology becomes news.

However, complexity and nonsense are by no means mutually exclusive. If the principles underlying the division of the zodiac into signs and houses within the signs are false; if the principles that dictate the ascription of meaning to the planets and to the relationships formed between them are purely arbitrary and based upon fancy, complexity becomes no more than an intellectual exercise. So let us look at those principles.

The Principles Underlying the Zodiac

The division of the zodiac into twelve sectors in Western astrology (or into eight, sixteen, or twenty sectors in other forms of astrology) is based fundamentally upon the belief that the universe is coherent and that numbers are not mere inventions of man allowing him to make purely quantitative distinctions. Rather they are the symbolic keys to *qualitative* laws that govern the coherent universe. Esoteric traditions are based upon the premise of multiplicity within unity. The expression of this doctrine has always involved the systematic and simul-

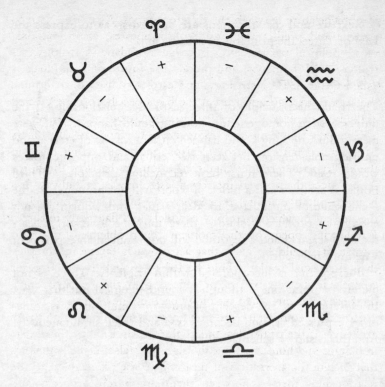

Figure 4. The signs of the zodiac, divided into polarities.

taneous use of numbers and symbols. Astrology is an ancient and particularly ingenious method of combining them.

The Law of Two

If we look at the way the zodiac is divided, we see that the signs are arranged in such a way as to express first the Law of Two, the law of duality, or of polarity; familiar to us as male–female, positive–negative or active–passive. We find that Aries is positive, Taurus is negative, Gemini positive, Cancer negative, Leo positive, and so on around the zodiac (see Fig. 4).

Next we find that the signs are divided so as to express the Law of Three, the principle of relationship.

The Law of Three

The triad, the principle of three, expresses relationship. If the universe were homogeneous, nothing could happen. If it were merely dual, nothing could happen either. A state of eternal and unbridgeable tension between two equal and opposite forces would result. There must be a reconciling principle, a Third Force. A sculptor and a block of wood will not produce a statue – the sculptor must have an idea; a man and woman are not enough to produce a child – there must be love, or at least desire; a scientist and a test tube will not result in an experiment – he must have curiosity.

But polarity is incorporated within triplicity. Three is not merely two plus one – though it sounds illogical put that way. In esoteric terms, the descent of unity into multiplicity is sometimes expressed as: one becomes two and three simultaneously. And this is shown schematically thus:

I

I   I

Though impossible to express in words unambiguously, the diagram shows how one becomes *both* two *and* three – depending upon the way the diagram is looked at.*

---

* This brief passage, in slightly different form, in our first edition, was singled out for censure by Culver and Ianna (*The Gemini Syndrome*, p. 84). It was featured in their attack upon astrologers who attempt to assume the mantle of scientific respectability by resorting to pseudo-scientific jargon; or who, as in our case, set out to hoodwink 'the uncomprehending public' with 'astrological jargon'.

We find this an interesting choice. To begin with there is no word in it unfamiliar to a bright high school student. More to the point, our italics make it clear that we are trying to get across an *idea* that does not conform to ordinary linear thinking, and

In astrology, the Law of Three finds expression in what are called the 'Modes of Action'. The signs, as we have seen, are either positive or negative, in accordance with the principle of duality, but at the same time they incorporate the principle of triplicity.

Man–Woman is a polarity, but Lover–Beloved–Desire is a relationship. Lover–Beloved are not the same as they were when they were merely Man–Woman, no matter that their external appearance is the same and their bills still come to the same address. The Law of Three is superimposed upon the Law of Two. The modes are superimposed upon the polarities; the polarities pervade the modes.

In astrology, the modes of action are called 'Cardinal' (that upon which all else depends), 'Fixed' (that which is acted upon), and 'Mutable' (that which effects the exchange of forces). Aries is cardinal, Taurus is fixed, Gemini is mutable, Cancer is cardinal, Leo is fixed, Virgo is mutable, and so on. And so the signs begin to differentiate themselves. Aries is positive and

---

that therefore calls for more careful consideration. Readers who have followed our elementary numerological argument to this point without difficulty may wonder what there might have been about it that posed insuperable problems to two professional astronomers. We wondered, too, at first, but think we can provide a constructive answer; an answer that uses this otherwise minor quibble to illustrate a major misunderstanding. We are talking about no less than the gulf that separates the artist from the scientist; the creative mind from the analytic.

From time immemorial, artists have been Pythagoreans, fascinated by number, harmony and proportion, and this is perfectly natural. The artist synthesizes, the scientist analyzes. And number, harmony and proportion are essential to synthesis. To put something together (synthesis), everything must fit; to take it apart (analysis), no such requirements apply. Evidently, the ability to follow our discussion calls for synthesis; and a faculty for holding two or more notions, notions that may appear incommensurable, in mind simultaneously. The predominantly analytic mind, however highly trained in its field, seems unable to do this (which is one of the chief reasons why astrology so outrages it). Evidently it cannot follow synthetic thinking even on the primitive level of our explanation. Culver and Ianna may be able to figure out the distance to the nearest quasar in staggering exponential numbers; but from the Pythagorean point of view, they cannot count past Two.

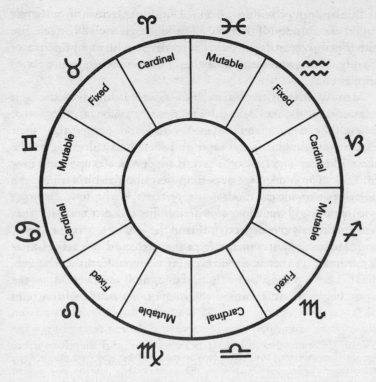

Figure 5. The signs of the zodiac divided into triplicities: the 'Modes'.

cardinal, but Gemini, though also positive, is mutable, and Leo is positive and fixed (see Fig. 5).

The Law of Four

Three terms, however, are insufficient to describe either a thing, or an event. A relationship is theoretical. It cannot be said to exist. Nothing has happened yet. Lover–Beloved–Desire is not a household or even an affair. For it to be a household, four terms are necessary, four terms which incorporate the three of the relationship within them. The four terms of a family might be Father–Mother–Responsibility–Household itself. But the fourth term is not merely tacked on and Father–Mother–Responsibility are not the same as Lover–Beloved–Desire (as all married men and women are well aware).

In most ancient traditions this foursome comprises the four 'elements': Fire, Earth, Air, Water – from which all matter is derived.

We are brought up on schoolbooks that deride and dismiss this notion as superstition. And of course, if taken literally, the four 'elements' do not adequately describe the physical world. They are not meant to. But the *principle* of the four elements was sound and remains sound, though the terminology may ring quaint and medieval to our ears.

Organic chemistry is principally concerned with the inter-action of four chemical elements: Hydrogen, Carbon, Oxygen, Nitrogen. The functions of these elements, the parts they play in organic life, can be shown to correspond neatly to the roles played by Fire, Earth, Air and Water.* Though imprecise from the modern scientific point of view, the ancient terminology has certain distinct advantages. It is more fluid and therefore more easily applicable to the manifold contingencies of life than our modern terminology. Everyday language continues to reflect the wisdom of the words chosen by the ancients to symbolize the 'elements'. It makes sense, still, to refer to personalities as 'Fiery', 'Earthy', 'Airy', 'Watery'. We all have a very good idea of what these words mean. Imagine the opposition that would greet an imposed esperanto designed to weed out old am-biguities; that would have us refer to people as 'hydrogenic' or 'carbonic'.

In astrology, then, the four elements are superimposed upon the modes and upon the polarities. Aries is Fire; Taurus is Earth; Gemini, Air; Cancer, Water; Leo, Fire, and so on. Aries is positive, cardinal, fire; Leo is positive, fixed, fire; Sagittarius is positive, mutable, fire (see Fig. 6).

* See Rudolf Hauschka, *The Nature of Substance* (Stuart & Watkins, 1966).

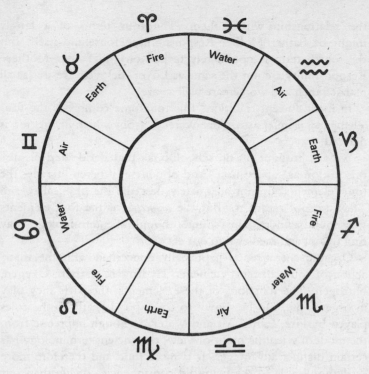

Figure 6. The signs of the zodiac divided into quadruplicities: the 'four elements'.

Each sign is different, no two are alike, there are no repetitions; all possible permutations of polarity, triplicity and quadruplicity work themselves out within a twelve-sign system. The modes – representing force – are linked together by the square, or cross – representing matter. The elements – representing matter – are linked together by the trine (triangle), representing force. And it is the combination of these numerically based metaphysical principles that imbue the signs of the zodiac with their meaning. Leo is Leo, and Cancer, Cancer, not because an imaginary lion and crab in the sky project their characters on to those signs, but because the qualities inherent in a sign that is positive, fixed, fire were best synthesized and symbolized by the

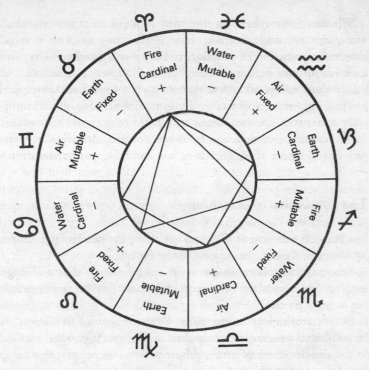

Figure 7. The zodiac divided simultaneously into polarities, triplicities and quadruplicities. Notice that the square or 'Cross' of matter will always connect each of the four 'elements'. Signs 90° apart are always of opposite polarities.

The trine of Force (or Spirit) connects like 'elements'.

Lion, while those of a sign that was negative, cardinal, water were best synthesized and symbolized by the crab (see Fig. 7).

So the diagram of the zodiac, constructed in this fashion, may be regarded as a matrix in which are embedded the consonants of a celestial language capable of expressing everything within our solar system. Upon this matrix, like moving vowels, the sun, moon and planets play, creating the inexhaustible and ever-changing 'words' that make up the world we call 'reality'.

It is this celestial language that astrologers claim to interpret.

Whether or not they can does not concern us at this moment. The point we wish to make here is that this system, with its simultaneous fusion of polarity, triplicity and quadruplicity, and its harmonically determined aspects and angles, is a whole. No amount of aimless observation, no matter how accurate or painstaking, could develop willy-nilly into such an elegant and internally consistent system. In short, astrology was never dreamed up by dreaming Chaldeans on watchtowers, nor was it motivated by 'a blend of imagination, fear and religious superstition'.

The Evolution of Astrology

But because this notion of astrology's origins persists it is worth looking briefly into the origins of the fallacy.

Scholars suppose, though upon no evidence, that astrology 'evolved' piecemeal and accidentally just as they suppose organic life to have done.

But whatever may be the value of the theory of evolution (as an accidental process) when applied to organic life, when applied to the development of ideas, religions or even superstitions it is a manifest impossibility.*

In the realm of man, nothing evolves mindlessly. No coherent body of knowledge – such as astrology – simply accumulates, taking form as it goes.

---

* There are a number of excellent books, none of them written by Creationists, that systematically expose the fallacy of the theory of evolution of organic life as a chance process. To the best of our knowledge there is no single book that covers every facet of the problem. But see: Marjorie Grene, *The Knower and the Known*, for a critique of Fischer's and Haldane's statistics; L. L. Whyte (ed.), *Aspects of Form*, especially the contribution by Albert M. Dalcq in which accident and selection are held to be insufficient to account for 'Form'; Wilhelm Schmidt, *Beginnings of Religion*, shows the inapplicability of Darwinian theory to the findings of anthropology. *Beyond Reductionism*, ed. A. Koestler, collects some of the biological evidence against the theory. Mathematician Arthur M. Young, in *The Reflexive Universe*, shows that organization is inconceivable without purpose or volition. See the bibliography for a more extensive listing.

Works of art, religions, scientific hypotheses, train schedules – all must be thought of. And only then can they be brought into existence – the perfection or imperfection of the manifestation depending upon the expertise of the creator and the basic validity of the idea. But without that idea, nothing can happen. (Plato was by and large right: wrong only in ascribing 'more' reality to the idea than to its manifestation. A 'higher' reality would perhaps have made his case clearer.)

In the history of man's institutions nothing has ever evolved in a Darwinian way – including the Theory of Evolution itself. *The Origin of Species*, in its formulation, was not first a comma, then a word, then a sentence, then a paragraph, then a chapter, then a theory. It was – like every other idea man ever had – an inkling, a sort of adumbration of the whole. And after much hard work, concentration, research, and the necessary period of gestation, it was 'born', as is everything else in the universe, whole (though, in this case, wrong). True, the actual writing progresses word by word and line by line, but this is, in a sense, the least important part of the process.*

How strange, then, that in science, in which above all else a theory must fit the facts of experience, scientists exempt the universe from obeying the same laws they themselves cannot escape. The universe happens by 'accident', it is 'coincidence', while man – the grand and sole exception – is forced to think first before he can do.

To return to astrology . . . if it is safe to say that it did not and could not 'evolve' accidentally, it is safe to challenge the accepted chronology of its origins as well. For not only is this chronology based upon scanty evidence but it is also dependent upon the 'evolution' hypothesis. Scholars maintain that

---

* Any number of esoteric schools and traditions hold that organic life 'evolved' in exactly the same way; for example, that the familiar cat is the final manifestation of the idea of catness. We must admit that we find it impossible to visualize a cat at a half-way stage of semi-corporeality, but this may well be our fault. In any case, this theory does have the merit of corresponding to invariable human experience, and if it is dangerous to anthropomorphize, quite possibly it is even more dangerous not to.

astrology as we know it today originated in Babylon no earlier than the seventh century BC, and was further developed in the orientalized Greece of the third and second centuries BC.

Traditional or legendary accounts of astrology's genesis say otherwise. In view of the inadequacy of the accepted theory, the traditional point of view merits closer examination.

Astrology's Origins According to Legend and Tradition

The gist of these accounts is that astrology was the product of divine inspiration, originally developed by the sages of a vanished prehistoric civilization (Atlantis). In developed form astrology was then passed on around the world. It was at all times a secret doctrine (hence the lack of written evidence), handed down orally from master to pupil. But it eventually leaked into the market-place, losing rather than gaining coherence and force as wars, natural disasters and generally degenerative influences contributed to mankind's increasingly despiritualized state.

It goes without saying that modern scholars have little sympathy for explanations based upon divine inspiration. Nor are they much inclined to look favorably upon Atlantis theories. And by calling upon 'secret doctrines' anything and everything can be accounted for.

The traditional or legendary account is therefore in every detail opposed to the accepted view. But as we have seen, that accepted view, logical and deceptively factual on the surface, is utterly without foundation. By contrast, the traditional account, at first glance a model of wooliness and hearsay, has much to commend it when subjected to similar scrutiny. Let us look at its chief elements.

Divine Inspiration

Obviously, this can't be proved. But neither can inspiration of any sort, and only diehard behaviorists today would deny its existence. Even scientists no longer pretend their discoveries are the result of deductive rational processes. They now reluctantly ascribe genuinely creative work to 'hypothesis formation' which is no more than plain old inspiration in respectably polysyllabic disguise.

From time immemorial poets, musicians and mystics have credited God or the gods as the source of their creativity. Truly creative atheists are actually a rarity, even today. Many, if not most, who profess no religious beliefs reveal themselves closet mystics when caught off guard. The few who are adamant and logically consistent in their materialism are scarcely better off. They may deny a divine source but are then stuck with the equally unaccountable fact of their own inspiration. There is no room for inspiration within a mechanistic, materialistic world model, or even for 'hypothesis formation'.

As a general rule, scholars try to apply a hit-or-miss trial-and-error explanation to all those advances that marked early civilization: the development of language, the domestication of grains and animals, agriculture, and religion itself. But the 'dreaming Chaldean' principle cannot account for these prodigious leaps of imagination any better than it can for astrology.

Over the past few decades, tacit support for the traditional view has been growing – though no one mentions divine inspiration as such.

Most of this work touches only indirectly upon the question of the origins of astrology. Nevertheless it has resulted in a gradual reappraisal of the scientific and intellectual achievements of early man. It has provided a new climate in which, without fear of automatic excommunication, scholars may cautiously suggest that ancient people actually knew something about the world they lived in. And in this altered climate, astrology, at least in its metaphysical, cosmological and theoretical form, looks rather less outrageous than it did, say, fifty years ago.

Noam Chomsky and a new school of linguists have argued that the structure of language is a complete, integral system from the onset. No language has ever been found that is rudimentary or incomplete; that is to say, under construction.

Mircea Eliade and Joseph Campbell, among others, have done much to reveal the coherent, cosmological thinking embedded in ancient myth and symbolism. Gerald Hawkins and Alexander Thom proved that Stonehenge and the megalithic monuments of ancient Europe served as astronomical observatories, spawning an entirely new (and now respectable) science called archeoastronomy.

Hamlet's Mill

Directly relevant to our theme is the book, *Hamlet's Mill* by Harvard philosophers Giorgio de Santillana and Hertha von Dechend (David Godine, 1977). For here is a carefully developed argument that proves beyond doubt that many of the principal myths of the ancient world have an *astronomical* basis.

Those strange, tangled, often incestuous tales that make no rational or sequential sense at all, become meaningful once their planetary or stellar nature is disclosed. The myths are, among other things, dramatizations of events in the heavens. Some of our most familiar biblical or mythical characters (whose stories are so full of absurdities and inconsistencies on the surface) prove to be universal metaphors for planetary or celestial phenomena. Samson, for example, a pure berserker on the surface, chronicles the violent and erratic course of Mars and the relationships that planet establishes on its wayward course. Noah is an embodiment of Saturn, which is one of the reasons why the ark is a cube – for the cube is Saturn's figure, and Saturn, like Noah, is the quintessential patriarchal symbol. Samson and Noah are among the original archetypes and what is most significant, they find expression *universally*. The same characters and the same stories recur again and again, modified to suit local surroundings. They pop up in the ancient Near East, in the Orient, in ancient Finland and Scandinavia, in native America and in Polynesia.

De Santillana and von Dechend do not pursue the astrological connotations of this astronomical interpretation – beyond acknowledging that they exist. But from our point of view this is the most important aspect of their study.

It proves that from the earliest recorded times, and before, ancient peoples not only carefully observed events in the heavens, but ascribed *meaning* to them. When that meaning is made systematic, astrology is born.

Two themes running throughout *Hamlet's Mill* relate to astrology's origins, and by extension, to its validity.

The first is the demonstration that the characteristics or meanings ascribed to the sun, moon and planets are as universal as the stories and characters themselves. They are written into the myths at their origins, at dates that cannot even be surmised. Mars figures have been violent and martial from time immemorial. Jupiter figures have been jovial (or autocratic), and Saturn figures saturnine. Since it is precisely this planetary aspect of astrology that modern statistical research corroborates so convincingly, the genesis of the mythical material becomes that much more important.

The second major contribution is the demonstration that knowledge of the precession of the equinoxes (supposedly a discovery of the Greek astronomer/astrologer Hipparchus in the second century BC) is also written into the myths. Since knowledge of the precession involves painstaking astronomical observation carried out over the course of long periods of time, this provides evidence for the systematic nature of ancient scientific interests, which in turn presupposes a highly organized society capable of underwriting long-term scientific research.

So, not only is astrology much older than is currently believed, but it comes out of a distant past in which the precession of the equinoxes was also known, proving that 'exact science', even by today's standards, existed.

It is only the *expression* of that real science in the form of myth that is not scientific in our sense of that word. This is perhaps one of the reasons why the extent and sophistication of ancient knowledge has eluded modern scholars.

Hamlet's Mill stops well short of concluding that the astrological content of these astronomically based myths corresponds to the truth.

For the moment that question can be set aside. The point is that the interest in astronomy/astrology (along with a no less passionate and profound interest in number, geometry, and mathematics) dates back into prehistory, seemingly coeval with those other titanic achievements of early man: language, agriculture, and the domestication of grains and animals. Since the 'dreaming Chaldean' hypothesis cannot be applied to any of these, we find ourselves forced back into a reconsideration of the traditional explanation: that ascribes these landmark advances to 'divine inspiration' or the direct descent of the 'gods' themselves to earth.

It is just possible that it is the terminology more than the concept that makes the idea seem so unacceptable. Let us try phrasing it another way: before the rational intellect came to dominate the consciousness of contemporary man, our ancestors perhaps had direct *experiential* access to universal principles and organized their world accordingly. In other words, what was experience to them (and still may be to traditional tribal societies such as the Bushmen and aborigines of Australia – as well as to saints, mystics and masters throughout the ages) looks like imagination or fantasy to us.

But whatever the truth may be, we are left with the *fact* of a profound, wide-ranging astronomical/astrological doctrine, expressed in myth, dating from some prehistoric time. With the 'dreaming Chaldean' hypothesis ruled out, the traditional or legendary account of its origins, however speculative, must stand as the best available at present.

The Sages of Atlantis

The theme of *Hamlet's Mill* is not original. Correlations between myth and astronomy/astrology have been recorded from classical antiquity, and de Santillana and von Dechend draw upon many old sources for their material. What distinguishes their study is the global range of its synthesis, and the insistence that myth has its origins in science rather than in primitive superstition, or even in some expression of a Jungian collective unconscious.

But it does not address the question of origins, beyond pushing them back into prehistory. This leaves a recurrent anomaly unanswered. Egypt, Sumer, India and other high ancient civilizations were largely devoted to perpetuating the status quo. Moreover most of these civilizations were at their height at, or close to their beginnings. It is generally conceded that their mythologies were also there at the beginning – the art and architecture came later. Where then did this science-based body of cosmological literature come from?

The mystery deepens when identical astronomical/astrological themes turn up in cultures with no interest in science and no apparent capacity for extended scientific inquiry. Specifically, how did the Polynesians, the native Americans, the rude, pre-Christian Vikings, and the Dogon and Bambara tribes of Africa acquire knowledge of this order?

Circumstantial the evidence may be, but it points to some prior civilization. This is in accord with the oldest traditions and legends themselves. The theme of a vanished 'Golden Age' recurs throughout the world, and the refusal of scholars to take it seriously is due more to the prejudices of researchers than to an actual lack of evidence.

Until very recently historians, anthropologists and all those looking into the distant past proceeded from the assumption that they, and only they had the capacity to arrive at 'objective' conclusions, no matter how fragmentary the records at their disposal. They simply dismissed out of hand the millennial memories of bards, chroniclers and priests whose job it was, after all, in pre-literate eras, to commit this material to memory and pass it on. De Santillana and von Dechend are not the first to condemn the arrogance and presumptuousness of this conceit, and it is just possible that the time is now ripe for acknowledging evidence that requires a total rewriting of ancient history; and a total re-appraisal of the order of knowledge available to humanity before historical records began. Gradually, gradually, over the past few decades, a new consensus begins to take hold.

Sacred Science in Ancient Egypt

Among those responsible for the new, upgraded picture of the past, a gently condescending, separate-but-not-quite-equal attitude has replaced that former arrogance. In effect these vanguard scholars are saying: 'Ah, yes, ancient man certainly had his science, and in its way it was real science, even though it wasn't quite *our* science. Just because ancient cosmological thinking does not correspond to our truths, we should not assume that these early efforts lacked system or intelligence.'

We suspect the ancients privy to the inner meaning of their own teaching would be dissatisfied with such a verdict. They might, in the face of our twentieth-century science, show an appropriate fear of the hydrogen bomb, and perhaps a momentary appreciation of the computer, TV set, automobile and electric toothbrush. But the enchantment would be brief. For they would instantly recognize the meretriciousness of the reigning materialist metaphysic, and they would regard the near-total absence of a sense of the sacred as an unmitigated tragedy – for which no amount of material comfort could begin to compensate.

In short, they would consider their own science superior to ours. They would find our notion of 'progress' misguided and our infatuation with it, infantile.

Throughout the history of the scientific revolution, this contrary view has had its adherents; it was they who preserved the traditional account of astrology's origins along with what may have remained of what once were the Sacred Sciences.

For proof of the existence of those Sacred Sciences we need only turn to ancient Egypt – not necessarily because the Egyptian civilization was more advanced than any other, but simply because there is so much left of it. That done, there are two ways to test the hypothesis. The first and most compelling is personal experience. All anyone has to do to be convinced of the level of ancient knowledge is to actually visit Egypt.

There in front of the Great Pyramid of Giza or meditating in the King's Chamber (if you can beg, borrow or steal a few moment's peace), or walking through the temple of Luxor or Karnak, it is only necessary to open yourself to the experience consciously built into these structures by the geniuses responsible for their construction to get an inkling of the reality of Sacred Science.

Even so, there is a catch involved, in fact, a double catch. The experience is only open to those able to travel, and the conditions have to be favorable as well. Ancient sacred art and architecture retains much of its magic, even in ruins, yet, even on the Egyptian scale, magic is fragile. Just as you cannot get anything out of Mozart played through a Walkman in Shea Stadium, so mighty Karnak may not convey its message when the great hypostyle hall is thronged and the guides are telling you how high the pillars are in a dozen languages simultaneously. Perhaps even more important, very few of us have come through our modern education with faculties unimpaired. Most of us have to some extent been brainwashed by the insistence upon physical demonstration and rational argument, and we no longer quite trust those faculties that provide us with the only kind of proof that is of real consequence. Thus, we may not quite trust the experience even if we have it.

For many of us, a carefully developed argument and empirical proof of some sort is required – and it is available. Over the past hundred years or so, a number of books have appeared devoted wholly or partially to this kind of demonstration.*

The work most relevant to our historical/astrological theme is the vast re-interpretation of the whole of ancient Egyptian civilization, developed by the French Orientalist, mathematician and philosopher, the late R. A. Schwaller de Lubicz. For it is Schwaller who provides final, incontrovertible evidence of the existence of a Sacred Science – which inevitably includes astrology – in Egypt and the manner in which its manifold aspects were expressed in art and architecture.

He provides the metaphysical, cosmological and scientific framework within which that postulated, early, highly advanced, pre-Babylonian astrology functioned. Moreover, he presents his case according to the prevailing ground rules – in so far as a subject of such profundity can be expressed within the limits of

* See the bibliography for a selected list of the best of these.

conventional scholarship. Everything is documented, nothing is left to chance or imagination. Anyone interested in disproving Schwaller's theories or providing alternatives has the material to work with readily available.

Symbolist Egypt

When the first edition of this book was written, Schwaller's work had not been translated from its original French and was effectively unavailable to the English-speaking world.

Because his interpretation is so diametrically opposed to all that we have been taught to accept about Egypt and ancient civilization in general, we devoted a substantial chapter to the subject. Though inadequate to the task of summarizing this vast work of scholarship with its wide-ranging ideas and their even wider-ranging implications, at least it provided the unspecialized reader with an inkling of what was involved.

Over the intervening years, however, the problem of access has much improved. Our original chapter provoked its own full-scale examination of Schwaller de Lubicz's ideas (*Serpent in the Sky: The High Wisdom of Ancient Egypt*, John Anthony West), and many of Schwaller's own works, those of his wife, Isha, his stepdaughter, Lucie Lamy, and of other scholars devoted to his ideas are now in print and available, albeit still known only to a small following. (Unfortunately, the massive, three-volume *Le Temple de l'homme*, key and masterplan for the whole *œuvre*, remains available only in French.)

So there is no longer any real need to try to do justice to Symbolist Egypt within the space of a chapter. Readers interested in devoting to this subject the attention it merits are referred to the bibliography. Here we pass over the evidence except as it relates to astrology, and content ourselves with a brief résumé of Symbolist Egypt and the Sacred Science that was responsible for its art and architecture.

Sacred vs. Secular Science

Sacred Science is based upon the premise of a pre-existent

Divine Consciousness. It takes as a given that the universe is a conscious creation. Within that creation, man has been created to play a specific role – which he is free to play or not play, according to his will, understanding and conscience.

Recognition and acceptance of that role is at the core of all the world's religions. The language may differ from tradition to tradition, but the message is the same. We are on this earth for a purpose. We are, all of us, born with the spark of Divinity within us, and it is our job and our privilege to transform that spark into a flame; to transform the carnal into the spiritual.

That process, the only human endeavor of consequence, has a spiritual, non-physical aim but takes place within the physical world.

The Sacred Science of antiquity, like today's rational science, studied the physical world, but for very different reasons. The sages of Egypt were not interested in facts by and for themselves, ripped out their living context. Their concern was to establish the relationship of Man to the Cosmos. For the Cosmos was the theater in which the human drama was played out. The study of the age of the universe, or the chemical constitution of quasars would have been an enterprise devoid of interest or value to them. They would have considered it, above all else, impractical. Whereas building a temple consecrated to a specific Divine Principle that put its priests in touch with that Principle was supremely practical, no matter how much effort went into the enterprise.

But this does not mean that the Sacred Sciences were not precise and in the true sense of the word, empirical; empirical, because based upon a study of those *principles* that make up our experience.

Fertilization, gestation, birth, growth, maturity, senescence, death and renewal – these make up the world of living, day-to-day experience. They represent the Why of creation. In the eyes of antiquity, they were not, as our rational science would have it, accidental effects of hypothetical, equally accidental Big Bang. Rather, they are aspects of the Divine Consciousness in action; the world of becoming in which we all play our part.

The modern scientific method, that so captivates Culver,

Ianna and their colleagues is – by definition, and by its own self-imposed limitations – incapable of studying those principles, and it therefore pretends they do not 'objectively' exist, although the results of their interaction are precisely what provides rational science with its facts.

The Principles correspond to Numbers (as we saw earlier – Two–Polarity, Three–Relationship, Four–Substantiality, etc.) which in turn find expression in harmony, proportion, and measure in art and architecture. Knowledge of the Principles is transmitted though myth and symbolism, their natural, proper languages. This is the source of the Egyptian *neterw*, those curious, composite animal-headed or human-headed figures (misleadingly translated as the 'gods') that look so strange to the uninitiated. The *neterw* are not – as orthodox Egyptology would have it – leftovers from some previous, animistic religious system. Rather, they are chosen as concrete embodiments of that Principle they are intended to symbolize . . . the dog, because of its uncanny homing instinct, guide through the limbo that follows death; the stork as glyph for the soul, since the stork returns year after year to the same nest, thus symbolizing reincarnation (and providing evidence that the Egyptians held this belief – which is customarily denied) . . . the pregnant hippopotamus as symbol for material gestation, for what could be more pregnant than a pregnant hippopotamus . . .?

The great achievement of R. A. Schwaller de Lubicz was to demonstrate, unequivocally, the precise manner in which Egyptian civilization is founded upon Sacred Science. Egypt, in the Symbolist interpretation, proves to be a mighty, comprehensive body of wisdom in which art, philosophy, science and religion are inextricably fused. There is no science that is not religious; there is no philosophy that does not find expression in art.

The Role of Astrology in Sacred Science

From the beginning of Egyptian civilization to its end, astrology plays a role – unmistakable, demonstrable, and yet impossible to define with precision.

There can be no doubt whatever that the Egyptians of the earliest dynasties knew there were correspondences between celestial and terrestrial phenomena, and that there was a connection between human consciousness and the heavens.

An intense Egyptian interest in astronomical phenomena is acknowledged. But because there are no *direct* references to astrological associations, scholars have concluded that this interest was simply astronomical. Were this the case, it would make the Egyptians unique among ancient peoples. But there cannot be the slightest doubt that, like all civilized human beings throughout history, the Egyptians were interested in astronomy primarily because of its astrological implications; that is to say, because of its relationship to the earth and to human life upon the earth.

At the moment it is impossible to say when astrology assumed its present form. None of its principal developments or transitional stages can be pinpointed. In Greek or Roman times it was already recognizably the astrology of today – with the same qualities attributed to the planets, the same correspondences between planets and the human personality, the same associations of the planets with colors and gems. According to accepted theory, the Greeks organized a chaotic body of superstition borrowed from Chaldea into systematic form. This is undoubtedly mistaken. The ancient association of planets and stars with deities, and of deities with numbers makes it clear that pre-Greek astrology had its own form of organization. It is possible, however, that the Greeks organized astrology into something resembling its *present* form. What is certain is that the Greeks took over a body of pre-existent knowledge pertaining to the nature of the planets and their relationships to earthly and human events.

Since some of the most important of these relationships can now be validated by modern methods, it is clear that a reappraisal of astrology (and of all ancient science) is in order.

A. Dreams the Chaldeans Never Dreamed

Astrology in Ancient Egypt
The Age of Aries and the Ram of Amon

Knowledge of the precession of the equinoxes (see p. 25) calls for organized scientific effort extended over long periods of time. When the evidence reveals such knowledge written into the mythologies of prehistory it presupposes an advanced science and a social structure capable of providing the necessary supporting conditions. It also proves these early scientists looked to the heavens for more than mere practical knowledge, such as that required to keep agricultural calendars – the standard explanation for early interest in astronomy.

The ascription of *meaning* to the precession proves that early astronomy and early astrology went hand in hand.

The Taurean Age (*c.* 4000–2000 BC) ushers in recorded history in Egypt and in Mesopotamia, and it is a fact that taurine imagery pervades the cultures of the entire area. Naturally, until very recently, this imagery was assumed to be part of the 'bull cults' prevailing in the area, and no one looked for a serious symbolic meaning behind the imagery. But the newest work is in the process of upgrading the cultures preceding the Taurean Age, and it will be most interesting to see if Geminian symbolism comes to light for these earlier societies (Schwaller suggested it could be read into the scanty remains of pre-dynastic Egypt, but as evidence it is necessarily conjectural). In any event, there can be no mistaking the prevalence of taurine imagery during the age astrologically associated with the Bull, and the preoccupation with monumental architecture during that period is also curiously apposite to an age ruled by an 'earth' sign.

Taken alone, all of this might be ascribed to coincidence. But de Santillana and von Dechend furnish several examples of the change-over from Taurus to Aries written into myth and legend, and these are difficult to interpret other than astrologically. Schwaller has produced perhaps the most convincing example of all.

In Egypt, at Thebes (modern Luxor), around 2000 BC, the

Bull of Montu was superseded by the Ram of Amon and the Ram of Amon continued to prevail in Egypt into Ptolemaic times (beginning 323 BC). The standard explanation for this event is that a priestly dispute took place in Thebes in which the priests of Amon ultimately emerged victorious.

The problem with this explanation is the total lack of evidence supporting it. There is nothing in known Egyptian history of the time to suggest such a feud; indeed, apart from the bizarre, brief, and mysterious interlude of Akhenaton, there is no evidence of priestly feuding throughout the 3,000 years of Egypt's history.

But astrologically on cue, the Ram of Amon replaced the Bull of Montu – also a solar deity. The celestial or astrological significance of the change in symbolism becomes clear once it is regarded in this light.

In complex, metaphorical language, Egyptian funerary texts related the passage of the Divine or Solar Principle through the hours of the 'night' of Death.

These texts are, in effect, manuals of transformation; they detail the stages of the process whereby the carnal is made spiritual; the goal of individual and collective human destiny in all valid religions. And it is this spiritual teaching that is painted or carved in the Royal tombs throughout the New Kingdom (*c.* 1500–1100 BC) and written out in innumerable papyruses of the epoch.

In these texts, the Solar Principle is generally depicted as a human figure with a ram's head. He is enclosed within a tabernacle formed by a coiled serpent, probably the origin of the metaphorical 'coils of time', and he sails on a boat through the celestial regions. He is called, 'The Flesh of Ra', in other words, the Solar or Divine Principle incarnated in matter. Texts that accompany these drawings and other texts in innumerable temple friezes refer frequently to 'the Ram in the sky'. Given the weight of the evidence, this can only be interpreted astrologically (otherwise it means nothing at all). And the conclusion is that astrology pervaded the entire Egyptian culture even though, at the moment, we cannot say what the transition from

Taurus to Aries meant to Egypt, nor how she incorporated her knowledge into ceremony and practice.

Egyptian Collective or Macro-Astrology

Modern astrology is based almost entirely upon interpretation of the individual horoscope. Even when astrologers practice mundane astrology in an attempt to predict national trends or events, they use the alleged individual horoscope of the nation or group as the basis for their analyses. Because nothing resembling an individual horoscope has shown up in ancient Egypt, scholars often insist the Egyptians had no astrology (a conclusion that under other circumstances might be taken as a compliment; that is, the Egyptians were too clever to be taken in. But in this instance the attribution is purely pejorative; the Egyptians weren't even clever enough to devise so elegant and systematic a superstition).

However, the Ram of Amon provides a clue. We can find instances of astrology in operation, even though as yet we do not know the thinking behind them. For the most part, what we see is a kind of collective, or macro-astrology deployed in a way that touched Egyptian civilization in its entirety. Let us look briefly at a few of these instances.

Dismantling of the Temples

The Pharaohs of Egypt were particularly prone to tear down temples erected by their predecessors and build new ones in their places, or to chisel the names of the original builders out of their cartouches (the oval 'Ring of Eternity' in which only the Pharaoh's name might be written) and instal their own. This has always been taken as an ancient instance of a modern commonplace: politicians, out of spite, egotism or psychological cunning, glorify themselves at the expense of their predecessors by tearing down or usurping their monuments.

But Schwaller proves that Egyptian temples were not destroyed. Rather, they were systematically and deliberately *dis-*

mantled. An old temple was not merely a quarry for the new; it was literally the progenitor. Stones and inscriptions were chosen from the superannuated temple as the symbolic germinal material from which the new temple grew. And this material was not simply built into the rising temple at random, but was carefully and with great care embedded in the foundations, in the cores of columns and in other strategic spots, sometimes invisibly, but always precisely.

The Egyptian temple was not an instrument of Pharaonic self-glorification. It was a living analog of the life process itself; a work of art in a state of perpetual renewal and perpetual consecration to the principle that engendered it in the first place. Though it cannot be proved at the moment, the deliberation involved strongly suggests an astrological motivation. When the principles to which a temple was consecrated had outlived their span of astrologically determined relevance, or changed to some new formulation, the temple was torn down and rebuilt. (The deliberation, though not the astrology, behind the dismantling has been tacitly acknowledged by a number of orthodox Egyptologists.)

Astrology and Medicine in Egypt

What we know of Egyptian medicine comes from only nine papyri, most of them fragmentary. The most important and informative appear to be copies of earlier documents. Considerable controversy has always surrounded the question of dating, as well as the assessment of the level of medical knowledge involved. Most recently it has been shown that when scribes made copies from earlier texts, the language of the original was preserved. Since the Egyptian language was constantly changing, and those changes are well documented, it is now possible to determine which of the papyri are older and which newer. This has in turn produced a disquieting paradox: the older the papyrus the sounder and more scientific the medicine, the newer the papyrus the more magical and incantatory. According to accepted theory, it is supposed to be the other way round.

In the fragmentary but impressive medicine that has come down to us from Egypt, the time at which remedies and medicaments are to be administered is of utmost importance, and precise instructions are given. Readers who follow developments in contemporary medicine will know that this subject is only beginning to draw the attention of our modern doctors. But the phenomenon is becoming generally acknowledged, though no one suggests planetary correspondences. An Egyptian treatise on eyes lists six different times for administering certain treatments. Along the same lines, elaborate instructions are given for the proper time to pick herbs and prepare remedies.

Presuming that these instructions were not mere caprice, their existence presupposes an astrological determination. It would seem the Egyptians believed, or knew, that different herbs embodied within them different principles corresponding to the principles symbolized by the planets and signs of the zodiac, as did the various diseases, and the human body itself. A very similar thinking pervades the work of the much misunderstood European herbalist, doctor, philosopher and mystic, Paracelsus.

Individual Astrology in Ancient Egypt

Though to date, nothing resembling an individual horoscope has been found in ancient Egypt, the accumulated evidence for what we have called macro-astrology presupposes an individual astrology of some sort, at least for the Pharaoh whose destiny would be linked to that of all Egypt. At the moment, we cannot prove that the Egyptians made the vital connection between the individual and the moment of birth, but since the 'birth' of temples was probably astrologically determined, it can hardly have been otherwise. What is certain is that Egypt understood the correspondence between man and the stars.

This is demonstrated in unmistakable fashion in a single Egyptian drawing whose significance has eluded scholars (even those interested in proving astrology existed in Egypt), until noted recently and interpreted by the pseudonymous Musaios

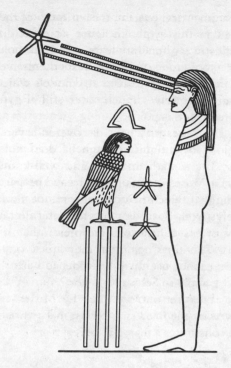

Figure 8. Mummiform figure in the shape of Osiris from the Second Shrine of Tutankhamen.

(Dr Charles Muses) in *The Lion Path*: Or *You* Can *Take It With You*, published in 1985.

Figure 8 comes from the second golden shrine in the Tomb of Tutankhamen. It is one of a row of identical mummiform figures, part of a complex and particularly enigmatic funerary text. But however puzzling the text and the reliefs, the astrological significance of this drawing cannot be misunderstood. Rays of force or energy connect the consciousness of the human individual and the stars; there is no other possible interpretation of this figure. Taken by itself, this little relief is enough to prove astrology existed in Egypt, and that is the main thrust of the argument in this chapter.

Within that historical context, the antiquity of the understanding enshrined in this symbolic figure deserves emphasis. The practice of illustrating funerary texts goes back only to the New Kingdom (*c.* 1500–1100 BC). But the texts themselves are derived from Old Kingdom (*c.* 2700–2200 BC) models which, by general agreement, are themselves much older still. Egyptologists are generally agreed on this point.

We think Dr Muses may have discovered several of the keys to the astrology of antiquity though he does not make access to them easy. As a mathematician, and well-known expert on cybernetics, Dr Muses is certainly aware of the scholarly ground rules according to which new theories are customarily set out. Unfortunately (from our point of view), he declines to follow them. Many of his conclusions are presented on a take-it-or-leave-it basis. This does not mean they are wrong. But it does mean that we cannot use them as evidence with the same kind of certainty we apply to Schwaller's work.

With that caveat set out, we think Dr Muses' explanation of the role played by the fixed star, Sirius, in Egyptian astrology is correct, and constitutes a major discovery.

The Role of Sirius

The fixed star, Sirius ('Sopdit' in ancient Egyptian), is the brightest star in the heavens. It is found at the mouth of the constellation Canis Major (The Big Dog, also, Orion's Dog) hence its popular name: the Dog Star.

As the brightest star in the sky, it is perhaps not surprising that it should play an important role in the star lore of many cultures, and none more so than Egypt. Moreover, in Egypt, there is a commanding physical reason why Sirius should be singled out for special attention.

Throughout the course of Egyptian history, the heliacal rising (first rising of a star after the period of invisibility following its conjunction with the sun) took place at the summer solstice, at or around the time of the first signs of the rising of the Nile – which was of course the lifeblood of Egypt.

But the nature of the attention lavished upon Sirius extends beyond this very obvious relationship; for Sirius also served as the basis for the extraordinarily sophisticated and accurate Egyptian calendar.

> Instead of attempting the formulation of a rigid calendar, the ancients knew how to take into account all celestial movements and to relate them to life on earth. We have seen that these sages gave consideration to both the lunar and the solar cycle, while keeping them separate one from the other. The solar cycle is complex in itself; in our day, use is made of both the *tropical year*, which is the time span between two consecutive returns of the globe to the spring equinox, and of the *sidereal year*, which is the time span elapsed between two conjunctions of the earth with the same star. But both of these periods involve fractions of days, minutes and seconds, and cannot be used as a fixed temporal unit because they need constant adjustments. Accordingly, the ancients adopted neither one nor the other, but rather based themselves on the *Sothic year* of 365¼ days exactly, the year determined by the periodic return of the heliacal rising of *Sirius*. It is a fact that among the extremely slow movements of the stars called 'fixed' in relation to one another, Sirius is the only one that allows the compensation of irrational discrepancy in time: therefore, it permits the establishment of a *fixed year* – or *year of God* – which serves as a measure of reference to keep track of all celestial movements. The heliacal rising of Sirius determined the New Year's Day, called 'opening of the year'.*
>
> R. A. Schwaller de Lubicz, *Sacred Science*, p. 172.

The ability to single out Sirius in this manner signifies a highly organized, observational astronomy, and of course the coincidence of the rising of Sirius with the rising of the Nile makes it an obvious candidate for special attention. But even these purely physical and astronomical observations do not account for the *symbolic* role Sirius played.

---

* For a detailed account of the astronomy involved, see R. A. Schwaller de Lubicz, *Sacred Science*, pp. 17–20, 287–90.

In particular, Sirius figures prominently in the funerary texts which employ celestial phenomena as analogies or metaphors for the processes of spiritual transformation. And these relationships are never arbitrary.

As we mentioned earlier, Egyptian symbolism is *never* arbitrary. Thus when Sirius is equated with Isis, personification of the cosmic feminine principle, we can look for a valid reason why. Sirius is also called 'The Second Sun', an intriguing appellation since it proves the Egyptians knew that stars were suns.

But the Egyptians also had a masculine form of Sirius (Sopdu) whom they equate with Horus, principle of resurrection. Dr Muses offers an explanation that, if correct, adds another dimension to what is already a major modern mystery involving Sirius and the Dogon, a West African tribe with many singular customs.

Marcel Griaule, a highly respected anthropologist, worked with, lived with and studied the Dogon. After several decades he was astonished to learn that a council of elders had decided to initiate him into their 'Deep Knowledge', an extensive body of secret, oral, cosmological lore whose existence he had never even suspected. (This is one of those telling pieces of evidence that validates the often denigrated notion of secrecy. If Griaule could live and work with the Dogon for twenty years without suspecting the existence of the doctrine upon which their entire culture was founded, it is clear enough that other societies throughout history could be equally secretive when deemed necessary.) His tutor was a blind, old man, Ogotemmeli, and the nature of the instruction was largely mythological and cosmological, incorporating a level of astronomical lore that the Dogon of the present era seemed incapable of developing for themselves.

But the single most astounding piece of information was not recognized at face value by Griaule himself.

Sirius is a binary star; the brilliant visible Sirius is accompanied by an incredibly dense invisible counterpart.

This was only detected in the West in 1862, by astronomer

Alvan Clark, working with the state-of-art telescope of his time. Many more years elapsed before a later generation of astronomers were able to gauge its astonishing density of 53,000 (the specific gravity of gold, for example, is 19.3).

In the Dogon 'Deep Knowledge', however, this dark and invisible companion of Sirius plays a major role. Not only did the Dogon know of its existence, but they also knew its orbit (50 years) and they described it as heavier than anything in the world.

How could the Dogon, without telescopes or technology, know of the existence of Sirius B (as it is rather unpoetically called)?

The question has provoked a variety of hypotheses. Robert Temple, an English writer and researcher, suggested in *The Sirius Mystery* that this knowledge was a residue of a corpus of higher learning bequeathed the earth by visitors from outer space, specifically from Sirius.

But this theory found little favor with academic astronomers who proposed an alternative. Carl Sagan suggested that the Dogon had been apprised of Sirius B by Jesuit missionaries working among them.*

---

* These two diametrically opposed explanations vividly illustrate the most common approaches to the many legitimate mysteries surrounding ancient societies. One camp romanticizes the problem, calling in visiting spacemen or Divine Providence, producing theories that appear impossible but are actually only implausible (after all, we go up into space, why shouldn't more advanced creatures come down? And who is there sufficiently knowledgeable to pass judgement on the existence or otherwise of Divine Providence?). The other camp systematically trivializes the mystery. This particular 'scientific' hypothesis presupposes an intense interest in modern astronomy by Jesuit missionaries, which is quite contrary to fact, coupled with the perfectly inconceivable determination to pass it on, and an even more passionate – though carefully hidden – interest by the Dogon ... who straightaway incorporated this piece of unsolicited information into their 'Deep Knowledge' only to reveal it decades later to Marcel Griaule. Upon close examination, this idea is substantially more absurd than its romantic alternative. It appears plausible but, given its context, is in effect impossible. The process responsible for generating it is the norm in academe, however, and because it is the norm, its absurdity goes generally unremarked. Banality is labeled

Thus the mystery remains: how did the Dogon know about Sirius B? One possibility, and one often raised, is that there must have been some ancient connection between the Dogon and ancient Egypt, for much else in their cosmology and mythology has an Egyptian flavor. Moreover, de Santillana and von Dechend and other sources supply interesting examples of other advanced metaphysical and cosmological African beliefs and were said by the tribesmen themselves to have come to them initially from Egypt.*

But did the Egyptians know of Sirius B?

Dr Muses believes that the masculine or Horus form of Sirius, Sopdu, is a reference to Sirius B and he brings powerful textual evidence from the ancient pyramid inscriptions in to support his argument. Isis and Horus are complementary but distinct, and the ancient pyramid texts very clearly distinguish between the masculine and feminine forms. It would be gratifying if references were made to size, density and luminescence, which would amount to formal, unchallengeable proof, but these do not seem to exist. An element of doubt must remain. Dr Muses' explanation accounts for the Isis/Horus duality of Sirius very reasonably, yet it is not the only possible explanation.

Egyptian mythology is complex. Translations are in every instance problematical. It would not be so very difficult to put forward an interpretation of Horus-in-Sothis that would make

---

'reason'. If 'reason' is responsible for a theory, and that theory has been put forward by a scientist, then other scientists will believe it. And once scientists believe it, then it can only be 'science' and therefore true. But in this instance, as in the 'dreaming Chaldean' theory and so many others, the very real and intriguing mystery is not actually addressed, and the proffered explanation is in reality no more than an expression of the level of creativity of its author.

* Another striking instance is recorded by Patrick Bowen, a writer who spent many years in Africa. He recounts in detail information passed on to him by a Zulu elder, concerning an elaborate spiritual psychology, called 'The Wisdom which comes of Old' initially furnished all the African tribes by what the Bantu called, The Brotherhood of the Higher Ones of Egypt. Cf. the comprehensive survey *Reincarnation: the Phoenix Fire Mystery*, Joseph Head and S. L. Cranston (Julian Press), p. 191.

sense and conform to the general symbolic method of the Egyptians, without calling in Sirius B.*

The theory may well rest finally upon the putative Dogon connection. For there can be no doubt about the Dogon knowledge of Sirius B; it is certain that the Dogon could not have discovered this themselves, at least given the present state of their society and there is a strong possibility of a Dogon/ Egyptian connection. We personally balk at the prospect of visitors from outer space while the alternative of astronomically enthusiastic Jesuits whispering secrets of Sirius B to the spellbound Dogon tribesmen is unworthy of consideration. We are left, therefore, with the probability that Egypt knew of Sirius B, and this hypothesis also provides the best possible explanation for the mythological context in which Sirius is equated with *both* Isis and Horus. It also receives indirect corroboration from de Santillana and von Dechend, who note that in various mythologies all over the world, Sirius is commonly associated with that culture's Isis/Venus figure and also with its equivalent of Pan. And once again we confront a situation in which advanced astronomical/astrological knowledge expressed as myth seems to date back to prehistory; or is encountered in cultures which, in their present state, could not begin to formulate or acquire it.

Since the 'gods' represent cosmic principles, and the planets and fixed stars were 'gods', astrology is involved. If Dr Muses is correct and the ancient Egyptians knew of the physical existence of Sirius B, an advanced astronomy was also involved, again bearing out the traditional account (although the manner in which this knowledge was acquired, without the aid of the modern telescope, remains as mysterious as ever). Thus, coming

---

* Schwaller de Lubicz did just this. Noting the similarity between the atomic nucleus with its dense neutron and light but massive positron and the structure of Sirius with its vast, luminous orb and dense companion, Schwaller saw this mirrored in the double feminine/masculine role played by Sirius: as both Isis and Horus. But it did not occur to Schwaller that the Egyptians might know of the actual *physical* Sirius B. *Sacred Science*, p. 28.

from still another direction, again we seem back on the track of a body of lost high knowledge, in which astrology played a paramount role. The specifics of this ancient astrology will therefore have more than academic interest.

Dr Muses finds clues to this lost knowledge embedded in the Egyptian language itself; a logical place to look – for those who recognize the richness of the ancient Egyptian symbolic method with its profusion of analogies and metaphors. What is dismissed by academics as a love of senseless punning is, for those able to 'think Egyptian', a means of making connections that would otherwise remain obscured.

Thus Dr Muses notes that the glyph for the star Sirius is also the sign that means 'to be prepared' or 'to be equipped with appropriate means'. At the same time, the word for star, *sb3*, with the determinative of a pair of legs means 'door', or 'to pass through a door'. This cannot be arbitrary. Since the stars represent cosmic principles, and Sirius is invariably referred to in exalted terms in the funerary texts, both the 'preparation' and the 'passage through the door' must be spiritual metaphors. Since Egyptian religion is entirely devoted to the transformation of the carnal into the spiritual (the most rigid academics would agree on this point, they would disagree only on the validity of the concept), the Egyptian language is here calling attention to an astrological process; one moreover that is perfectly consonant with the contemporary astrological understanding of transits (the passage of planets over emphatic or senstive position in the horoscope). In other words, in Egypt, the star, Sirius, is tied to spiritual preparation and to crossing over spiritual thresholds in some sense or another.

Dr Muses accounts for astrological 'influence' through the principle of resonance (more on this later, under The Question: How? See pp. 364–94).* He maintains that at certain critical or

---

* In the first edition of this book, we also suggested that resonance provides a valid physical explanation for astrological effects. But this possibility was ignored by critics of astrology Culver and Ianna, Jerome and Bok and others who preferred to

sensitive points, when planets formed conjunctions or other aspects to Sirius, those undergoing schooling in the mystery religions would take advantage of these critical and sensitive moments to 'prepare themselves' and to pass through those 'star windows' or 'doors'.

Apart from this interpretation of the astrological significance of Sirius, Dr Muses also re-examines the roles of the planets as they apply to the days of the week. He points out that throughout the world, the same correspondences between planets and the days exist.*

In all cultures and societies, Sunday is assimilated to the sun, Monday to the moon, Tuesday to Mars (our English days combine Teutonic and Latin names for the planets/gods concealing the planetary sequence. Tuesday is from the Teutonic 'Tiw' or Mars, Wednesday from 'Wodin' or Mercury, Thursday from 'Thor' or Jupiter, Friday from 'Freya' or Venus). These universal attributions again suggest a common source older than the fragmented, unconnected societies about the world who make use of them, and perhaps provide further important clues to this lost, ancient astrology that made conscious use of such correspondences in ritual and ceremony.

For reasons too technical to go into in a book of this general nature, Dr Muses is convinced that we are presently in one of these crucial astrologically sensitive periods (extending through July 1994), and that individuals who have taken steps to 'prepare' themselves may use this period for their own development, as did the ancient Egyptians. Readers interested in pursuing the subject are referred to *The Lion Path: You Can Take It With You*, also Murry Hope, *The Lion People* (Thoth Publications, 1988).

---

dismiss astrology on the basis of Victorian physics. In all fairness to astrology's opponents, its devotees were no quicker to seize upon what may ultimately provide the acceptable physical *modus operandi* accounting for astrology.

* Prediction and analysis in Burmese astrology, little known in the West, is based upon the day of the week the individual was born and the planetary significance of that day.

Astrology in the Egyptian Funerary Texts

In other words, to the ancients responsible for setting out the funerary texts, astrology was not primarily a system of fortune-telling even though its earliest overt appearance (in Assyria in the Second Millennium BC) is in that role. Nor was it primarily a means of analyzing character, a diagnostic and therapeutic tool, as the more responsible ('humanistic') astrology of today tends to be. According to Dr Muses, this ancient astrology, encoded into the texts, provided the practical framework for people on the path. These astrologically determined periods were opportunities to tune in to personally resonant moments. Astrology opened the doors, it was an Open Sesame, into the spiritual treasure (incidentally, the symbolic meaning of *Aladdin and the Lamp*, the familiar but profound *Arabian Nights* tale).

If what Dr Muses calls 'resonantly assisted theurgy' (theurgy: communication, or working with God; from the Greek *theos*, God + *urgos*, working) is the original function of astrology, and if it is valid, then it may also throw new light upon that most ancient of puzzles: astrology's origins.

How did it begin? An observation made many years ago by John Addey, one of twentieth-century astrology's most original and influential thinkers, may furnish the answer – even though Addey was not addressing this particular problem when he made his observation. Talking about astrology in general at a convention, and speaking from personal experience, Addey remarked that on many occasions he would get the feeling 'that there was rather a lot of Mars about' and then, checking his ephemeris, learn that, indeed, Mars was just then involved in some significant planetary configuration. For no apparent reason, this innocent-sounding observation stuck in our minds over the years. When it is examined in the light of the Muses work, it leads to an intriguing hypothesis. If even today it is actually possible to develop a heightened sensitivity toward celestial 'influences' or correspondences then it may not be implausible to suggest that the ancients, living in closer communion to the natural world than ourselves, and with their heads less full of clutter, might well have been able to experience astrological effects directly and routinely. This would seem to apply particularly to the astrological significance accorded the planets which, as we have pointed out, are common to all cultures despite the quite different astrological systems. And, as we shall see, it is these planetary 'personalities', and to date, only these (out of the vast and unwieldy body of astrological doctrine) that have survived modern testing more or less intact.

In other words, the ancients ascribed specific powers to the planets for the very simple reason that they could *feel* those powers directly. (People following the Lion Path as developed by Dr Muses sometimes report similar direct experiences.) Though no doubt impossible to prove, this hypothesis has the double advantage of plausibility and simplicity – though it does not address the development of astrology's Pythagorean and metaphysical framework.

In any event, an initiatic astrology is in keeping with the actual physical accomplishments (temples, tombs, pyramids) of the ancient societies that practiced it. The pieces all now fall into place. That single little figure from Tutankhamen's shrine (see p. 57) proves the existence of astrology in Egypt. There is no possible satisfactory alternate explanation for this figure. The astronomical/astrological basis of the mythologies throughout the world independently corroborates that interpretation. By general agreement, these mythologies pre-date recorded history. Thus, astrology also pre-dates recorded history and astrology is found everywhere. With the texts beginning to reveal the nature of that lost astrology, and statistical studies validating its premises according to today's ground rules, we stand on the threshold of recouping what once was a valid and crucially important aspect of the ancient initiatic discipline, the great Sacred Science of individual human transformation – without which no civilization in any meaningful sense is possible.

If this new interpretation of astrology's origins is valid, it adds a new dimension and a piquancy to the already complex role played by astrology throughout Western history.

B. The Whore of Babylon

★ When Jupiter stands in front of Mars there will be corn and men will be slain, or a great army will be slain.

★ When Mars approaches Jupiter there will be great devastation in the land.

★ When Mars approaches Jupiter, in that year the king of Akkad will die and the crops of that land will be prosperous.

★ When the Moon rideth in a chariot, the yoke of the king of Akkad will prosper.

★ When the Moon is low in appearance, the submission (of the people) of a far country will come to the king.

★ When Mercury culminates in Tammuz, there will be corpses.

★ When Leo is dark, the heart of the land will not be happy. Long live the Lord of Kings . . . from Asandu.

★ When Jupiter goes with Venus, the prayers of the land will reach the heart of the gods. Merodach and Sarapanitum will hear the prayer of the people and will have mercy on the people. Let them send me an ass that it may ease my feet . . . From Nirgatitir.

From *The Reports of the Magicians and
Astrologers of Nineveh and Babylon*,
ed. R. C. Thompson

Assurbanipal (668–626 BC), King of Assyria, received the above as daily reports from his magicians and astrologers. Marked confidential, and intended only for the king, these reports, inscribed in cuneiform upon clay tablets, were among the thousands recovered from the ruins of the library at Nineveh. Marked 'unconfidential' and put in less orotund language, it might come right out of a contemporary newspaper. No esoteric interpretation as far as we know can be made of most of these reports.

However, recent research has also determined that much of the material found in Assurbanipal's library was copied from earlier sources, dating back another thousand years to Hammurabi (1728–1686 BC) who in turn derived his famous code of laws and presumably much else from the still-earlier Sumerians. Astrological, astronomical, magical tablets and omens have all come to light mixed together. Scholars examining this farrago regard the closely observed, accurate astronomy as a signal that science was emerging out of the welter of ancient superstition. But given the evidence of *Hamlet's Mill*, Schwaller de Lubicz, Dr Muses and others, it might be argued rather more persuasively that the science was the old element and was giving way, in Assurbanipal's time, to magic and superstition.

We do not know and cannot know the status of all this material within its own context. If a portion of the New York Public Library should be found in the ruins of New York three thousand years from now, who would be able to determine the seriousness with which the wildly heterogeneous material was regarded? Who would suspect that books on Darwinian evolution were taken seriously, while Schwaller de Lubicz and Gurdjieff were ignored? The fact that the material was found together tells us very little. And some of the most outrageous-sounding of the omens smack of a possible alternate or symbolic explanation. 'If a ewe gives birth to a lion and it has two horns on the left – an enemy will take your fortress.' Was this meant to be taken literally? It doesn't seem possible. But how can we know? On the other hand, 'If a man goes on an errand and a falcon passes from his right to his left – he will achieve his goal' sounds like simple superstition of the seven-years-bad-luck-for-breaking-a-mirror type.

In these, the very oldest direct astrological references we have so far, the planets already have their traditional characteristics; in particular, Venus corresponding to love and affairs of the heart, and Mars to violence and warfare. But beyond this, to draw conclusions and pretend that astrology grew willy-nilly from this collection of disparate material is not scholarship, but prejudice and imagination, particularly with evidence of an earlier astrology in Egypt readily available.*

Nor has anyone apparently entertained the possibility that Assurbanipal's astrologers/magicians made accurate predictions; at least often enough to retain possession of their heads – since Eastern despots were not renowned for their patience and soothsayers were expendable. The point worth stressing is: even when confronted by a situation like this involving a body of intermingled omens, magic, astrology and accurate astronomical observations, it is not quite legitimate to jump to the conclusion that this represents the only or the highest level of learning then available in Babylon in the seventh century BC.

It is from Babylon, in the centuries following Assurbanipal, that the first actual horoscopes and zodiacs are found. And while it is impossible at the moment to prove that an esoteric, higher astrology was practiced at the same time that the court soothsayers and street-corner prophets flourished, the appearance of horoscopes and zodiacs makes it nearly a precondition. It is also culturally highly plausible. The existence of such an astrological tradition in Egypt is now, in our opinion, undeniable. (In Egypt, in fact, as far as we can tell, it was only that esoteric astrology that was permitted to flourish.)

Babylon was historically and culturally a far more chaotic society than Egypt ever was. But it is well established that there were cultural links throughout the whole of the ancient world, and it is unlikely that the tradition directing Egyptian civilization in its entirety would not have had its counterpart in Babylon, even if it functioned – as esoteric traditions so often are forced to function – invisible to the public eye.

There are a few Old Testament references that lend a degree of credence to this idea. The prophet Daniel, living a century later than Assurbanipal, was reputed wiser than the magicians and astrologers at their own game, and was made master over them

* Cf. Culver and Ianna, *The Gemini Syndrome*, pp. 12–19.

– though the Book of Daniel does not make it sound as though wisdom was the salient characteristic of Nebuchadnezzar's court.

Then, in 597 BC, the prophet Ezekiel, along with King Johakin of Juda, was exiled to Babylon. Prophesying the sufferings of Israel (a pretty safe bet all things considered), Ezekiel (4:6) testifies, quoting the Lord, as He appeared before him in a vision: 'I have appointed thee each day for a year.'

To an astrologer this looks very much like a reference to a system of prediction still generally used, in which a day on one scale is equated with a year in another. That is, the position of planets on the thirtieth day after the birth of a child will reflect the situation that will be prevailing in his or her thirtieth year. Though this may look distinctly unscientific, psychologists are beginning to place considerable importance on the events of the first few weeks or months following birth, on the birth trauma itself, and even on prenatal conditions as factors in the individual's eventual personality. And since the strongest pro-astrology evidence we have concerns the relationship between the position of planets at the moment of birth and subsequent personality, it is at least conceivable that celestial factors play a particularly significant role in those earliest weeks of life, in which case, the day-for-a-year system of 'progressing' the horoscope may have a physical basis.

THE WHORE OF BABYLON: *She Seduces Greece*

Though impossible to document or even deduce an advanced esoteric astrology in Babylon in the same way that we can in Egypt, it is legitimate to assert that astrology is always an element in ancient Sacred Science, and it was a high form of Sacred Science that found its way to Greece and took root as Pythagoreanism.

Pythagoras (*c.* 580–500 BC) may well have been the single greatest force in the development of Western thought. Like so many of the world's great teachers, he left nothing in writing, and subsequent accounts of his work and his life have been distorted to the point where, for many years, even his historical existence was questioned. But it is now generally accepted that he is not merely a compendium of legend, and that he taught his famous doctrines at his school in Croton, opened after his return from prolonged – if formally unauthenticated – travel in Mesopotamia and Egypt.

Pythagoras has always been credited with the discovery of the laws of harmony and the geometrical Rule of Pythagoras. At the same time he has been severely criticized for fostering the notion that numbers have *meanings*. This in turn led to a veritable Pandora's box of despised superstitions, among them the infamous doctrine of the 'Harmony of the Spheres' – central to astrological thinking.

It is, however, impossible to avoid Pythagoreanism. Even the logician, in his monochrome world of yes-or-no, pays tacit homage. For if two were not different in meaning from one, there could be no distinction between true and false; while, in the subtler worlds of mathematics and physics, 'Neo-Pythagoreanism' is a recognized movement.*

It is not known if Pythagoras himself taught astrology, or practiced it. Victorian and classical scholars, tracing their intellectual genealogies, and, like nouveau-riche industrialists, anxious to prove themselves of noble lineage, successfully pretended for several centuries that the Greeks were untainted by astrology altogether; at least until Alexander brought it back with him from his conquests; at which point it was supposed to have spread unchecked.

But by 1900 this view was contested by Franz Cumont.

> ... another pupil of Plato, the astronomer Eudoxus of Cnidos, declared: 'No credence should be given to the Chaldeans, who predict and mark out the life of every man according to the day of his nativity.' Certain modern philologists – who doubtless look upon Greek history as a kind of experiment in a closed vessel,

---

* See E. T. Bell, *The Magic of Numbers* (McGraw-Hill, 1946) for an interesting if emotionally inconsistent account of Neo-Pythagoreanism in contemporary science.

which providence anxious to exclude every disturbing element conducted for the fullest instruction of the savants of the future – certain philologists, I say, have doubted whether Eudoxus in the fourth century could really have known and condemned oriental genethlialogy (prophesying from the moment of birth). But like Eudoxus, Theophrastus, a little later, spoke of it in his treatise on 'Celestial Signs': he regarded with surprise the claim of the Chaldeans to be able to predict from these signs the life and death of individuals, and not merely general phenomena, such as good or bad weather. The insatiable curiosity of the Greeks, then, did not ignore astrology but their sober genius rejected its hazardous doctrines, and their keen critical sense [1] was able to distinguish the scientific data observed by the Babylonians from the erroneous conclusions which they derived from them. It is to their everlasting honour that, amid the tangle of precise observations and superstitious fancies which made up the priestly lore of the East, they discovered and utilized the serious elements, while neglecting the rubbish. As long as Greece remained Greece, stellar divination gained no hold on the Greek mind, and all attempts to substitute an astronomic theology for their immoral but charming idolatry, were destined for failure. The efforts of philosophers to impose on their countrymen the worship of the 'great visible gods', as Plato terms them, recoiled before the might of a tradition supported by the prestige of art and literature.

> Franz Cumont, *Astrology and Religion Among*
> *the Greeks and Romans*, pp. 30–31

... And the time comes when the son of the nouveau-riche industrialist repudiates his father's crasser pretensions and owns up to the scoundrel at the root of the family tree ... insisting, however, that he was Robin Hood.

How are we to reconcile that 'sober genius' and 'keen critical sense' [1] with a concomitant belief in idolatry – be it never so charming or immoral?*

---

* Even allowing for the subjectivity of language; to call, say Kronos – who castrates his father and devours his children, or Oedipus – who slays his father and commits incest with his mother, 'charming' would seem somewhat inappropriate.

How could these Greeks on the one hand sift the science out from the superstition of Babylon and on the other bestow 'prestige' upon an art and literature founded entirely upon idolatry?

It is obvious that a nation of such sub-Sagittarian creatures (half-genius, half-jackass) never existed. Sober genius and a keen critical sense have nothing to do with a belief in or a repudiation of astrology. Socrates had sober genius and a keen critical sense, but the bureaucrats who put him to death, and who expressed the will of the Greek majority at the time, did not. And it was Plato, after all, who called the planets the 'great visible gods'. So it was hardly the sober genius of the average Greek in the *agora* that rejected the doctrine when the soberest genius of them all embraced it.

A widespread passion for prophecy is one of the telltale signs of a decadent society. If the Greeks did not succumb to this particular form of national despair for several hundred years, it is not because their sober genius prevented them, but because they were too busy fighting enemies and each other to spend time this way.

In Cumont's time, no pre-Christian horoscopes had been found. Yet the testimony of Eudoxus and Theophrastus proves that genethliacal astrology *must* have existed at least as early as the fourth century BC. And it is not unreasonable to suppose – accurate astronomical data being available – that the Chaldeans had at their disposal some systematic method of calculating and prophesying, conceivably dating from antiquity. But because, until very recently, pre-Greek societies were not allowed to practice science in our sense of the word, the notion of an early systematic astrology was strenuously contested.

Robert Eisler, one of the most vituperative critics astrology ever had, declared in his inimitable prose:

> It follows then that the claim of the various 'Chaldean' and 'Egyptian' star-clerks, writing in Greek for a Hellenized public able and willing to pay for 'nativities', to base their forecasts on the secular, nay, millennial experiences of their respective ancestors,

was and is no more than a good, healthy bouncing lie. Never at any time did an early Sumerian, Assyrian, Babylonian, or, for the matter of that, an old Elamite, Hurrite, or Hittite astrologer writing in cuneiform script on clay tablets ever establish any relation whatsoever between the position of the planets in the various zodiacal signs and the fate or character of any individual child royal, noble or plebeian-born or conceived at a given hour.

Robert Eisler, *The Royal Art of Astrology*, p. 166

Yet despite the conviction with which this view is expressed, it rests upon the assumption that Eisler had read all the Sumerian, Assyrian, Babylonian, Elamite, Hurrite and Hittite tablets that were ever written, and that ever will be found. This assumption turns out to have been premature.

More recent discoveries (1952) have brought to light the postulated horoscopes of the Babylonians, in which planetary and zodiacal positions are noted. The earliest of these horoscopes can be dated back to 29 April 409 BC.*

The discovery of these early horoscopes tells us that personal, genethliacal astrology (as well as the mundane astrology of Nineveh that predicted national or local events in relation to the future of the king) existed centuries before it was supposed to have begun; and in Babylon. Despite such evidence, it is the erroneous view of astrology's origins that remains current.

* * *

Reduced to essentials, history may be seen as the struggle of civilization against barbarism, with barbarism predominating – since it takes a thousand civilized men a hundred years to build a cathedral while a single barbarian with a howitzer flattens it in a minute. Certain societies – Egypt was surely one of them – effect a balance for a time. In others, civilization runs like a thick visible thread through the barbarian tapestry, holding it together – the cathedral builders of the Middle Ages, for

---

* Neugebauer and Van Hoesen, 'Greek Horoscopes', American Philosophical Soc., vol. 48 (1959).

example. In a truly dark age, the thread is invisible. Scholars cannot legitimately talk about 'religion', 'art' or 'astrology' without specifying which level of religion, art or astrology they mean.

> By patiently following the connections of mathematical and astro-nomical theory we moved from period to period and from civiliza-tion to civilization. Our road often went parallel to the road pointed out by historians of art, religion, alchemy and many other fields. This is not surprising. It only underlines the intrinsic unity of human culture. The role of astronomy is perhaps unique in so far as it carried in its slow but steady progress the roots for the most decisive development in human history, the creation of the modern exact sciences. To follow this specific aspect of cultural history seems to me worthy of our efforts, however fragmentary our results may be.
>
> O. Neugebauer, *The Exact Sciences in Antiquity*, p. 177

But 'the road . . . of religion, art and alchemy' goes in exactly the opposite direction from that of the exact sciences which in any case are not exact, but merely quantitative. 'Decisive' is not a synonym for 'valuable'. The A-bomb was the most 'decisive' event in the history of Hiroshima. Civilizations operate upon a number of levels simultaneously. Pop music, often accomplished in its own right, is not of the same *order* as Bach; Fundamentalist Christianity bears absolutely no resemblance to the Christianity of a Meister Eckhart or Thomas Merton. That such a hierarchy exists is unmistakable. To overlook it is to falsify or mis-understand history hopelessly. But the hierarchy cannot be measured – not by any instrument that is an extension or refinement of the five senses. And it is this that provides our modern scholars with their loophole.

Arbitrary, metaphysical standards – such as measurability – are erected. Everything is then subjected to this standard as a qualification for 'serious' consideration. When the standard is inapplicable, the fault is held to lie in the subject. A vote may be taken, true, except that in the discussion preceding the vote all who point back to the long-since-forgotten original arbitrariness of the standard are branded cranks or dreamers and excluded from the vote . . . If it cannot be measured, if it does not fit into the plan, then, in a revisionist's version of the famous fairy tale, it is the obnoxious, whistle-blowing little child that is declared non-existent. The universe is, by a unanimous vote of experts, decreed spiritually flat . . . And the Empire lived happily ever after, devoting itself wholeheartedly to the manufacture, promotion and distribution of the Emperor's New Clothes . . .

Did the Pythagoreans actually have and teach astrology, but, like the Egyptians, keep it to themselves? It is common knowledge that the Pythagoreans took pledges of secrecy.*

Was a knowledge of astrology among the secrets? We don't see how it could have been missing. Pythagoras, and Plato after him, taught that man is a microcosm, and that in him are contained all the laws applicable to the macrocosm of the universe. This is a fundamental principle of astrology. Empedocles, a fairly early Pythagorean (*c.* 450 BC) has been credited with the invention of the 'four elements'. But the four elements play a significant role in the symbolism of Egypt (and in the symbolism and cosmology of various cultures of the Orient and elsewhere). They are also central to the astrological doctrine. Pythagoras taught that musical harmony was but that expression of cosmic harmony to which our organs of sense had access; an early taste of the 'music of the spheres'. The same mathematical ratios of the musical scale, applied to astrology, produce the astrological doctrine of 'aspects'. Was all this unknown to the Egyptians and Pythagoreans themselves? Only grafted on to the Chaldean superstition later by clever eclectic con-men? Our own

---

* 'The mysteries most jealously guarded by the Brotherhood (of Pythagoras) were of supposed cosmic and practical importance. It is both tragic and ironic that they were preposterous nonsense.' E. T. Bell, op. cit., p. 198. And doubly tragic and ironic that E. T. Bell did not know the nature of those secrets, and so was talking through his hat.

guess would be that Pythagoras and his followers knew the principles of astrology, but that their study of it was confined to the symbolism of the zodiac and the planets and the harmonic relationships between them; an early Pythagorean would be more interested in the abstract meaning of Mars in Scorpio than he would be in the way in which Mars in Scorpio manifested itself in the personality of X, born under Mars in Scorpio. And if he concerned himself with whether X, born under Mars in Scorpio, should buy a poodle when Jupiter stood in conjunction with Sirius because Sirius was also known as the 'Dog Star' and Jupiter symbolizes good fortune, he would be dismissed from the Brotherhood. And he might then set up business in the *agora* as a 'Chaldean'. It is also conceivable that the Pythagoreans knew the secret of 'resonantly assisted theurgy' as well.

*   *   *

The wave of genuine civilization initiated by Pythagoras and then brilliantly formulated by Plato passed swiftly over Greece, leaving as mementoes the Greek temples, Greek art, a number of streams of Pythagorean teaching in varying degrees of impurity, and a thriving but chaotic astrology.

By the third century BC, improved astronomy and geometry permitted astrologers to make more precise calculations when erecting horoscopes, though it is impossible to gauge the effect this had on their interpretative skill. (The master chef can do more with an open fire than the novice with a gas range.) And this scientific-looking astrology was carried throughout the then-known world by Alexander.

Aristotle's most famous pupil largely succeeded in the physical realm in emulating the intellectual achievements of his master. Self-proclaimed as a harbinger of enlightenment, Aristotle managed to misunderstand, pervert and destroy nearly all that was valuable in the work of his predecessors. And just as Aristotle distorted the teaching of the Pythagoreans and substituted the arrogant and false notion that man, through the exercise of intellect alone, could arrive at a knowledge of the real world, so Alexander, pursuing a parallel path, burned to the ground the palace of Darius, and with it the great library then containing the wisdom that had managed to survive all other conquerors and catastrophes. By way of compensation he established the city of Alexandria in honor of himself. Nor did the parallel quite stop there. The particularly malignant aspect of Aristotle's teaching mentioned above did not infect the West until it was falling apart from other causes anyhow; while through no fault of Alexander's, Alexandria became in its turn the spiritual capital of the world, melting-pot of cultures, and a thriving centre for the exchange of all manner of astrological and esoteric knowledge.

Over the course of several centuries, scholars collected and studied ancient and modern scripts and tablets. Undoubtedly, new work was undertaken; and another famous library, the Museion, grew to a reputed 700,000 volumes . . . But if horse-racing is the sport of kings, then book-burning is the sport of conquerors; and it is partially due to this pastime that knowledge of the teaching of the past is so hopelessly fragmentary. During Caesar's wars, the Museion was burned, destroying most of the astrological texts. Babylon, over its long history, was destroyed repeatedly, as was Nineveh, and all the seats of ancient culture. In the second century AD, the Emperor Septimus Serverus pillaged the Egyptian temples of all their sacred literature, which was subsequently destroyed or scattered about the world. The Serapeion, the library slowly built from the remains of the Museion and from the accumulated memories of scholars, incurred the wrath of the Bishop Theophilus three centuries after Caesar; 200,000 offending scripts were lost. Remnants found their way to Byzantium where they were momentarily safe. Meanwhile, the Emperor Constantine decreed that his version of Christianity – which bore a certain resemblance to the Christianity of today, but none to that of Christ – was to be the only and official religion of Rome, and burned all the pagan archives. In Byzantium, Theodosius II followed suit in the fifth century; not only closing all the universities still teaching Greek philosophy, but putting to the torch what had come to Byzantium from Alexandria. In

B. *The Whore of Babylon*

Alexandria itself, however, the indefatigable nth generation of scholars was piecing together what was left of what was left of . . . and for several centuries lived in peace to enjoy the fruits of its labors. In 641, however, Alexandria again fell. Scholars begged the Arab general, 'Amr (or Omar) to spare the library. But 'Amr, a proto-Logical Positivist, declared the matter a pseudo-problem. 'Either,' he reasoned, 'these books contain what is already written in the Koran, in which case they are unnecessary; or else they contain what is not in the Koran, in which case they are false.' And the library burned. (This legend, alas! is held to be apocryphal.)

THE WHORE OF BABYLON: *She Corrupts Rome*

The earliest complete astrological treatise that has survived to our own day is the *Tetrabiblos* of Claudius Ptolemy, Alexandrian Neo-platonist, astronomer, geographer, mathematician, astrologer, of the second century A D. Seven centuries had elapsed since Pythagoras – the span of time separating the Magna Carta from ourselves. During this time, astrology flourished on every level – with increasing emphasis on the lower – and in every corner of the Hellenized world. Out of these seven centuries comes astrology as it is practiced today – not much has been added or changed, at least until very recently. Yet the steps involved in its supposed development remain absolutely unknown, making the history of astrology more elusive than ever. Indeed, however romantic it sounds on the surface, it is only that postulated Sacred Science of a remote, lost antiquity that provides reasonable answers to the myriad questions surrounding astrology's origins.

Who first decided that Mars should be God of War; and that the planet Mars should therefore be important in the horoscopes of soldiers? And by analogy (Mars/Iron/Weapons/etc.) the planet of butchers and surgeons? Saturn was already playing his traditional role in the earliest of the Egyptian myths. Mercury, the Hermes of the Greeks, and Thoth (or Djehuti) to the Egyptians is invariably messenger of the gods; he rules the intellect; is the planet of writers (and of magicians, jugglers, pickpockets). Who first thought of this? And upon whose authority was it accepted? Did hundreds and thousands of independent astrologers scattered over the Hellenized world all suddenly agree that this was Mercury's function? If the scholars are right, and the meanings assigned to both the signs of the zodiac and the planets are utterly arbitrary, without even a grain of truth, then the historical fact that in two thousand years these meanings have gone unchallenged – and by the best, not the worst minds – stands as a psychological enigma too great to ignore. In the pre-Christian era no known single astrologer, and no known astrological or esoteric school, possessed the authority to impose decrees upon hosts of independent astrologers of every possible philosophical and religious persuasion. (Of course, the now-proven *universal* character of these planetary attributions makes a Greco-Roman development of astrology impossible, not just improbable.) And in the Hellenized world there was no organization big enough or stable enough to carry on systematic astrological observations – which would require the detailed records of generations. Eisler (op. cit., p. 79) scoffs at the Chaldeans for boasting that their divinatory art was the fruit of millennial experience. What has happened to those records? Why is there no single instance of such massive statistical compilation extant? These are legitimate objections. And the astrologer cannot meet them. But his oblique defense is interesting. Putting aside for the moment the aesthetic satisfaction of astrological symbolism, astrologers have actually been working with the material for two thousand years. Yet, in these millennia no one has seriously attempted to revise the astrological canon. No one has claimed that Venus was really saturnine in character, or Mars jovial. Assume for the moment that astrology is absolute rubbish, and that the results it returns are always and inevitably false. Is it possible then, that for two thousand years all who practiced it were so benumbed by its symbolism, so awe-struck by the imaginary authority of remote Chaldean dreamers, that not only did they fail to repudiate the doctrine, but they did not even attempt to radically reorganize it upon a more effective basis?

The answer to all of these questions is that, however astrology may have been developed, it was developed by people with access to the truth. These truths were understood intuitively, and subsequently verified through personal experience by those with the gift, throughout the ages. And though even more prone to abuse, corruption, popularization and bastardization than other art forms or religion itself, astrology's metaphysical truth and practical validity sufficed to preserve it to the present day.

Though impossible to document categorically, certain hints and fragments give clues as to how this astrology may have managed to percolate down through the centuries, more or less intact.

There was, for instance, Berosus, a Babylonian priest of Baal who opened an astrological school on the island of Cos in 280 BC. We do not know what he taught, or how, but there is usually something behind a reputation that becomes legendary.

The greatest teacher of the pre-Christian era was Posidonius. Nothing remains of his work, but second-hand reports and a number of works from other writers who were indebted to Posidonius for their ideas, provide clues. So it is known that his teaching was based largely on Plato's *Timaeus* – which is Pythagorean in its entirety – and that he incorporated into his doctrine elements of the rather ornate mystical doctrines then coming in from the East. In his day, only Epicurus (preaching an altogether different doctrine) rivalled him as a teacher. A number of the great men of the age were his pupils, among them Cicero (who later bitterly repudiated astrology). Posidonius was by repute one of the most ardent advocates astrology ever had. Apparently he inspired a long astrological poem by the Roman, Manilius, which in turn had a long-lasting influence among astrologers.

Hipparchus, the greatest of Greek astronomers, was an astrologer – much to the regret of contemporary historians. But it would appear that the Greek contribution to astrology was technical, not interpretive. The advanced astronomy and mathematics of the Egyptians of the early and Middle Kingdoms had been lost, or was still successfully kept secret. The complex astronomical/astrological content of extensive reliefs in the late Ptolemaic Temples of Dendera, Esna and Edfu suggests the old knowledge was still available to the Egyptian priesthood. But the Greek mathematicians and astronomers Aristarchus, Seleucis, Hipparchus and others were forced to rediscover it for themselves. (The information may well have been available in some form in the library of Alexandria, to which scholars would have had access.) The application of improved astronomy and geometry permitted the calculation of an accurate horoscope. And to this was applied the already extant canon of zodiacal symbols and planetary meanings – no doubt to some extent adulterated and confused by this time.

As the founders of Stoicism, the Greeks also provided a philosophical atmosphere in which an astrology could flourish that was not Pythagorean symbolism, nor cheap market-place prophecy, nor even psychological study, but a philosophical prop used to support Stoical pantheistic materialism; a doctrine in many ways similar to the atheistic materialism prevalent today (in its varying guises of 'Humanism', 'Existentialism', 'Ethical Religion', etc.).

Like modern materialism, Stoicism was influential among the ruling and intellectual classes of the day; and astrology served Stoicism in the same emotional capacity that modern science serves modern materialists. Astrology was to the Stoic the study of manifestation of divine will; modern science is to the materialist the study of the manifestations of undivine accident – but both presuppose the ineluctable operation of cause and effect.

Like their modern counterparts, the Stoics denied or were unaware of the principle of 'level' ('Never speak of the higher or the lower in evolution.' Charles Darwin, quoted by Marjorie Grene, in *The Knower and the Known*, p. 266). Having taken this step, the Stoics were unable to reconcile the idea of free will with that of cause and effect.

In a universe entirely pre-determined by divine will, just as in one in which meaningless effect follows automatically upon accidental cause, an interest in the nature of the causes is an absurdity. Still, the Stoics, like their modern counterparts, could not help wanting to know which effect would follow which cause. Astrology, like our science two thousand years later, was pressed into providing this cheerless and futile information.

By the time of Claudius Ptolemy, astrology had 'developed' or perhaps more accurately 'conglomerated' into the recognizable parent of the astrology still practiced today. Christianity was, at this time, just one of many conflicting religions vying for prominence; all of which in one way or another concerned the supposed nature of the 'soul', and all of which in one way or another took astrology into account. But if astrology could be cast into every imaginable philosophical image, its techniques were settled – never to the satisfaction of its skeptical practitioners but, as we have said, in such a manner that no subsequent revisions have been made that withstood the test of time.

For all his excellence as a geographer, astronomer and mathematician, Ptolemy's knowledge of the physical universe was as scanty as anyone else's of his age. But in his astrological works he attempts to account for astrological 'influence' by scientific explanations. He replaces the personalities ascribed to the planets with the de-humanized terminology of Aristotle's 'primary qualities', which to the modern ear sounds ridiculous. (Hot, cold, moist, dry are so-called 'primary qualities'.)

Ptolemy does not invent astrology; he attempts to apply what he believes to be physical science to the vast corpus of rules-of-thumb that have come down to him from unknown or rumored sources.* Thus, explaining how the planets determine the kind of death to be expected, he maintains:

---

* 1,800 years later, Robert Eisler ridiculed Ptolemy's explanation of how astrology worked, and then went on to explain how it didn't work by means of the identical explanation. An amusing aside: the fourteenth edition of the *Encyclopaedia Britannica* is so solicitous of its modern readers' sensibilities that it refrains from mentioning that Ptolemy was an astrologer – though, as far as the West is concerned, he was the most important one who ever lived. This is like writing a biography of Oedipus and for reasons of delicacy forbearing to mention his strained family relationships.

. . . if the dominion of death be vested in Saturn, he will produce death from the super-abundance of cold. Jupiter effects death by quinsey, inflammation of the lungs, apoplexy, spasm, pains in the head, morbid performance of the heart, and by all diseases arising from superabundance of air, and from immoderate and impure respiration.

Mars causes death by constant fevers, semitertians, sudden and spontaneous wounds, diseases of the kidneys, expectoration of the blood, and haemorrhages of various kinds; by miscarriage, or abortion, and by child-birth, by erisipilas, and in short, by such diseases as proceed from abundant and immoderate heat.

Venus produces death by disorders of the stomach, and of the liver, by scurvy and dysentery; also by consumption or wasting away, and by fistula and poison, and by all diseases incident on the superabundance or poverty of moisture, and its corruption.

Lastly, Mercury causes death to proceed from fury, madness, melancholy, epilepsy, falling fits, coughs and obstructions, and by all diseases as arise from superabundance or disproportionate dryness.

. . . if it happen that Saturn be in fixed signs, and in quartile or opposition to the Sun, and contrary in condition, he will produce death by suffocation, occasioned either by multitudes of people, or by hanging or strangulation . . . If he [Saturn] be posited in places or signs of bestial form, the native will be destroyed by wild beasts, and, if Jupiter also offer testimony, being at the same time badly afflicted, the death will then occur in public, and by day; for example, by being exposed to combats with wild beasts. If Saturn be posited in opposition to either of the luminaries in the ascendant, he will cause death in prison: if he be configurated with Mercury, and especially if near the constellation of the Serpent in the sphere, and in terrestrial signs of the zodiac, he will produce death by venomous wounds or bites, and by reptiles and wild beasts. And, should Venus also attach herself to Saturn and Mercury thus combined, death will then ensue by poison or female treachery. If Saturn be in Virgo or Pisces, or watery signs, and configurated with the Moon, he will operate death by means of water, by drowning and suffocation; and if found near Argo, by shipwreck . . .

> Mars, if in signs of human form, and posited in quartile or in opposition to the Sun and Moon, and contrary in condition will operate death by slaughter, either in civil or foreign war, or by suicide: if Venus add her testimony, death will be inflicted by women, or by assassins in the employment of women: and should Mercury also be configurated with them, death will happen from robbers, thieves, or highwaymen . . .

> Ptolemy's *Tetrabiblos*,
> translated from the Greek paraphrase by Proclus
> by J. M. Ashmand, pp. 198–200

What has happened to Pythagoras? Is this the legacy of the Egyptian sages? How could Ptolemy's *Tetrabiblos* remain an astrological textbook for sixteen centuries? And how could a man commit such nonsense to papyrus in the first place?

Half the men in the world are born with Saturn in a 'bestial sign'. Of those, at least one in twenty are in 'malefic' aspect to Jupiter. Even allowing for a high incidence of violence in second-century Alexandria, are we to believe that twenty-five out of every thousand men were torn apart by wild beasts in public combat?

How could such a notion arise? Is it possible that at one time half a dozen men were killed by wild beasts in the arena? Examining their horoscopes, astrologers discovered that all happened to have Saturn in 'bestial signs' in malefic aspect to Jupiter; hence it passed into the astrological canon that all men born under such conditions would be torn to bits by wild beasts, and having been incorporated, went unchallenged forever after? Could it have been that, at another time, four different men were done in by their women; each was found to have a similarly unfavorable Venus; and it was concluded that all who have ill-aspected Venuses are doomed to die violent female-inflicted deaths?

Modern scholars believe that this is the answer. And, certainly, it must be part of the answer. A keen, critical sense has never been the general rule among astrologers. Thus, even today, statements such as the following are much less rare than they ought to be:

Saturn has a reputed temperature of 270 degrees below zero; and is therefore the 'icy' planet of the heavens. As every schoolboy knows, heat expands while cold contracts.

When, therefore, a woman is born with Saturn mixing his ray with either the Sun or the Moon, her life becomes much too restricted and cramped . . . Saturn is a very sincere and conscientious planet, but he is essentially the planet of fixity.

This was written, incredibly enough, in 1954, and appeared in print in *Prediction* Magazine (November 1954). Its perpetrator, A. W. Pole, in a subsequent advertisement calling attention to his services, described himself as 'The World's Most Praised Astrologer'.

But it is not the whole story. First, it must be realized that a complete textbook on astrology is an impossibility; a fore-doomed attempt to quantify the qualitative. Each horoscope is a whole. Each horoscope is individual.* And every astrologer knows (Ptolemy certainly knew) that to abstract individual elements from the horoscope is to eliminate part of the truth. Thus, it is misleading to say that Venus in opposition to Saturn means 'thus-and-so'.

For it only does under special circumstances when a myriad of other factors enhance the probability of its working out. But to talk about the subject at all, the astrologer is obliged to generalize. And in generalizing it is impossible to talk in the sort of infinite conditional tense the subject demands.

Putting aside Ptolemy's Grand-Guignol sense of illustration for the moment, not many men are actually murdered by women, or even by assassins hired by women. But there is a recognizable *type* of man who lives his life at the mercy of women. He has been known to caricaturists and dramatists from time immemorial. Obviously, every henpecked husband has his own peculiarities, but a modern astrologer would not be

---

* Later (pp. 195–6), we will discuss the very real problem posed by 'Time Twins' – children born the same minute but otherwise unrelated.

surprised (if a test group could be selected upon some pre-arranged, mutually agreed-upon scale of henpeckedness) to see this validated by statistical methods, and, indeed, to show a high incidence of Mars/Venus/Saturn affliction, perhaps (given the results of Gauquelin's work) in relation to the angles.

Ptolemy and other astrologers of his age took astrology seriously. Though even from this era very little written evidence has come down to us, a number of sources attest to the efforts astrologers were making to improve and refine their art. Vettius Valens, a near contemporary of Ptolemy, tried to make statistical observations, unaware of the subtleties of statistical techniques. Doctors made use of astrology in their diagnoses and prescriptions, without great success one gathers. The high science of Egypt had long since disappeared. And by the end of the second century the impetus to perform original astrological work had died altogether.

The demise of the Roman Republic and the inauguration of the Empire was the beginning of a heyday for the market-place astrologer that lasted four full centuries.

The accession of Augustus to the throne had been predicted by astrologers, despite heavy odds, and Augustus was so impressed he had coins cast bearing his sun-sign (Capricorn). Subsequent emperors relied heavily upon their star-gazers.

But Rome never was a civilization in our sense of the word. Though civilizing currents ran through it – early Christianity, the purer forms of Neo-Platonism, certain gnostic sects – civilization never reached the Roman population at large; a generalization defensible upon grounds of the paucity of Roman literature, the vapidity of its art and sculpture, and its dreary if monumental architecture. Art invariably mirrors the spirit of its age. To understand the soul and spirit of any civilization, study its art; its history does not matter much. Which is probably why the true civilizations of the past did not pay much attention to their history.

By the time of Christ the fervor of the Republic had died; the Empire replaced it with its famous three-ring bureaucracy ('the grandeur that was Rome'). And in this atmosphere of bored frenzy the masses turned to the street-corner soothsayer for advice and solace.

Instant horoscopes were cast in the streets. If a client did not know the exact moment of birth – and few did – a stick was thrown upon the soothsayer's marble zodiac; where it fell marked the ascendant. It was believed that if the stars impelled the passer-by to inquire into his destiny, the stars would see to it that the stick indicated the correct degree.*

Pythagoras played no more of a role in this astrology than he does in today's newspaper astrology. But it would be a mistake to draw too close a parallel between the corner 'Chaldean' in Rome (every pop astrologer called himself a 'Chaldean') and his apparent descendant. The Chaldean was no mere journalist-cum-psychologist. His economic and psychological role in society was greater. He combined in himself the triple function of manufacturer, advertising agency and retail outlet; and his product of garbled mysticism and spurious hope differed from the material products of today principally in that, when it had served its emotional purpose, it left no disposal problem in its wake.

The situation was by no means new. Centuries earlier, the prophet Isaiah had issued his famous pronouncements against the astrologers:

> Sit thou silent and get thee into darkness, oh daughter of the Chaldeans ... Stand now with thine enchantments, and with the multitudes of thy sorceries wherein thou hast labored from thy youth ... Thou art wearied in the multitude of thy counsels. Let now the astrologers, the star-gazers, the monthly prognosticators stand up and save thee from those things which have come upon thee.

But resounding prose has little effect upon the course of empires. Jerusalem fell in due course, and Rome in her time followed

---

* 'People fashioned their lives on astrological predictions ... To submit to astrology intellectually implied absolute submission to fate. Adepts disputed whether there was any free will at all.' C. A. Burland, *The Magical Arts* (Arthur Barker, 1966), p. 70.

suit. Whether astrology added or subtracted as much as a day from their lifespans must remain an open question.

FOOLISH DAUGHTER CARRIES ON:

Islam and the Early Middle Ages

For several centuries the Christian church at least tolerated astrology, if not actually embracing it. The fundamental doctrine of astrology presumes the coherence of the universe, and purports to be the means of understanding the divine will of the macrocosm as it manifests itself in the microcosm of men. There can be no fundamental rift between astrology and any genuine religion. But the actual practice of astrology is quite another matter.

St Augustine, in the third century, had consulted astrologers himself before his conversion, and did not deny that their predictions were often accurate. But being more theologically astute than his predecessors or contemporaries he understood the dangers. To the philosophically naive, astrology appeared to replace the will of God with the purely mechanical motions of the stars. It could lead men to resign themselves to fate instead of struggling towards grace; and it appeared to deny free will – which Augustine held to exist only in so far as it granted man the freedom to choose or refuse salvation.

The potential evils of astrology heavily outweighing its potential good, Augustine threw the full weight of his authority against it: a wise move theologically and politically – judging from the level of astrology then practiced throughout the Empire. Astrology was not banned by the Church, nor quite driven underground; but its de-emphasis was sufficiently strong to preclude its resuscitation in European Christendom, a situation that prevailed into the Middle Ages. But the long fall from grace applied only to Western Europe.

The Neo-Platonists of Alexandria were chiefly responsible for the survival of astrology in the West. Plotinus, the great expounder of Plato and Pythagoras (third century AD) argued against a fatalistic interpretation of astrology. And it is due to Plotinus and a number of gifted followers that astrology as a serious study continued. Proclus, the most distinguished of the later Neo-Platonists (fifth century), wrote a paraphrase of Ptolemy's *Tetrabiblos* and it was largely through this work that what remained of the tradition was handed on.

While there is little evidence of actual astrological practice by the Neo-Platonists, it may be that a certain amount was going on behind the scenes. What has come down to us as the *Hermetic Writings* are of Alexandrian origin. By repute, the extant fragments were once part of a gigantic work allegedly containing two thousand volumes, which burned with the Museion in Caesar's time. The Platonists of the Renaissance thought the *Hermetic Writings* were the remnants of the library of Thoth (Egyptian Hermes), containing the ancient sacred science of the Egyptians. But more exacting contemporary research has dated them later, to the second and third centuries A D. These strange and tantalizing books are more Neo-Platonic than Egyptian, but older, Egyptian elements have been assimilated. The *Hermetica* is a mixture of alchemy, astrology, magic, medicine; much of it obscure, and apparently deliberately so.

There is however one astrological point in the *Hermetica* of great interest. A common objection to astrology is that, even granting the possibility of stellar influence, the important moment should be the moment of conception, not the moment of birth. The compilers of the Hermetic texts were aware of this problem, and there are formulae, attributed to the legendary author of the texts, Hermes Trismegistos (Thrice-Blessed Hermes), for determining the moment-of-conception horoscope from the birth horoscope. Throughout the history of astrology, the importance of the moment-of-conception horoscope has been a matter of keen debate. All astrologers agree that it ought to mean *something*, but few agree what that something should be. A few astrologers insist upon working with the (necessarily putative) moment-of-conception horoscope alone. But the majority believes that the moment-of-conception determines what a person inherits from his or her parents (agreeing with modern genetic theory) but insists that the moment of birth nevertheless determines character (very much disagreeing with modern genetic theory).

Meanwhile, in other corners of the dismembered Empire, interest in astrology was undiminished, and of course throughout the Orient it was star business as usual. Aetius of Amida, physician to the court of Byzantium (sixth century) published his *Tetrabiblion*, largely a compilation of excerpts from earlier works. Much respected, and popular, this book brought about a revival of Ptolemy's ideas which had been forgotten in the East, including his idea of the earth as a sphere. Aetius also drew attention to the much older works of Philolaus (d. *c.* 390 BC), a Pythagorean who, Aetius asserted, designed a cosmological system in which the earth was merely another planet, similar to the sun and moon, whirling about a somewhat abstract 'eternal fire'.

In Western Christendom the direct stream of Pythagorean thought was kept alive by Boethius, the last philosopher who could be called technically a Roman. Writing at the turn of the sixth century, when Rome itself was a crumbling town with but a few thousand inhabitants, and what remained of the Imperial Court had moved to provisional safety in Ravenna, Boethius in two books, *De Institutione Aritmetica* and *De Institutione Musica*, attempted to reconstruct what was then known of the teachings of Pythagoras. Boethius wrote with that brilliance and fervor that seems to settle upon a few chosen men at the dissolution of a civilization. His books exerted a persistent influence throughout those over-maligned 'Dark Ages'. (Though crude, incommodious and politically chaotic, the Dark Ages were pitch-black only to those who believe 'illumination' contingent upon electricity: the art that survives this period, the *Book of Kells*, for example, was not created by ignoramuses. For two centuries the Celtic Church was a brilliant center of learning and true spirituality, and there were other bright spots throughout Europe.) Though not directly astrological, Boethius' work at least served to keep alive the numerological and harmonic principles upon which astrology is based.

Among the various pejoratives hurled at astrology perhaps

the most common is 'medieval' (see p. 6). But in fact the medieval resurgence of astrology was due entirely to the Arabs.

Unlike almost every other great religion, Islam did not begin as an esoteric discipline. Rather, the warlike faithful of Mohammed first reconquered and unified the Eastern and African territories of the former Roman Empire, and it was only afterwards, when the martial enthusiasm abated, that the Mohammedan mystics (the Sufis) – the astronomers, doctors, scholars and mathematicians – came to the fore. A great astronomical observatory was built in Baghdad and systematic observation of the heavens began; many new fixed stars were discovered and named. And, because the Arabs, like every other pre-industrial people, did not understand the value of compiling facts for the pure quantitative joy of it, astronomy was unthinkable without astrology.

Muslim Spain was the greatest of the Arab centres of learning. And in Granada and Seville astrology, along with the other ancient sciences, was studied on its symbolic and psychological level, with particular emphasis upon its supposed relationship to medicine. Throughout Islamic Spain, the Jews were among the foremost philosophers, astrologers, and physicians. Tolerated by the Arabs as 'Children of the Prophets', and not yet vilified by the Catholic Church as the cause of all its woes, for several centuries the Jews lived unmolested amid the Arabs, yet were free to travel in Christendom, and so served as unofficial go-betweens and transmitters of culture between the two irreconcilably opposed forces. Welcomed for their learning and their medical lore, the Jews also brought the rejuvenated Arab astrology into Europe.

The debased soothsayers of Rome had been forgotten. The Augustinian objections – valid for their time – were no longer binding; the greatest of the medieval churchmen with almost no exceptions warmly embraced the study of astrology, especially for its symbolic meaning. St Thomas Aquinas, one of the more hesitant, gave it his blessing only in principle, not in practice; Grosseteste, first chancellor of Oxford, championed it, as did Roger Bacon, the 'father' of the experimental method.

Astrological and alchemical symbolism pervades the great Gothic cathedrals (cf. *Le Mystère des cathédrales* by the twentieth-century alchemist, Fulcanelli).

There can be little doubt that the medieval concept of the world was one-sided. But the contempt in which the Middle Ages are now held is a measure of the misunderstanding of the epoch; and the result of a world view that is no less distorted.

To the modern Rationalist mind, the universe is a gigantic fact, reducible to an infinity of constituent facts. To the medieval mind it was a gigantic symbol; in which phenomena in all their diversity were but reflections of the will of God. Indifferent, or downright hostile to matters of fact, the medieval mind was interested only in the principle behind the fact. To the modern mind, only facts count (see Culver and Ianna, p. 157) and principles take care of themselves. The scientist distrusts or even denies the reality of inner experience; (see the Abraham Maslov quote, p. 160). He relies upon the evidence of his senses. If he can measure it, it is 'real'. The medievalist called the world of sense an illusion; only inner experience was real. He may have believed the world was flat but he understood the universe to be a hierarchy of values, because that was his experience. Our modern thinkers may *know* the earth is round, but they think value is 'subjective', a mere invention of man (perhaps because their own inner experience is so poverty-stricken and disordered they cannot trust it). The medieval mind ignored the facts of the physical world, and so produced a society that was all cathedrals and no sanitation. The modern mind ignores the values of the spiritual world and so has produced a society that is all sanitation and no cathedrals. Rationalists rejoice and call this progress. But the increasingly fraught psychological state of our sanitary society suggests that in the end cathedrals may prove to be the necessity, sanitation the luxury.

For the two extremes are not opposite and equal. Fact pursued to the exclusion of value is insane and produces H-bombs and striped toothpaste indiscriminately. Value pursued without reference to fact is merely misguided – though, as in medieval Europe, it may ultimately produce an environment so unhealthy and uncomfortable as to make the values themselves appear irrelevant to many.

Perhaps more important, thinking about values is not the same as acting upon them. The same order of mind responsible today for linguistic philosophy and the various 'philosophies' of science, in the Middle Ages was engaged upon the construction of vast and equally inutile conceptual schemes. The famous angelologies and demonologies were in effect attempts to apply reason to the recorded experiences of the great saints and mystics, despite the admonitions of the same saints and mystics that this was impossible.

Roughly speaking, the world was an arena in which the forces of Good, or order, were engaged in eternal battle with disruptive forces of the Devil (the quaint name given by the medievalists to the Second Law of Thermodynamics). And astrology, studying and purporting to explain the multiplicity of interactions between the movements of the heavenly bodies and the things of earth, became the instrument *par excellence* for the establishment of prodigiously complex systems describing the operations of the forces of order.

The danger, for the medievalists, lay in their indifference to the way the disorderly physical facts conformed to the neat theory. When harmony is the *only* criterion for judging an idea, there is nothing to restrain the imagination. The symbolic hierarchical cosmology of medieval thought may well have been an accurate *schematic* plan of the structure of the spiritual world, but there was nothing to prevent the addition of every manner of imaginary connection when applied to the physical world – though not much of this fanciful 'science' applied to astrology.

The enduring principles of astrology had been established in the distant past. The alchemists had long associated the metals with the planets.* The Osiris legend with its lead coffin (fashioned by Set, who was equated with Saturn) shows the Saturn/lead connection stemmed from earliest antiquity; and the

---

* Sun/gold, Moon/silver, Mercury/mercury, Venus/copper, Mars/iron, Jupiter/tin, Saturn/lead.

other traditional relationships may be Egyptian or even pre-Egyptian as well. The planet/herb connections were studied by the Arabs, and by the Jewish astrologer-physicians; while Ptolemy, the greatest geographer of his time, carefully attributed zodiacal dominion to the various states and cities of his time, in all likelihood continuing a much earlier practice – the Egyptian nomes, or provinces, were each consecrated to their own divinities, which were in turn associated with specific stars or planets.

The Hermetic texts proclaimed, 'As above, so below', and medieval thinkers sought replicas of the zodiac everywhere and in all things. Man, the microcosm, contained the zodiac within himself, and the various members and organs of his body were supposed to be under the dominion of the various planets and signs. The four humors – phlegm, blood, choler and black bile – corresponded to the four elements, and diseases were held to result from imbalances, excesses and deficiencies of one humor or another. A proper balance was called a 'good humor' and medicines were prepared that were supposed to effect such a balance. Though medieval medicine seems to have been somewhat less appalling than currently reputed, it was far from efficient. The medieval ignorance of the empirical method along with its blithe disdain of elementary hygiene must have helped stave off the over-population problem.

The principal astrological correlations were ancient, but the medieval mind, with its obsession for classifying and pigeon-holing, was responsible for attempting to make a single tapestry of the innumerable threads that had come down to it from Arab, Neo-Platonic and Byzantine sources. Because it made little difference if the physical facts corresponded to the principle, it does not seem to have bothered astrologers unduly that their astrology was unsatisfactory, and they did not attempt to improve it. It was spiritually more rewarding to look for as yet undiscovered connections and correlations. At its worst, this produced such theories as the one claiming that because there were seven planets there were, necessarily, seven orifices in the human body.

A determination to see connections everywhere may be

absurd, but it is no more absurd than the equal and opposite determination to see connections nowhere. For example, the well-known physicist, K. von Weisaecker (*History of Nature*, Routledge and Kegan Paul, 1951, p. 24) alertly contrasts the crudity of the first man-made stone implements to the incredible complexity of the hand that fashioned them. He then marvels that the hand should be the product of 'unconscious forces', a conclusion put forward in the service of 'the search for objective truth'. But the objective truth is that in the face of such reasoning the medieval numerologists and demonologists need not hang their heads.

Indeed, in certain respects, medieval numerology was not only justified, but, under the circumstances, logical within the context of the then-known physical world. The number seven had been invested with magical and mystical significance since time immemorial, as the sum of Heaven and Earth, or Spirit and Matter, respectively symbolized by the numbers three and four. The folklore of innumerable people and the traditions of all the great civilizations are rife with seven; the seven Pleiades, the seven-headed dragons, the seven-branched candelabra, the seven strings of Orpheus' lyre, the seven Sirens of the seven spheres. The periodic table of elements with its octaval structure, the discrete energy levels of quantum theory, would come as no surprise to the medieval mind, but above all, and by far the most evident and conclusive proof of the significance of seven, was the apparent fact that there were seven planets, Sun, Moon, Mercury, Venus, Mars, Jupiter, Saturn, each in its crystal sphere, circling serenely about the earth. Who will blame the medievals for accordingly looking for seven everywhere and in all things?

Astrology in the Renaissance

Astrology went out of fashion. It was not, nor has it ever been, disproved, either in fact or in principle. The reasons for its falling into disrepute are complex.

The decline of astrology is generally attributed to the

rediscovery of the heliocentric system by Copernicus, to Kepler's laws, Newton's mechanics, the discovery of Uranus and Neptune, and, last but not least, to modern man's healthy skepticism and more considered deployment of his intellectual faculties. This account of the decline of astrology has become so general it is no longer questioned. But like the similarly unquestioned account of astrology's origins, it is quite without foundation.

With the exception of the discovery of the new planets, the other scientific advances in no way affect either the principles or the practice of astrology; a fact known and accepted by Copernicus, Kepler and Newton.

For several centuries – roughly from the time of the cathedrals to the break-up of medieval society around the end of the fifteenth century – astrology's practical limitations were less important than its symbolic soundness. Astrologers were far more interested in the many numerological, mystical, alchemical, and cabalistic implications of their art, and Roman-style fortune-telling had not yet regained its hold over the masses.

But in the increasing chaos of Europe, largely brought on by the simultaneous growth and power of states, and by disenchantment with the corrupt and manifestly unspiritual Church, astrological prophecy again became fashionable. Most of the Renaissance popes consulted astrologers on a more or less openly acknowledged basis. Melancthon, Luther's right-hand man, was an ardent astrologer, and Luther himself was not above providing the preface to an astrological work by Johannes Lichtenberger – in which he declared the signs in the heavens to give warning to the godless.

Meanwhile, a few individuals were attempting to refine the techniques of astrology. Johannes Müller (1436–76), mathematician and astronomer, improved upon the crude theory of 'houses' that had held sway since Ptolemy. It was Müller, writing under the euphonious Latinized pseudonym, Regiomontanus (Müller came from Königsberg), who provided the astronomical basis for the twelve houses, and related them in function to the twelve signs. The basis for this had been established by Ptolemy's division into Ascendant, Mid-heaven, Descendant and Nadir, but it was Regiomontanus who worked out the rather complex mathematics involved. In theory, the twelve-house division was accepted by astrologers all over Europe; in practice unfortunately, defining the exact boundaries of the houses between the angles is a problem that bedevils astrologers today as much as then.*

So, with interest in the spiritual side of astrology declining, and with an augmenting public demand for astrological prophecy, the very real inadequacies of astrology and, even more so, astrologers, became increasingly apparent to thinking men. A situation was created in which the worst aspects of astrology came to predominate just as a new breed of secular and cerebral thinkers was coming to the fore. These men, like their contemporary descendants, were incapable of comprehending symbolism and the principles of hierarchy, and so an increasingly debased astrology was seized upon and ridiculed for being what it was never intended to be.

This is a far cry from the customary contention that Copernicus, Kepler and Newton 'destroyed' astrology between them.

Copernicus, Galileo, Brahe, Kepler and Newton

Copernicus (1473–1543) in fact was led to his demonstration

---

* For a variety of technical reasons, there are arguments for and against the different methods of division, and while almost everyone agrees as to where the angles should be, and that there should be twelve houses corresponding to the twelve signs, the conflicting systems may make a difference of five, ten, or even more degrees to the boundary or 'cusp' of one of the houses. Thus, a powerful configuration of planets in the first house, the house of 'personality' by one method of house division, may by another method of division fall in the second house (or house of attachment and attitude towards the corporeal world). Obviously, this ought to make a big difference in the interpretation given to the whole horoscope; and the problem of house division remains an embarrassing and unsettled one. But the problem tends to disappear if Dr Muses is correct and astrology's original function was initiatic rather than interpretative.

(demonstration, *not* discovery) of the heliocentric system by his study of Pythagorean ideas, which he encountered first in Italy, at the school begun by the theologian and mystic, Nicholas de Cusa (1401–64), whose teaching was based upon Boethius.

Thus the heliocentric theory was very much a topic of discussion among the scholars of the Renaissance;* but it remained for Copernicus to go to the considerable trouble to confirm it through observation.

Ultimately, opinions on astrology – Copernicus', Einstein's, Shakespeare's or anyone else's – are of no importance: either Mars in Scorpio means something or it does not. But since historians and all of astrology's opponents insist that the great names of early science failed to repudiate astrology only through force of habit, muddled religiosity, or fear of public reproach, it is worth devoting some time to this otherwise barren controversy.

Trained as a diplomat, Copernicus was able to apply that training to his life, and recognizing the psychological potency of his rediscovery, wisely refrained from publishing during his lifetime – a caution that seems to have been characteristic. We do not know, for instance, what Copernicus thought of astrology, or of the effect he thought his theory might have upon astrology. We do know, however, that among his close friends was Joachim Rheticus (who saw to the posthumous publication of Copernicus' ideas), an ardent astrologer and author of *Narratio Primo* (1540), a book that used the Copernican theory to make astrological predictions of the imminent Second Coming of Christ.

These being the inclinations of his closest friends, it seems unlikely that Copernicus should have been particularly hostile to astrology. But the situation is ironical. Copernicus, taking his cue from the Pythagoreans, proved the point that was to usher in four centuries of rational, anti-Pythagorean thought. And the

---

* See the discussion of the problem posed for astrology by the heliocentric theory, in Culver and Ianna, *The Gemini Syndrome*, pp. 55–65.

Copernican theory, which in no way affects astrology – beyond allowing astrologers to base their interpretations upon more accurate observations – is credited with bringing about its downfall.

No one remembers Joachim Rheticus. Surely there are few today who study *Narratio Primo*. But in reality it was the flood of books of this genre, books conceived in support of astrology, that were responsible for astrology's decline. There was no Second Coming. And skeptics were increasingly disinclined to give credence to the astrologers who predicted there would be.

Galileo (1546–1642), responsible for the final public triumph of the Copernican theory, was a practicing astrologer (famous for predicting a long and happy life for his then patron, the Duke of Tuscany, who died a fortnight later), and he nowhere intimates that he practiced only to make a bit of money on the side, or that he privately repudiated the subject. Since Galileo was willing to stand up to the whole of the Inquisition to defend his beliefs (up to the point where he was forced to choose between them and his continued physical existence), it is unlikely that he would keep a disdain for astrology secret.

Tycho Brahe (1546–1601) was an outspoken champion of astrology, yet, as an astronomer, made the one discovery that did more to disrupt the psychological faith in astrology than any other single scientific advance. Brahe proved that a Nova which flared in the sky was a fixed star.

Since Aristotle, astrologers and everyone else had believed that the fixed stars were eternal, unchangeable, immutable and that they were gods. Astrologers had always welcomed a new light in the sky with a noisy abundance of predictions – usually dire – but a strange silence fell over them when they learned that here was a supposedly 'fixed star', living a life, and apparently dying a death of its own. And while this new fact was seized upon by astrology's opponents who, just then, were beginning to voice their objections, most astrologers managed to overlook it altogether. Particularly vulnerable was the elaborate system of relationships built up by the medieval astrologers upon numerological and theological grounds, and which the astrologers as well as their opponets by this time took literally, not symbolically.

Facts change, but principles are eternal; atoms and galaxies disintegrate but the harmonic principles responsible for their formation remain. Yet our intellect seems incapable of accepting this in good grace. The history of religion is invariably a story of man's attempting to intellectualize what must, by rights, be understood through experience. Our modern science goes to the extreme of virtually deifying the conditional and transitory (but visible, tangible and measurable) facts while denying the existence of eternal but intangible principles.

In Brahe's time, the mass of believers in astrology – almost everyone – as well as the astrologers themselves, believed astrology to be the *effects* of causes which could now be shown as illusory: the literal hierarchy of the seven spheres, the literal geocentricity of the solar system, the literal immutability and divinity of the fixed stars and so on.

Confronted by the confirmed experimental results of Copernicus and Brahe, most astrologers turned their backs, stuck their heads in the sand, shouted 'fraud' or simply rationalized away the fact – for example, the astronomer who refused to countenance the moons of Jupiter because if they were too small to be seen by the naked eye they were unimportant, and if they were of no importance, they did not exist. In short, astrologers reacted to these unwelcome observations exactly like modern scientists faced with verified accounts of ESP phenomena, or Gauquelin's massive statistical surveys proving conclusively that the position of specific planets at birth corresponds to eminence in specific professions.

Brahe himself was no exception. Though able to reconcile his own discovery of exploding Novae with his astrological beliefs, he was never able to countenance the Copernican heliocentric theory, which he repudiated on theological grounds; and to account for undoubted observed data, invented an elaborate geocentric theory of his own.

By this act of willful obtuseness, Brahe not only kept his pet belief intact, but made it easy for future historians to classify him. Though an indefatigable observer and experimenter, and endowed with great technical ingenuity,* Brahe's anti-Copernicanism and unabashed advocacy of astrology make him a 'forerunner' of science – not a scientist, but a man of the transitional period. 'With the overthrow of the authority of Aristotle and Ptolemy and the ever-increasing emphasis placed on accurate observation and experiment, a new phase in men's outlook developed. Full freedom of speculation, unhampered by religious limitations, took many centuries to mature ...' (Colin Ronan, *Changing Views of the Universe*, p. 97).

That is to say, man had not yet degenerated to the point where the exercise of pointless curiosity (the same that killed the cat) would take precedence over understanding. Indifference to value – called 'intellectual freedom' – had not yet supplanted an interest in values themselves. No one had as yet tried to graft two heads on to a dog just to see if it could be done.

Brahe is classified: Not a Scientist. But his successor at the Observatory of Prague, Johann Kepler (1571–1630), keeps getting his elbows stuck outside the pigeon-hole. Kepler made observations and experiments and let the chips fall where they might. Yet he was, at the same time, an intensely religious man, a Neo-Platonist, whose scientific approach was part of a grander scheme to provide empirical confirmation of the harmony of the spheres.

Because his salary depended upon the emperor, and because the emperor had other matters on his mind and did not take kindly to being reminded. Kepler was in permanent financial straits. To supplement his erratic income he wrote astrological almanacs predicting events in the coming year, and cast personal

---

* It was Brahe's astronomical instruments that first brought him to the attention of his patron, the Emperor Rudolph II. And it was his observatory and the access to his instruments that made Kepler covet the otherwise difficult and thankless post of court astrologer at Prague.

A quarrelsome and belligerent man, Brahe had his nose cut off in a duel and utilized his technological skills to fashion a new one for himself.

horoscopes. He regarded both as a waste of valuable time, but for very different reasons.

The invention of the printing press made yearly almanacs sure-fire bestsellers. These almanacs were specific to a region or country and, in the absence of not-yet-invented newspapers, contained a variety of useful information: dates of fairs and markets, ferry schedules, money exchange rates, holidays, dates of full and new moons, and, most popular, extended weather forecasts. This was the domain of the astrologers. And even though as early as the latter fifteenth century, the influential Renaissance thinker and Kabbalist, Pico della Mirandola (the 'Scourge of Astrology'), effectively proved that these forecasts were useless, people still clamored for them. It was this kind of astrological prediction (equivalent to the pop astrology in today's newspapers) that Kepler despised. This was the 'bathwater' that he was at pains to dispose of.

But his attitude towards personal horoscope interpretation was more complex. That he believed in their efficacy is attested by his published correspondence with Wallenstein, the ablest and most powerful of the Hapsburg generals in the Thirty Years War. In particular Wallenstein was anxious to have Kepler's predictions for his own future. But since the directions in Wallenstein's horoscope were by no means favorable, Kepler, knowing the old story about the fate of the messenger who brought bad tidings, was loathe to comply, particularly since Wallenstein was something of an amateur astrologer in his own right, and not easily fooled. But eventually, in 1625, after a long period of ratiocination, a Wallenstein agent approached Kepler, offering both money and threats, and Kepler complied with a list of predictions extending to the end of 1633.

He suggested that in early 1634, Wallenstein might experience certain difficulties, but that he, Kepler, did not have time to make calculations extending beyond this period. And he larded his forecast generously with advice not to take anything too literally or seriously.

It is this reading (with all those reservations and conditions) that, preserved among Wallenstein's papers, has furnished generations of Kepler scholars with the evidence they so desperately sought to establish Kepler's putative disbelief in the efficacy of horoscopes. But Kepler's own writings flatly contradict such a conclusion; and Wallenstein's own fate cannot be taken as negative evidence for horoscope interpretation either.

Kepler's forecast was cautiously worded but not inaccurate: early 1634 was certainly a difficult period for Wallenstein; in February of that year he was assassinated.

'Astronomy, the wise mother,' Kepler wrote, 'astrology the foolish little daughter, selling herself to any and every client willing and able to pay so as to maintain her wise mother alive.'

Had the matter actually stopped there, had there been no further Kepler writings on the subject, subsequent scholars might have been justified in attributing Kepler's astrological interests mostly to outside pressures; but the matter does not stop there, and the value of this passage as evidence for the prosecution is also contingent upon a piece of gross mistranslation. The key German word Kepler used in that famous 'foolish daughter' paragraph was '*buhlerische*' which means 'unchaste', 'whoring' or 'wanton' rather than 'foolish'. This obviously puts Kepler's famous comment in a totally different light. It is the amorality or immorality of astrological practice *not* the invalidity or foolishness of astrology that Kepler is criticizing. (Since generations of Kepler scholars have mistranslated '*buhlerische*' as 'foolish' – a mistake no college German student would be allowed to get away with – in order to make Kepler's beliefs correspond to what these scholars feel so eminent an early scientist ought to believe, it would be cumbersome to break with tradition and we have retained 'Foolish Daughter' for our section heads).

Kepler considered writing almanacs an absolute travesty of astrology, but he held the predictive powers of horoscope interpretation in high regard – it was just that it took him away from his real aim, which was the attempt to prove the physical reality of the 'harmony of the spheres'. And trying to deal diplomatically with powerful (and doomed) egomaniacs like Wallenstein was not only time-consuming, but dangerous.

On the subject of horoscope interpretation he wrote, 'A most unfailing experience (as far as it can be expected in nature) of the excitement of sublunary natures by the conjunctions and aspects of the planets has instructed and compelled my unwilling belief' (*De Stella Nova*, Cap. 28).

Kepler repeatedly writes to friends of his intention to separate the 'gems from the slag'. He issues 'a warning to certain theologians, physicians and philosophers who rightly reject the superstitions of the astrologers, not to throw the baby out along with the bathwater'. And declares: 'nothing exists and nothing happens in the visible heavens that is not echoed in some hidden manner by the faculties of Earth and Nature: the faculties of the spirit of this world are affected in the same measure as heaven itself' (*De Stella Nova*, Cap. 28).

Yet upon this basis of such crystal-clear affirmations Kepler scholars find it possible to write:

> Kepler's attitude to astrology is as inconsistent, irrational and ambiva-
> lent, as are most people's attitudes towards dying institutions, or to
> institutions in periods of rapid change . . . Beside being a great math-
> ematician and scientist and an obstinate if not profound religious
> philosopher, Kepler was a great mystic and dreamer, an ingenuous
> personality without a trace of slyness, cant or insincerity in him.
> Much of astrology is mysticism, poetry or harmony to him, and cer-
> tainly by no stretch of the imagination natural law . . . He certainly
> struggles with astrology at every turn because he is a lover of its
> folklore . . . But his efforts are those of an animal trapped in a
> cage, or more correctly of a man trapped in the web of his beliefs.
>
> Mark Graubard, *Astrology's Demise and its*
> *Bearing on the Decline and Death of Beliefs*, p. 230

But Mr Graubard's club-footed figures of speech, meant to be complementary, only trip each other up. The animal trapped in a cage struggles because it knows it is trapped. The man trapped in the web of his own beliefs never struggles because he does not know he is trapped. The man trapped in the web of his own beliefs believes himself to be free, enlightened, sentient and progressive, and when he is not putting Galileo on trial, signing anti-astrology manifestoes, carrying revolutionary placards or setting up concentration camps for people trapped in opposing webs of belief, he may be found hard at work on paragraphs such as Mr Graubard's, quoted above.

Kepler's attitude towards astrology was entirely consistent and is expressed unmistakably in the passage already referred to: 'An unfailing experience . . . has compelled my unwilling belief . . .'

'Now that Kepler had been, as it were, on the couch before us,' Graubard continues, 'the most conspicuous feature of his attitude is inconsistency . . . It is obvious that those parts of astrology which he accepts, he believes in because he inherited them and his personality finds harmony with their tenets.'

This is so 'obvious' that it is exactly the opposite of what Kepler himself says. According to Kepler, he was initially skeptical of the matter in its entirety, and only after having *practiced* it did he find that it compelled his unwilling belief. It was the blind and unempirical belief in astrology – the heritage of his age – that he inveighed against.

Experience and observation is not in itself any guarantee of objectivity (see L. Johnson Abercrombie, footnote to p. 18). People see what they want to see; what they are prepared to see. Scholars have spent countless hours studying Kepler only to misrepresent views that could not be less unambiguously stated in the first place. On the positive side, many scientific discoveries have come from one person's seeing in a new way what everyone had always seen but overlooked.

So it is possible that Kepler managed to delude himself over all his decades of astrological practice. But scientists and historians of science value experience and observation as the best and usually the *only* valid method of acquiring knowledge. Kepler was one of the very greatest of scientists, a man who fully understood the value of experiment and observation. Kepler made his living as a practicing astrologer, and after a lifetime of astrological experience and observation concluded there was something to it. The scientists and historians of science have never erected a horoscope. Yet on this basis they call Kepler 'irrational, inconsistent and ambivalent', and rejoice that modern man no longer lives in an age of ignorance and superstition.

... as a serious and systematic world view claiming the allegiance of many of the best intellects in every rank of society, astrology is dead. If it be asked what dethroned astrology the answer lies in the general progress of science and scholarship. Astrology had been born in a geocentric world and the Copernican revolution dealt it a shattering blow. The predictions of the astrologers do not survive the test of the experimental method. Scholarship, in its concern with the history of ideas, shows how easily genuine elements of knowledge can combine with illusory notions to form grandiose systems of thought in which the mind is content to dwell for a time.

Benjamin Farrington, *Encyclopaedia Britannica*, 1967

So shattering was the blow of the Copernican revolution that its two greatest exponents, Kepler and Galileo, were practicing astrologers! Somewhere along the line it may not be disrespectful to question the putative 'general progress of scholarship' if not of science. The final sentence of this passage should be particularly illuminating to students of psychology. Mr Farrington is a Marxist.

Kepler's astronomical discoveries (of the elliptical orbits of the planets, and of the ratios between their distances) were part of his life's work to find the literal, physical proof of the Pythagorean notion of the harmony of the spheres. He attempted to demonstrate that the distances between the planets could be related to the perfect solids (see Figs. 9 and 10) which in turn bore harmonic relationships to each other – relationships that were believed to be not coincidence but keys to the meanings of these shapes and forms. Using rather complicated mathematics, Kepler tried to calculate the exact literal sound emitted by the planets and contended that this music could only be 'heard' by the sun, which stood as the embodiment of the Divine Principle.

Copernicus put the sun back where it belonged. Brahe's instruments made it possible to accurately observe and calculate the orbits of the planets. Figures 9 and 10 are Kepler's own drawings and show what he hoped to prove: the planets in circular orbits forming precise harmonious relationships and the

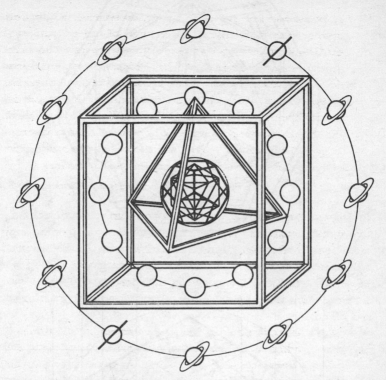

Figure 9. Nested Platonic solids.

whole system of planets forming a structure of nested platonic solids.

What he actually found were only very rough approximations of those harmonic relationships since the planets followed elliptical not circular orbits. While elliptical orbits did not invalidate the theoretical conception of the 'harmony of the spheres' it meant that those harmonies were infinitely more subtle and varied than Kepler or anyone else had anticipated. Contemporary astrologers still do not know what, if anything, the physical fact of elliptical orbits signifies for astrology. Gauquelin's statistics, categorically proving a relationship between position of the

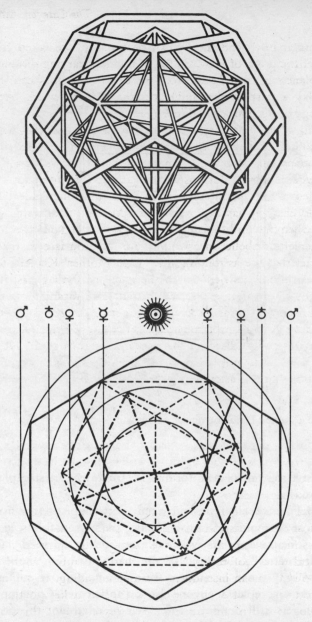

Figure 10. Orthogonal projection. Orbits of Mars, the Earth, Venus, and Mercury around the sun.

planets at birth and the human personality, are taken from a geocentric point of view. So far, the widely varying distances of the planets in their orbits from the earth have not been shown to play a part in the 'influence' the planets wield. See our analogy of the concert hall (pp. 174–5).

And when he thought that he had found the key to it all, he exulted, believing he had re-discovered the secret of the Egyptians; an interesting remark in that it shows that Kepler believed these relationships were known to the Egyptians.

These being his interests, it is quite understandable that he should chafe at having to cast horoscopes to finance his work. But, when the 'foolish daughter' quote is trucked out as evidence of Kepler's disbelief in astrology, no mention is ever made of the fact that the astronomy, the 'Wise Mother' Kepler praises, was astronomy carried out in the name of Pythagoras; it was not the quest after ever more distant and meaningless astronomical facts. It was an attempt to get to the *principles* behind the facts. And to experimentally verify those principles it was first necessary to discover the relevant facts. In short, Kepler's astronomy was not what a modern astronomer would call astronomy: it was astrology.

FOOLISH DAUGHTER: *In Disgrace*

Astrology's decline was a complex affair. But if we deal with it on three levels – (1) Spiritual and symbolic astrology, (2) Psychological and medical astrology and (3) Fortune-telling – a clear picture emerges.

Since Ptolemy, no one had given a satisfactory account of the physical basis of astrology: the *How?* of it. In medieval Europe this didn't matter; the emphasis was on the spiritual not the physical nature of reality. To the medieval mind, astrological symbolism was an instrument for understanding. It was not so much a system of acquiring knowledge as a key to the hierarchical nature of the universe. To make use of this sort of astrology, the ability to think in terms of 'level' is essential. By Kepler's time, the ability had largely vanished. In principle, the quest for factual knowledge and the quest for spiritual understanding should go hand in hand. In practice, in the Western world, they have been by and large mutually exclusive. Kepler was one of the few men who attempted to combine the two quests, but the tide had already turned.

Religion was swiftly degenerating into Fundamentalism (the belief in the literal truth of Scripture), dogmatic Catholicism, and various systems of empty ethics. The spiritual quest went on, not exactly underground, but in isolation and opposed to the intellectual current of the time (splinter groups of Rosicrucians, Alchemists and Freemasons – however much or little they may have retained of the old traditions; Boehme, William Law, Fenelon, Swedenborg, Blake, Goethe). But apart from a few individuals, no one was interested in or capable of understanding the astrological symbolism.

To pass muster in an increasingly scientific age, astrologers were expected to provide a satisfactory physical explanation for astrology, and this they could not do, though not for lack of ideas. One respected old theory held that the stars transmitted their influence through the dew – that pervasive fluid which at night dripped from the stars influencing everything it touched; the influence changing according to the position of the star. With the realization of the nature of condensation this theory was abandoned.

A more serious notion, holding till the sixteenth century, was that the stars and planets exhaled winds and vapors according to their sign and position, and the newly born inhaled his 'soul' as it were. Upon learning that the atmosphere does not even reach the planets, this theory was abandoned in turn.

The Renaissance astrologers had 'explained' astrology in terms of the principle of musical resonance: just as glass vibrates in the room when a violin is played at a certain pitch, so the 'soul' vibrates to the music of the spheres. This, of course, is not an explanation but an analogy, and the intellectuals of the seventeenth and particularly the eighteenth century would have none of it. (Later, however, we shall see that this idea has a renewed lease of life.) But astrologers could no more explain how their astrology worked than musicians could explain how their music worked, and the temper of the time was such that the musicians were allowed to keep fiddling with no questions asked, but the astrologers were not.

Kepler had warned skeptics not to throw out the baby with the bathwater. But few were in a mood to listen, and there was an inordinate quantity of bathwater in the tub. Astrology on its psychological and medical levels was essentially Ptolemaic. Only two technical refinements – and those disputed – had been applied to the astrological method. One was Regiomontanus' method of house division, the other Kepler's contention that the harmonic basis of the aspects demanded its logical expansion. That is: if the 90-degree angle (corresponding to the fourth harmonic) was operative, then its harmonic fractions and multiples of those fractions, the 45-degree and 135-degree angle, should also be sensitive points, and should be incorporated in the interpretation. But these were minor improvements in view of the general nebulousness of the accumulated doctrine.*

Unable to explain how astrology worked, honest and less credulous astrologers were forced to admit that it did not work very well, and that to make it work at all required not science (which by definition can be taught to one and all) but artistry. In the end it was the interpretation that counted, but on this basis it was impossible to come to any sort of definite conclusion or to take practical action. In other words, while the advice not to throw out the baby with the bathwater may have been sound, in practice it was impossible to distinguish categorically between what was baby and what was bathwater.

In little over a century astrology declined from a serious pursuit practiced by the best minds of the age to a parlor game.

---

* A thriving school of contemporary German astrologers, following the ideas of Baldur Ebertin, has jettisoned the theory of 'houses' altogether, but places great emphasis upon the harmonics of the 'hard' angles, very much in keeping with Kepler's ideas.

John Dee (1527–1608), astrologer, magician, occultist, and early experimenter in ESP phenomena, had been the trusted adviser and confidant of Queen Elizabeth. But by 1638 astrology had become so unfashionable (at least in France) that the astrologer Morin de Villefranche had to be hidden behind the arras to record the exact moment of birth of Louis XIV. A generation earlier, protocol would have given him the place of honor over the physician.

By the time John Aubrey (1626–97) was writing, it had become necessary to adopt an unmistakable defensive tone when favoring astrology: 'We have not that Science yet perfect, 'tis one of the Desiderata. The way to make it perfect is to get a Supellex of true Genitures in order whereunto I have with much care collected these ensuing . . .' (Aubrey's *Brief Lives*, ed. Oliver Lawson Dick, Penguin Books, 1962, p. 52).

Aubrey's empirical approach was admirable, but it was not acted upon; and even had it been, nothing would have resulted: the application of statistical methods to astrology is a delicate matter, far beyond the resources of the seventeenth-century science.

Meanwhile, as astrology's prestige diminished, no really brilliant astrologers appeared. Granted that for every Kepler there were a thousand fakers and incompetents, still, the sixteenth century had produced a number of erudite and impressive men who, as practicing astrologers, had established widespread reputations for themselves. Also, there can be no doubt that the predictive and analytic aspects of astrology depend to a certain extent upon the mood of the recipient. The most widespread of all astrological prophecies – the prediction of a deluge of Noachian proportions following the grand conjunction of all the planets in Pisces in 1524 – failed to materialize. The rich built arks and all Europe was in a turmoil, but nothing happened, and the astrologers continued plying their trade; 1588 was supposed to be a particularly grim year. Yet apart from the single spectacular event of the Spanish Armada (which was, after all, only bad for Spain) nothing untoward happened. And the astrologers were not put out of business.

But eighty years later, the last of the renowned astrologers, William Lilly, specifically and accurately predicted both the Plague and the Great Fire which devastated London in successive years in 1665 and 1666. What happened was that Lilly was brought before the House of Commons suspected of having provoked these disasters.

A learned and in many ways admirable man, Lilly included the following in his *Epistle to the Student of Astrology*, which, along with Kepler's incessant invective, tells us something about the true state of astrology in its decline.

> Be humane, curtius, familiar to all, easie of access: afflict not the miserable with terror of a harsh judgement; direct such to call on God to divert his judgements impending over them: be civil, sober, covet not to an estate; give freely to the poor, both money and judgement; let no worldly wealth procure an erroneous judgement from thee, or such as may dishonour the art.

From this, we may justifiably conclude that the astrologers of the day did commonly all those things Lilly admonishes the student not to do.

But Lilly's example inspired no new school of ethical and enlightened astrologers. With no champions of intellectual stature, the decline went on apace.

Contemporary scholars in general (see Benjamin Farrington above) attribute all this to the 'progress of science and scholarship'. And it is true that by 1685 most members of the educated classes were skeptical of astrology. However, the subject that occupied these progressives at that particular time in lieu of astrology was witchcraft. Were there, or were there not witches? Chief Justice Hale declared that there had to be witches, since there were laws against them. Others were not so sure. Meanwhile, any number of witches were tried and put to death. And it was in this climate of scientific progress and improved scholarship that Newton's *Principia Mathematica* was published (1687), a work which – it is contended – demolished astrology once and for all.

Curiously enough, this corollary to his work does not seem

to have occurred to Newton, which brings up an anecdote famous in astrological circles. It is said that the astronomer Edmond Halley once berated Newton for his alleged defense of astrology, at which point Newton is supposed to have loftily replied: 'I have studied the subject, Mr Halley, and you have not.' There is no concrete evidence in support of this tale. On the other hand, historians maintain with varying degrees of indignation that Newton was immune to such superstitious interests, and this is patently untrue. Newton's interest in alchemy never flagged, and over a long life more of his time was spent studying what would now be called 'occultism' than what would now be called 'science'. As a young man, at any rate, he had studied astrology.

> Newton's last undergraduate year was the seminal period of his mathematics when his interest in astronomy and, on his own admission, astrology, needed a fair knowledge of contemporary mathematics for their proper understanding.
>
> Sir Harold Hartley, FRS, *New Scientist*,
> 11 May 1967, reviewing *The Mathematical Papers
> of Isaac Newton*, vol. I, 1664–6

This division of labor may have been science's loss, but it was not occultism's gain. For all his mathematical brilliance Newton had no inkling of the principle of 'level'. Devoutly religious, his religion was a barely mitigated Fundamentalism. It was Newton who popularized the notion of the universe as a Divine mechanism. It remained only for still less comprehending minds to extract the Divinity from the mechanism to initiate the reign of Rationalism.

It is, however, worth repeating that if Newton does not defend astrology he does not condemn it either. The Copernican revolution was already a century and a half old and yet Newton, the greatest scientific mind of the day, did not claim that Copernicus', or any of the discoveries following, including his own, invalidated astrology.

The Eighteenth Century and the Triumph of Reason

In the false dawn of the Enlightenment, men believed that through the exercise of reason, all problems could be solved. Reason could not get at the Kingdom of Heaven (reputed by Scripture to be not here nor there, but within) and therefore reason dispensed with the Kingdom as a primitive illusion. Instead, reason would establish such a Kingdom democratically, right here on earth; a faith which, carried to its logical conclusion, culminated in the mystic illumination at Hiroshima.

Of these early champions of reason, there was none more outspoken than Jonathan Swift, none less capable of applying that faculty to the conduct of his own life.

Astrology at its highest is irrational, expressing the harmonic relationships whose fundamental irrationality is intrinsic to life itself. At its lowest, astrology is both irrational and unreasonable. By the time Swift arrived on the scene, there was only this lower astrology in evidence – and even if a higher astrology had existed it would have been incomprehensible to him, and equally a matter for derision.

But it so happened that a popular almanac-maker, who went by the name of Partridge, incurred the Dean's displeasure. And taking the name of Isaac Bickerstaff, Swift published a rival almanac in which he promised to go one better than the pusillanimous prophets of the day.

Bickerstaff claimed that he would avoid the vague generalities indulged in by ordinary astrologers, and instead would publish precise and verifiable forecasts. At that time (1708) feeling was running high against France, and Bickerstaff predicted the deaths of most of the French notables. Included amongst these forecasts there was one predicting the death of Partridge, the almanac-maker, on 29 March 1708.

Partridge uncooperatively lived through the fateful day in perfect health. But Bickerstaff refused to acknowledge the fact and published a pamphlet entitled, 'An Account of the Death of Mr Partridge, the Almanac Maker, Upon the 29th Instant, in a Letter from a Revenue Officer to a Person of Honour'.

Partridge published a furious rebuttal, but in vain. The joke had acquired a life of its own, and people refused to believe Partridge's testimonies to his continued existence. He would be stopped in the street and asked for money for his coffin, etc.; while, at the Stationers' Hall, Bickerstaff's tract had been taken seriously (bureaucrats never change) and Partridge's name had been stricken from the rolls. Public derision actually forced him out of business (he returned unrepentant, several years later, with a new almanac). While few could understand Newton, there was no mistaking Swift, and astrology had been subjected to a bout of ridicule which made it taboo in educated society.

In France the same process was at work, its finishing touches applied by Swift's brilliant counterpart, Voltaire, another who sedulously managed to keep separate the preaching of reason from its practice.

Two astrologers, the Comte de Boulainvillier and a professional astrologer called Colonne, had independently predicted Voltaire's death at the age of thirty-two. And some thirty-four years after this time had elapsed Voltaire, in a published letter, begged the humble pardon of these gentlemen for upsetting their predictions. As a literary gimmick, it lacked the magnificent ingenuity of Swift's campaign. But the letter set all literary France laughing, and served to hasten astrology on its way as a 'serious' interest there.

Voltaire, however, forgot to mention that at the age of thirty-two – the year of his predicted death – he was insulted by the Duke of Rohan, and replied with his customary acerbity. Not long after, he was set upon by thugs, and bastinadoed, with the Duke of Rohan looking on. Finding nobody to take his part, after some three months Voltaire found himself obliged to challenge the Duke to a duel, which he most assuredly would have lost. But on the morning of the duel he was providentially arrested and sent to the Bastille (for some past libel), in all likelihood saving his life and granting him the opportunity of jeering at the astrologers thirty-four years after the fact, for failing to distinguish between his demise and this closest of possible shaves . . .

Two centuries earlier, this story would have been cited from one end of France to another as an example of *good* predictive astrology.

In the fifteenth century, men would believe anything about astrology; in the eighteenth and nineteenth they would believe nothing.

The alleged predictive power of astrology is, historically, its chief popular attraction. But it is difficult to defend in court at present. No serious and concerted attempts have been made to test astrological prediction – a survey of newspaper predictions run by Culver and Ianna (see p. 199) was too broad-based and crude to qualify as the 'disproof' it is claimed to be. Devising a genuinely fair test requires ingenuity, co-operation (just what constitutes an 'accurate' prediction?) and it must be run under conditions that are mutually agreeable to astrologers and their opponents.

On the basis of long personal experience, we are cautiously optimistic about a fair test producing results favorable to astrology. But even if the statistical number of 'hits' proved disappointing, it is undeniable that over the long course of astrology's history there have been so many accurate, precise and documented predictions that to dismiss them all as 'coincidence' is indefensible and not a little silly. For instance: in the Austrian court of Maria Theresa, the court astrologer still found employment. At the birth of Marie Antoinette (the same day as the Lisbon earthquake in 1740) the reading of the horoscope was so dire that the celebration which would have ordinarily taken place at the birth of a royal princess was called off, and the entire court was plunged in gloom.

Now, in all of history there can be few characters whose lives were more ill-starred and unhappy than Marie Antoinette's. Yet this story is cited by Hilaire Belloc, in his biography of Marie Antoinette, to illustrate the unenlightened state of an Austrian court, still believing in that exploded superstition, astrology. This is rather like attacking medicine as a fraud and as evidence citing all those who have been cured.

B. The Whore of Babylon

SLEEPING BEAUTY AWAKES:

Astrology in the Nineteenth Century

For two centuries Newtonian theory was so successful in solving mechanical problems that it was generally believed all problems would ultimately yield to a mechanical explanation. This notion was hotly and effectively contested by a minority of thinkers – most brilliantly perhaps by Goethe (1749–1832), whose scientific work is not generally known to those familiar with his literary reputation (see Erich Heller, *The Disinherited Mind* for an excellent account of this aspect of Goethe's work). But the Newtonian view prevailed until twentieth-century physics showed it to be mistaken from a purely physical point of view.

Secure in this mistaken cosmology (scientists 'make mistakes', everyone else is 'superstitious') and the philosophy that accompanied it, astrology had been dismissed from serious consideration long before the one discovery was made which really did affect both its theory and its practice: the discovery of Uranus by Herschel in 1787.

Of all the septenary examples furnished by nature, none had been more convincing to the medieval mind than the seven planets. Though the Copernican system made it clear that the arrangement of the seven did not conform to pleasing geocentric notions, there were, nevertheless, seven (not counting the earth) and astrology itself remained self-contained and in need of no revision. The discovery of Uranus, and subsequently Neptune and Pluto, while not invalidating the principle of celestial 'influence', most certainly threw the matter open to question and these questions remain open today.

Throughout the nineteenth century, astrology was accounted dead. But it was merely in a state of suspended animation. While popular and even psychological astrology had nearly vanished – with the exception of a few almanac-makers and gypsies – a localized but intense interest in the Pythagorean level of astrology was maintained. Goethe himself took pains to note his exact moment to birth; he cast horoscopes, seems to have considered them of some value, and was pleased to note the relationship between his own radix sun (5 degrees Virgo) and the radix moon in the chart of Christiane Vulpius, perhaps the most important of his mistresses. And followers of Goethe's scientific work (itself descending from Swedenborg, alchemy, and surviving fragments of traditional teaching) never ruled out astrology. 'Astrology is astronomy brought down to earth and applied to the affairs of men,' wrote Ralph Waldo Emerson, once again demonstrating the historical fact that throughout the ages it has been the best minds who have endorsed astrology, while the mediocrities sneered. The well-known, and otherwise much-respected psychologist, Fechner (1801–87), held that the stars and planets had 'souls' and were not merely the sum of their physical constituents – a view that was not sympathetically received. A scientist named Schleider, in a rebuttal entitled 'Moonshine Phantasies of a Natural Philosopher' (1857), replied forcefully:

> Except the forces of gravity, light and heat, we know of no powers which pass down from the heavenly bodies to our earth. All our scientific investigations, astronomy and physics with their tremendous resources of observation and experiment have not enabled us to perceive the slightest trace of further influence. Thus, today, for the man of sound judgement no other opinion is possible. Dreamers, however, and fools would conspire with 'the man in the Moon' against healthy human intelligence.

> Quoted by L. Kolisko in *The Moon and Plant Growth*
> (Anthroposophical Publishing Co., 1938)

And today, in a world of cosmic rays, X-rays and gamma rays, bathed by proton streams and refreshed by the solar wind, exploring the ever-greener pastures of the interplanetary electromagnetic fields, there is also but one possible opinion for the man of sound judgement: which is that the man of sound judgement of a century ago would have done well to have expressed his only possible opinion with a bit of caution.

But men of identical sound judgement prevailed a century ago and interest in astrology was virtually invisible; though it must have existed, since the one-thousand-page book *Astrology*, compiled by E. Sibly around the end of the eighteenth century, was reprinted in 1812 and again in 1826. Little societies of gentlemen took a dilettantish but perhaps not altogether superficial interest in astrology along with the 'occult' in general, and as a pure surmise for which we can offer no concrete evidence, it seems possible that somewhere in Europe splinter groups or even isolated individuals were passing on the tradition handed down from the builders of cathedrals. There is no point in pursuing this point further beyond remarking that it is difficult to imagine the coherent and systematic exposition of ancient tradition set out by R. A. Schwaller de Lubicz, Rene Guenon, Matila Ghyka and others cooked up out of thin air. It is scientific to explain a mystery by attributing its cause to 'coincidence' but romantic to postulate the possibility of an esoteric tradition coming to the surface only when the time is ripe for it – still, it remains a possibility.

The revival of astrology itself, however, owes itself to more traceable causes.

Somewhere, the positivist philosopher, August Comte (1798–1857) had observed: 'Quality is of no importance; quantity is the only positive criterion' (or words to that effect). This assertion is itself a value judgement, and therefore qualitative, and therefore, by Comte's own standard, of no importance; but despite its unimportance it may be safely regarded as the motto of the modern industrial state, down to and including our own day.

This philosophy and the way of life it engendered inspired the revolt in literature and the arts called romanticism. This was but part of a larger but inchoate distrust of 'progress' that was bound up with a renewed interest in matters that might be lumped together as 'the supernatural'.

One specific manifestation of this interest was the group of people who, beginning in 1848, used to gather in the house of a Mr Fox in America to investigate 'spiritism'. This was an unsystematic approach to what now has attained quasi-respectable status as 'parapsychology'. Back in Fox's day, however, the Zener card was undreamed of and it was out of 'spiritism' that the familiar seance was developed with its spirit guides, ectoplasm, mysterious rappings and the rest. Twentieth-century

'Channeling' is much the same phenomenon in slightly different dress.*

How much of all this was real we cannot say, but not all was fake, and spiritism attracted the attention of a number of otherwise sane and educated men and women.

Enter Mme Blavatsky

By 1873 interest was running high in America and in Europe. But as yet 'spiritism' was not a 'movement', a philosophy or a religion, but more of an emotional reaction against that materialism which in its fabulous hubris, imagined it had all the answers,† and yet furnished so little satisfaction.

And into this emotionally fertile chaos, with characteristic fanfare, came Madame Blavatsky – declaring that everything that everyone was trying to do along these lines was wrong, but that she possessed the answers, having been vouchsafed the esoteric secrets by initiates in Egypt, Tibet and India.

Helena P. Blavatsky (née Hahn) (1831–91) was forty at this time, and her history, though known only from what she chose to tell of it, was incontrovertibly exotic. Born of wealthy parents in Russia, as a child she displayed remarkable 'psychic' faculties.

---

* Spiritism began in 1848 with a rash of poltergeist (from the German for 'noisy ghost') disturbances in Fox's house. There were knocks on the walls and thumps on the floors. Furniture rearranged itself and toppled over, pots and pans sailed through the air, and people with a respect for evidence gathered to study the matter. It was discovered that the phenomena took place only when Fox's two pubescent daughters were around. (Later researchers found this typical of poltergeist visitations. Hundreds of such cases have been studied and they have never been satisfactorily explained.) The lives of the Fox daughters were much affected by all the attention. First they were trotted around the country as a kind of circus act, and then, when their ability to summon up the phenomena disappeared as they reached maturity (typical again of poltergeist visitations), they started faking them. When eventually exposed, they became perhaps the first to give mediums a bad name.

† The chemist, Berthelot, in 1888, declared that science had discovered everything of importance that there was to be discovered; only details remained. Lord Kelvin expressed a similar opinion.

At the age of seventeen she married the seventy-year-old general, Nikifor Blavatsky, who bestowed upon her her invaluable name, legally conferred upon Helena the freedom to leave the parental home and then, it would seem, vanished from the scene.

From this time on (1848), Mme Blavatsky roamed the world, seeking out esoteric knowledge. She spent time in Egypt where the otherwise unknown 'Brothers of Luxor' initiated her into their doctrine. In 1855 she went to Tibet, then virtually inaccessible to foreigners (this trip seems to have been authenticated by outside sources) and studied under the Lamas for seven years. From Tibet she went to India and studied there. Her appearance in America caused a sensation, and a wave of publicity which though largely derisory did not prevent her from converting into a recognizable movement the energy being wasted in milling about with 'spiritism'.

Meanwhile, Mme Blavatsky threw her energies into teaching her doctrine, ferociously but gleefully battling her hosts of detractors, and yet somehow finding time to churn out her voluminous *Isis Unveiled* (1877), *The Secret Doctrine* (1888) and a number of minor works in which she made her knowledge public.

At a century's distance it is still not easy to determine Mme Blavatsky's true stature. Certainly, her endless talk of 'adepts' and 'initiates' is disconcerting; and her sources cannot be traced or checked. We do not think it improbable over the course of history that special knowledge has been vouchsafed to special individuals to accomplish special missions. But was Helena Blavatsky one of these? Perhaps it is not for us to judge. She was a woman of great personal power and prodigious learning. Her claim was to effect a synthesis of the esoteric traditions of the world, but the result is more conglomeration than synthesis. Yet, a century later, some of her more outrageous-sounding statements look luminously prophetic,* while the initial distrust engendered by her ecstatic and convoluted prose style abates significantly upon re-reading.

---

* When it was believed that the major problems had all been solved, Professor Philip Spiller summed up the almost unanimous conception of the structure of matter: 'No material constituent of a body, no atom, is in itself originally endowed with force,

Whatever the judgement of history (which is by no means necessarily correct in any event) it is to Mme Blavatsky and the Theosophical movement she founded that astrology owes its revival.

> Yes, our destiny is written in the stars! . . . This is not superstition, least of all is it fatalism . . . It is now amply proved that even horoscopes and judiciary astrology are not quite based on fiction, and that stars and constellations consequently have an occult and mysterious influence on, and connection with, individuals. And if with the latter, why not with nations, races, and mankind as a whole?

As a piece of Blavatsky prose this is somewhat unrepresentative, both for its clarity and relative restraint; but it is

---

but every atom is absolutely dead, and without any inherent power to act at a distance.' P. Spiller, *Der Weltaether als Komische Kraft*, p. 4; quoted by H. P. Blavatsky, *The Secret Doctrine*, vol. II, p. 232.

Blavatsky, however, asserted: '. . . Matter is the most active when it appears inert. A wooden or stone block is motionless and impenetrable to all intents and purposes. Nevertheless, and de facto, its particles are in ceaseless eternal vibration which is so rapid that to the physical eye the body seems absolutely devoid of motion; and the spatial distance between those particles in their vibratory motion is considered from another plane of being and perception as great as that which separates snow flakes or drops of rain. But to physical science this will be an absurdity.'

If a recognized scientist had made that statement twenty years prior to the development of Relativity, he would have been (a) hounded out of the scientific community of his day and (b) reinstated as a misunderstood genius-ahead-of-his-time by the scientific community of today. But Blavatsky's description of atomic structure, both prophetic and precise, has somehow escaped the notice of science.

Her extraordinary insight was equalled if not superseded by two of her most eminent followers, Annie Besant and Charles Leadbeater. In *Occult Chemistry*, originally written in 1908, Besant and Leadbeater claimed to have used psi faculties to scry the inner structure of matter. Their descriptions and their drawings did not coincide with the Rutherford–Bohr model of the atom that appeared a decade later, but it matches in many significant ways the quark model with its 'string' theory that is currently the favorite among physicists. (Cf. *Extrasensory Perception of Quarks*, Stephen N. Phillips, Theosophical Publishing House, 1980; also, 'Extrasensory Perception of Subatomic Particles', *Fate*, May 1987.)

typical of the way she draws conclusions from purely assertive premises. It is by no means 'amply proved' that horoscopes are not quite based on fiction, and to maintain that it is, is simply to reverse the commonly held, equally mistaken notion that astrology is amply disproved.

But had Mme Blavatsky been a model of coherence and caution the skeptics would have been unimpressed (as they have been when confronted by far more cautious and coherent work covering similar ground), while the elimination of the movement's apocalyptical flavor would have restricted its appeal ... In any case, theosophy, in one blow, brought knowledge of the existence of ancient and Eastern traditions to a multitude of people, and it inspired a renewed and serious inquiry into astrology, first in England, then not long after in Germany, France and America.

By bringing in ideas prevailing in Indian astrology, and Indian philosophy (or perhaps due to Blavatsky herself – it is very difficult, without going into the matter in great detail, to know what is tradition, what Blavatsky), the question of the new planets, Uranus and Neptune, was side-stepped, and the rigid numerology of the medieval Church shaken loose.

Indian astrologers had always maintained that man manifested twelve 'layers' of consciousness, corresponding to the twelve signs of the zodiac, and twelve postulated planets – which are there whether we see them or not. Dr Charles Muses, in *The Lion Path*, argues that Egyptian texts should be read to take into account twelve planets, as well. (Should the eventual planet count go beyond twelve, these schemes would encounter the same problems as the seven-planet model.)

As a conceptual scheme, the twelve-planet model was particularly useful since it seemed to answer some of the more embarrassing questions facing astrologers. Part of the appeal of theosophy, in any case, depended upon its high disdain of experiment and observation.

Following Blavatsky, a new wave of astrologers, led by the English theosophist, Alan Leo (1860–1920), was gathering force – appearing as a tsunami to the astrologers concerned it did not yet constitute a visible ripple in the world of science: 'Astrology is already dead. It has been dead so long that it no longer stinks,' announced Dr Charles Arthur Mercier in the Fitzpatrick Lectures before the Royal College of Physicians in 1913.

How this statement struck Alan Leo we cannot say, but his astrological works were, by this time, a considerable financial success. Leo combined a sincere and by no means shallow interest in the esoteric side of astrology with a keen commercial sense and a crusading spirit. Under his aegis the Astrological Lodge of the Theosophical Society was founded, dedicated to a serious study of the matter.

Leo's brand of astrology had about it that whiff of well-meaning-old-lady and anti-vivisection that hangs over theosophy to this day: reading a 'good book' was a means of combating malefic planetary influences; seaside and country walks were also high on the list of antidotes (scientifically sound advice as it turns out: country and seaside air being charged with bracing negative ions). Contributors to Leo's magazine had the disconcerting habit of taking grandiose pseudonyms for themselves: Sepharial, Charubel, Aphorel.

Leo and his associates stirred up interest. They developed and refined a number of predictive techniques still popular with astrologers today. Their strong emphasis upon astrology as a means for describing and analyzing character attracted a number of people discerning enough to distrust the latest developments in Freudian psychology then coming into vogue.

Societies were founded in France and in Germany; and little magazines of varying quality appeared, airing innumerable differences of opinion on innumerable unsettled astrological questions.

Meanwhile, in the universities of Europe, orthodox scholars were laying out the presumed corpse with Procrustean solicitude, and a quite fantastic concern for detail in view of the lack of mourners. Since, *a priori*, there was nothing to be learned from astrology itself these multi-volume histories stand as landmarks to inutility. Their scholarly nature kept them safe from the public (see the books cited by Robert Eisler, p. 152). Other scholars were already convinced both that astrology was superstition and that it was dead. And the one question that was worth asking was left open (as by Cumont; see p. 3) or not posed at all: how could men otherwise not dissimilar to ourselves have believed in such nonsense for millennia?

Ironically, the only beneficiaries of this scholarship were the astrologers. Putting the scholarly prejudices to the side, they were able to make use of the scholarly facts and their possible application to astrological practice.

World War I to World War II

After the First World War interest in astrology increased sharply, particularly in Germany. The weird atmosphere of inflation, military defeat and moral and psychological chaos seems to have invaded even the universities, and in this unsettled air it was possible for a fully qualified Herr Doktor not only to become interested in astrology but to own up to it without undue loss of prestige or position, a situation that prompted Jung to predict that the acceptance of astrology as a serious academic study was just around the corner.

This was certainly premature (and possibly altogether mistaken). The theosophical cast of most of the new astrology was enough in itself to scare off the orthodox.*

---

* 'Because of the comparative silence of astrology for a great number of years, it became the fond belief of the mentally timid and the conventionally minded – those enamoured of dogma and artificiality – that it had lapsed into a desuetude quite too eternal for resurrection. Some there were who even boasted that 'science' had knocked it into a cocked hat, by such an impact exploding it into smithereens. But because a cloud has momentarily obscured the light of the sun, is it any reason to believe that central luminary has gone out of business? No more can truth be suspected of withholding one ray of its effulgence from the glory of the world. Only a casual glance down the corridors of time is necessary to note the persistency with which this spiritual searchlight periodically illumines the human journey. Astrology is the same yesterday, today and for ever, though humanity, impelled by a recessional law along the under arc of its evolution, may for a time lose consciousness of its divinity – albeit the beacon be still shining from the opposite zenith – and so believe to have totally vanished from mortal ken. But anon we come again to the horizon,

Meanwhile, it had become fashionable among astrologers to call astrology a 'science'.* But despite attempts to up-date the medieval terminology and to incorporate the new planets into the astrological scheme, it was essentially the astrology that had come down from Ptolemy. Skeptics were not converted.

In Germany, in the 1920s the situation was squarely faced.

---

and behold! there in the heavens still shines the Star of Interpretation, doubtless somewhat strange to us because of enforced separation, but none the less scintillant in its majesty and grandeur. Racially, humanity is once again touching the rising point in its circle of motion, hence the recrudescence in the theme of the stars, and in all that concerns the spiritual weal of the body politic.' John Hazelrigg, *Astrosophic Principles* (Hermetic Publishing Co., New York, 1917), pp. 11–12.

This comic bombast is by no means atypical of turn-of-the-century astrological prose. That astrology can survive the Hazelriggs in one camp, and the Rationalists in the other may be taken as a sign of its unquenchable appeal, if not of its validity.

* Culver and Ianna, *The Gemini Syndrome*, p. 202, would have their readers believe that the principal aim of astrologers today is to win acceptance in the world of science; and that all astrologers maintain astrology is a science, albeit an imperfect one at present. They cite the titles of several books to support that contention: *Astrology: the Space Age Science*, *Astrology: the Divine Science* and *Scientific Astrology*. But this is both misleading and irresponsible. There is certainly a generalized yearning for academic respectability, especially among those who think the subject susceptible of the kind of investigation that only a recognized educational or scientific institution could fund. A very small number of astrologers (for reasons ranging from expedience through envy to ignorance) have tried to jump on the scientific bandwagon. But astrologers with an understanding of the scientific method have at best an ambivalent attitude towards it. They respect it as a powerful but intrinsically limited, investigative tool. They have contempt for its claim to be the best – or only – means for arriving at the truth of this rich, multi-leveled universe we live in. They are dismayed at the world engendered by a widespread belief in this most pernicious of superstitions.

The first edition of this book, liberally cited by Culver and Ianna when it suits them, represents a broad consensus of the astrologers' reservations about science, and is widely regarded in astrological circles in this light. We can hardly be accused of trying to get on to the scientific bandwagon! Yet, we are curiously unmentioned in this context, as are the dozens of other astrologers who share our attitude. In fact, it is Culver and Ianna who turn the spurious authority of science to their own ends. *The Gemini Syndrome* is subtitled *A Scientific Evaluation of Astrology* as though that settled the matter. That is just about as valid a concept as *A Scientific Evaluation of Love* or *A Scientific Evaluation of Music* might be. Nor is *The Gemini Syndrome* a 'scientific evaluation' in any legitimate sense; rather it is an evaluation by two scientists.

Attempts were made, some of them bizarre, to bring astrology into the twentieth century. New theories proliferated, the most remarkable being the 'Hamburg School' of Alfred Witte which postulated no less than eight planets beyond the orbit of Neptune. Precise ephemerides (astronomical tables listing the daily latitudes and longitudes of the planets) were calculated for these hypothetical planets, and predictions made upon these calculations, claiming impressive results.

No single tenet in the astrological canon was held sacred; everything was thrown open to question. The spate of erudite and highly technical astrological magazines reached amazing circulation figures.

But the concerted effort to turn astrology into a science was not successful. A few seeds were sown that today bear modest fruit. The chief lesson learned was that traditional astrology, for whatever it was worth, did not readily lend itself to the quantitative methods of science. Aubrey's old idea of 'a Supellex of true Genitures' was a naive over-simplification.

Naturally, in Germany as elsewhere, a popular interest in prophecy flourished alongside the more 'serious' astrology. (Many 'serious' astrologers made their livings out of this sort of thing as had Kepler and others from antiquity – astrologers have to eat, too.) The frenetic political situation throughout the 1920s ensured a constant market for mundane astrology, and there was a keen public interest in the horoscopes of the various political leaders, most of which were public knowledge.

An astrologer, Frau Elsbeth Ebertin, had scored a bull's eye on Hitler's horoscope, though she had been given only his date of birth and not the precise minute. In her book of predictions for the year 1923 she had predicted that this was a man who would bring trouble to Bavaria (common sense, perhaps, as much as astrology) but that any attempt he made to seize political power would end disastrously. This was the year of the famous *putsch*, which culminated with Hitler in jail. Frau Ebertin and other astrologers were *personae non grata*, and several leading Nazis opposed astrology on ideological grounds. In the years immediately preceding the war the little erudite magazines vanished. Astrologers with any sense of self-preservation said nothing in public about Hitler's horoscope.

It was, however, only in Germany that concerted efforts were made to put astrology on a respectable footing. In France, a few individuals were attempting to justify astrology on a statistical basis, claiming impressive results, but finding almost no one willing to give them a hearing. In France, too, a number of unorthodox and brilliant psychologists began looking into astrology, not so much as a means of prediction, or even as a means of analyzing character from the actual birth data, but as a tool for the description and understanding of human nature far subtler and yet more comprehensive than the rigid and ultimately unsatisfactory attempts at 'typology' current among psychologists. Valid enough as far as they went, they invariably stopped short before they divulged anything of value. For example, what good is it to know that both Tennyson and the strong-man in the circus were mesomorphs? Or that Kafka and the shy grocer around the corner were both introverts? Psychologists such as Rene Allendy and Adolphe Ferrière saw, and saw rightly, that character approached through the symbolism of astrology suddenly acquired perspective. It is this extraordinary psychological profoundity and elegance that has commended astrology to so many contemporary psychologists as a working tool in therapy. It is probably safe to say that even if there were no scientific evidence to back up astrology at all, its future would be assured – simply because professionals in a variety of psychological fields find that it works.

And on a still-higher plane, a small number of scholars and teachers (Schwaller de Lubicz, René Guenon, P. D. Ouspensky, Alice Bailey and Krishnamurti among them) were setting out the inner meaning of the various esoteric traditions coherently, thoughtfully, unsensationally (see the bibliography), making it possible to see – among many other things – that astrology once functioned as an integrated part of all civilizations based upon sacred science.

In England, Alan Leo had died, and his thriving astrological lodge was taken over by the late Charles E. O. Carter.

Articulate, practical, and personally impressive, Carter managed to put astrology into acceptable modern terminology, something few other contemporary astrologers had even come close to.

Carter was, however, skeptical, even distrustful, of the attempt to make astrology too scientific. After a few rather amateurish sallies into statistics, he settled for a traditional approach. Carter relied upon personal or collective intuition tested against experience as the best means for improving astrology, setting a stamp upon a school of British astrologers which, at its best, was characterized by solidity and practicality at the expense of adventurousness.

Re-enter the Corner Soothsayer . . .

Yet it was in England that the current craze for newspaper horoscopes began. The British seem to have a knack for being respectable to the point of comedy and at the same time flagrantly indiscreet – the man in the bowler hat carrying his umbrella rides up the escalator in the London tube past advertisements that until recently a 42nd Street bookshop would have had to sell under the counter.

In 1930, rather in the spirit of a joke, the *Sunday Express* printed an astrological article upon the horoscope of the newly born Princess Margaret, which incited such an avalanche of mail that the astrologer responsible for the article, R. H. Naylor, was commissioned to write a series. The response was enormous, and quite unexpected; circulation soared, and so eager were rival papers to inform and enlighten their readers that, first in England, then in France, Germany and America, columns of astrological predictions became a feature of the popular press.

This early pop astrology was not the blanket-prediction sort prevalent today (in which all those born under Leo will suffer financial losses, while Scorpios will meet an attractive stranger), but time-honored largely inaccurate mundane astrology, the same that Isaiah inveighed against.

Naylor, the first of the astrologers to make a splash, was also the most colorful, certainly the most courageous, and, in the end, perhaps no more inaccurate than most. Unlike the majority of his colleagues, he dared to make precise and verifiable predictions. When right, none crowed louder than Naylor; when wrong, none rationalized faster: 'Since 1919 I have consistently predicted that peace would be maintained between the great nations of the world. My astrological researches now convince me that we no longer have the same assurance; the shadow of the war darkens the world' (*Prediction*, March 1936).

April 1936: Naylor predicted that Edward VIII would marry within three years, but that he would be idolized as no kings had been before. (Interestingly enough, the famous palmist, Cheiro, predicted Edward's abdication.)

August 1936: Naylor predicted that Roosevelt would 'squeeze' in but that it was improbable he would finish his second term. In October 1938, however, he predicted a third term for Roosevelt.

'TEN YEARS' PEACE! WORLD TO DISARM: More astounding Prophecies' read the cover of *Prediction* for June 1939.

September 1944: 'The days of Franco are numbered.'

On the other hand, Naylor, in 1944, disagreed with a US forecast based upon a statistical study, calling for a European war between 1966–70. Naylor instead saw the US during this period in a state of internal chaos and a war in Asia.

June 1951: Naylor predicted a Russia–China clash.

*   *   *

This fever of public interest accomplished very little for astrology on any of its meaningful levels. But it provoked infuriated rebuttals from rationalists of all stripes, from the science-minded and, most interesting, from eminent scientists, none of whom can be said to have acquitted themselves with distinction (see pp. 141–7).

The astrologers were unable to reply to these rebuttals without a note of hysteria, but once the emotional brushwood is cleared aside the argument was simple: the scientists demanded proof upon acceptable scientific terms that astrology was valid. The astrologers admitted that there was no such 'proof', but that this was not the fault of astrology – if the scientists wanted 'proof' let them put the matter to the test themselves, which had never been done, and, until producing disproof, reserve their opinions.

By the 1930s, from a scientific point of view astrology was at least conceivable – relativity and the quantum theory having shattered the simplistic purely material universe of Newton and Laplace – but there were no scientists willing to look into the possibility directly, even though by the late 1930s there were also a number of scientifically attested facts that had begun to look suspiciously astrological.

In that ivory tower where the academic community keeps itself safe from events in the real world, the putative death of astrology remained and remains a cause for smug celebration. Reviewing *A History of Western Astrology* by S. J. Tester, a classicist from Bristol, England, in the October 1988 issue of *Sky and Telescope*, Harvard Astronomer Owen Gingerich, wrote:

> Despite the recent flap over horoscopes in high places (referring to the Reagan brouhaha) astrology is defunct as a serious system for understanding human impulses. As the *Britannica* aptly puts it, 'In short, modern Western, though of great interest sociologically and popularly, generally is regarded as devoid of intellectual value.' In the end, Tester concludes, astrology was not killed. It simply died 'like a plant or animal left stranded by evolution'.

The sheer existence of thousands of contemporary practicing astrologers and their hundreds of thousands, perhaps even millions, of clients, bears witness to the exemplary fatuity of these pronouncements. Moreover, Owen Gingerich was one of the 186 signers of the 1975 manifesto, 'Objections to Astrology' whose opening statement declares, 'Scientists in a variety of fields have become concerned about the increased acceptance of astrology in many parts of the world . . . acceptance of astrology pervades modern society. We are especially disturbed by the uncritical dissemination of astrological charts, forecasts and horoscopes by the media and otherwise reputable newspapers, magazines and publishers. This can only contribute to the growth of irrationalism and obscurantism.'

Evidently, a Harvard astronomer sees nothing amiss in declaring astrology defunct as a serious system for understanding human impulses on the one hand and, on the other, signing a statement expressing deep concern over the pervasive acceptance of astrology throughout the world. But certain irrational obscurantists might perceive an element of quite inadmissible contradiction there, and perhaps the jury will, too.

Hitler's Astrologer

The Second World War put a temporary halt to astrological activity, such as it was, but added to its history the strange footnote of Hitler and his alleged astrologers.

In Germany, since Hitler's accession to power, astrologers had been looked upon with disfavor. Nevertheless, in England, a rumor had been assiduously circulated by a refugee astrologer called Louis de Wohl that Hitler personally consulted astrologers and that he followed their advice – a not-implausible contention, since it was known that a number of higher-ups in the Third Reich maintained an interest in the more grotesque aspects of magic and the 'occult', including giving credence to the cosmological scheme that held we live not on the surface of the earth but inside it, and look out towards its surface. According to de Wohl, Hitler's astrologer was K. E. Krafft, an eccentric but in his own way quite brilliant man who, since the 1920s, had been on a one-man campaign to put astrology on a sound statistical basis.

After the war it was pretty well established that Hitler had not had a private astrologer and that he never took astrological advice. Krafft, it appears, had toyed with Nazi ideas in the beginning, and had been given some subordinate and temporary position in Goebbels' propaganda ministry. But when he learned to his surprise that the political leaders did not share his interest in pure astrology (he was ordered to turn out predictions on the defeat of the Allies) he refused to co-operate. The reward of foolish integrity was prison, and he died, finally, on the way to Buchenwald in 1945.

B. The Whore of Babylon

In England, however, de Wohl succeeded in convincing the British High Command that Krafft was in the pay of the Nazis and was giving them astrological advice and accordingly the British created a one-man counter-astrology agency, giving de Wohl the rank of captain, and he went through the war attempting to advise the high command on the moves Hitler would be making according to astrological interpretation.*

Apart from its value as a historical curio, there is one aspect of the Hitler astrology affair that is of genuine astrological interest. In a review of Hitler's rise to power, his brilliant coup at Munich in 1938, his swift campaigns in Poland and Scandinavia, there is one moment of glory that stands out above all others, one brief period during which he was unmistakable master; his blitzkrieg invasion of Holland, Belgium and Luxemburg, followed by his humiliation of the French.

The moment may be pinpointed to 10 May 1940, and, oddly enough, this moment is written into Hitler's stars so unmistakably that any astrologer might well conclude that Hitler was acting upon the advice of his own astrologer; or, learning that this was unlikely, use Hitler's campaign as a singularly impressive example of a man being compelled by his stars to act.

In this book it is the principles and functions of astrology, the evidence for and against it, that concern us, rather than its technique, but since astrology as a means of prophecy is the role with which most people are familiar, we shall use this opportunity to describe briefly the methods used by astrologers in attempting to make their forecasts.

The first, simplest, and most logical method, is to look at the 'transits'. The position of the planets at birth are known as their root or 'radix' positions. In the course of their revolutions about the heavens the planets cross or otherwise form 'aspects' with these radix positions which are held to be sensitive points.

* The ramifications of this story are such that it is impossible to condense without destroying its nightmarish quality. The details are exposed with commendable thoroughness by Ellic Howe, *Urania's Children* (William Kimber, London, 1967).

Naturally, the varying speeds of the planets in orbit mean that a predictable but infinitely varied sequence of transits is forever in progress, and from the various combinations the astrologer attempts to make forecasts.

Looking at Hitler's horoscope, we can see that on the night of 10 May 1940 his transits could not have been better.

As Fig. 11 shows, Saturn was forming trines first to Hitler's well aspected moon, then to his radix Jupiter. The transiting Mars – planet of war – made a trine to the Ascendant, and a sextile to the radix Mercury. Jupiter – planet of success – was moving into a conjunction with the radix sun, traditionally the position, above all others, standing for success in undertakings. While the moon, which moves so swiftly that it runs through the gamut of aspects once a month, was in exact trine to Uranus – planet of revolution, surprise, 'blitz', of the unexpected – on the very hour the attack was launched.

Yet an astrologer advising Hitler would not have restricted himself to prophecy on the basis of transits. He would also look into what are called 'secondary directions'. It is this that astrologers think Ezekiel is referring to when he talks of 'one year for one day' (see p. 71). Thus the position of the stars on Hitler's fifty-first day of life makes it possible to predict – within broad bounds – what will happen in his fifty-first year. These indications were far less favorable than the transits, and it was by incorporating the secondary directions with their own wishful thinking that so many astrologers kept predicting peace before the Second World War. Astrologers tried to make themselves believe that the stars would not allow Hitler to act fatally against his own interests. Yet, having made his moves, without taking the astrologers or anyone else into consideration, it does remain a fact that Hitler's one brightest moment was easily detectable, astrologically, and coincided with his actual moment of triumph.

If there is any history of the future, it will mark the Second World War as the turning point of civilization, and, depending upon the state of the new civilization, it may well mark the turning point for astrology.

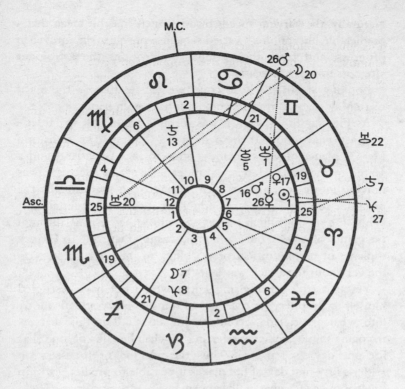

Figure 11. Hitler's horoscope with transits (see Fig. 1). Further salient features and their interpretation: Saturn high in the sign of Leo, in the tenth house; traditionally the symbol of a man who climbs high, with burning ambition, but is in danger of losing his position. Saturn in double square to Venus and Mars: danger will become reality. Mercury in opposition (180° distance) to Uranus: an indication of misguided (at times brilliant) ideas and violent hysteria. Saturn in a not very strong sextile (60°) from Uranus gives a tendency to use these (disagreeable) traits profitably in furthering the ambition. Uranus less than 6° from the Ascendant, but in the twelfth house leads to violence. Neptune and Pluto are close to each other in Gemini in the eighth house; death and destruction caused knowingly, and possibly an indication of suicide. On the positive side: Sun in Taurus in trine (120°) to Moon and, less powerfully, to Jupiter, the latter two being in a benevolent conjunction.

Astrology Moves into the Age of Aquarius

It is an astronomical fact that, due to the precession of the equinoxes, the sun will soon rise (around 2200 AD) at the spring equinox in the sign of Aquarius, binging on what astrologers call 'the Age of Aquarius'. Now astrologers have always held that this astronomical fact is of profound significance, and that the period of transition between one age and another is invariably one of chaos, conflict and indecision; old traditions crumble, new formulations are born; in between it is impossible to say with any certainty what is happening or will happen.

That we stand at such a historical moment is a truism. But there is, naturally, no need to believe that this has anything to do with astrology. Perhaps, like the Golden Section in nature, like the appearance and evolution of organic life on earth, like the harmonics of the periodic table of elements and the spiral shape of galaxies, the current chaos and the astronomical shift of zodiacal signs may be explained by 'coincidence'– that Sherlock Holmes among principles, to whom the solution of all mysteries, big and small, is 'elementary'.

Still, it is interesting, and perhaps not altogether coincidental, that the same war that polished off the past also provided the impetus to science, whose disclosures over the past forty years

---

This is not only the 'animal-lover', but also lends the personality of a strong attraction and, with Sun in 7, a public appeal. This man 'married' his public with high ideals, then deceived it (unfavourable Mars and Venus also in 7) for his own ambitions (Saturn), and in the end was impotent and unable to fruitfully consummate this weird marriage. (It is interesting that many planets in the seventh house is a feature in the charts of many dictators, among them Mussolini and Stalin.)

The symbols drawn on the outside of the chart signify the positions of the planets as they actually were on 10 May 1940, 1.15 a.m. Greenwich Mean Time. Broken lines mark the principal aspects.

have made it possible to prepare a defense of just that despised astrology an earlier science had prided itself upon discrediting.

But before embarking upon our defense, the jury should be thoroughly familiar with the Prosecution's argument. As we mentioned earlier, this argument is invariably misrepresented. The prosecution never owns up to its true identity but rather pretends it is the Judge, weighing the evidence for and against astrology with scientific impartiality. So let us look in detail at the actual argument to see what is valid and what is not.

II.

OBJECTIONS TO ASTROLOGY

A. *Witnesses for the Prosecution*

The Queen of Humbug

In our first edition we selected a number of typical objections to astrology, mainly voiced by scientists – since it is science that has arrogated to itself the role of sole arbiter of truth. (Our poisoned, polluted, trivialized and nuclear world bears witness to the success of that campaign.)

Our objections came from two sources: first a representative sampling taken from the many critics who spoke from the position of authority vested in them simply by practicing science; and, second, a detailed analysis of the single critic we could then find who claimed to have actually studied the subject.

Over the intervening years the situation has changed somewhat. In general the same basic objections have been reiterated by numerous critics who make no claim to have studied astrology, and who do not feel it necessary to do so. This attitude was illustrated vividly when the Reagan story broke, and journalists around the world trotted out the familiar objections virtually in chorus (we will look at some representative samples in Part IV, Heresy in the Church of Progress.

But as it happens, for the most part, our earlier critics voiced their criticisms in more detail. Therefore, in republishing most of our original selections intercalated with a few newer passages we are in no sense mispresenting our own case, or the prosecution's, by using dated material. Rather, we are providing the most representative sample we can assemble.

A. *Witnesses for the Prosecution*

We have, however, taken the liberty of replacing the Chief Prosecutor. It is with considerable regret that we relinquish most of our excerpts from Robert Eisler, author of *The Royal Art of Astrology*.

From our point of view, Eisler was the ideal opponent. His stated aim was of course the aim of all critics of astrology: the demolition of superstition (that is, belief in ancient, outmoded, invalid gods). His unstated aim was the unstated aim of all critics of astrology: the replacement of the false gods by the one and only true God, Reason.

But the successful proselytization of Reason calls for at least the illusion of reasonableness, and *The Royal Art of Astrology* is a torrent of unrestrained, erudite invective; a parody of everything that has ever been wrong with scholarship; an exaltation of Reason so gloriously unbalanced that it could not take in even the most gullible unbeliever. Thus, it is an assault upon astrology that amounts to an inadvertent defense . . . for if this be Reason let us have Unreason at any price, even if it should mean accepting astrology . . .

Over the intervening years, Eisler's arguments have been largely replaced by those of a more contemporary but less colourful breed of missionary, and our case is the duller for it. It can't be helped.

[A.] 'The Queen of Humbug', by Dr Harold Spencer Jones, HM Astronomer at the Royal Observatory, Greenwich (*News Review*, 3 August 1939):

> Astrology claims that the heavenly bodies – the sun, moon, planets and stars – have an influence on human affairs. It is asserted that the disposition of these bodies at the moment when a person is born is a direct influence on his personality, and that by studying their positions at any time after birth, guidance for the future can be obtained.
>
> These claims are sufficiently extensive and startling. But they do not nearly exhaust what astrology can do. Diseases can be diagnosed. The course of world events can be foretold. Weather can

be predicted. Some people even believe that seeds grow better if planted according to the state of the heavens.

Such claims are absolute rubbish. No astronomer could possibly say anything else [1]. But they pander to the desires of many people to peer into the future. They foster the primitive instinct to cling to the belief that our lives are directed to some extent by supernatural forces.

The astrologer will cast a horoscope and will advise about the future – for a fee, of course. It is significant that I do not know of any astrologer who is an observer of the stars, nor do I know of any serious observer of the stars who is an astrologer.

It is the task of the astronomer to observe and to study the stars, and by slow and patient observation to learn something about them. On the basis of what he has learnt, it is his duty to come into the open and to declare firmly and unreservedly that astrology is rubbish, a mere collection of empirical rules that have come down through the dim mists of the past . . . [2]

Any serious student of science could not help being amused if he were to read any book on astrology. I have never yet seen any argument put forward in support of it which would bear the least scientific investigation [3].

I have sought to find in books on astrology some justification for the supposed all-pervading effects of the heavenly bodies on human life and activities. I have found general statements, such as that there is a coincidence of earth events with those taking place elsewhere in the solar system (the only exemplifications given for this is that weather on earth is influenced by sun spots) and that all men are subject to the laws by which the earth is governed.

I have found nothing more substantial. As an astronomer I do not hesitate to say that I consider that altogether too slender a foundation on which to base such far-reaching assertions [4].

Unfortunately, there are many people who believe implicitly in astrology. I have had shoals of letters, many of them tragic, telling how the belief in it has ruined homes which until one of the partners took it up were happy ones. I would say that whereas astronomy is the Queen of Sciences, astrology is the Queen of Humbug . . .

[B.] Astrology ... still has millions of followers, but is so far removed from anything resembling science that it does not seem worthwhile to discuss it. The theory that sun spots cause depressions ... is the last respectable survival of the ancient view that human affairs are linked with astronomical phenomena.

Martin Gardner, *Fads and Fallacies in the Name of Science*
(Dover, 1957)

[C.] The belief in astrology is excusable; it is an indolent man's philosophy. The advantage of a belief in astrological absurdities is that one's acts are predetermined by the motions and 'influences' of the sun, moon and stars ... Obviously, if we can convince ourselves that we are not responsible for our acts, our morality deteriorates, and we cease to worry. Astrology is a comforting philosophy, adapted to the needs of timorous people and idiots.

Alfred Still, *Borderlands of Science* (Rider, 1964)

[D.] *Astrology:* A pseudoscience which deals with the influences of the stars upon human affairs and the foretelling of future events ... From the middle of the seventeenth century (in Europe) the interest in this pseudoscience has declined. It still flourishes however, in Asia and Africa and is a means of livelihood to many charlatans who prey upon the ignorant classes in all countries.

Encyclopaedia Britannica, 1957

[E.] *Synthetic Superstitions and Bogus Science:* One definition of superstition is 'Other People's Religion'. I certainly disagree with many points in other people's religious opinions, but I am not going to attack them here. Religious doctrines, even when they are untrue, are generally part of a system in which some intelligent and thoroughly decent people believe. I propose to discuss the synthetic superstitions which are being manufactured as 'opium for the people' particularly astrology. Large numbers of Sunday newspapers keep a tame astrologer, and I sometimes take a look at their columns. Now I don't despise real astrology. It began thousands of years ago in an attempt to link up happenings in the earth with those of the sky. It led to the keeping in Babylon, and other cities of what is now Iraq, of exact records of eclipses and other celestial events which have been of the greatest use to modern astronomers.

And in the late middle ages, it developed into an art with elaborate rules. In order to cast a horoscope you had to know all the positions of all the planets at the time of a person's birth. Indeed for accurate predictions the exact hour is needed. Each planet was supposed to have had a good, bad or neutral influence.

And the sky was divided into 'houses' concerned with various aspects of human life. Thus, if at the time of your birth Saturn and Mars were in conjunction in the House of Death, you were likely to meet with an early and violent death. A given day was or was not lucky for a person whose birth-hour was known, according to very complicated rules.

The rules were supposed to embody the wisdom of the ancient Chaldeans. Astrology had a great influence on the thought and language of ordinary people. Such common words as 'consider', 'disaster', 'influenza', and 'conjunction', all derive from astrological theory.

Astrology received shattering blows when two large new planets, Uranus and Neptune, were discovered, not to mention one moderate-sized one, Pluto, and about a thousand dwarf planets [1]. The wise men of the East had never discovered them, and the attempt to fit them into a horoscope is like putting a motor car into a coat of arms.

For astrology, like heraldry, has its rules, and is a quite amusing, though rather futile hobby. If I were a genuine astrologer following the great tradition of the 'science', I should be even more angry with the Sunday newspaper practitioners than with complete sceptics.

These ladies and gentlemen predict your lucky days on the basis of the month in which you were born.

I was born when the sun was in the constellation called the Scorpion. Now, according to traditional astrology, this alone doesn't tell me much. But if the lucky planets, Venus and Jupiter, were there too, then I may look forward to certain kinds of good luck.

But, if astrology is true, it is as ridiculous to predict a person's fortune from the position of the sun alone as it would be to diagnose a disease by looking at a patient's tongue without taking his temperature or pulse rate, or making any other examination. Another of these bogus sciences is palmistry . . .

If the astrologers and palmists want to convince scientists of the truth of their 'sciences', they have an easy task. No doubt (if their claims are right) they must have discovered that millions of young men were going to die between 1914 and 1918 [2]. So they ought to be able to predict the dates of future wars. When they get a few dates right, I shall take them seriously. But I am not much impressed by a few lucky shots.

However that may be, astrologers and palmists are very useful to the cause of capitalism. They help to persuade people that their destinies are outside their control. And, of course, this is true as long as enough people believe it. But if enough people learn how the joint fate of all of us can be altered, things will begin to happen which will mean the end of capitalism as well as of astrology and palmistry [3].

J. B. S. Haldane, *Daily Herald*, 29 September 1938

[F.] . . . China and India have ancient astrological traditions just as impressive as the West's yet based upon entirely different star patterns. If one tradition is right, the other two are wrong [1]. If birthcharts can give subtle insights into personality and destiny, why are they unable to tell a person's sex, intelligence, or race, or recognize the criminally insane? Why is there no clustering of birth dates of thousands who are killed in a single earthquake [2]?

What about people born in northern countries where some astrological signs never rise? Why do astrologers not adjust for changes in the zodiac caused by the precession of the earth's axis? As Eysenck and Nias write, 'In the time of Ptolemy, the sun was in the constellation Aries on the day of the spring equinox . . . today it is in Pisces.'

Martin Gardner, reviewing *Astrology: Science or Superstition*
by H. J. Eysenck and D. K. B. Nias,
in *Discover*, October 1982, p. 12

[G.] Astrology, in its broad version, unfounded and irrefutable, barely articulated, is a potential opium for the semi-intellectual.

Mercury, Journal of the Astronomical Society of the Pacific,
vol. X, no. 1, January/February 1981

[H.] . . . astrologers have tried to rationalize astrology in terms of science. They are continually combing the scientific literature, or at least popular accounts, for all kinds of physical experiments, expecially bizarre ones that seem to indicate some causal relationship between celestial objects and things on the earth.

When magnetism was discovered, it became a favorite thing. And of course astrologers like to talk about the tidal forces. We know the sun and moon make tides on the earth and we understand that very well as a gravitational phenomenon. Astrologers do not. They argue, 'Look at the tremendous tides the moon produces on the ocean. Think what it can do to humans – humans are mostly water.' It turns out, however, that a three-pound book located six feet away exerts about 50 millions times as strong a tidal force on a man as does Mars when that planet is at its closest to earth. Tidal forces exerted by the planets are completely negligible on something as small as a human being. Also consider electromagnetic radiation. The light and other radiation from the planets combined is trivial by factors of millions compared to even small fluctuations in the sun's output.

Astronomer George Abell,
interviewed in *Mercury*,
Journal of the Astronomical Society
of the Pacific, March/April 1976

Commentary

It is clear that all these critics, without exception, are ignorant of – or deliberately ignore – the Pythagorean principles that actually provide astrology's foundations. To them, pop astrology is the only astrology that exists. But even upon this assumption, the attacks that are levelled are devoid of fact and almost as free of legitimate objections. Some amount to deliberate distortions of the astrological argument while others are shot through with logical absurdities and inner contradictions. Let us look at these objections in order.

The Astronomer Royal (A) can find no statement that 'will

bear the least scientific investigation'. That is: there has been no scientific investigation. And he dismisses the sun-spot correlation – as does Gardner (B) – as 'too slender a foundation on which to base such far-reaching assertions' (A4). Perhaps so. But it *is* a foundation. Many of the major advances in science have been initiated by no less tenuous and inexplicable discrepancies. Modern physics, for example, can be traced to the critical but extremely delicate Michelson Morley experiments in which the speed of light failed to diminish as predicted under controlled laboratory conditions, destroying the theory of the luminiferous ether (required to buttress the then-prevailing dogma of the structure of matter), paving the way for relativity theory. Earlier we quoted a few assertions made by eminent nineteenth-century authorities concerning the 'absolutely lifeless' structure of matter (pp. 124 ff.). We suspect the objections to astrology voiced by their twentieth-century counterparts will look no less naive and mistaken to the science of the next century.

The Astronomer Royal then goes on to dismiss all claims that astrology can diagnose disease, foretell world events and weather and provide propitious times for planting. 'Such claims are absolute rubbish. No astronomer could possibly say anything else (A1).'

Now these claims may be unfounded, but since when is an astronomer an authority on disease, agriculture, or prophecy?*

According to Patrick Moore (see p. 6), 'astronomy studies the universe' and upon that basis, presumably, an astronomer has the authority to pass judgement upon anything within that universe. But realistically speaking, astronomy is concerned only with the mechanical motions and the physical constitution of the celestial bodies. (Spencer Jones admits that himself,

---

* Though an astronomer, Dr Spencer Jones represents an exception to the rule since he was perhaps best known for his prophetic skills. When asked by a journalist in 1957 what he thought of the possibility of space travel, Spencer Jones replied: 'Space travel is bunk.' Two weeks later the first Sputnik was launched.

cutting the ground out from under his own authority two paragraphs after asserting it. 'It is the task of the astronomer to observe and to study the stars, and by slow and patient observation to learn something about them.')

The question of *meaning* lies permanently outside the limited field of the astronomer's expertise. Unless he has studied astrology itself, an astronomer is no more fit to pass judgement upon it than a radio repairman is fit to pass judgement upon Mozart.

Moreover, there are now and were then a few astronomers who did not automatically dismiss astrology. From time to time, astrological journals publish letters from astronomers who admit to an interest in astrology but who elect to remain anonymous for fear of professional repercussions. At least one astronomer, Percy Seymour, Principal Lecturer in Astronomy at the Plymouth Polytechnic and Director of the William Day Planetarium in England, has betrayed his colleagues and not only admitted an interest, but published a book on the subject. In *Astrology: The Evidence of Science*, Seymour – whose specialty is planetary magnetism – develops his theory that planetary motions affect the extreme sensitivity of the earth's magnetic field, which in turn could account for the proven astrological 'effects'. We will be discussing this interesting hypothesis under The Question: How? in The Evidence (see Part III.D).

Alfred Still (C) and the editors of *Mercury* (G) find astrology a proper philosophy for 'timorous people and idiots' and a 'potential opium for the semi-intellectual'. Since these timorous semi-intellectuals must necessarily include Plato, Plotinus, Kepler, Goethe and Jung, to name a few, it does make us wonder at the philosophical credentials of Mr Still and the literary accomplishments of the editors of *Mercury*. Mr Still's views are particularly instructive. He thinks belief in astrology brings on moral deterioration and 'we cease to worry', which would seem to imply that worry and high morality must necessarily go hand in hand.

Out of the considerable verbiage, it is only the geneticist, Haldane, and the mathematical gamesman, Gardner, who, despite numerous inaccuracies, present a few genuine objections. The discoveries of the new planets (E1) were and remain a problem, but hardly the 'shattering blows' claimed. (We shall be dealing with legitimate objections to astrology in detail shortly.)

Both Haldane and Gardner detect a major astrological stumbling block – the relationship between individual destiny and large-scale events . . . the millions killed in a war, or the thousands in an earthquake.

But this objection is offered as though, over the course of astrology's millennial history, astrologers had never thought of it on their own.

In fact Ptolemy devoted considerable time to just this problem. He contended, and modern astrologers would agree, that the destiny of the individual is subsumed in the greater destiny of the state, nation, race, tribe or geographical area. Accurately determining the 'horoscope' of a race, state, or geographical area is another problem. Perhaps it cannot be done. But this does not invalidate the astrological *principle* of terrestrial/celestial correspondence. All it means is that astrological prophecy is unreliable. Few astrologers would maintain the contrary – though it is true not many would want to dispense with it altogether.

Gardner (F) thinks the astronomical fact that in the extreme north and south certain signs never rise, invalidates astrological effects. But this assumes a direct one-to-one causal relationship between the constellation and the human being born under it. Most astrologers do not believe such a direct relationship exists, and are certainly aware of the problem. In any event, this objection applies only to 'houses'. Using certain house systems, people born in these extreme latitudes could not have their ascendants in those signs that never rise, theoretically producing less variety in external appearance and public behavior than in people born in more southern latitudes. It's not inconceivable that research among Lapps and Eskimos could bear out such a theoretical possibility. Otherwise, those born in the far north have horoscopes with the same twelve sun signs as everyone else.

Gardner (F) argues that since different astrological systems are used in China and India, only one can be true. Identical devastating logic was used by Bertrand Russell in his argument against religion (*Why I am Not a Christian*). Russell argued that since all religions disagreed with each other, logically, only one could be true. This is exactly equivalent to saying, 'six chefs give different recipes for apple pie, therefore only one can be apple pie', or, 'musicians in the West, China and India all use different musical scales, therefore, only one can be music,' or 'democracies all have different constitutions, therefore, only one can be a democracy'.

Finally, Haldane's objection to astrology on left-wing political grounds should be savored for itself (E3), but it may also be regarded as an object lesson in the trustworthiness of the scientific mind when it ventures outside its own constricted little sphere.

Astronomer George Abell (H) dismisses astrology on the grounds that the known 'forces' (gravitational and magnetic) exerted by the planets are much too feeble to produce astrological 'effects'. Though it sounds authoritative and scientific, it is a pseudo-objection, based upon a false and antiquated vision of the world. Briefly, Abell and his colleagues have chosen a demonstrably incorrect model of 'reality'. We shall be devoting considerable time to exploding this objection, which is at the core of the extended assaults upon astrology.

Over the past two decades, a number of books have appeared, including our own, that deal fully and systematically with all the objections raised so far. The latter-day opponents cited (Martin Gardner, George Abell and the editors of *Mercury*) have had ample opportunity to acquaint themselves with the arguments and refute them if possible. No mention is made of this readily available material, by them or by other contemporary critics of astrology. It is a curious situation. For these writers would express nothing but contempt for people criticizing their own fields who had not done their homework and familiarized themselves with the current arguments pro and con.

Why should astrology's critics feel no obligation to do so? A telltale and typically apoplectic passage from Eisler accounts for what otherwise appears a serious dereliction of duty.

> To this day the devotees of astrology never tire of repeating the bitter complaint of Alfred John Pearce, who wrote in his *Textbook of Astrology* (1911), 'Why is it that the great majority of learned men of the nineteenth and the present century have denied that there is any truth to astrology? The reply is: Because they had never investigated it, being too prejudiced against it to do so.'
>
> This wanton accusation against modern scholarship is in itself sufficient proof of either an absolute lack of good faith or an almost unbelievable ignorance of all the learned work dedicated to the study of astrology from the time of the great Frenchman Saumaise (Salmasius, 1648), the correspondent of Milton, to our own age which saw the deciphering, editing and translating of the most important Mesopotamian and Egyptian astrological texts, the publication in more than a dozen volumes of the *Catalogue of Greek Astrological Manuscripts*, under the direction of Franz Cumont and Wilhelm Kroll, the rediscovery and publication of the *Sphaera Barbarica* by Franz Boll (1904), of the astrological texts of Hermes Trismegistus by Wilhelm Gundel (1936) and the searching investigation of all the available material by such men as A. Bouche-Leclercq (1899), Carl van Bezold (1914), Reginald Campbell Thompson (1900), Charles Virolleaud (1905 ff.), Aby Warburg and a whole group of younger men inspired by their example. Not one item of the list of their books given below, is ever quoted by any one of the defenders of astrology. They will not acknowledge honestly the decisive fact that their futile practices have been investigated with the greatest care and impartiality by the foremost scholars of the leading Western nations for almost three centuries, and that not one has failed to condemn them as the stale, superstitious residue of what was once a great, pantheistic religion and a glorious philosophical attempt to understand and rationally to explain the universe . . .

> Robert Eisler, *The Royal Art of Astrology*, p. 27

So great was the care and impartiality with which these scholars studied astrology that in the preface of his work Bouche-Leclercq excuses himself from actually attempting to work with astrology and examine the basis of its symbolism with: 'We do not waste our time in studying upon what others have wasted theirs'; an attitude commended warmly by Eisler. Franz Boll, challenged at a lecture with never having himself erected a horoscope, replied impartially, 'We are not yet mad enough to waste our time in this way.' The impartial and careful Franz Cumont has already been discussed.

To the best of our knowledge, *no* critic of astrology has *ever* attempted to put astrology to the test of experience. As we mentioned earlier (p. 6), this in itself would not amount to decisive scientific proof or disproof, either. (Tone-deaf children, given violins, seem to disprove the possibility of music.)

But because the element of interpretation (that is, artistry) is fundamental to the practice of astrology, it is illegitimate and deliberately misleading to dismiss the entire subject as a pseudo-science (D) – especially when its most eminent practitioners insist that astrology is inherently irreducible to a pure quantitative science. (And the notion of a pure quantitative science is an illusion to begin with; recognized as such by all scientists who subscribe to the established theories of modern physics.)

In practice, what this means is that those careful and impartial nineteenth- and early twentieth-century scholars commended by Eisler, starting from the premise that 'astrology can't work, therefore it doesn't', produced a voluminous body of original, scrupulously biased works (based in their entirety upon the indefensible 'dreaming Chaldean' historical model and the then-reigning billiard-ball cosmology of Newtonian physics).

Though largely unread and forgotten today, their conclusions have been taken up, summarized and paraphrased by popularizers and the contributors to textbooks and encyclopedias. With almost no alteration, it is this account that prevails today. It has been accepted unquestioningly as authoritative by all critics quoted so far. And it is by and large the uninformed pronouncements of these second- and third-hand sources that get parroted on television and radio whenever astrology is the subject, and a scientific 'authority' is consulted. (We shall be looking at some typical specific comments in our section devoted to Astrology and the Press, pp. 416–40). In other words, there is no need for anyone to look into newer works, especially those written by astrologers or by those scientists who have studied the evidence, found it unassailable and acknowledged those conclusions formally in writing. It has all been taken care of by that earlier generation of 'experts'.

Even so, despite their bias and their incomprehension of astrology's metaphysical basis, if called upon today to defend their attitude those earlier scholars might plead extenuating circumstances. There was nothing in the science of the day hinting at the energetic rather than material nature of matter. In their Newtonian billiard-ball universe, with planets whirling about in absolutely empty space, there was no theoretical framework within which astrological 'influence' might operate. Nor was there a conceptual framework that would have allowed them to test those quantitative aspects of astrology amenable to such analysis.

Of course, those turn-of-the-century scholars could have turned to the readily available work of Blavatsky, Besant and Leadbeater for valid insights into latter-day high-energy physics. But it would be ungenerous to demand it of them.

Since those extenuating circumstances no longer apply, it is instructive to look at the objections to astrology now raised by critics who claim to have studied the subject; not merely looked up outdated references in encyclopedias.

Several books wholly devoted to discrediting astrology have appeared since our first edition was published. The two most highly regarded within the scientific community are *The Gemini Syndrome: A Scientific Evaluation of Astrology* by astronomers R. B. Culver and P. A. Ianna, and *Objections to Astrology* by astronomer (the late) Bart J. Bok and science writer Lawrence E. Jerome. A third massive work, *Recent Advances in Natal Astrology* by Dr Geoffrey Dean and Arthur Mather, is, despite its title, more of an attack on astrology than a defense, yet comes (astonishingly) from within the astrological camp itself and represents a special and important case. We shall be discussing a number of its conclusions in the course of our argument.

Excepting the contribution by Lawrence E. Jerome (which

criticizes astrology from a different and particularly valuable angle) both *The Gemini Syndrome* and *Objections to Astrology* raise in detail essentially the same scientific objections as those raised by critics quoted at the beginning of this chapter. So, rather than go through these books, addressing individual objections as they arise, forcing us to repeat ourselves, we will itemize the objections in one list at the end and deal with each in appropriate detail in turn.

The importance of both *The Gemini Syndrome* and *Objections to Astrology* lies, not so much in the specific scientific objections they raise which (the Jerome entry apart) are standard, but in the insights both provide into the psychological, philosophical and metaphysical issues astrology inevitably involves. These are at least as important to our case as the objections themselves, and merit extended treatment.

Objections to Astrology is the document endorsed in 1975 by 186 leading scientists including 19 Nobel Prize-winners. Though socially conscious scientists will on occasion band together to support some politically sensitive issue such as the anti-nuclear movement, it is rare that they feel obliged to defend their basic philosophy as scientists. Seen in this light, the Bok/Jerome book takes on an importance it might not otherwise have. *The Gemini Syndrome* serves a complementary function. It spells out the premises upon which *all* objections to astrology are based; premises other critics take as axiomatic. Once the premises can be exposed as false, it then becomes possible to argue a case for astrology even without available hard evidence in support of it (though there is no shortage of such evidence). By spelling out those premises, Culver and Ianna provide an invaluable service. There is no longer a danger (as there was in the original *Case for Astrology*) of our putting words into opponents' mouths; nor do we have to look to outside sources in order to detail the premises upon which the prosecution case is built.

Our discussion of *The Gemini Syndrome* and of *Objections to Astrology* will be as thorough as space permits. But *The Gemini Syndrome* in particular is a long, densely argued work.

In their attack upon astrology, Culver and Ianna often refer to the original edition of this book; sometimes quoting us out of context, sometimes pruning quotations in such a way that our argument is misrepresented. More important, the reader is given no inkling that the central scientific and psychological elements of our argument have been ignored. A powerful impression is created: all that supports astrology has been disposed of. The exhaustive treatment of those arguments that are addressed, cleverly reinforces that impression.

We are not crying 'foul', or seeking redress. Culver and Ianna are conforming to standard academic procedure, particularly as it prevails in science when a fundamental challenge to dogma presents itself. Indeed, any other kind of treatment would prove an embarrassment. It would suggest a level of integrity and objectivity among astrology's opponents. That would oblige us to deal with *The Gemini Syndrome* as an exception to the rule, which would seem to be special pleading, complicating and weakening our case.

But we have been provided with an object lesson, and we pass it on. Culver and Ianna specifically call attention to the dangers of bias.

> No one likes to be wrong. Yet we are all wrong for one reason or another from time to time, when we were quite confident we were right ... It is a complicated world out there – lots of shades of grey, vested interests, incomplete information, calculated risks. You have to be very, very careful. Right? Right.
>
> *The Gemini Syndrome,* p. 28

Though we do not consciously intend to misrepresent their argument, perhaps we will not prove careful enough? It is not for us to say. Readers interested in examining the evidence in depth are therefore enjoined to get themselves copies of both *The Gemini Syndrome* and *Objections to Astrology*.

The Gemini Syndrome: A Scientific Evaluation of Astrology

Culver and Ianna take the common view that whatever cannot be demonstrated through the scientific method is invalid, or does not exist. Their criticism of astrology is largely based upon astrology's (alleged) inability to prove itself through the application of the scientific method. It is the scientific method that is final arbiter.

> Briefly the scientific method is a sort of cyclic trial-and-error approach to the investigation of nature. Here, accurate experimental results and carefully observed phenomena are the only 'truths' . . . The theory must be used to make experimentally verified predictions which can then be subjected to the appropriate tests. If the prediction and the experimental check agree, the theory is shown to possibly be not incorrect . . . it is a procedure that clearly works. About this there is no doubt. *No bit of established knowledge about the world around us or of modern technology has come about in any other way but through the scientific method.* [Italics ours]
>
> *The Gemini Syndrome*, p. 29

Strong words! But brought up, as are we all, on the scientific paradigm, there seems little to argue with. Especially convincing is the tone of authority . . . '*No* bit of established knowledge . . . has come about in *any* other way'. Not much room for discussion there!

Yet subjected to closer scrutiny minor flaws appear. Perhaps Culver and Ianna are not following their own advice; they are not being careful enough? For example, we seem to recognize a difference between a cat, a dog and an elephant. Most of us would term this knowledge 'established'. It seems to take place in 'the world around us'. And we do not seem to have used the scientific method to arrive at our knowledge; it did not come to us via 'a cyclic trial-and-error approach to the investigation of nature'. We know not to touch a hot stove, or to eat rotten fish. This is also knowledge of the 'world around us'; anyway, it seems to be, and it comes to us directly, through experience. We do not even need a scientific explanation for verification. That we can produce one does not seem very important. At least not to most of us.

Knowing how to play the violin is another form of knowledge, and knowing how to explode a sequence of asinine philosophical assertions masquerading as science still another. Both involve 'knowledge of the world around us' in some legitimate sense. Neither involves the scientific method. Indeed, when the situation is examined more closely, it becomes possible to suggest the exact contrary of Culver and Ianna despite that uncompromising tone: *none* of our knowledge of the world around us (that is of consequence in dealing with it) comes through the scientific method; *all* of it comes through personal experience,.

But it is not necessary to go to this extreme. Or to broach the epistemological and philosophical questions the Culver/Ianna passage may raise. It will suffice to acknowledge that if Culver and Ianna are right; if *only* knowledge obtained through the scientific method is valid, then the scientific method is reduced to triviality – since this knowledge has little bearing upon the conduct of our normal daily lives. On the other hand, if other forms of knowledge are recognized, then the scientific method is but one of any number of valid means for acquiring knowledge, in which case, criticisms based upon the scientific methodology are *a priori* partial and conditional and apply *only* to those areas of inquiry that may prove susceptible to it.

Indeed, Culver and Ianna pay lip service to this established fact.

> [1] It is widely known that quantum theory has encouraged a somewhat different viewpoint wherein there is not a strict cause–effect relationship between events in the real world, at least on the microscopic or atomic level ... Nevertheless, it still seems that a large part of the search for explanations of things in the real world is usefully described as the identification of 'plausible physical relationships' between events ...

But within the space of just one paragraph this cautiously expressed opinion has developed assertive muscle: (2) 'In summary we would say again that science is the best way to find truth known to mankind . . .' (p. 37)

And just two short paragraphs later, what began as modest opinion is transformed into dogma that brooks no argument. (3) 'The evidence – objective descriptions of nature – is the only basis for truth.' (p. 37)

The left brain knoweth not what the right brain thinketh . . . That such mutually exclusive and self-contradictory statements should occur within the space of three paragraphs, surviving scrutiny by both authors through proof-reading and two editions of their book, is a testament to the level of their critical faculties. Here, we are not dealing with a situation analogous to our six chefs giving different recipes for apple pie, or composers all producing music using different scales. These statements are logically, mutually exclusive and self-cancelling, and they appear just a few pages after a patronizing chapter in which scientific logic is explained and spelled out for us poor ignoramuses who are not scientists and who therefore do not understand it, and who therefore might be inclined to look favorably upon astrology and other superstitions.

(1) is a not unreasonable assessment of the strengths of the scientific method (given a rigorous definition of such loaded terms as 'things', 'real world' and 'plausible physical relationships', which is next to impossible to set out). A few loopholes are left for that which might not be amenable to treatment by this method. (2) is obviously a value judgement: science is 'the best way to find truth'. But by definition the 'best way' is not the *only* way (3) 'The evidence – objective descriptions of nature – is the only basis for truth' is pure, unvarnished credulity, unsupported and unsupportable. It is belief held in open contradiction to the observed facts.

For there are all kinds of truths: truths of art, truths of philosophy, truths of love, truth in the witness stand – virtually all that comprises our living experience – that cannot be reduced to 'objective descriptions of nature' and that are yet part of 'the real world'.*

---

* It might be possible to define truth narrowly and limit it to that which can be supported by science – leaving out virtually everything we call 'life', thereby reducing truth to triviality. But Culver and Ianna's inclusion and endorsement of the quote from Abraham Maslow (see p. 160) makes it clear they are not using truth in this restricted but legitimate sense.

Culver and Ianna have not developed the faculty for distinguishing between facts and their own beliefs. Elsewhere on this same page they declaim: 'To believe without evidence is imagination; to believe in spite of evidence is delusion.' *Ipse dixit* . . . we find ourselves in rare agreement.

The Anatomy of Inconsistency

But to better understand the level of their attack upon astrology – and to forestall accusations of quoting out of context ourselves – it is worth looking in detail into the illuminating page that provides the passages above.

> In summary we would say again that science is the best way to find truth known to mankind. It is fair and objective, even if scientists are not; we certainly don't claim to be totally free of bias. This is partly why the scientific search for truth is so important. It transcends bias and personal opinion and rejects merely psychologically satisfying explanations and produces evidence for anyone to see and judge. It is not limited to 'hard' science. Abraham Maslow has advocated the broadest application of science, writing that science

> '. . . need not abdicate from the problems of love, creativeness, value, beauty, imagination, ethics and joy, leaving them altogether to 'non-scientists', to poets, prophets, priests, dramatists, artists, or diplomats. All of these people may have wonderful insights, ask the questions that need to be asked, put forth challenging hypotheses and may even be true much of the time. But however sure *they* may be, they can never make mankind sure. They can convince only those who already agree with them, and a few more. Science is the *only way we have of shoving truth down the reluctant throat* [our italics]. Only science can overcome characterological differences in seeing and believing. Only science can progress.'

> *Toward a Psychology of Being*, p. viii

The evidence – objective descriptions of nature – *is the only basis for truth*. It is not what we think the world is like, it is what the world reveals to us whatever our preconceived ideas. To believe without evidence is imagination; to believe in spite of evidence is delusion. *Only empirical evidence counts* [our italics throughout]. Whatever criticism and objections may be raised, the 'proof' of the idea must be that it works. We must demand of any hypothesis that it passes every empirical test we can pose for it. We demand no more or less from astrology. (p. 37)

The assertion that science is fair and objective even though scientists are not may well be among the silliest statements ever made by human beings. It is like saying justice is impartial, even though judges are corrupt.

The system, any system, is only as good as those who run it. The history of science is the story of bold, innovative thinkers who have persisted in their convictions against the massed opposition of their colleagues (who, for the most part, refused to acknowledge sound evidence). Impartial experiments can be conducted only by those who are impartial to begin with, or at least open to the possibility of being proved wrong. More important, an experiment can only be conducted if directed toward some preconceived aim. There is no such thing as a random experiment. Rare serendipitous discoveries apart, science can only find what it is looking for. When astrology is at issue, or extrasensory perception, or any other subject that challenges the spiritually flat inner world of the rationalist, the scientific method is drafted into service as a means of preserving dogma, not as a means for discovering truth. Experiments may be performed, but only those that *a priori* can be expected to produce negative results. Only those data are carefully examined which enforce the preconceived position. (Soon we shall describe the delicious furore caused when such a pre-judged experiment goes awry and produces contrary evidence.)

What Big Eyes You Have, Grandma

The Maslow passage, cited with approval, might win a prize for woolliness at the local sheep-judging but cannot qualify as thought. The notion of setting scientists loose on poetry, prophecy, joy and ethics is of course terrifying (or ludicrous, depending on the point of view), and also betrays a perfect incomprehension of precisely that quantitative scientific method championed by Culver and Ianna.*

(On the other hand, this is not to say that art, religion, literature and the rest cannot be approached systematically. The cathedral of Chartres is an example of such a systematic approach. But this is not the banal quantitative science of Culver and Ianna. It is the Sacred Science of the ancients.)

Less amusing is the wolf leering out from under all that wool ... (Actually, we apologize to the world of wolves for this misuse of an old image. Wolves are not Fascists.)

Who is Abraham Maslow that he would have his truths shoved down our reluctant throats? Presumably, even the throats of those who have examined his truths and found them conditional at best; at worst inconsequential or dangerous. Do Culver and Ianna endorse this scientific authoritarianism? Obviously they do or they would have cut the quote short. They are very good at cutting quotes to suit their needs (and, indeed, here take a most unrepresentative passage from Maslow – who more commonly writes at length, though just as fuzzily, about the futility of trying to apply hard science to human psychology).

In deference, then, to the Holy Scientific Method, we are not to trust conclusions based upon the results of our own hard work and inner conviction. Only when our results have been verified by empirical proof produced by impartial, scientific outsiders are we to have confidence. But since, as Culver and Ianna admit, scientists are biased, we are foredoomed to perma-

---

* Happily, not all scientists share the Maslow, Culver and Ianna conviction about an indefinitely extended scientific domain. Astronomer George Abell, an arch-foe of astrology, interviewed in *Mercury*, declared, 'Science is a procedure for exploring nature and for finding the laws by which nature behaves. Science must obey very specific rules in this investigation. It's very restrictive for this reason. There are many areas of human endeavor that science has nothing to do with – such as art, religion, literature and so forth . . .' (*Mercury*, March/April 1976)

nent insecurity ... poor souls in purgatory awaiting that scientific Second Coming when the biased scientists disappear and the impartial system takes over. Upon this basis Beethoven would have thrown out all of his Late Quartets, and very little in science would have happened either.

It is this cheerless scenario that Maslow, Culver and Ianna would inflict upon mankind in the name of Progress – for as Maslow insists 'only science can progress'. Yet in the world of everybody's living, day-to-day experience (Maslow's, Culver's and Ianna's included), the exact opposite applies. Only the individual can progress. Learning to play the violin is progress. Learning a martial art is progress. Learning to distinguish between the (conditional) facts of science and indefensible opinions arbitrarily drawn upon those facts is progress. Flying to the moon may be progress (giving it the benefit of the doubt), but only for those who fly there. For the rest of us such progress is as vicarious, as fleeting, and as meaningless as the pleasure derived from a *Penthouse* centerfold – and considerably less intense. When large numbers of individuals are doing the kind of inner work that results in individual progress, a progressive society becomes possible; more accurately: civilization ... but this is not the place to discuss the crucial distinction between what Maslow, Culver and Ianna call progress (which is no more than shiny barbarism) and what once prevailed as civilization.

Its introductory chapters stamp *The Gemini Syndrome* as a farrago of inconsistency, inner contradiction, psychological absurdity, hubris and (following the definition laid down by Culver and Ianna themselves) delusion. But because it attacks astrology and calls itself 'a scientific evaluation' no questions are asked. 'Amid the flood of literature promoting the current craze for astrology, this volume is one of the few books that provide a hard look at astrology by professional scientists ... Recommended for science collections and for most public libraries' (Jack W. Weigel, University of Michigan Library, Ann Arbor).

Obviously, *The Gemini Syndrome* is not science. The fairy-tale transformation of a description of the scientific method into dogma within the space of three paragraphs, and the endorsement of science as a means for shoving the truth down unwilling throats, reveals its true nature.

Winning Converts for the Church of Progress

Culver and Ianna are missionaries, carrying the gospel of the Church of Progress into infidel territory. Many of their colleagues are even less circumspect about their aims than themselves.

> The more serious-minded among us are starting to ask what is going on. Why the sudden explosion of interest, even among some otherwise sensible people, in all sorts of paranormal 'happenings'? Are we in retreat from the scientific ideas of rationality, dispassionate examination of evidence, and sober experiment that have made modern civilization what it is?
>
> In the past, the raising and answering of such questions has been left to commentators and journalists. This time around, however, some scientists are beginning to fight back . . .
>
> Flyer advertising the *Skeptical Inquirer*

> So let us do our best to get rid of this ideological garbage, lest it inundate the earth . . . If we save even a few from the lure of the higher nonsense, our efforts will have been worthwhile.
>
> L. Sprague de Camp, *New Humanist* #6, p. 8

> I'm trying in my way, to bring society to a rationalist point of view . . . and I am waging a battle here, and I have lots of troops on my side.
>
> James 'The Amazing' Randi, *The Humanist*, #6, pp. 16–22

The paradox of these irrational rationalists, these passionate crusaders for dispassion, is of course the stuff of which satire is made. It also should establish for the jury the real nature of the opposition to astrology, by Culver and Ianna, and by almost all other critics we have yet to discover.

Now, in principle, there is nothing wrong with missionary work performed in the hope of convincing others of the truth of one's own deeply held religious convictions. But this becomes suspect when the campaign is unwittingly described in martial language: 'I'm waging a battle here, and I have lots of troops on my side.' When the missionary expresses his willingness to shove the truth down unwilling throats, the prospective convertee may well begin to suspect ulterior motives. And when the stated aim of all this proselytizing zeal is the inculcation of 'scientific ideas of rationality, dispassionate examination of evidence, and sober experiment that have made modern civilization what it is?' even the most benighted of natives may find themselves unconvinced. And they may be accordingly unwilling to give up comfortable superstitions for this new faith whose most salient characteristics are obvious, wholesale self-delusion and/or hypocrisy.

On the other hand, the alert among the unconverted will realize that the personal, individual psychological imbalance prevailing among astrology's opponents does not of itself invalidate their argument.

B. The Case Against Astrology According to Culver and Ianna

The Premises

Though detailed and elaborate, the argument raised against astrology is only as good as the premises upon which it is based. As we have already noted, Culver and Ianna acknowledge that

> 'quantum theory has encouraged a somewhat different viewpoint wherein there is not a strict cause–effect relationship between events in the real world (1). Astrologers, having recently recognized this [actually, as we have seen, Blavatsky and the Theosophists recognized it long before the scientists did, and Blavatsky acquired that recognition from ancient India, Egypt and Tibet], believe they have found support for the view that no physical connection need exist between the planets and people for astrology to work. However, there is little solace for astrology here. It is true on the quantum level that individual events are not predictable, but one can establish probabilities for given events and see the collective results fulfilled for many events. Astrology, after 3000 years, doesn't seem to have yet reached this stage . . . The quantum level effects, at any rate, do not extend upwards to the scale of the solar system. . .'   (p.36)

It is true that astrologers have sometimes tried to use quantum theory as an explanation for astrological correspondences, and this is probably illegitimate. However, the ground rules laid down by Culver and Ianna are even more illegitimate. The key to their illegitimacy is the constantly reiterated reference to 'the real world' (1).

The 'real world' of Culver and Ianna, and of science in general, is the world extending upwards of the quantum level. Sometimes this 'real world' is called 'nature'. In this 'real world', or 'nature', all effects have measurable causes, and can be subjected to measurement; they must be predictable. To be valid, indeed, to qualify for a place in the 'real world', Culver and Ianna insist astrology must also be susceptible to the same kinds of treatment.

But there is one big problem with this 'real world' of Culver and Ianna: there are no people in it. This is a 'real world' that excludes both consciousness and volition or purpose. In other words, the very faculty that allows Culver and Ianna to measure, predict and quantify does not count as part of 'the world out there'.*

---

* '. . . mind is not only not locatable, *it has no location*. It is not a thing in space and time, not measurable, hence . . . not assimilable as science. Yet it is not to be dismissed as an epiphenomenon. It is the foundation, the condition that makes science possible. The entire point of science is to bring ever deeper and subtler aspects of reality to recognition in our consciousness. That recognition is itself virtually an act of creation . . . Our consciousness is not alone the precondition for science, but for reality. What exists is what has become manifest to our consciousness . . .

'I have propounded two riddles: one, the very peculiar character of a universe such as ours, that breeds life, and two, the problem of consciousness, mind, a phenomenon that lies outside the parameters of space and time, that has no location.

'A few years ago it occurred to me . . . that mind, rather than being a very late development in the evolution of living things, restricted to organisms with the most complex nervous systems – all of which I had believed to be true – that mind instead has been there always, and that this universe is life breeding because the pervasive presence of mind had guided it to be so.

'That thought, though elating as a game is elating, so offended my scientific possibilities as to embarrass me. It took only a few weeks, however, for me to realize that I was in excellent company. That kind of thought is not only deeply embedded in millennia-old Eastern philosophies, but it has been expressed plainly by a number of great and very recent physicists.

'So Arthur Eddington (1928): "The stuff of the world is mind-stuff . . . the mind-stuff is not spread in space and time . . . recognizing that the physical world is entirely abstract and without 'actuality' apart from its linkage to consciousness, we

B. The Case Against Astrology According to Culver and Ianna

But in the world where the people live, and where the astrological correspondences take place (following Culver and Ianna, this can only be the 'unreal world'), events are most assuredly unmeasurable and unpredictable. More important, there are innumerable effects, measurable effects, that have no measurable physical cause, and no 'plausible physical explanation'. Let us take a hypothetical example.

The Effect Without a Cause

An astronomer is having breakfast. He is enjoying himself, daydreaming, as astronomers will, of the objective truth. He is imagining himself winning a Nobel Prize, or perhaps thinking of ways to cut out a rival at the observatory and get tenure first, or perhaps he is wondering if a galaxy or at least a black hole will ever be named after him.*

---

restore consciousness to the fundamental position" *Nature of the Physical World* (Cambridge University Press), pp. 276–7.

'So Erwin Shroedinger: "Mind has erected the objective outside world of the natural philosopher out of its own stuff. Mind could not cope with this gigantic task otherwise than by the simplifying device of excluding itself . . . withdrawing from its conceptual" *Mind and Matter* (Cambridge, 1958).

'I like most of all Wolfgang Pauli's formulation: "To us . . . the only acceptable point of view appears to be the one that recognizes both sides of reality – the quantitative and the qualitative, the physical and the psychical – as compatible with each other, and can embrace them simultaneously . . . It would be most satisfactory if physics and psyche (i.e., matter and mind) could be seen as complementary aspects of the same reality" *Interpretations of Nature and Psyche*, C. G. Jung and W. Pauli (each writing separately), Bollingen, 1955, pp. 208–10.

George Wald, Nobel Laureate and Harvard Professor Emeritus in Biology, in *Noetic Sciences Review*, Spring, 1989, p. 12.

Excerpted from *Synthesis of Science and Religion*

* '. . . is it really true that a good or genuine scientist is, or should be, indifferent to matters of priority, caring only for the Advancement of Learning and nothing for who causes it to come about?' P. B. Medawar, *The Art of the Soluble*, p. 126

'. . . some eminent scientists become almost paranoid about protocol, and are capable of sensing a deliberate slight in the failure to be invited to a conference . . .

Then he comes across a leading article in his otherwise reputable newspaper. A massive statistical experiment appears to verify a correspondence between the position of the planets at birth and eminence in certain specific professions. According to the article, the data has been checked by eminent statisticians who were unable to fault it. But this is astrology! A return to ignorance and superstition! This represents a challenge to the spirit of dispassionate experiment and rational inquiry that has made modern civilization what it is! Our astronomer's reverie is broken. He feels the adrenaline flow; he gets red in the face, his heartbeat and pulse rate soar and he breaks out into a nervous sweat. He shouts at his wife. He rushes to the phone to alert similarly rational colleagues of this new development. The lines are all busy. All the rationalists have read the article and are trying to get through to each other. And soon there is an official edict published by the Church of Progress itself, disclaiming astrology, signed by 186 scientists, 19 of them Nobel Prize-winners.

In the 'unreal world' where the human beings live, there are most assuredly effects, effects that can be measured, even predicted – adrenaline flow, heartbeat, volume of perspiration – but that have no physical cause. What is it that has ruined our astronomer's morning? Black ink on a newspaper? This can be measured, of course. But there does not seem to be a 'plausible physical relationship' between the measurable quantity of ink

---

their typical vanity is to attend more conferences than they can grasp the significance of . . .' Prof. John Ziman, *Public Knowledge*, p. 134

'What is good for General Motors is not always good for the nation, but once science is understood, it turns out that what is good for the individual scientist is by and large good for science.' In other words, says Mr Hull, those scientists who seem to be unusually selfish, egotistical and aggressive may be our biggest benefactors. They're the ones who get things done . . . Scientists don't cite their peers out of a sense of honor or modesty, Mr Hull claims. They do so to buttress their own work . . .' Natalie Angier, reviewing *Science as a Process: An Evolutionary Account of the Social and Conceptual Development of Science* by David L. Hull (University of Chicago Press, 1988), in the *New York Times Book Review*, 6 November 1988

and the effects produced. Still, there was the adrenaline flow! It can't be the ink! Well then, perhaps it is the light reflecting from the page. This can also be measured. Light from a measurable source falls upon the page and is reflected into the retina of the eye. These light waves are then processed by the nervous system which determines that this particular visual pattern poses a threat to the astronomer's biological survival, triggering selective processes built up over millions of years of evolution . . . Actually, this explanation might well satisfy scientists. Evolutionary arguments employ a similar logic. But it does not actually address the problem of the 'plausible physical relationship' that Culver and Ianna insist is a prerequisite for determining scientific truth – and if a truth is not scientific then, according to Culver and Ianna, it cannot be 'true'. 'The evidence – objective descriptions of nature – *is the only basis for truth . . . Only empirical evidence counts* [our italics]. Whatever criticism and objections may be raised, the "proof" of the idea must be that it works. We must demand of any hypothesis that it passes every empirical test we can pose for it.' So, here in our hypothetical example we have empirical evidence aplenty for the effect, but literally nothing to account for a cause.

Here are a few more examples from the same 'unreal world': the solo flute playing Mozart at a distance, barely audible, that can move the listener to a state of exquisite and inexpressible gratitude, while a wash of nineteenth-century strings played full-volume by a second-rate provincial orchestra produces no effect at all beyond mild boredom. On another front, there is the national anthem, sounding through the static of a primitive radio, that electrifies deluded patriots and has them all up in arms ready to kill each other . . .

Where is the 'plausible physical relationship' that Culver and Ianna demand as a prerequisite for events in the 'real world'? There is a physical medium, the air, through which the sound waves are carried. But the cause (the genius of Mozart) cannot be called a 'plausible physical relationship', while the undeniable and measurable physical effects are out of all proportion to the measurable physical disturbance; sound waves falling upon the ear. This is the 'unreal world' where the living, sensitive, functioning human beings exist; where consciousness and will determine physical events. In this 'unreal world' quantity and quality are inextricably intertwined. Our flute and our wash of violins *can* be quantified – up to a point. But this applies only to the medium through which the effect is produced. We can measure the sound waves, the vibrations of the eardrum, and all the rest. It tells us nothing of the cause.

In the 'unreal world' where Mozart moves us, it is *frequency* rather than magnitude that is significant. Magnitude may or may not play a role (as in rock music). But there is no known modern scientific way to judge the significance of frequency, even though it can be measured very precisely. The secret of 'quality' (in music, art, architecture and to a lesser extent in poetry and literature) resides in frequency, harmony and rhythm and our inherent ability to respond. What is involved is the phenomenon of Resonance. When we deal with frequency, harmony and rhythm, or Resonance, what we are actually dealing with is Number, and the interplay of *principles*; the same principles upon which astrology is based (see pp. 31–8). And it is this same 'unreal world' of people that astrology concerns. We will return to this crucial point later in The Question: How? (see pp. 364–94).

So to pretend to 'disprove' astrology without even having broached this question of frequency and its attendant phenomenon of resonance (universally accepted in other areas of scientific inquiry) is to beg the issue.

Culver and Ianna cannot be unaware of this argument; it has been around at least since Pythagoras (the Music or Harmony of the Spheres). It appeared in modern dress in our own first edition, and also in other books cited in *The Gemini Syndrome*. They do not attempt to address it.

> Offered the choice between the hypothesis that you feel depressed today because Neptune is transiting your sixth house and you feel depressed today because of the low barometric pressure, we are likely to not consider the former very seriously owing to the lack

of physical causation. This does not 'prove' that the first hypothesis is wrong. Indeed, there is no established discipline that rejects causality as completely as astrology (at least some astrologers).*

This has been a major factor in preventing its acceptance, and we shall feel inclined (but not compelled†) later to examine astrology for any plausible physical relationships.

(p. 37)

By ignoring the notion of the Harmony of the Spheres, and the sciences of number, harmony and rhythm, by ignoring the undeniable fact that, in the 'unreal world' of people, innumerable effects exist for which there is no physical causation, Culver and Ianna slip out of the obligation of providing a legitimate third choice to their anti-astrology illustration. Here is one: you are feeling depressed today because your lover has just told you he/she is leaving. Following Culver and Ianna, of course you are not likely to consider this hypothesis very seriously either, owing to the 'lack of physical causation'.

But compared to the wholly immaterial nature of the leaving lover (who has not even left yet, but has only threatened to leave) the transit of Neptune takes on a kind of quasi-materiality, and this is no illusion‡ Neptune is part of the solar system, and the solar system is a *system*. In a system, any system, there is an interaction between constituent parts.

---

* Elsewhere, Culver and Ianna accuse astrologers of crawling shamelessly on to the causality bandwagon. Clearly, those criticized here for denying causality ought not to be included in that earlier attack. In their defence, it might be pointed out that in this unusual instance, Culver and Ianna require well over a hundred pages to contradict themselves.

† Astrologers commonly confront the age-old problem of free will vs. astrology with the saying: 'The stars incline but do not compel.' Here, Culver and Ianna are indulging in levity.

‡ Astrologers do not commonly associate Neptune with depression, and certainly not with daily mood swings – since Neptune moves very slowly, and would take, on average, fourteen *years* to transit a house! Though ludicrously ill-chosen for the point it is intended to make, this sixth-house Neptune transit poignantly illustrates the level of scholarship generally prevailing in this 'scientific evaluation of astrology'.

Selecting the System

Systems vary enormously in subtlety and complexity. The rules that apply to a simple system cannot be applied directly to a more complex system. Beyond a certain level they probably cannot be applied at all. Satisfactorily defining a system presents a problem no less grave than defining the 'real world' of Culver and Ianna, and this is not the place to go into the elaborate semantic and philosophical issues involved. But a system, any system, is inconceivable without a directing intelligence or consciousness.* The more sophisticated the system, the subtler the manner in which physical forces are deployed, and the more inescapable — and mysterious — the conscious or volitional element. In a mainly physical system, the conscious element is concealed, while in a mainly conscious system, it is the physical element that eludes detection.

To use a homely example, let us say we want to drive a nail into a block of wood. This represents a very simple and ephemeral system, lasting no longer than the act itself. It barely qualifies as a system in the usual sense of the word. Still, simple as it is, it is nevertheless ineluctably metaphysical. A decision motivates it, and that decision has no physical measurable properties. But because it is so simple, calculating its dominant, constituent physical factors — force, velocity, resistance — is a relatively straightforward procedure. There is an easily under-stood relationship between the effect (nail driven into wood) and its 'plausible physical explanation' (hammer hitting nail). But if we want to move a ton of steel with a cup full of gasoline, a more sophisticated system is called for. The energy potential of the gasoline is finite and easily worked out. But if it

* See Arthur M. Young, *The Reflexive Universe* and *The Geometry of Meaning*, for a particularly convincing argument on the fallacy of attempting to describe an organized system without including the element of intention, or volition; that is to say, consciousness. Young, a mathematician and inventor of the Bell helicopter is one of those rare thinkers equally at home in ancient mysticism and modern science.

is ignited on top of our ton of steel nothing much will happen. If, however, the ton of steel is organized into a Porsche, then the same cup of gas will send it from o to 6o m.p.h. in six seconds. Here, the element of consciousness involved in organizing the system is much more intense and conspicuous. And the relationship between the amount of energy expended and the effect produced, far more complex. The effect is purely mechanical, of course, traceable and comprehensible on the basis of known physical laws. Intention or consciousness plays no role in the operation of the completed system in this case. The element of consciousness has stayed back in the factory in Stuttgart. But there would be no Porsche without it.

When we revert to our image of the concert hall, the consciousness or intention (Mozart's genius in this case) plays the commanding role while the physical forces involved become much more difficult to quantify and impossible to understand analytically. This is the opposite pole to our hammer/nail system.

The concert hall filled with people is also a system – once the music starts to play. The faintest quaver of the solo flute then becomes significant. Before the music started, the orchestra shuffling around and tuning up had no effect at all, though it made much more noise.

The concert hall also provides a useful model for countering a number of other anti-astrological arguments; chiefly: 1) that the planets are too far away to produce effects; 2) that the forces exerted by them are too small; 3) that astrologers do not take into account the variable distance of the planets in their orbits; and 4) that the planets vary enormously in size amongst themselves and also in their distances from earth, and astrologers take little or no note of these differences. But in the concert hall, as in astrology, there is no 'plausible physical explanation' to account for the effect produced. The cause is metaphysical (the genius of Mozart). Physical musical instruments act as the medium for transmitting the message. They cannot be called 'a plausible physical explanation' of the music. And, indeed, considered apart from the metaphysical cause, they are mere mechanisms, pieces of wood and brass. They exert no measurable force; they simply create disturbances within the self-contained air of the system, and like the planets, they act at a distance. Yet, the distance itself, and even the magnitude of the disturbance, that is to say, the volume of the music, are of secondary importance ... For if the concert hall is well designed, we will hear the music, and be moved by it, in the last row of the top balcony, and we will hear it even if there is a pillar blocking our line of vision to the orchestra, or if we happen to find ourselves sitting behind a team of sumo wrestlers. Along the same lines, the massive tuba and thunderous tympani are no more or less important than the diminutive flute and violin. *People* are involved in the concert hall model, as they are in astrology. The primitive hammer/nail model of reality will not suffice. And that 'plausible physical explanation' required to account for astrological effects (more accurately 'correspondences') no more depends upon large magnitudes of gravitational or magnetic force than the effects produced by Mozart's music depend upon quarts of soundwaves.

Once people are allowed to play some role in the 'real world', the importance of that 'plausible physical explanation' that Culver and Ianna cannot do without or see beyond, declines dramatically. It depends, ultimately, upon the order of consciousness prevailing in the system under consideration.

There is today not the slightest possible doubt that the solar system is a system; interrelated, delicately balanced and dynamic; and curiously analogous to the system represented on the human scale by the concert hall. Leaving aside for the moment the question of the consciousness responsible for the system in the first place or prevailing within it, we think it not implausible to suggest that we are inextricably bound up within that system. And from remotest pre-history, astrology has been the discipline devoted to studying our part in it.

Summary

The premises upon which Culver and Ianna base their criticism are false, and their argument accordingly invalid. The scientific method is *not* the only valid means we have for acquiring knowledge of the world; nor do all physical effects require 'plausible physical explanations' to qualify as phenomena. By ignoring the crucial element of consciousness in the 'real world' and by failing to take into account the need to apply different criteria to different classes or orders of systems, Culver and Ianna simply evade those arguments that adequately account for astrology. Since they quote (selectively) from sources that present these plausible accounts it means they are aware of them. Their refutation of astrology is therefore not only wrong, it is dishonest. They deal only with those objections that can be refuted within the arbitrary ground rules of a limited and inappropriate methodology.

Thus, despite the extraordinary detail of their objections, what is trumpeted as *A Scientific Evaluation of Astrology* is, upon close examination, not scientific at all. It is little more than the elaborated biases of a couple of uncomprehending scientists. *The Gemini Syndrome* is a long and tortuous trail of red herrings – carefully smoked; laid down (it must be acknowledged) with admirable solicitude, but red herrings none the less.

C. Objections to Astrology: *Bart J. Bok and Lawrence E. Jerome*

This is a rather different kettle of fish. It begins with a statement drafted by Jerome and Bok, and endorsed by 186 leading scientists, 19 of them Nobel Prize-winners.

Scientists in a variety of fields have become concerned about the increased acceptance of astrology in many parts of the world. We, the undersigned – astronomers, astrophysicists, and scientists in other fields – wish to caution the public against the unquestioning acceptance of the predictions and advice given privately and publicly by astrologers. Those who wish to believe in astrology should realize that there is no scientific foundation for its tenets.

In ancient times people believed in the predictions and advice of astrologers because astrology was part and parcel of their magical world view. They looked upon celestial objects as abodes or omens of the Gods and thus intimately connected with events here on earth; they had no concept of the vast distances from the earth to the planets and stars. Now that these distances can and have been calculated, we can see how infinitesimally small are the gravitational and other effects produced by the distant planets and the far more distant stars. It is simply a mistake to imagine that the forces exerted by stars and planets at the moment of birth can in any way shape our futures. Neither is it true that the position of distant heavenly bodies makes certain days or periods more favourable to particular kinds of action, or that the sign under which one was born determines compatibility or incompatibility with other people.

Why do people believe in astrology? In these uncertain times many long for the comfort of having guidance in making decisions. They would like to believe in a destiny predetermined by astral forces beyond their control. However, we all must face the world, and we must realize that our futures lie in ourselves and not in the stars.

One would imagine in this day of widespread enlightenment and education, that it would be unnecessary to debunk beliefs based on magic and superstition. Yet, acceptance of astrology pervades modern society. We are especially disturbed by the continued uncritical dissemination of astrological charts, forecasts, and horoscopes by the media and by otherwise reputable newspapers, magazines, and book publishers. This can only contribute to the growth of irrationalism and obscurantism. We believe that the time has come to challenge directly and forcefully the pretentious claims of astrological charlatans.

It should be apparent that those individuals who continue to have faith in astrology do so in spite of the fact that there is no verified scientific basis for their beliefs and indeed that there is strong evidence to the contrary.

Objections to Astrology, pp. 9–10

Careful readers of this statement of purpose may have wondered at the astonishing times we live in, as set out by Bok & Jerome. In one sentence we are told that 'in these uncertain times people long for the comfort of having guidance in making decisions' and two sentences later, we are enjoying 'a day of widespread enlightenment and education' in which it ought to 'be unnecessary to debunk beliefs based upon magic and superstition'.

Is it possible to imagine times that are simultaneously uncertain and enlightened? To us such times seem inconceivable. But 186 eminent scientists evidently found no flaw in such thinking.

While this does not directly affect the evidence for or against astrology, again it provides insight into the level of discernment prevailing among its opponents.

Meanwhile, that undercurrent of authoritarianism, overt in Culver and Ianna, is present here as well. While Jerome and Bok and the 186 eminent scientists do not specifically enjoin shoving truth down unwilling throats, it is clear they hope their collective authority and prestige will induce 'otherwise reputable newspapers, magazines and book publishers' to perhaps refrain from disseminating the work of 'astrological charlatans'.

Before approaching the formal objections to astrology raised by Bok and Jerome, several elements within their signed statement deserve discussion.

Notice that Bok and Jerome do not share the Culver/Ianna view of astrology's origins. They do not see astrology arising out of a 'blend of imagination, fear and religious superstitition'. Rather they see it as part of a 'magical world view'. Now, to Bok and Jerome (and to the 186 signers of their document) a 'magical world view' is in no way superior to a 'blend of imagination, fear and religious superstition'. But, as we shall soon see, it involves a radically different philosophical conception, which in turn is reflected in ancient and modern views of science, and the role of astrology within that view. We shall return to this point in detail soon.

Here let us deal with the scientific rationale given by Bok and Jerome for astrology's development. They contend that the ancients did not realize how distant were the sun, moon and planets. In other words, not knowing the distances, it was logical in its way for the ancients to ascribe power to planets and stars, while modern people do so only because they have been coerced into it by 'astrological charlatans'.

Yet when the above statement was issued, a much-revised and upgraded estimate of ancient astronomical knowledge was already widely accepted by most scientists. The proven astronomical function of Stonehenge and other ancient monuments demonstrated beyond any possibility of doubt the sophisticated astronomy prevailing in the ancient world. In *The Place of Astronomy in the Ancient World*, A Joint Symposium of the Royal Society and the British Academy, ed. F. R. Hodson, one contributor after another finds that ancient astronomy, wherever it may have been practiced, ancient East, Near East, Europe, Polynesia or America, was far more advanced than earlier scholars cared to acknowledge. Ancient Egyptian astronomy generally receives low marks compared to Babylon, yet in his discussion of the Egyptian treatment of the planets, R. A. Parker remarks (p. 60):

> How early the five planets were identified is not known to us. The first monument on which they all appear is the astronomical ceiling of Senmut (*c.* 1450 BC) but they surely were known well before then ... the usual order is Saturn, Jupiter, Mars, Mercury and Venus, that of most distant planets to the one nearest the sun. The first three planets are frequently separated from the last two ...

This, in turn, suggests (though it does not prove) a commensurate understanding of planetary if not stellar distances. In all likelihood the Egyptians kept the planetary groups separate because they knew that Jupiter, Saturn and Mars orbited outside the earth's orbit and Mercury and Venus within it.

In other words, there is every reason to believe the ancients knew perfectly well how far the planets were from the earth, and this knowledge did not preclude their belief in astrology. This means in turn, that Bok and Jerome will have to find some other rationale to account for the ancient belief in astrology. And, actually, they have one: when they ascribe astrology to 'a magical world view'.

But they have forgotten that such a magically based astrology operates independently of distances. Thus their objections are self-cancelling and doubly wrong: 1) the ancients probably knew how far the planets and stars were from us, and 2) this is absolutely irrelevant to a world view based upon the principle of correspondences, or magic.

As with Culver and Ianna, illogic and inconsistency are paraded as 'science' and of course the scientific method is the final arbiter of truth. Without a verified scientific basis, in the Bok/Jerome view, there can be no valid astrology. But as we have already pointed out at length, this argument does not apply. It is as illegitimate to look for a scientific basis (in the narrow, quantitative sense intended by Jerome and Bok) to astrology as it is to look for a scientific basis to love or art.

On the other hand, there *are* scientifically verifiable aspects or elements to astrology. The Gauquelin data alone, accruing over two decades prior to the publication of *Objections to Astrology*, should have been enough to induce any scholar interested in truth to at least call for further study. And there is a body of available indirect scientific evidence establishing correlations between celestial and terrestrial events that has undeniable astrological connotations. This was also well known and readily available at the time *Objections to Astrology* was published. So when Jerome and Bok claim 'there is no verified scientific basis' to astrology, they distort the truth to make it conform to their own narrow definition of astrology. When they claim 'there is strong evidence to the contrary', they lie.

Meanwhile, their scientific objections to astrology follow a pattern now familiar to readers of this chapter. But because of the widespread press attention paid to *Objections to Astrology* and the eminence of many of the signers of the statement (the list is reproduced in the Appendix) that is the pretext for the book, it is essential that the salient points are quoted at length.

The Objections According to Bart J. Bok

Many believers in astrology speak glibly of the forces exerted by the sun, moon, and planets. I should mention here that these forces – according to astrology, critically effective only at the precise moment of birth – can hardly be gravitational or radiative in nature. The known forces that the planets exert on a child at the moment of birth are unbelievably small. The gravitational forces at birth produced by the doctor and nurse and by the furniture in the delivery room far outweigh the celestial forces. And the stars are so far away from the sun and earth that their gravitational, magnetic, and other effects are negligible. Radiative effects are sometimes suggested as doing the job. First of all, the walls of the delivery room shield us effectively from many known radiations. And, second, we should bear in mind that our sun is a constantly varying source of radiation, radiating at many different wavelengths, variations that are by themselves far in excess of the radiations received from the moon and all the planets together.

Many believers in astrology have suggested that each planet issues a different variety of special, as-yet-undetected radiations or 'vibrations' and that it is the interplay between these mysterious forces, or quantities, that produces strong effects of an astrological nature. If there is one thing we have learned over the past fifty years, it is that there is apparently conclusive evidence that the sun, moon, planets, and stars are all made of the same stuff, varieties and combinations of atomic particles and molecules, all governed by uniform laws of physics. We have samples of the moon that are similar to rocks on earth, and as a result of our space probes, we have been able to study the properties of samples from the surface of Mars. It seems inconceivable that Mars and the moon could produce mysterious waves, or vibrations, that could affect our personalities in completely different ways. It does not make sense to suppose that the various planets and the moon, all with rather similar physical properties, could manage to affect human affairs in totally dissimilar fashions ... Astrology demands the existence of totally unimaginable mechanisms of force and action.

(pp. 30–31)

That last sentence provides a suitable coda to the litany of incomprehension and obfuscation produced by astrology's critics in general, and by Bok and Jerome here. It also reiterates the single most commonly voiced objection to astrology (see George Abell, p. 147), and we shall deal with it shortly in the section that addresses the standard objections – rather than those peculiar to a specific work. Bok voices only one objection that merits individual attention. Actually, even this is not a new objection, but a common one cast into fresh terminology particularly useful to our case.

The Same Stuff

According to Bok,

the sun, moon and planets ... are all made of the same stuff, varieties and combinations of atomic particles and molecules, all governed by uniform laws of physics ... It seems inconceivable that Mars and the moon could produce mysterious waves, or vibrations, that could affect our personalities in completely different ways. It does not make sense to suppose that the various planets and the moon, all with rather similar physical properties, could manage to affect human affairs in totally dissimilar fashions.

But our familiar chemical elements are also all made of 'the same stuff', of *identical* stuff in fact, atomic particles, electrons, etc. and all governed by the 'uniform laws of physics'. Yet they manage to behave in totally dissimilar fashion, in spite of those same uniform laws of physics. Their *quantitative* composition – in terms of atomic weight, number of electron shells, positive or negative charge and so on – determines their highly specific individual *qualities*. But those qualities, precisely measurable as to their effects and interactions, remain utterly mysterious in their essence. In other words, nothing in the uniform laws of physics tells us *why* iron behaves as it does, and helium the way it does. The solution to those mysteries resides in the Laws of Number, the metaphysical principles whose interplay results in 'the uniform laws of physics'.

While these metaphysical principles cannot, by definition, be verified, or understood, or even approached through a science that restricts itself to the physical, there are our familiar chemical elements, all made of 'the same stuff', and all behaving in dissimilar fashion – rather in the way astrologers contend the planets differ. The organs of the human body are made of 'the same stuff', and they, too, behave in dissimilar fashion and perform dissimilar though ultimately complementary functions. The carburettor and speedometer of the Porsche are made of the same stuff and behave in dissimilar fashion; and a mouse and a tiger are made of quite identical stuff and they behave in dramatically dissimilar fashion. Woe to the rationalist who thinks otherwise.

Finally, and closer to astrology, the instruments of the symphony orchestra are made of the same stuff, 'varieties and combinations of atomic particles and molecules, all governed by the uniform laws of physics', and they not only behave in dissimilar fashion but produce notably dissimilar effects – merely through fluctuations of frequency, volume and rhythm. We can think of no lullabies written for the trumpet, nor marching songs for the flute.

While none of these analogies or examples corresponds exactly to the astrological model, all bear similarities in one way or another. In some ways the solar system resembles an atom, with its relatively tiny but dense nucleus counterbalancing its complement of electrons; the whole occupying a relatively gigantic amount of space compared to its mass (to illustrate the relative size of the nucleus to the whole atom, scientists commonly compare it to a pingpong ball in Madison Square Garden). From another angle, the solar system looks rather like an organic or mechanical system with the sun as 'heart' or 'engine'. But in its astrological context it most closely approximates the concert hall, with its instruments all made 'of the same stuff', all behaving in dissimilar fashion and producing measurable, physical effects independent of a physical 'cause'.

Bok, along with all his colleagues, rejects astrology, using as a model the one physical system to which it has absolutely no resemblance whatsoever; the primitive hammer/nail, cause/effect system. When a more complex, and more valid model is used, the objection simply evaporates. The fact that the planets are made up of the same stuff is irrelevant to astrology and does not amount to an objection at all.

But Bok's raising the issue, and its tame acceptance by the 186 leading scientists, highlights a curious phenomenon. Between themselves, scientists, are in agreement (up to a point) on the profound implications of relativity theory, quantum physics, Goedel's Theorem and other acknowledged advances that have forced a total revision of the scientific view of the physical world. Though there is no agreement precisely how the new physical world view should alter our perception of 'reality' it is acknowledged that that change is radical and philosophically profound and compelling.

Yet when the subject of astrology comes up, an instantaneous philosophical myopia settles upon them all and quite suddenly they seem unable to see past the end of Newton's nose.

Objections in the Broader Arena

Just as the resurgence of astrology has philosophical, social and spiritual implications extending far beyond the acceptance of astrology as a serious study, so has the story of the opposition to it. *Objections to Astrology* by Bok and Jerome represents a particularly good example of what is at stake. As science it is of course without merit. But this is not really significant in itself. Not all science can be good science, and there is undoubtedly an unconscionable lot of nonsense written in the name of astrology.

But you do not see 186 leading astrologers signing a manifesto endorsing the maunderings of astrology's lunatic fringe. Leading scientists evidently have less discrimination in such matters.

So let us look now at those standard objections, raised by all astrology's critics, and based upon a world model that these same critics willingly repudiate as partial and outmoded.*

At the same time, let us again emphasize the crucial distinction between the astrological premise — that correspondence or correlation between celestial and terrestrial events and between the positions of planets at birth and the human personality — and astrological practice, which invariably involves interpretation of the horoscope.

This distinction is never made by astrology's opponents, and

---

* 'In the early twenties, Sir James Jeans said: God must be a mathematician. The very notion of mathematics is inexplicable in terms of mechanism. You don't understand mathematics by looking at matter. It's an extremely abstract theory; almost a spiritual thing.

'There have been other non-mechanistic currents within physics such as represented by Heisenberg, who took the Pythagorean/Platonic view and Pauli who took a somewhat mystical view closely associated with Jung. There is also a great deal in modern physics which does not suggest the validity of mechanism and reductionism. But unfortunately, the prevailing trend is toward mechanism and reductionism. I think that the most original and creative scientists and the leading physicists who made the innovations were not mechanists whereas those who followed and who were less original and creative tended to be more mechanistic.'

Physicist David Bohm, in *Resurgence*, March/April 1987

seldom by astrologers, putting them in an unnecessarily defensive position.

For it is the validity of the astrological premise that legitimizes astrology in principle. And it is the validity of the astrological premise that undermines the materialistic foundations of the Church of Progress – which is of course why it meets with such intense hostility from its priesthood. The practice of astrology is, philosophically, a matter of lesser consequence, and can be developed or redefined in due course.

It is not so very difficult to project a situation in which *all* current astrological practice is shown to be not so much invalid, as totally insusceptible of scientific verification (which is not the same thing by any means!), while the astrological premise as defined above stands indisputably confirmed.

So it is the objections designed to discredit the astrological premise that we devote the most attention to.

The Standard Objections to Astrology

1. 'Astrology demands the existence of totally unimaginable mechanisms of force and action.'
2. Copernican heliocentric theory exploded astrology, which was based upon a geocentric conception.
3. The discovery of the new planets, Uranus, Neptune and Pluto cannot be incorporated into traditional astrology, and disrupts and invalidates a system based upon the septenary of the ancient planets.
4. The sun is nothing but a mass of incandescent material; the planets are nothing but globes of more or less solidified mineral, metallic and gaseous matter. Therefore they cannot influence life on earth.
5. According to genetic theory, all that we inherit comes to us at the moment of conception, when sperm and ovum join. It is at this moment that physical and, by and large, mental characteristics are permanently fixed. If there were anything to astrology at all, it would base horoscopes upon the moment of conception,

which is impossible to determine since fertilization may take place as much as twenty-four hours after the sexual act.

5a and b. Twins and time twins: babies born the same minute in the same place would be identical, following astrological theory.

5c. Induced births: if astrology is valid, it would have to contend that induced birth radically alters the subsequent character of the child whose birth is induced.

6. How can astrology account for mass tragedies? For example: did all the Jews murdered by Hitler have death written into their stars?

7. What about people born in far northern countries where certain signs never rise at all?

8. The zodiac is an imaginary circle, and all other astrological principles such as houses, aspects and the meanings attached to the planets are purely arbitrary and have no basis in empirical fact.

9. Astrology fails to take into account the precession of the equinoxes and therefore bases itself upon a zodiac that is doubly imaginary.

Answers to the Objections

1. '*Astrology demands the existence of totally unimaginable mechanisms of force and action.*' Bart J. Bok puts this primary objection succinctly. Culver and Ianna elaborate upon it, carefully working out and tabulating the gravitational effects of all the planets to show how infinitessimal they are.

The fact of the matter is, and that fact has been acknowledged by any number of scientists with no particular interest in supporting astrology, that this principal objection is without substance. Precisely what astrology does *not* require are those 'totally unimaginable mechanisms of force and action'.

And to understand why this should be so, it is only necessary to recognize the illegitimacy of the hammer/nail, cause/effect model applied to astrology. No less 'unimaginable mechanisms' would be required to account for the difference in effect produced by the trumpet and flute.

And yet even scientists would find themselves hard pressed to deny that such differences exist. The human personality – the principal subject of astrology – cannot be quantified in acceptable scientific fashion, or even defined. The subject of human consciousness – of consciousness in general – is equally unsusceptible of scientific explanation. It is most certainly elusive and subtle, and yet most of us would find it difficult to deny that we have personalities, that personalities are part of the 'real world', that we are conscious in some sense. There is no known mechanism to account for consciousness; while the mechanism of genetics accounts only for the transmission of hereditary characteristics; not for the different characteristics themselves nor for the glaring differences between those with the same hereditary make-up.

Astrology does not require 'unimaginable mechanisms of force and action' to account for its validity. Enough is now known about the interconnectedness of the solar system and the extreme sensitivity of living organisms to minute fluctuations in the geomagnetic and electromagnetic environment to put this objection to rest once and for all. Rather, what astrology requires is a plausible model for the transmission of *meaning*. As we shall see, there are several approaches to such a model.

2. *Copernican heliocentric theory exploded astrology* . . . This objection affects the practice not the premise of astrology. The rediscovery of the heliocentricity of the solar system destroyed medieval cosmology and dealt a blow to the faith of the Medieval Age. But astrology studies the 'influences' of the planets as they stand *relative to the earth*. No doubt, European astrologers were unhappy to learn that the sun did not revolve about the earth, but their astrology was none the worse for it. Neither Copernicus, Kepler or even Newton ever suggested that astrology was affected, much less destroyed, by the Copernican discovery. Moreover, among the major world civilizations, it was only the medieval Europeans who subscribed to the geocentric theory. The ancient Egyptians, Pythagoreans, Hindus, Chinese, constructors of Stonehenge and others, knew better all along. And all practiced astrology.

3. *New planets.* This presents a philosophical problem. It does not affect the astrological premise.

In traditional number symbolism, the Law of Seven is held sacred as the sum of Spirit (Three) and Matter (Four); it is the number associated with Process or Growth, and plays that role universally in the mythologies of the world. The happy instance of seven planets circling serenely round the earth seemed to medieval thinkers just such a splendid physical 'proof' of the sacred nature of the law. And this was incorrect.

The discovery of the new planets, Uranus, Neptune and Pluto, actually does nothing to invalidate the law. It means only that the law does not manifest itself in the solar system the way medieval astrologers thought. In fact there are many instances in the physical world in which processes are fulfilled having undergone seven stages. The fertilized ovum, for example, divides seven times before it becomes the blastocyst; the chemical elements arrange themselves naturally into the sevenfold periodic table, according to their valences.

In a general way astrologers have reached agreement on the subject. Uranus is the planet of revolution, violent change, intuition, 'democracy' and technology. Neptune is appropriately 'watery' and somewhat mysterious; a planet of the occult, of mass movements, drugs, romanticism, of subtle reaches of the mind. Pluto is responsible for the unleashing of explosive subterranean powers; it is connected with the state beyond death and the 'underworld', and is connected to totalitarianism and cataclysm.

How did astrologers arrive at these conclusions? By a kind of collective hunch; by the 'feel' of the new planets; by assuming that their names, however apparently fortuitous, were chosen correctly on some intuitive or superconscious level;* and finally,

---

* Pluto is a particularly interesting case in point. One account has it that Pluto was made up from the names of its discoverers, Percival Lowell and C. W. Tombaugh. Another account has it that a little girl wrote the astronomers and suggested naming the new planet (discovered in 1933) after Walt Disney's famous dog, Pluto, a suggestion with curious repercussions.

Despite a number of unlovely personal traits, and an addiction to cuteness, there can be no doubt that a vein of extraordinary innate esoteric understanding ran

principally, by referring back to the symbolism appropriate to each.

Many of the difficulties posed by the new planets in western astrology do not actually apply to Hindu astrology which always postulated twelve planets, and which described the traits or characters of the missing five in some detail.

In Hindu astrology, the twelve planets are endowed with increasingly spiritual functions corresponding to the increasingly spiritual nature of the twelve signs. A combination of these factors has led to a general consensus on the natures of the new planets – and to some extent upon the still-undiscovered but postulated two planets still missing from the twelve-planet schema, the one infra-mercurial (between the sun and Mercury), and the other trans-Plutonian. Opponents would of course dismiss the process (of ascribing meaning to the new planets, or to any planets) as pure and unmitigated fantasy, but astrologers

----

through Walt Disney's genius and ability to communicate with the widest possible public on every level. His *Pinocchio* took a dreary nineteenth-century Punch and Judy story and turned it into a luminous gnostic quest by the created Son for his Father; its separate incidents finding parallels with those of teaching tales of Gnosticism and other esoteric doctrines. Almost certainly, Disney was not acquainted with this arcane literature. And his settling on the name 'Pluto' for his famous dog is similarly apposite. Pluto in Greek mythology is guardian of the Underworld. He is not a dog, of course, but his ward, the three-headed dog Cerberus is keeper of the gate. But Pluto's close equivalent in Egyptian mythology is Anubis the dog/jackal, 'Opener of the Way' and guide through the Underworld – no matter that Disney's Pluto was not associated with embalming and the passage through the 'night' of death to ultimate illumination, there is an ancient association linking the Greek Pluto to the dog.

Now rationalists will surely scoff at any attempt to read meaning into the choice of the name 'Pluto' for the P. Lowell/Tombaugh planet. Yet had Lowell been named Lawson, we may be absolutely certain the new planet would not have been called 'Plato' following identical anagrammatic thinking. 'Pluto' sounded right, both to its discoverers and to the astrologers. Along the same lines, attempts to call Uranus 'Herschel' after its eminent discoverer have never taken hold. And Herschel initially wanted to name the planet he'd discovered 'George', after the King. A rose by another name would no doubt smell as sweet but its value for poets if not lovers would be drastically curtailed.

might well call it 'hypothesis formation'. Given the presently unsinkable status of the massive Gauquelin tests, the astrologers have a theoretical basis for their belief that the new planets symbolize specific qualities or personality types. Until or unless adequate controlled tests are devised and carried out, the matter is unresolvable. But the objection is invalid.

4. *The sun is nothing but a mass of incandescent material* . . . This is another version of the objection put forward by Bart J. Bok – that the planets and stars are all made up of the same 'stuff'. As we explained earlier, this is not an objection, nor is it science. It is simply an expression of the materialist dogma, a statement of negative faith, the insistence that the universe is meaningless. It ignores the absolute inability of science to deal with the central question of consciousness. Astrologers, and those responsible for all the high civilizations of the past would maintain that the sun and planets are physical vehicles in which the celestial consciousness expresses itself; just as the human body is the physical vehicle in which the soul is destined to transform itself into spirit. To the soulless such an argument will be condemned as 'unscientific', and so it is. But no more so than the contrary assertion that consciousness is a particular rather than a universal aspect of existence, and that it has reached its (purely accidental) apogee in the human race, or more specifically, in the person of the enlightened Rationalist.

Actually, the latter argument is less scientific than the former. It is consciousness, albeit in a debased form, that makes the Rationalist philosophy possible in the first place. Without consciousness, Rationalism, and all experience as well as all mental activity would be inconceivable. It is therefore far more scientific to assume (as the observant ancients did) that consciousness is universal and central to all existence; rather than that it should be peculiar only to man, and to a lesser extent to organic life on earth.

It is true we cannot prove the consciousness of the sun or the earth for that matter (though James Lovelock's widely accepted Gaia hypothesis – of the earth as a self-regulating mechanism – stops just short of postulating the latter, and indeed, is practically unthinkable without it).

But imagine the analogous situation of a cell traveling through the blood stream of our body. The cell has a form of independence and sensitivity to change; it performs a number of complex intelligent roles (when it rebels and demands its own 'freedom' of course we come down with cancer or AIDS). In any event, imagine a scientifically inclined cell that tries to develop a valid philosophy and cosmology. It would be very difficult, maybe impossible for our cell to find or prove the twin faculties of consciousness and will that motivate so many of our activities. Indeed, without a giant leap of imagination, our cell would be unlikely to look beyond the largely mechanical bodily systems in which it was locked and played its own role. So, from a strictly observational point of view, our cell might conclude that its universe was nothing but a 'mass of organic material'. Only by extrapolating from its own level of consciousness, from the 'curiosity' that impelled its scientific investigations in the first place, would our cell discover the truth.

So while we may not be able to 'prove' that the sun is anything more than a mass of incandescent material, it would be both short-sighted and arrogant to insist that our limited observational powers settle the matter.

5. Genetic theory . . . all that we inherit comes to us at the moment of conception with the mingling of genetic material from both mother and father . . . If there is anything to astrology at all, horoscopes should be erected for the moment of conception which is of course impossible to determine by and large, ergo, astrology is a fraud . . .

This is the only scientific objection to astrology that is based upon science, rather than scientific prejudices, and it is the only objection that has any real substance to it. Astrology's opponents raise it as though the possibility has never occurred to astrologers throughout the ages. In fact, a considerable astrological literature exists on the subject. Detailed rules for astrologically determining the moment of conception, in order to erect a moment-of-conception horoscope, are supposed to date back to the fragmentary Hermetic texts (assembled by Neo-Platonic scholars in Alexandria in the third-century AD but containing older elements). The Theosophists and later, Alice Bailey, devoted much time to working out real and symbolic pre-natal 'epochs' that were supposed to implement if not supplant the usual birth chart. But astrologers disagree violently among themselves as to the validity or necessity for such pre-natal charts, and, certainly, there is no scientifically sound astrological answer to the commanding scientific argument that everything we inherit comes to us at the moment of conception.

But what is it precisely that we inherit? What is it that the mingling of genes at the moment of conception produces? Certain physical characteristics, certainly; predispositions toward certain diseases, intelligence to some extent no doubt . . . And is that all we are? A chance combination of genetic material donated equally by our mothers and fathers? Most geneticists would probably support such a view. But as is so often the case, such support has nothing to do with actual science; it is merely a belief held by scientists masquerading as science.

The problems posed by genetics for astrology are intricate and delicate, and lead inescapably to profound philosophical questions on the nature and genesis of the 'self' or soul. There is no need, however, for us to enter this arena in order to counter the objection that developments in genetic science invalidate astrology.

Michel Gauquelin's work (see pp. 232–318) establishes a correspondence between the human personality and the position of planets at the moment of birth. There is of course nothing in modern genetic theory that can possibly account for such a connection. But that astrological connection exists – incontrovertibly and apodictically. Astrology's opponents try to make astrologers defend their practice in the light of modern genetics. But the shoe is actually on the other foot. Whatever problems genetics may pose for astrology, those posed by astrology for genetics are still more severe and intractable. The astrological correspondence is proven. It's up to the geneticists and the biologists to account for it, not the astrologers.

5a. *Twins. Identical twins (identical genetic structure) are notoriously alike, however many hours apart their births. Fraternal twins (different genetic structure) are no more alike than ordinary siblings even though they may be born within minutes of each other.*

Both situations pose problems for the interpretation of a horoscope. In astrology, in theory, every minute counts. Ten minutes difference in birth can mean that the ascendant of one twin is in a different sign from the other, and with that all the other 'houses' change as well. On the other hand, the same ten or twenty minutes can make no discernible difference if the ascendant falls in the middle of a sign. (Rotating once in twenty-four hours, any given spot on the earth stays in a sign roughly two hours, depending upon latitude.) In practice astrologers cannot distinguish between those twins that seem virtually identical in all respects, and those that are psychologically quite different. At the same time, fraternal twins, born close together, are generally more different than any 'blind' horoscope analysis would detect. To complicate the matter further, the question of 'house division' is unsettled.

If the problem admits of an astrologically satisfactory answer, it must lie in a refined interpretation of the individual degree areas. As we have seen, the zodiac is divided into polarities, triplicities, quadruplicities and the dodecad, following Pythagorean principles.

In harmonic terms, this corresponds to the second, third, fourth and twelfth harmonics. But if these divisions are significant, then it follows that their multiples must resonate with them. Indeed, from ancient times, astrologers have worked with these finer divisions. Ancient Egypt divided the 360 degrees of the zodiac into 36 sectors, or 'decans' (thirty-sixth harmonic); Hindu astrologers work with specific three-degree areas (120th harmonic) while a number of systems, old and new, exist ascribing specific – usually symbolic – significance to each individual degree. So, twins born even a few minutes apart would indeed differ in the ranges of these higher harmonics. But attacking the matter practically; figuring out why identical twins born hours apart are nevertheless identical in so many ways, and why fraternal twins born minutes apart are so different poses a legitimate interpretational problem.

Though a *tu quoque* argument does not resolve the problem, astrologers are certainly within their rights to remind critics that the so-called 'exact' sciences are filled with inexactitudes (see the 'Piccardi Effect', p. 337), and the hardest of 'hard' sciences have soft underbellies when turned over, as a browse through any geological journal will soon demonstrate. This does not disqualify them as sciences. On the contrary, as Culver and Ianna admit (just before declaring the opposite), the truth in science is never absolute, but rather represents a high statistical probability.

The twin problem applies *only* to astrological interpretation (not to the astrological premise), and it becomes a serious problem only if astrologers try to call astrological interpretation a science – which not many do. To give a concrete example: if astrologers were being tested 'blind' (that is, having no personal contact with the people to whom the horoscopes belonged) they probably would not be able to distinguish effectively between the horoscopes of fraternal twins born within a few minutes of each other or between identical twins born hours apart, and make valid character analyses and/or predictions. But if astrological interpretation is accepted in its rightful role as an art with a scientific basis, and astrologers have their normal personal access to the people whose charts they are to read, the problem is much mitigated.

5b. *Time Twins . . . Babies born the same minute in the same place ought to be identical, no matter that they are from different mothers and fathers.*

An astrology that does not take genetics into account (which in practice is not uncommon) would have to take this outlandish stance. But if the genetic make-up is determined by the moment of conception, then astrology need defend only the notion of identical personalities, which is perhaps rather less of an assault upon reason and experience; and more difficult to prove or disprove. In principle, Time Twins represents a rich, and relatively easily researched field for both supporters and opponents of astrology. It would not take more than a certain amount of time, effort and money to acquire satisfactory samples of time twins, and devise appropriate psychological/physical tests to look for similarities. Yet, to date, virtually no organized work has been done. The astrologers, in general, lack the time, the money, and the organization to carry out work of this sort (though in fact at least a few expensive organized experiments have been run in less promising areas, with negative results). Astrology's opponents, meanwhile, would rather scoff than work, and have shown themselves loath to engage in any astrological experiment they are not certain will fail beforehand.

Nevertheless, in a disorganized fashion, a certain amount of anecdotal material has been collected in which time twins share a wide variety of features: they may have the same names, and marry wives with the same names, succeed or fail in the same businesses, and die of the same or similar causes at the same time. In some cases, time twins born under very different social strata live out their lives according to a near identical pattern. In our first edition we included a number of these 'case histories'. Subsequently, many (but not all) were 'debunked' in the *Skeptical Inquirer* (Eriksen, #7, pp. 43–4). But to the best of our knowledge, no one has taken the trouble to look into Eriksen's data, or into those examples he neglected to debunk. Given the proven unobjectivity of so many other *Skeptical Inquirer* inquiries, it would be naive to accept 'Eriksens' data as definitive without independent corroboration. Perhaps the wisest course is to consider the matter effectively open.

Most practicing contemporary astrologers hold that the birth horoscope represents, not so much a catalog of predetermined characteristics, as a map upon which tendencies are written. Time twins, according to astrological theory, should share these tendencies, but the maps would be different – because of their different genetic make-up, social environment and so on. What is needed is a study that gathers data for a large group of time twins, and that looks systematically for psychological and other similarities between them.

5c. *Induced births: Do astrologers maintain that a child whose birth is induced will have a different character than if it had been born normally?* Difficult as it may be to countenance, astrologers have no choice but to maintain it. There is some suggestive material to back up the notion, though by definition it cannot be proved or disproved – since the same baby cannot have both an induced and a natural birth. The Gauquelin data reveals that the significant planetary relationships that normally obtain between parents and their children disappear when the births are induced. Since other Gauquelin data proves a correlation between personality and position of planets at birth, there is reason to prefer the astrological to the logical position.

6. *Mass Tragedies: did all the Jews murdered by Hitler have death written into their horoscopes, etc.?* This common and valid objection was voiced by J. B. S. Haldane and Martin Gardner and briefly discussed earlier. But it is an important point that deserves elaboration. Astrologers contend that the individual's destiny is subsumed in the greater laws governing the city, state, nation or even race. But in practice astrologers seem unable to distinguish satisfactorily between the general and the particular. As we have argued, the evidence suggests that astrology originally was part of a highly developed initiatic discipline rather than a system for character interpretation or divination.

But at least since the second millenium BC in Mesopotamia, astrology has been most visible as a system of divination, and it remains so. That is the essence of its popular appeal at its most superficial and yet most persistent level, and astrologers have no satisfactory answer to objections directed at this mundane astrology level.

On the other hand, however scientifically unsatisfactory, mundane astrology deals with matters of legitimate human interest that science cannot or will not address. What is it actually, that makes for the differences between races, nations, regions, even between neighboring villages? All people vaguely awake to their own sensitivity know that 'character' changes from one region to another; that the 'atmosphere' at one point on the river is altogether different from another point two miles distant; that one city seems hostile and another benign. National and racial stereotypes are disavowed by liberal thinkers everywhere, but they survive because something in them rings true. No matter that all are extrapolations, exaggerations and simplifications of only the negative traits. It cannot be measured, yet the Germans are incontrovertibly Germanic, the French irredeemably French, and no sane human being would argue otherwise.

When science turns its attention in this direction at all, everything is blithely ascribed to the interaction between genotype and environment. But this is not an explanation, it is a description: a label applied to a mystery. It does not tell us why the Germans are different from the French, nor does it begin to account for their respective Germanness and Frenchness.

Astrologers cast horoscopes for the dates of important historical events, the signing of treaties and constitutions, dynasties of kings or lines of successive leaders and ministers, and for the dates of important geological and climatic phenomena (earthquakes, floods, famines, plagues), looking for striking frequencies within the signs, recurrent positions, aspects or patterns of planets and specific degree areas to which a particular city, nation, or race is 'sensitive'. Their reasoning is not logical, but analogical and perhaps none the worse for that. As Samuel Butler once remarked, 'Though analogy is often misleading, it is the least misleading thing we have' (*Notebooks, Music, Pictures and Books: Thought and Word*) . . . The nation or race is more than merely a conglomeration of individuals; it has its own mysterious integrity (its Frenchness, Germanness, etc.), and is therefore a unity in its own right. If the individual is sensitive to astrological influences, then it follows that the greater (but more amorphous) individuality of the state, race, corporation, team, etc. should also be sensitive. When the ancient Egyptians shifted from the symbol of the Bull to the symbol of the Ram, in keeping with the New Arian Age, they were working with mundane astrology but we do not know what criteria directed their moves, nor the effects produced. Modern astrologers try to erect horoscopes for nations and organizations on the basis of key charters, treaties or incorporation documents, in other words the 'birth' of the organization. But the results would not be likely to impress scientists. On the other hand, the results of economic forecasters should not impress scientists either, and to date there have been no impassioned documents signed by 186 eminent scientists warning the public about the dangers of believing economic charlatans.

Finally, there are those attested and undeniable instances of accurate predictions. Culver and Ianna logged the 3,011 predictions by a number of popular American astrologer/psychics over a five-year period, and were delighted to find them right on average just 11% of the time. They then gleefully contrasted this to the 100% accuracy of astronomical predictions, unaware of the self-evident fact that, short of a cosmic collision, there are no major unforeseen variables involved in astronomical predictions so that 100% accuracy is to be expected. While in astrological situations, the situation is infinitely more complex.

Certain situations might be called near-sure bets (renewed hostilities in the Middle East), others might be amenable to some sort of calculable statistical probability (Elizabeth Taylor gets remarried) while still others would defy placing odds on. In other words, a 'hit' against infinite odds becomes rather more interesting than a hit in astronomy, where there is effectively but one horse in the race.* And a number of hits against infinite odds starts getting very interesting indeed, even if the statistical frequency of these hits is unimpressive as a figure. Culver and Ianna make no attempt to distinguish between these categories of prediction, and unfortunately destroyed their files after a five-year period had elapsed, before we began rewriting this book. A new, updated version is in progress, but is also unavailable for comment as this is written, so it is impossible to say how many of those 11% of correct predictions are made against long or infinite odds.

The point is that accurate astrological predictions are made,

---

* When the comet Kahoutek was first spotted in the late 1980s, astronomers unanimously predicted that it would light up the night sky in the most spectacular comet display since Halley's comet early in the century. Kahoutek turned out to be a dud, barely visible to the naked eye. We have already mentioned Spencer Jones's prescient pronouncements on space travel. The moral is: when there is more than one horse in the race, astronomers are no better at picking the winner than anyone else.

and not all that infrequently. It is highly probable that an even less scientific faculty than astrology is involved in the process as well; intuition, precognition, telepathy, call it what you will. For if purely astrological factors were at stake, we should expect much more unanimity among mundane astrologers than we actually find. But the subject is not one that can be resolved or even satisfactorily studied by science. A single astrologer scoring hits relatively consistently effectively counteracts negative results by all the others. And this is a possibility to be borne in mind whenever we look back at those supposedly 'superstitious' ancients. How do we know how often the court astrologers of Nineveh and Babylon were right? There is no way we can know. But who are these omniscient modern scholars that they can simply assume the ancient astrologers were always wrong? It is not inconceivable that they were right at least as often as today's economic forecasters; indeed, to keep their jobs as well as their heads, perhaps more often.

In conclusion then: astrology as a set of complex rules, as a teachable discipline, is most certainly not capable of predicting events such as mass tragedies in advance; but this is not to rule out the possibility of an individual astrologer doing so, and on a consistent basis. Out of such stuff are prophets made. Scientists who claim astrology is invalid because it cannot consistently predict mass tragedies deliberately ignore its necessary interpretational nature as a practice. They are reversing Cinderella. For here, it is Cinderella's toes that are being cut off by the wicked step-sisters – to make her foot fit into their own shoe, and a narrow, little, hob-nailed jackboot it is.

7. *What about people born in far northern countries where certain signs never rise at all?* This common objection refers to the astrological houses, discussed briefly on p. 150.

If the sun, making its (apparent) circuit of the sky, comes under the 'influence' of the constellations of the zodiac in turn over the course of a year, then, following this logic, the earth, turning on its own axis once a day, comes under the same 'influence' in a 24-hour period. Ultimately, then, houses can only be valid if the signs themselves are valid. But even if the signs are valid, houses present a physical problem that does not apply to the (apparent) circuit of the sun through the zodiacal signs.

Due to the tilt of the earth's axis, the amount of time spent under each constellation for a given spot on earth varies according to its geographical location. So if there is a physical, astronomical basis to the houses, they must differ in size according to location. But this creates complex physical problems; for example, in extreme northern latitudes certain signs never rise at all. Since houses theoretically determine personality, how are astrologers to analyze personality for people with whole constellations missing from their horoscopes?

Houses are probably the weakest and most vulnerable piece in the astrological puzzle. Culver and Ianna in particular miss no opportunity to exploit the many contradictions involved, and the heated disputes the many, mutually contradictory house systems provoke among astrologers.

Their discussion of the house problem is well handled and useful, particularly for anyone looking seriously into the technical problems houses involve.

But the objections are only as valid as the premises; and the premises are invalid. As we have stressed repeatedly, astrology does not require a 'plausible physical explanation' on the terms laid down by Culver and Ianna and other objectors. Nor are the houses absolutely essential to astrology (certain systems work without them), as these critics would have readers believe. The postulated correspondence between events on earth and events in the heavens, and between the human personality and the position of the planets at birth is scarcely affected by the astrological dispute over houses.

Meanwhile, even that disagreement is used as implicit condemnation. That is: the astrologers disagree among themselves, therefore all must be wrong, including those who have abandoned houses altogether, and those who use the equal house system. (This is an instance where there may be a significant difference between the apple pies produced by our chefs, and some may not be using apples.) Similar criteria do not apply to scientists – where violent disagreement and disarray carries no onus. There it is called 'healthy debate'. Consider the recent controversies over cold fusion and superconductivity.

In any event, the problem of houses affects *only* the interpretation of the horoscope; it does not touch upon the basic astrological premise of a correlation between the position of planets and the human personality; it has no bearing upon the metaphysical concept of the Harmony of the Spheres, nor does it in any way interfere with the practice of astrology as an integral part of the initiatic quest; the ancient discipline of the transformation of the soul. If the houses are nothing but bathwater, they may eventually go down the drain, sped on their way by astrology's critics. The baby is alive and kicking.

8. *The zodiac is an imaginary circle, and the other principles of astrology – houses, aspects, etc. are equally arbitrary and correspond to no objective realities.* This is, of course, the master objection. It is true, at the moment, that the strictly scientific evidence supporting the validity of the zodiac is indirect and tangential – though there is plenty of evidence to prove an overall correspondence between events in the heavens and events on earth, as well as evidence supporting the traditional meanings ascribed to the planets.

So, even if the reality of the zodiac is acknowledged *dis*proved, the validity of the basic premise of astrology is not disturbed. But, such an acknowledgement would be premature as well.

The tests carried out to date have been relatively crude. More finely tuned experiments may yet come up with positive results. It is also possible that although valid, the reality of the zodiac lies outside the pale of scientific proof. As we have argued throughout, the scientific paradigm pertains only to a narrow band of the spectrum of human experience. Outside that band it has no rightful authority. Putting definitive limits to the band poses problems. And astrology is a discipline that is occasionally within the band, more often without, and sometimes hovering about in that grey borderline area.

9. *Astrology fails to take into account the precession of the equinoxes;* another objection that concerns astrology's practice not its premise. The so-called 'Tropical' or Greek Zodiac, the one used

by most Western astrologers, is fixed. Each astrological year begins with 0° Aries. However, due to the precession of the equinoxes (see p. 25), on the actual day of the vernal equinox – the spring day that is divided equally between day and night, (21–22 March) – the sun no longer rises in 0° Aries, but has gradually precessed and at the moment rises in 5° Pisces. This means, in practical, astrological terms, that a child born on 24 March is said to be born under Aries, but in fact the actual, physical sun, is rising deep in Pisces. Is this child Arian or Piscean?

As is so often the case, critics raise this objection without checking its status in astrological circles. Astrologers have in fact been aware of the problem for centuries. Ptolemy may have known of it. The Egyptians certainly knew of it, and following Di Santillana and Von Dechend (see pp. 42–5), so did everyone else in the ancient world.

But recognition of the problem and its resolution are two different matters. Astrologers are by no means in full agreement on the subject, and in India, it is the Sidereal Zodiac that prevails. In the West, the familiar, Tropical Zodiac is used by all but a handful of quite passionate Siderealists who have assembled statistics to buttress their arguments.

Opponents contend the statistics lend themselves to alternative interpretations, and insist that their collective experience validates the traditional, Tropical Zodiac.

The two zodiacs are not in fact inimical and mutually contradictory. It is crucial to remember (astrologers themselves often forget) that neither zodiac is intended literally, as an actual configuration of stars whose imaginary resemblances to animals, people and a scale provide the signs with their meanings. Most dictionaries claim that the world 'zodiac' is derived from the Greek for 'circle of animals' but the same Greek words also yield the meaning 'wheel of life' and it is in this sense that the zodiac should be understood. The zodiac is a *symbolic* representation of the continuous and eternal cycle of creation. And the meanings of the signs (see pp. 31–8) follow inescapably from the interplay of numerical principles (duality, triplicity, quadruplicity) upon which the zodiac is constructed. The Arian personality is not Arian because its symbol is the Ram, but rather because this initial sign is masculine/cardinal/fire, and so on around the zodiac. Ram, Bull, Twins, Crab, etc. were chosen as representations, or embodiments of the qualities and functions dictated by the interplay of principles. In other words, the principles come first, the animals second.

The Tropical or fixed Zodiac pertains to laws governing life on earth, and these have not changed. The vernal equinox still occurs on 22 March, and that is the first day of spring, o° Aries. Spring does not start earlier because the sun is actually in 5° Pisces. So, if that fusion of numerical principles that underpins astrology is valid, and the Tropical Zodiac is a legitimate expression of those principles, it follows that astrologers are justified in retaining it.

On the other hand, if the Tropical Zodiac is valid for life on earth, then the Sidereal Zodiac cannot be without its own significance. It is the precession of equinoxes around the Sidereal Zodiac that brings about the Taurean, Arian, Piscean and shortly, Aquarian Ages; events that, in ancient civilizations, had profound implications. Like Ezekiel's vision (which has strong astrological connotations) the two zodiacs may be thought of as a wheel within a wheel.

An analogy may help illustrate the manner in which the two zodiacs operate simultaneously. Imagine a self-contained village within an enormous empire. The village has its own feasts, holidays, local saints and heroes; its own rhythm of life. To the casual observer it may appear altogether autonomous and unchanging. But actually, the village is inextricably bound and responsive to the greater laws governing the empire. From time to time messages and instructions arrive; minute but progressive changes are made in the rites and regulations. To the villagers themselves it may not appear that significant change has taken place. It is only through a study of records and monuments left by ancestors that the extent of the change becomes clear. The village of course corresponds to the Tropical Zodiac, the empire to the Sidereal. Or to put it another way; the person born

23 March will be an Aries personality whatever the Sidereal Age; but that Aries personality will be subtly different today, on the cusp of the Aquarian Age, from the Aries personality in Caesar's day, against a background of Pisces, which would in turn be different from what it would have been 1000 years earlier against a background of Aries.

In so far as horoscope delineation is valid, Western astrologers can justify sticking to the Tropical Zodiac – though Hindu astrologers can also justify their own use of the Sidereal. Making use of the leisurely imperatives of the Sidereal Ages may well have been a possibility for the ancient Egyptians, but it is not for us. If it were, we should now be busy building appropriate sacred structures consecrated to the Aquarian Age, designed to attune men to their time. Instead, we work on star wars.

The Negative Evidence

Astrology's opponents insist that astrology has been disproved, and it is this claim that has had the widest media coverage. Indeed, as we have seen, the Prosecution has undertaken an extensive campaign not only to discredit the defense (which is its legitimate task) but to silence it (which is not). 186 leading scientists have tried to use their prestige to prevent 'otherwise reputable publishers' from publishing the works of 'astrological charlatans'.

Strictly speaking, the negative evidence should be entrusted to the Prosecution, and ought not to concern us. Under the circumstances, however, it is in our interests to look at a few typical examples to let the jury see the kinds of tests that have been run, just what it is, specifically, that has been disproved, or rather, unproved, and the manner in which this material is interpreted by the Prosecution.

Unfortunately, in this instance, we shall be forced to suspend our customary practice of allowing the Prosecution to speak for itself.

Andrew Fraknoi of the Astronomical Society of the Pacific has, for undisclosed reasons, declined to give us permission to quote from his copyrighted pamphlet (from his letter: 'We do *not* grant you permission to quote from our pamphlet, *Astronomy and Astrology*' . . .). Whether or not taking an academic Fifth Amendment will prove effective in court we leave to the jury to decide. Since even careful and extensive paraphrase may also be construed as a provocation subject to litigation we find ourselves reduced to an unactionable summary and recapitulation of the pamphlet's material. Jurors interested in verifying for themselves the accuracy and fairness of our reportage are encouraged to procure copies of the pamphlet for themselves.

Professor Ivan Kelly of the University of Saskatchewan discusses negative results from a number of sources. Snell, Dean and Wakefield (*Psychology*, Vol. 16, p. 471) using a sample of 1,500 names drawn at random from leadership biographies tested for the correspondence between leadership qualities and the specific sun signs associated with those qualities by astrologers. Virgo, for example, is held to be a sign unconducive to leadership. But in the study leaders with their sun in Virgo were no less common than others. Taking a related tack, in a 1978 Ph.D. dissertation at North Texas State University, J. Noblitt tested the relationships between the astrological aspects and personality traits. His hypothesis was that individuals with a preponderance of disharmonious aspects should – if astrological theory had substance –return higher scores on a stress/relaxation index. They failed to do so, providing what Kelly called 'fairly decisive' evidence against astrology.

Roger Culver tested the hypothesis that signs of the zodiac correspond with a variety of physical traits. Using a sample of 300 he examined arm size, baldness, bicep size, blood type, bust size, calf size, chest size, finger size, foot size, hair color, handedness, freckles, height, hip size, reach, leg length, neck size, wrist size, skin color and weight against the zodiacal signs. No significant relationships were found.

G. A. Tyson (*The Journal of Social Psychology*, Vol. 110, p. 73) looked for a correspondence between date of birth and career and found none.

Kelly also discusses at some length Michel Gauquelin's attempts to link the zodiacal signs to professions and to heredity, and his efforts to show a correspondence between positive signs of the zodiac and extraversion and negative signs to introversion. Kelly reports that all these studies produced negative results. Finally, Kelly cites the massive compilation of evidence that comprises Dean & Mather's *Recent Advances in Natal Astrology*, and declares that 'in balance' tests designed to probe astrology's validity have been 'generally negative'.

Commentary

The surveys cited by Kelly are not so much evidence against astrology as evidence for the ability of astrologically illiterate scientists to wheedle research money out of their universities.

Snell, Dean, Wakefield and Tyson might have employed their time more destructively. Gauquelin's exponentially more thorough and sophisticated work had long since established the lack of a one-to-one relationship between specific traits or propensities and the zodiacal sign traditionally associated with it.

Noblitt's attempt to correlate harmonious/inharmonious aspects with personality scores for relaxation/tension was a bit less simplistic. But had Noblitt done his astrological homework, he might have known about John Addey's experiment with nonagenarians in which significant results turned up only when separating and applying aspects were examined separately (see pp. 318–27). Addey's results are at least as 'fairly decisive' in favour of astrology as Noblitt's are against. Needless to say, they go unmentioned.

It is a pity that Roger Culver's detailed inquiry into zodiac-related baldness, freckles and hip size did not come to the attention of Senator William Proxmire while he was handing out Golden Fleece awards for fatuous scientific research projects. But traditional astrologers would expect most of these external features to relate to the ascendant, not the sun sign. Gauquelin's results (well known to Culver when carrying out his own test) would in any case dissuade any researcher seriously interested in discovering anything new from pursuing such an avenue. It is only in academic life that people get paid for flogging dead horses – presumably that is one of its attactions.

More important is Kelly's flagrant misrepresentation of the evidence as a whole. The phrase 'generally negative' is used to evade even mentioning the positive evidence – though the existence of this evidence is emphasized in unmistakable fashion by Dean and Mather themselves, despite their own negative attitude towards astrology as a practice, and their curious incomprehension of its principles.

But it is Kelly's treatment of Gauquelin's work that provides a good taste of the limitless subterfuges the Prosecution will resort to in order to keep up the pretense that positive evidence does not exist at all. The Gauquelin tests cited do indeed fail to validate the astrological zodiac. But to describe these negative results without any reference at all to his commanding positive evidence is a scholarly sin of omission of cardinal proportions, and manifestly deliberate. In an earlier century Kelly would doubtless defend the flat earth by citing a dozen failed attempts to circumnavigate the globe but omit mention of Magellan.

In the same pamphlet, Jay Paschoff discusses negative results compiled from several other sources. Bernie I. Silverman, a psychologist at Michigan State University, tested the validity of specific values traditionally associated with sun signs: Libras and Aquarians – equality, Sagittarians – honesty, Virgos, Geminis and Capricorns – intellectual pursuits, etc.

Sixteen hundred graduate psychology students filled out questionnaires and rated these specific values. When compared to their sun signs no significant relationship was found.

In another test, Silverman studied signs held by astrologers to be compatible for marriage. His sample included 2,978 marriages and 478 divorces. He found that couples born under 'compatible' signs were no less likely to be divorced than others born under 'incompatible' signs.

In still another test, James T. Bennett and James R. Barth, economists at George Washington University, found no correspondence between soldiers born under signs ruled by Mars and military re-enlistment rates.

Having cited these tests, Paschoff then goes on to address a self-posed question: If astrology is meaningless, why does it command so large a following? One possibility Paschoff considered was the bandwagon effect. A test, labeled 'ingenious' by Paschoff and conducted by Silverman, supported this contention.

Twelve typical sun sign personality descriptions were taken from astrology books. One group of individuals were told which signs the descriptions belonged to. More than half of these people thought that the descriptions applied to themselves. In other words, individuals born under Cancer thought the description of the Cancer personality was among the four best descriptions offered.

But another group of individuals was not told which personality description matched which sign. When these picked the description that best matched their assessments of their own personality this apparent correspondence between sign and personality type disappeared.

Still, Paschoff continues, citing an unnamed historian of science, the bandwagon effect alone is not enough to account for the astonishing historical persistence of astrology. He reasons that astrology, like other pseudosciences, must satisfy the 'intuitional needs' of the unenlightened who do not understand what science is, what its basis is, and what it holds out for us.

He declares that from an astronomer's point of view astrology is meaningless, unnecessary and impossible to explain within the context of known physical laws; that astrology is contrary to pure science, and besides it obviously doesn't make good its promises; that if people want to subscribe to it as a religion, or apply it as therapy, they shouldn't pretend that it is science; that the only reason people may think they've seen it work is that they have deluded themselves; that astrology was developed long ago when people did not understand what was happening in the universe, and finally, that we should study the stars, but we should learn the truth.

While we feel certain that the lengthy passages excerpted from the works of Culver & Ianna, Bok & Jerome and their colleagues have already effectively conveyed to the jury the quality of the Prosecution's thinking, it is with real regret that we comply with the enforced omission of this concluding paragraph of Paschoff's. No summary by us can quite capture the low level of its science, the commensurate level of its prose style, its weak scholarship, muddled hubris and the evangelical religiosity of its call to science as arbiter of truth.

The Carlson Experiment

In 1985, Shawn Carlson, a graduate student in physics at the University of California, devised an experiment intended to test astrologers' ability to delineate character on the basis of the horoscope.

One hundred and sixteen college student volunteers filled out a standard personal inventory called the CPI (California Personality Inventory) which assesses traits such as sociability, dominance, femininity and masculinity. Psychological profiles were then erected on the basis of the answers and sent to participating astrologers in groups of three along with a horoscope belonging to one of the profiles. The astrologers were to pick out the profile that matched the horoscope.

The astrologers scored at the chance level.

Carlson's lengthy description of the experiment was published in the prestigious English science magazine, *Nature* (vol. 318, 5 December 1985). The jury may think it odd that none of the positive experiments, including Gauquelin's thirty years of work, have ever been reported in this unbiased journal.

In summing up, Carlson concluded:

> Great pains were taken to insure that the experiment was unbiased and to make sure astrology was given every reasonable chance to succeed. It failed. Despite the fact that we worked with some of the best astrologers in the country ... despite the fact that every reasonable suggestion made by the advising astrologers was worked into the experiment ... astrology failed to perform at a level better than chance. Tested using double blind methods, the astrologers' predictions proved to be wrong ... The experiment clearly refutes the astrological hypothesis.

Commentary

Though astrologers did not pass this test, Carlson's conclusions are illegitimate and do not follow from his own description of the experiment.

The crux of the problem is the CPI test itself. Designed to be used by professional psychologists, the Interpreter's Syllabus accompanying the test includes the following proviso:

> ... the diagnostic implications of the profile are not always self evident; for this reason IT IS IMPORTANT THAT SCORES ON THE TEST BE INTERPRETED BY A COMPETENT PSYCHOLOGIST WHO HAS BECOME FAMILIAR WITH THIS PARTICULAR DEVICE [caps belong to the Syllabus]. Validity-in-use is not something that resides purely in the inventory itself; it is an outcome that derives from the interpreter's skill and insight in making manifest what is inherent in the instrument.

According to the designers of the test itself, then, the profiles derived from it cannot be expected to provide useful information to untrained non-psychologists.

That this is the case was proved by Carlson himself. Commenting on another part of the test in which participants were asked to pick their own profile out of a group, and could not do so above the chance level, he writes: 'However, we cannot use the result (chance scores by the astrologers) to rule out the astrological hypothesis, because the subjects were also unable to select their own CPI profile at a better-than-chance level.'

This means that the profile returned by the CPI was absolutely meaningless unless in the hands of trained professional psychologists. Without prior training in the use of the tests, the astrologers could not begin to get a clear picture of the personality they were supposed to match to the horoscope. Moreover, though a number of astrologers did indeed participate in devising the test, Carlson's claim that 'every reasonable suggestion made ... was worked into the experiment' is demonstrably false. Many astrologers dropped out because their suggestions were not incorporated into the test, and they realized they were being conned. Chief among their objections was that the gender of the subject was not disclosed. The CPI scores differently for the same traits depending upon whether the subject is male or female. For example, the category 'high femininity' for men includes the following traits: 'Appreciative, complaining, feminine, formal, meek, nervous, self-denying, sensitive, weak, worrying'. But 'high femininity' in a woman is characterized by significantly different qualities: 'Conscientious, discreet, generous, gentle, helpful, mature, self-controlled, sympathetic, tactful, warm'. Given such differences within the test itself, no psychologist could hope to interpret scores without knowing if the subject was male or female. But astrologers allowed themselves to be tested on that basis.

Conclusion

Carlson's sweeping assertions do not follow from the results. Astrology was not being tested, nor was the astrologers' ability to delineate character on the basis of the horoscope. What was being tested was the ability of a scientist to hoodwink astrologers into believing their abilities were being tested. Since Shawn Carlson is also a professional conjurer, that is to say, an expert in deception, it is perhaps not surprising that he should succeed in his efforts. What is surprising is that so many astrologers should prove so hoodwinkable, and so grossly overconfident of their abilities that they should walk wide-eyed into so obvious an ambush.

Also tested was the willingness of the science press to abandon its normal standards and publish the unrefereed results of a fatally flawed experiment run by a scientist with no training in the subject under consideration (Carlson is a physicist not a psychologist) – as long as those results were anti-astrology. Apart from *Nature*, Carlson's experiment was also reported by *Science 86* (March) under the heading: 'Astrology: Down for the count'.

Summary of the Objections and the Negative Evidence

These, then, are the chief, common objections to astrology. All but one (the genetic argument) are based upon a thoroughly discredited physical conception of the universe and the solar system; a conception that is barely Newtonian; closer actually to the crude atomism of Democritus and Leucippus.

There is, in truth, nothing whatever in modern science that invalidates astrology from a theoretical physical point of view; and a number of highly qualified scientists have acknowledged that fact. Here is one example with a curious story attached.

The mathematician Warren Weaver was one of America's most eminent scientists, with a number of important discoveries to his credit, including proving that gravitational waves from the center of the galaxy enter our solar system. Weaver was Vice-President of the Rockefeller Foundation for the Natural Sciences; a scientist universally respected, with impeccable credentials. His daughter, Helen Weaver, is an astrologer. For years Weaver declined to listen to arguments advanced by his daughter supporting astrology. But at a certain point, perhaps unwilling to acknowledge her as 'semi-literate' and 'an idiot' he began listening to her reasoning, examining closely the basis for his own opposition. Weaver died before coming to firm and developed conclusions on the subject, but in the preliminary notes to what was intended to become a book jointly written with his daughter he noted:

> As a wholly reasonable reaction, many persons and presumably all orthodox scientists, find it difficult to conceive of any way in which the configuration of the planets, at the time of birth, can affect the personality traits and talents of that child. What conceivable 'forces' could bring that about?
>
> However, to some scientists, at least, it may seem reasonable to assume, and to believe that the entire universe is an inter-related unit, every part of which is related to and affected by every other part, whether or not we have a reassuring name or any description of the 'force' which carries out the effect. The universality of this assumption is entirely comparable to the universal law of gravitation. In the classical scientific instance, we have a name for the law, and a neat simple formula for its magnitude. It may, however, be well to remember that in the case of gravity, the name and formula

are *all* that we have. Not even Einstein, popularly supposed to have 'explained' gravity, had any basic understandable explanation for *why* there should be such a force.

Thus at the moment of birth – i.e., the moment when a human being becomes a full fledged portion of that overall unity – the whole of the universe, however distant and in however unimaginable a manner, may exert some influence on that new member of the overall unity. What forms that influence may take, and how that influence may be correlated with certain aspects of the overall unity (in particular, with the geometrical configuration of certain celestial bodies at the moment of birth) will be discussed in later chapters of this book.

The projected book was cut short by Warren Weaver's death and never completed. But it is clear from the passage above that one of America's most respected modern scientists, upon due reflection, could find nothing inherently implausible with the astrological premise, and proposed developing a theory that might account for it.

We repeat: the theoretical objections are invalid in their entirety and the claim that negative evidence exists to disprove astrology is a wildly irresponsible overstatement. The Prosecution's only viable card in a doomed hand is the inability of astrologers, to date, to support the validity of the zodiac, the cornerstone of modern, Western astrological interpretive practice. A considerable number of tests devised to prove the validity of the zodiac have come out negative, and none have been unconditionally positive. While this admittedly represents an embarrassment to astrologers, it chiefly affects astrology's practice; it does not touch upon its premise. Moreover, when we look into the positive evidence, there are plenty of straws left for astrologers to clutch at. Even if direct positive scientific or statistical evidence fails to materialize, it may still be possible for astrologers to insist upon the validity of the zodiac by inference. For example, a number of rigorously run tests have shown astrologers able to delineate character on the basis of the horoscope. All of those astrologers employ the traditional zodiac in interpreting the chart. If, further, even stronger evidence continues to accumulate, at a certain point it may be possible to infer with confidence that the zodiac is valid but that proving it directly remains beyond the pale of science – just as science cannot prove a difference between Spaniards and Swedes or prove that a Bach cantata is a better piece of music than 'The Star-Spangled Banner'.

But even as these familiar, invalid objections get trotted out and restated by self-styled experts and the media, the only objection that legitimately applies to the premise of astrology (apart from the genetic objection) is routinely overlooked. This is the argument developed by Lawrence E. Jerome, following the essay by Bart J. Bok in *Objections to Astrology*.

Astrology and Magic

Can astrology be disproved? Literally thousands of volumes have been written on the subject over the ages, attacks and defenses, apologies and interpretations. Proponents have claimed astrology as a 'science' and an 'art', a true interpretation of the inner workings of the universe. Opponents have mostly attacked astrology on physical grounds, citing the old classical arguments: the question of twins, the time of birth versus the time of conception, the immense distances to the planets and stars, and so on.

But very few writers have come to the nub of the matter: astrology is false because it is a system of magic, based on the magical 'principle of correspondences' . . . (pp. 37–8)

The purpose of this article, then, is to try to provide that 'final disproof' of astrology. The plan is simple: I shall demonstrate that astrology arose as magic and that physical arguments and explanations for astrology were only attempts to associate the ancient 'art' with each important new science that came along . . . I shall prove that astrology is magic because its interpretations are based on the 'principle of correspondences', the very basic law of magic. I shall show that it was not until the Greeks – and then later in the Renaissance – that astrology began to be ascribed to physical influences of the stars, long after their magical characteristics had been established. (p. 39)

In their opening joint Statement endorsed by 186 leading scientists, Bok and Jerome were trying to have it both ways, disavowing astrology because of the distances of the planets and also because of the magical world view that is astrology's foundation. But as we pointed out earlier (p. 179), these objections are mutually self-canceling. If there is no commanding physical reason to disavow astrology (and there is not if the correct model is employed), then the magical basis of astrology does not affect its plausibility. In other words, the magic might be wrong but astrology would still work because the physics was right. While from the magical world view proposed by Jerome 'the old classical arguments' are irrelevant and do not apply. We are pleased to find Jerome not only in full agreement with us on this point, but also pulling the rug out from under his own colleague's feet. For Bart J. Bok was among those writers guilty of erroneously attacking astrology on 'the old classical grounds . . . distances of the planets and so on'. Indeed, Bok's entire argument is based upon those grounds. It is illuminating to see these two mutually contradictory views expressed within the same book by its co-authors and endorsed by 186 leading scientists.

Jerome then goes on to provide his own version of astrology's beginnings, drawing upon anthropologist Alexander Marshack's thesis, developed in his influential book, *The Roots of Civilization* (Weidenfeld and Nicolson, 1974). Originally raucously derided but subsequently generally accepted, Marshack's argument is that Paleolithic notations originally believed to be hunting tallies were in fact records of lunar observation (postulating an apparent scientific interest in astronomy in Paleolithic times, hence the initial antagonism. Primitive man is not supposed to have had scientific interests). Out of these lunar notations Jerome believes astrology developed, as magic supplanted early science: 'The association of lunar notations with the seasonal advent of - certain plants and animals also helps explain why abstractly shaped constellations have animals' names: there was a long history of associating objects with animal life ...' (p. 41)

The constellations Gemini (Twins), Virgo (Virgin), Sagittarius (Centaur), Libra (Scales) and Aquarius (Water-Bearer) immediately spring to mind as examples of such animal-life associations. Even more convincing is their well known seasonal advent. Twins characteristically appear with the moon in June, virgins with the moon in September, balance scales proliferate in October and, as so many astrologers have observed, centaurs become a nuisance when the moon sails through Sagittarius in December, trampling lawns underfoot with their hoofs and shooting arrows into the houses of innocent people.

Identical commanding logic supports Jerome's account of the development of those specific magical correspondences that, he claims, astrology is based upon. 'Thus Pisces (the Fish) is called a water sign, red Mars is associated with war, quick and elusive Mercury governs the metal quicksilver (mercury), planets in opposition are in disharmony, and so on.'

Presumably, it is the 'and so on' that explains why Aquarius, the Water-Bearer, is an air sign, why Scorpio, the Scorpion (an insect found only in the desert) is a water sign, and why Gemini, the Twins, must be an air sign, since early man would quite naturally associate twins with the air, as well as with the moon in June – how should he do otherwise?

While this reasoning is obviously good enough for 186 leading scientists, 19 of them Nobel Prize-winners, it will not satisfy nitpickers, who in this instance, may have a point. But this does not automatically invalidate Jerome's insistence that magic is the basis of astrology,

> One may well ask, Why would magic develop along with civilization? As in the case of lunar notations and seasonal time-keeping, one can only suggest that magic arose because it was of selective advantage. Perhaps magic gave the burgeoning city-state cohesiveness; one could easily make a case for magic being the power wielded by priests to keep the citizens in line, convincing them that

only by working for the good of the state could they keep the 'powers of nature' in check.

This interpretation would further suggest to a hard-core skeptic that civilization does not have a rational basis, but rather an irrational basis of *selective* value – irrational at least in terms of the twentieth century. For magic is based on the 'principle of analogies', or the 'law of correspondences', as it is generally called in astrology. As we shall see, this 'principle of correspondences' is merely a product of the human mind and has no physical basis in fact.

Later, Jerome will claim that the chief danger associated with belief in astrology is that it 'robs man of his rationality, his most human feature'. Perhaps it is not only astrology that has that effect? We find the notion that magic, that is, superstition, has 'selective advantage' especially engaging. The alert reader may well wonder, as do we, why magic should then subsequently have lost this original selective advantage? Presumably because eventually Reason accidentally arose, and Reason had even greater selective advantage? But noting that the impetus behind the Bok/Jerome book with its prestigious endorsement is precisely the Rationalists' irrational fear of a resurgence of superstition, this latter argument becomes difficult to support. The forces of Reason (Jerome) and the forces of superstition (astrologers) are both co-existing without the biological survival of either at stake. The question then imposes itself: how can two such mutually opposed forces co-exist in modern society, when both have a selective advantage? As everyone knows, a selective advantage presupposes the physical demise of the selectively disadvantaged.

But it would be uncharitable to continue in this vein. It seems to us odd no one noticed that, like 'the principle of correspondences' itself, Jerome's entire argument is 'merely the product of the human mind and has no physical basis in fact'. Nor has anyone picked up on the implications of that extremely interesting latter sentence.

Astrology is indeed based upon the Principle of Correspondences; but Jerome does not understand this principle or 'the physical basis in fact' that is ostensibly his criterion. One hundred years of relativity theory and high-energy physics has made it absolutely clear that matter (the 'physical basis in fact') is itself a form of concretized energy. Every high school student knows this. Since matter is a form of energy, the question of 'reality' takes on a new, pressing and philosophical significance. How 'real' is Reality? is a question currently raised by physicists and philosophers of science everywhere. It is not easily answered within the context of modern science. But one aspect of the situation is absolutely clear and agreed upon by scientists and laymen alike: what we call Reality is largely (if not entirely) a consequence of our perception.

That is to say, we *know* that a table is comprised of atoms (whose provenance remains a total mystery, incidentally). And we know those atoms are in an eternal state of furious motion. But we perceive the solid, immobile table. The physical basis, that sacred 'fact' before which Jerome and his scientific colleagues genuflect, is demonstrably an artefact of the senses, undeniably and scientifically 'a product of the human mind' in some very profound if mysterious way. All ancient metaphysical systems understood this. It is most familiar through the Hindu concept of Maya, the illusion of the world – which, incidentally, does not mean that the world itself *is* an illusion; rather that our perception of it is illusory. No physicist would disagree with this, and a number of the most renowned physicists have explicitly written to this effect (for example, Sir Arthur Eddington famously remarked that 'the world more resembles a mind than a machine').

How then to account for our perception of the world? What is it that is responsible for our irremediably subjective notion of the physical 'facts'? It is the Principle of Correspondences.

We perceive the world as we do *only* because the atoms at their eternal dance *correspond* in a particular way with our own perceptual faculties. In other words, if our perception were different, the physical world (and all those facts that comprise it) would be different as well. And it is the facts that would have to change accordingly. If our perception were exponentially quickened, the table would lose its solidity. We would witness a rhythmic whirr of atomic particles. If our perception were prodigiously slower, a tree would live and die within a few blinks of an eye. We would perceive it in motion (time-lapse photography furnishes a less extreme example of this) as a flickering green flame; the seasons might then appear as music, and music would be a solid.

In practice, it is very difficult to give up the conviction that the table is a fact, and has a physical basis. As all the ancient teachings insist, the grip of the senses is strong. Nevertheless, the true, energetic nature of the table is a point on which all scientists agree. Matter is but energy in infinitely varied states of harmonic equilibrium which correspond to, or resonate with our perceptive faculties in a particular way. What is responsible for that 'physical basis in fact' is the ancient Principle of Correspondences in operation. It is the Principle that is real, if anything can be said to be real. It is 'fact' that is subjective, conditional, provisional, 'illusory'.

Now it is quite true that the Principle of Correspondences is the basis of magic, and of astrology. Jerome is quite right to undermine his own collaborator's credibility on this score. But he then proceeds upon the double assumption that he understands magic, and that it is invalid, neither of which are true.

Understood correctly, Magic is a name applied to the human endeavor to consciously make use of the creative powers of nature. It is the attempt to master or mimic the fundamental laws of resonance that have produced the cosmos. Whether or not such mastery or mimicry is possible on the human level does not concern us here, but the ancient understanding is certainly correct. The basis of Magic is the Principle of Correspondences. It is this principle that makes possible the transformation of energies; the mysterious phenomenon underlying all natural processes, biological, organic, and celestial.

For example, when we eat a potato, its energy is transformed, into blood, bone, muscle, tissue, and finally thought and emotion. Biologists like to call this process 'digestion' but that is just a name applied to a specific form of natural or organic magic. What is responsible for the miraculous transformation of nutrients into thought is a fabulously complex array of chemical and molecular *correspondences*. On a more fundamental level, the same principle mediated the transformation of the indigestible minerals in the soil into the organic nutrients of the potato, and on a more fundamental level still, it made possible the initial transformation of energy into its basic mineral form. Thus it is Magic that makes possible creation, indeed, all conscious, organic life. In a quite literal sense, all of perceived reality is Magic.

The ancients understood this perfectly, and in great detail. The Egyptians personified Magic and called him Heka, the primordial transforming power. It was Heka who accompanied Consciousness (Sia) at the rudder of the Solar Boat, on the fabulous journey that led from Death to Resurrection or Rebirth, since it is the transformation of the physical into the spiritual that is the only human activity of real consequence. Today, Heka is put to mundane and destructive tasks, but even so he makes science possible. Without Heka, the Principle of Correspondences, mediating between the conditional physical world and the observer, there would be and could be no science. The higher and more rarefied the energy level, the less predictable, repeatable and measurable the phenomenon, and the less exact or 'hard' the science (it is only in contemporary science that 'hardness' in this sense is a virtue; in most other human activities it is a form of stupidity. A repeatable violin virtuoso would be a laughing stock, and a predictable samurai would soon be a dead one).

Living organisms are less predictable than rocks, so biology is notoriously less 'hard' than geology, while psychology is 'softer' still – so much so that the geologic-minded are loath to call psychology a science at all. And from their point of view they are quite right. But it is Heka, Magic, the Principle of Correspondences that makes even geology possible. Meanwhile, since the study of people tends to have more immediate relevance to many of us than the study of rocks, abandoning psychology in the interests of uniform scientific hardness is not necessarily a move in the right direction. In fact, Heka has not really been disenfranchised, despite the Church of Progress. He is still very much with us. Only his role in all creative activity is no longer recognized at face value. On the cosmic and planetary level he has been deprived of consciousness, and his name has been changed to Evolution. On the human level he continues to function more-or-less sporadically as Art.

Art is magic, literally and technically. Sacred Art is objective, sacred magic, consciously based upon cosmic principles, and it works on everyone whose faculties have not been stunted or destroyed by modern education. Secular art is subjective, secular magic and it works only upon the converted; those directly affected. Bad art is bad magic, and it works only on the gullible or not at all. (Advertising, incidentally, is sorcery, which works on the will as opposed to the emotional centers.) But Art is really just a name for a specific form of magic. It is Heka, the Principle of Correspondences that allows the inspiration of Mozart or Beethoven to manifest in soundwaves (through in-animate instruments made of wood and brass) and transform itself into that exquisite rush of emotion within us. It is Heka who heals. If sick, even terminally ill patients, change their attitude towards their malady, they can sometimes be cured. The medical profession grudgingly has come round to admitting the truth of this ancient understanding, though it is not yet perhaps prepared to acknowledge the force responsible. It is Heka, Magic, the Principle of Correspondences, that effects the interchange between 'attitude' and the afflicted organs – which is an example both of 'action at a distance', and of an effect without a 'plausible physical explanation'. Try to measure 'atti-tude'. Astrology (when it is not debased to its pop level) operates in the upper reaches of psychology; those necessarily rarefied realms where human consciousness interacts with realms higher than our own, and to which we may aspire – if we do not restrict ourselves to the joyless scientific paradigm of Jerome and Bok, and Culver and Ianna and the world 'out there'. And inescapably, it is Heka, Magic, the Principle of Correspondences that sees to it that Divine Inspiration (Will or Intention), made manifest in the planets, transmits itself (by virtue perhaps of their chemical make-up, size, speed and orbits) in subtle frequencies and amplitudes. These in turn produce fluctuations in electromagnetic or geomagnetic fields – as yet not clearly understood or specifically identified but whose existence is acknowledged. These fluctuations are physical in a sense directly analogous to the fluctuations in the air, the soundwaves, that the ear inteprets as music, or the fluctuations in light that the eye interprets as color. In this case, those fluctuations represent celestial harmonies, and they manifest on earth as 'meaning'.

The study of this meaning is astrology. It was not developed by aggrandizing priests taking selective advantage of the buffaloed masses by converting lunar notations into animals such as twins, virgins, scales, centaurs and aquatic scorpions. It is the Principle of Correspondences that validates the astrological premise and that makes possible its study.

So when Lawrence E. Jerome says 'astrology is false because it is a system of magic', he is not only wrong, but very precisely wrong: astrology is *true* because it is a system of magic. And when he says, 'the "principle of correspondences" is merely a product of the human mind and has no physical basis in fact', he has actually managed to incorporate into that sentence the principal elements of the astrological situation – something other critics have not done. But he does not understand its implications. It is 'fact' that is 'entirely the product of the human mind'. All modern physicists would agree. And fact's 'physical basis' is a consequence of the operation of the Principle of Correspondences, mediated through our own perceptual faculties. So, while Jerome is correct in saying, 'the principle of correspondences does not have a physical basis *in* fact', the statement is both meaningless and deceptive. For it is the Principle of Correspondences that is the basis *of* fact.

Having set out to provide the 'final disproof' of astrology; to show once and for all why astrology does not work, Jerome has unwittingly furnished the information necessary to show why it does; and that it must – for the Principle of Correspondences is universal. A system by definition presupposes the mutual interaction of its separate components. And the solar system is most assuredly a system. 186 leading scientists have endorsed Jerome's argument. History will accord them the respect they deserve.

Postscript to the Objections

Meanwhile, again acknowledging the importance attached to a scientific imprimatur, it is particularly interesting when scientists make general statements that inadvertently reflect favorably upon astrology.

As a complement to the Warren Weaver passage above, it is well worth contemplating the following lines, written in 1954, by the eminent mathematician and physicist P. A. M. Dirac:

> With all the violent changes to which modern physical theory is subjected, there is just one rock to which one can always hold fast – the assumption that the fundamental laws of nature correspond to a beautiful mathematical theory. This means a theory based on simple mathematical concepts that fit together in an elegant way so that one has pleasure working with it.
>
> 'Quantum Mechanics and the Aether',
> *Scientific Monthly*, LVIII, 1954, p. 142

This appeal to the human aesthetic sense as final arbiter of truth is interesting. There is nothing 'rational' about it. And, in the historical absence of what we today would call 'hard' evidence, it is precisely astrology's aesthetic appeal that has commended it to all those superior intellects from time immemorial, and that has ensured its survival into modern times, despite the opposition of the Church of Progress (see Cumont, p. 3).

According to Schwaller de Lubicz, the ancient Egyptians distrusted thinking that came from the head only. To get to the truth, they insisted, it was essential 'to think with the heart'. When Dirac says that 'the fundamental laws of nature must correspond to a beautiful mathematical theory', he is unknowingly talking pure ancient Egyptian.

Yet this appeal to aesthetics is thoroughly unsentimental. Ultimately even the most unregenerate materialism is based upon value judgements – that is, unproven and unprovable assumptions. For example, the assumption that life on earth is an accident is no more logical, no more scientific, and no *less* metaphysical than the assumption that it is not. We live in a very peculiar age in which whatever is trivial, meaningless and hopeless is deemed 'reasonable' while whatever is not is called 'superstition'. It would be difficult to imagine anything that matched Dirac's definition of a 'rock' better than astrology: 'a theory based on simple mathematical concepts that fit together in an elegant way so that one has pleasure working with it'. If Dirac's criterion is valid, given the difficulties of proof and disproof involved with astrology, it would appear that even scientifically, it is more 'logical' to accept a theory that is aesthetically satisfying than one that is not.

But there is no need to combat Rationalists on an aesthetic basis. For there is an accumulation of direct and indirect evidence substantiating the fundamental premise of celestial/terrestrial correlations, and very powerful evidence substantiating the oldest and most universal aspect of astrology; the meanings assigned to the planets.

III.

THE EVIDENCE

Will the Defense Please Take the Stand

The attempt to put astrology into terms acceptable to modern disciplines, and to apply what is valuable in these disciplines to astrology, has occupied the time of a number of astrologers since the revival of interest about the turn of the century. The aims of astrology in the light of science and the modern world were summed up by John M. Addey, President of the Astrological Association of Great Britain, in an address in 1959:

> Most think of the present century as having marked the beginning of a gradual rebirth or re-emergence of astrology. The position today is that some useful advances have been made in various branches of practical horoscopy and that thanks to the work of many astrologers there is now a widespread curiosity abroad in our science – a kind of latent interest, widely diffused but as yet unfocused. Nevertheless, what has been accomplished looks rather small when set against the work waiting to be done. So far as the practical rules of horoscopy are concerned, there are a host of uncertainties – the zodiac, the houses, aspects – all present intractable problems which can only be solved by careful, persistent work; the philosophical basis has yet to be adequately re-expressed in modern times; the metaphysical laws and principles of our subject are uncoordinated; our records are scattered and contain many errors; valuable traditional elements lie buried in the writings of the past which need translating, and new developments at home and

abroad are neglected for want of those who can follow them up and interpret them to us ... The chief obstacle [in acquiring more students] is the opposition of the scientific fraternity, and to silence or check their criticism would seem to be the first step in presenting our case to a wider public and so attracting more students ...

Addey goes on to successfully adumbrate astrology's elusive requirements: no sooner does one call it a 'science' than it looks like an art; no sooner does one call it an art than it becomes apparent that a scientific approach is what's needed. Meanwhile, the jury might like to briefly reflect upon Addey's clear, considered, cool approach in the light of charges leveled earlier: astrology as 'an opium for the semi-literate', a 'proper philosophy for timorous people and idiots'.

But having recognized the need to apply the scientific method to astrology, a number of factors come into play to complicate the matter.

To begin with, research into astrology, like every other form of research, requires money and trained personnel, both of which are conspicuously lacking. Then, direct astrological experiments are intrinsically unrepeatable. The relationship of the planets to each other is in a state of perpetual change, and it is therefore impossible to isolate completely any one factor, or group of factors and study them apart from the whole.

As an example, let us suppose it is decided to try to determine scientifically the meaning of Mars in Scorpio. It would be a simple matter to collect a test group of individuals born during the time that Mars is transiting the sign of Scorpio. But, except for relatively rare time twins (people unrelated but born at the same time in the same place) each of these individuals will have Mars in different relationship to all the other planets, particularly the swiftly moving ones such as the moon, Mercury and Venus. Ascendants and Mid-heavens will be spread around the zodiac, and if the attempt is made to narrow the test group to, say, those with Mars in Scorpio in conjunction with a Scorpio ascendant, then the test group will be so narrow that it would be extremely difficult to draw generalized conclusions from the results.

Compromise is possible, but it requires recognition of the fact that astrology can never be reduced to a strictly quantitative study. Quantitative elements exist, certainly, and can be abstracted from the whole with some degree of statistical significance, but it is essential that the meaning of the whole is not forgotten in the process of studying the part.

As the situation stands today, there are two principal types of positive evidence supporting astrology; statistical evidence proving the existence of correlations between personality types and the positions of planets at birth, and physical evidence, not necessarily related directly to astrology, but proving the existence of physical relationships between celestial and terrestrial events.

A. Statistical Evidence

Early Inquiries

With the development of statistics, astrologers have attempted to make use of this potentially useful weapon. But until quite recently, those organizing the experiments had but little training in statistics, and it is only from their mistakes that today's astrologers have begun to realize how difficult it is to apply statistics to astrology – largely due to the multiplicity of factors to be taken into account and to the difficulty of isolating those factors being tested. To give just one example of the sort of thing experimenters overlooked initially: due to the elliptical orbits of the planets and their varying velocities relative to the earth, they often appear to be stationary in any given sign, or may appear to move backward through a sign in a retrograde motion. This means that over limited periods of time each of the planets will spend varying amounts of time in each of the signs, all of which must be taken into account when making calculations for, say, the number of musicians born with Venus in the sign of Libra.

The eminent psychologist Carl Jung made an interesting but elementary attempt to look for astrological factors in the horoscopes of married couples. He studied the mutual relationships of the sun, moon and ascendant and initially was achieving impressively significant results, but as his experiment continued and his test group grew, his results tailed off, though even so they remained statistically significant. But Jung seems to have lost interest in the experiment and pursued it no further.

It seems odd that in running his test Jung should have failed to look for mutual relationships between Mars and Venus, traditionally the planets of the male–female attraction. But in any case, in an inquiry of this sort, the difficulty is in defining what is meant by 'attraction'. Surely, it is safe to say that some relationship must exist – or must have existed – between married couples that does not exist between unattached men and women. But defining the precise nature of the attachment in astrological terms is another matter altogether.

Other experimenters made similar mistakes. Before the Second World War, an American professor, Farnsworth, out to disprove astrology, collected the birth dates of seven thousand musicians. Music is traditionally linked to Venus; Venus is supposed to 'rule' the sign of Libra. But Farnsworth found no more musicians born under Libra than under any other sign and therefore considered that he had disproved astrology. This was premature. To effectively discredit the music/Venus relationship, it would be necessary to look into the other roles Venus may play in the charts of musicians – aspects, houses, angles, etc. – and this Farnsworth failed to do. Again, the problem is knowing what to look for. It is true that musicians have their music in common, but music is a broad subject. Astrologers would not expect the tympanists to have much in common with the flautists, and factors linking flautists with each other and tympanists with each other – if they exist – would be submerged in the statistics.* Admittedly, astrologers would be delighted if statis-

---

* While astrologers may regard the sun in its zodiacal sign as a starting point in the interpretation of a horoscope, it has never played the commanding role assigned it by popular belief, which is, in turn, what astrologically illiterate scientific opponents are at pains to disprove. The sun is in one of twelve signs but also in one of the twelve houses. This gives 144 possible combinations, or psychological 'types' each of which is viewed differently by any practicing astrologer. The Sun conjunction Saturn means something quite different to Sun conjunction Jupiter while squares, oppositions and other aspects to these planets also have their own meanings. Thus, just considering the sun in its sign, house and the aspects it forms to the various planets involves many thousands of combinations and permutations, which are multiplied by considerations of the individual planets, each in its sign, house and the aspects each forms to the other planets. It is this bewildering multiplicity of factors that makes scientific

tics did show more soldiers born under Aries than under other signs, and more musicians under Libra, but after a number of such statistical onslaughts it has become clear that the universe demands a certain finesse before deigning to reveal its astrological secrets.

Two other early statistical attempts are worth mentioning, principally because – though subsequently shown to be inadequate – they led to experiments in which, at last, genuine results began to appear.

K. E. Krafft, the Swiss who was thought to have been Hitler's private astrologer, spent years accumulating data of every imaginable sort in an attempt to put astrology on a scientific basis as it related to heredity, physiology and psychology.

And Paul Choisnard, a well-known French astrologer, devoted much time to the compilation of statistics claiming to prove astrological factors at work in heredity, in the position of the ascendants of 'superior' persons, and in the position of the planets in the horoscopes of those who had suffered violent deaths. Choisnard claimed that his statistics proved significant astrological factors at work in such astrological concepts as Sun–Mars relationships in the charts of early mortalities; Mercury–Moon relationships in the charts of philosophers; Sun–Moon aspects in the charts of celebrities and aspects of Mars in the charts of soldiers.

Though the academic establishment ignored the work of Krafft and Choisnard, astrologers for many years firmly believed that this statistical work was sound and that astrology had been vindicated.

Michel Gauquelin and the Mars Effect

Eventually, in 1950, the work of Krafft and Choisnard came to

---

inquiry into astrology so difficult to perform. But this does not mean that accurate astrological interpretations do not take place.

the attention of Michel Gauquelin, a young graduate in statistics and psychology from the Sorbonne, who decided to put their claims to the test. This in turn led to a quest thirty-seven years in duration as this is written, and by no means resolved. The Gauquelin data, and the saga of the data, taken together, make up one of the more important scholarly episodes of the century. As saga, told in detail, it reveals, perhaps better than any other single story, the true Inquisitorial nature of the Church of Progress and the general level of disregard in which the search for truth is held by many eminent scientists and academics. At the same time, as data, the voluminous Gauquelin files contain the single, major corpus of (apparently) unassailable positive scientific evidence supporting astrology . . .

Without Gauquelin, on the basis of the energetic make-up of matter, and the necessary interactions between the parts of a functioning system, it might be possible to construct a theoretical defense of astrology. It would also be possible to defend it if certain metaphysical premises could be agreed upon between opponents – an unlikely event. But without Gauquelin, there would be no point in insisting, as we do, that the fundamental premise of astrology now stands vindicated – according to the ground rules laid down by science itself.

However, to date, opponents steadfastly refuse to acknowledge the validity of Gauquelin's work. While a minority with some vestige of professional conscience intact admit it cannot be faulted, even they do their best to belittle it; or they pretend that astrology is not involved, but some brand-new, hitherto unrecognized science (a misrepresentation to which Gauquelin himself, in his early years, contributed).

But the majority of opponents either lie about it (see Martin Gardner's review of the Eysenck/Nias book, pp. 435-7) or they ignore it, citing only those experiments that have yielded negative results. On this basis, they contend astrology has been 'disproved'.

This is categorically untrue. Very little, actually, has been disproved. What remains unproved (unless or until tests are devised that arrive at contrary conclusions) is the ability of astrologers to scientifically and quantitatively interpret the horoscope – a very different matter.

In the chapter on objections to astrology, Witnesses for the Prosecution, we described a number of typical examples, including Carlson's trumped up but widely trumpeted experiment. Later in this chapter we will look into a few better-designed tests that indicate astrologers can in fact substantiate their claims to delineate character, though they may not be able to do so consistently under test conditions.

Since the aim of this book is to present the positive evidence, intimate details of the bulk of the negative evidence do not really concern us. These experiments have been described at length in a number of books and the reader interested in pursuing the matter further is referred to them.* For our purposes it will do to freely acknowledge the negative results of these tests and their failure to date to validate standard astrological practice and beliefs. If our opponents extended the same courtesy to Gauquelin's work, there would be little need for this book and modern science would be in a most interesting turmoil.

Traditional Astrology Disproved?

The important question is: do all these negative results mean that all traditional astrology that is not Gauquelin is thereby disproved? Astrology's opponents of course entertain no other possibility. Even the critical but eminently fair-minded psychologists, Eysenck and Nias, strongly suggest that this is the case. The title of their book: *Astrology: Science or Superstition?* pretty much describes their position: if it isn't science then it must be superstition. Nevertheless, they do not shut the door on what, to date, has resisted verification, and leave loopholes open for future tests.

---

* For an excellent overview see *Astrology: Science or Superstition?*, Eysenck and Nias. For an exhaustive (if hypercritical) examination of *all* attempts to validate astrology see *Recent Advances in Natal Astrology*, Dean and Mather – soon to appear in an updated edition.

Within the astrological camp itself, its extreme science-oriented wing, most vocally represented by analytical chemist and astrologer Geoffrey Dean, views the lack of positive results as critically as do Bok, Jerome, Culver, Ianna and their scientific colleagues . . . Whatever does not yield to scientific investigation is not science, and therefore not true – though (in Dean's estimation) astrology may perhaps serve in some unscientific (*ergo*: lesser) context such as art or healing or counseling. In other words, even if it's false, if it makes people feel better, it can't be entirely useless. But it's not science, which is all that really counts to these people.

Astrologers Answer

Earlier, we described the problems involved in approaching astrology through science (p. 227). Given the accumulated volume of negative evidence, the question imposes itself: are astrologers now compelled to abandon the chief components of their tradition, or can they find a legitimate (as opposed to a merely pig-headed) means for preserving that tradition despite the negative results?

The answer, we think, is a qualified 'no' to the first half of the question, and a qualified 'yes' to the second. But much has to do with recognizing the profound psychological gulf that separates the kind of understanding involved in astrology and the thinking prevailing in science.

Astrologers, in the main, argue that the negative results are due to extracting elements from the horoscope and attempting to study them in isolation. This, they say, negates a basic principle of astrology, which is that the horoscope is a *whole*, a 'meaningful *Gestalt*' in the jargon of psychologist, Zipporah Dobyns. The parts cannot be studied separately, without reference to the whole.

There are two problems with this argument. First, it is a weak position to defend in the light of the Gauquelin data. There, strong statistically significant relationships between planets and personality show up independently, with no reference whatever to the whole. No *Gestalt* was required. Why one set of positive results and another negative using identical criteria? If the positive results stand as proof, should the negative results not count as disproof – of sun signs, rising signs and the rest of the astrologers' ancient arsenal?

This is, of course, the view of the opposition, but it is not necessarily valid. It may be that the statistical net employed was too coarse to catch anything but the biggest fish. As Eysenck and Nias admit, more sophisticated tests may yet turn up positive results. Science is full of major discoveries that were only revealed through fine-tuning research technique.

The second problem with the holistic argument is that most scientists seem incapable of understanding it. Yet nothing could be clearer. Certainly, it is possible to take the carburettor out of a car and work on it alone. But only if its function within the whole car is understood to begin with. It would be difficult to imagine a more cogent or elemental argument, yet when it is broached by scientists strange things happen.

Here is Dr Geoffrey Dean (in his postscript to *Written in the Stars: The Best of Michel Gauquelin*, by Michel Gauquelin, Aquarian Press, 1988): 'Astrologers argue that signs and aspects cannot be studied in isolation (which is like arguing that overeating won't make you fat), and that what matters is the birth chart as a whole. But recent studies have shown that the whole chart doesn't work either; in fact astrologers do not usually agree on what that means in the first place.'

Now this view is particularly interesting since it is voiced by a scholar who is an outspoken (even vituperative) critic of traditional astrology and, by his own reckoning, an astrologer as well – a unique combination that should result in balanced, informed criticism but that often doesn't.

Dean is something of a master of the inappropriate analogy, and the one above illustrates, better than any reasoned argument on our part could do, the gulf between two types of thinking, holistic or synthesizing and linear or logical. To argue that 'the chart is a whole' is not in any imaginable sense like arguing that 'overeating won't make you fat'. The one bears absolutely no relationship to the other.

To say that the chart is a whole and cannot be studied in isolation is more like arguing that you cannot understand the carburettor without understanding the car; nor can you understand musical virtuosity just by measuring the hands of pianists.

It is not inconceivable that valid musical relationships might be revealed by a thorough study of pianists' hands. But if no physical measurable relationships at all were found between pianists' hands and their virtuosity, it would not cast doubt upon the existence of musical virtuosity – though this presumably would represent Dean's scientific position. The parts do not yield scientific data, therefore the parts are imaginary and the whole invalid. Culver and Ianna present an identical argument in characteristic irrelevant detail in *The Gemini Syndrome* (p. 150).

However discomfiting the negative results (for astrologers), they do not actually invalidate sun signs, aspects, and other elements of the traditional astrological canon. It is, as we said above, possible that refinements of technique will produce positive results. It is also possible that, even though valid, these elements of astrology will *never* prove amenable to scientific inquiry – because they cannot be quantified.

This is not quite special pleading either. There is no shortage of recognized qualitative distinctions made universally in everyday life that science cannot or can only barely detect. For example, until very recently no tests had ever been devised that showed up psychological and characterological distinctions between nationalities. The newest tests have succeeded in showing up differences in the attitudes of Orientals and Westerners, but that is as far as they go. Does this mean, therefore, that no distinctions exist between Swedes and Spaniards? Dean, Culver and Ianna and their colleagues could draw no other conclusion. Since science has revealed no distinctions, and science is the only way to arrive at truth (see p. 160) it follows that Swedes must be the same as Spaniards . . . who are, of course, the same as Eskimos who are the same as Bushmen. Good science no doubt but it makes for boring travel . . .

Mostly, it is astrological experience that convinces astrologers (ourselves included) that Cancers and Arians are as different as Spaniards and Swedes. If science can detect no measurable difference between the latter pair, then astrologers are under no compelling obligation to relinquish their conviction that equally glaring differences exist between the former. Thus, lack of proof in this instance may be as much a limitation of science as a shortcoming in astrology, and it may well be both.

Who Picks Up the Stick?

In *In Search of the Miraculous* (pp. 366–7), P. D. Ouspensky relates an interesting demonstration of astrology in action, provided by his teacher, the Armenian mystic, G. I. Gurdjieff. Gurdjieff was asked about astrology by a pupil but did not immediately reply. Instead, the group of pupils continued on their walk through the woods. Suddenly Gurdjieff dropped his walking stick. All the pupils reacted differently to this event. One jumped for it, another jumped but too late, another, wrapped up in the ideas under discussion, didn't notice the stick had been dropped. Still another saw Gurdjieff had done it intentionally and watched to see what the others would do. Everyone took note of their various and unique reactions to the same event. 'That,' Gurdjieff explained, 'is astrology.'

Psychologically, the instinctive reaction to the dropped stick provides a key to the lives of the individuals concerned. Each one will react instinctively to everything that comes up in life as he (or she) did to the dropped stick, and so will each of the rest of us. It would be difficult to envisage a more poignant and telling little demonstration. And if it is this information that is astrologically written into the horoscope (Gauquelin's work effectively proves this to be the case on the statistical level), its study can be a crucial factor in the lifelong process of acquiring self-knowledge, and possibly a major key to plumbing the secrets of the human psyche.

Yet to science, Gurdjieff's lesson is meaningless. There is nothing to measure, nothing to replicate, nothing to prove, and therefore nothing to shove down unwilling throats.

Surely, it is a grave mistake (and many astrologers make it) to ignore the scientific results to date. The Gauquelin data and the stuffed file of failed experiments must be faced. It can no longer be business as usual in the astrology tent. One major lesson may be that astrologers have overestimated the importance of sun and rising signs; that it should be the position of planets at birth that represents the basic signature of the horoscope; the Martial, jovial, saturnine, lunar or Venusian character. If so, then perhaps sun sign, rising sign, aspects and the rest determine subtler and yet pervasive parameters; these traditional factors perhaps determine who will notice that the stick has been dropped, and who will pick it up . . .

Thus, we now *know* that as many great athletes will be born under Cancer as under Aries. This is proven. It is a fact. It is the position of Mars at the moment of birth that is (statistically) significant in the charts of great athletes, that distinguishes them as a group, that sets its seal on a particular personality type conducive to success in sport. But the athlete born under Aries may well manifest his essential Mars personality in a very different way from the Cancer athlete, a subtle distinction that may be scientifically undetectable (therefore non-existent) but a matter of consuming interest to the athlete himself, his family, his team and everyone else he deals with.

Astrologers remain convinced that the horoscope, viewed as a whole, provides insight into these niceties. Whether or not they can be elicited from statistics remains to be seen. Meanwhile, in a world that still grossly over-rates the validity and the importance of scientific proof (though it should have learned better long ago), astrologers would do well to talk circumspectly about those crucial elements (sun signs, rising signs, aspects, houses) of traditional astrology that remain unproven. They may, however, with equanimity, insist that these elements are unproven, not disproved. There is a big difference.

Gauquelin's Background

Michel Gauquelin was born in 1928, and brought up in a home where astrology was a familiar subject (rare in those times).

Though enjoying no more than parlor game status with his father, visitors to the house took it more seriously, and young Michel was an early and passionate convert. At seven he was asking people their birthdays, and giving them a character-reading on the basis of their sun sign. Later, in school, he was 'Nostradamus' to his classmates.

It was not until he found himself at the Sorbonne, studying psychology and statistics, that he became aware of the import-ance of scientific proof. This in turn raised questions about astrology's validity. Young Gauquelin decided to put his newly acquired expertise to work on the claims of Krafft, Choisnard and others.

Very swiftly, and to his intense chagrin, he found their methods faulty and their claims invalid. After several years of effort Gauquelin could show that *all* scientific claims made on behalf of astrology were false, and that not a single element of the astrological tradition withstood statistical inquiry.

As he describes it himself, it was like being betrayed by a lover. Gauquelin now turned against astrology with much of the ardor of his original embrace. In particular, he condemned the astrologers' pretensions to science and their refusal to ex-amine negative evidence. Indeed, so complete was his disenchant-ment that when, in his methodical statistical stalk through the starry hunting grounds, he encountered a striking celestial cor-respondence, he declined to call it astrology, sparking a con-troversy that has not yet entirely quieted down.

Having disposed of the validity of sun signs, rising signs and the rest to his own satisfaction, Gauquelin was looking into a possible relationship between position of planets at the moment of birth and the subsequent choice of profession. This facet of astrology is incorporated in the thorny question of 'houses' but Gauquelin was looking at it independent of any specific house system.

Gauquelin compiled a list of 576 eminent French doctors from medical directories, using objective criteria to avoid bias in the selection process. He then set out to get their birth-times from town archives throughout France, a laborious, expensive, thankless and infinitely tedious task that would occupy much of his time in the years to come. Heroism and statistics seems about as likely a combination as charisma and accounting, but the story of Michel Gauquelin in pursuit of his data has unmistakable heroic overtones . . .

As the earth rotates, the planets appear to rise and set just as the sun and moon do. A given planet rises on the eastern horizon, reaches its zenith, or upper culmination, midway between rising and setting, and then sets and passes below the horizon. The house system in astrology is based upon this diurnal (daily) rotation of the earth, but Gauquelin was ignoring the customary interpretation imputed to houses and to planets in houses.

Without making allowances for retrogradation and other astronomical or demographic complicating factors, if the ideal orbit of the planet is divided into twelve sectors, it means that planet would spend one-twelfth of the day, or 8.33% in each sector. This means that if only chance were operating, and births are equally distributed throughout the day (they aren't – which is one of a multiplicity of conditioning factors that have to be taken into account), 8.33% of a given group of people would have a given planet in each sector. 16.7% of the people would have a planet in a given pair of sectors. This would be distribution according to chance.

How the Statistics Work

But according to the laws of statistics, if an appreciably greater (or appreciably lesser) percentage of people are born with a planet in a given pair of sectors, the researcher is then tipped off to the possibility that factors other than chance may be involved. Formulae exist for calculating the odds against chance, which take into account both the percentage above or below the chance level, and the size of the sample group.

The size of the group is a crucial element in statistics. A group that is too small returns untrustworthy data. It is not difficult to see why this is so, looking at the simplest illustration of probability in action: the toss of a coin. Obviously, there is an exactly even chance that the coin will come up heads or tails. But if you tossed a coin ten times and got eight heads, you would only consider that rather good luck – if you happened to be calling heads. But if you tossed the same coin 100 times and got 80 heads you would consider that fantastic good luck, especially if you were calling heads. If you tossed it 1,000 times and got 800 heads, someone would ask to examine the coin, and rightly so. Even though the percentages are the same for each individual toss, the chances of tossing eight heads out of ten are quite good, but the chances of tossing 800 heads out of 1,000 extremely remote. This is common sense. It is not difficult to understand why this is so.

The same logic applies to the sample groups in statistics. In a group of 120 people, say, chance would have it that 10 people would be born with Mars in a given sector, or 20 people with Mars in a given pair of sectors.

If 30 people were born with Mars in a set of sectors it might appear significant (to a non-statistician) since 50% more people were born with Mars in a given pair of sectors than chance would allow. But this would not be the case in any reliable sense when the sample group is this small. Just as throwing heads eight times out of ten would be nothing remarkable. Statistics is a kind of mathematically justified common sense.

Gauquelin's group of 576 eminent doctors was large enough to give statistically significant results. So, when appreciably more than 16.7% of them were found to have been born with Mars and Saturn in the sectors representing the planet's rise and upper culmination or zenith (henceforth referred to as Sectors 1 and 4), factors other than chance became a possibility.

Gauquelin first checked to make sure that all known demographic and astronomical factors had been taken into consideration. Failure to do this had led many of the earlier would-be astrologer/statisticians astray. For example, births do not take place randomly around the clock. There is a pattern to births. In general, if births are allowed to take place naturally and are not induced, more babies are born in the morning than in the afternoon. This pattern has to be accounted for in the calculation of statistics for it can significantly raise or lower the levels that actually represent chance. Then, the location of the births will affect the calculations. One thousand births in Finland would require different treatment than 1,000 births in France. Astronomical factors such as the retrograde motion of planets and the path of their ellipses had to be factored in. But that done, Gauquelin's results were still highly significant.

In statistics, the odds against chance become degrees of significance. The degree of significance increases with the odds, and can be calculated. And the degree of significance is cumulative; multiplication rather than addition is involved.

For example: if the odds are correctly calculated, you have a 1 in 10 chance of winning if you pick a horse at 10–1. But the chances against picking two 10–1 winners in a row are not 20–1, but 10–1 multiplied by itself, or 100–1, and 1,000–1 against picking three 10–1 winners in a row. You don't actually need statistics to tell you that the odds against picking three 10–1 winners in a row are not good. Statistics formalize that correct intuition. A similar logic underpins the calculation of the odds for the position of planets in sectors. If the group is small, deviations are meaningless (unless they prove to be repeatable). If, however, the sample group is large enough, relatively small deviations from chance become statistically highly significant. Gauquelin's groups were mostly in the 500–1,000 range. In groups this size, a 20% deviation above or below chance takes place at odds of around 1,000,000–1 against chance.

This is precisely what Gauquelin found with his initial group of 576 eminent professors of medicine. A statistically highly significant number of the eminent doctors were born with Mars or Saturn in Sectors 1 and 4 (and lesser, but still significant numbers were born when Mars and Saturn were in the sectors directly opposite the rise and culmination. See Fig. 12).

Now it is a truism of statistics that if enough factors are tested for, sooner or later something is going to show up that looks statistically significant. There is always the possibility of a high-level fluke as it were. Or, put another way, even though the

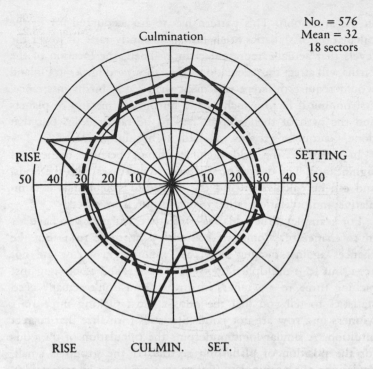

No. = 576
Mean = 32
18 sectors

Culmination

RISE

SETTING

50 40 30 20 10   10 20 30 40 50

RISE   CULMIN.   SET.

Figure 12. Members of the Académie de Médecine: Mars
Gauquelin's first positive evidence for the Mars Effect. This graph shows
the distribution of Mars in the horoscopes of 576 eminent French
medical professionals. If chance alone were involved, roughly 32 individuals would be born in each sector, and the graph would show a
ragged line roughly hugging the broken-line circle drawn at 32. It is the
pattern formed by the jagged points just after the rise, extending to near
the 50-circle culmination, and lesser extensions at the setting and nadir,
that alerts the statistician to the strong possibility of a non-random event.
A subsequent second test of 508 more eminent medical men produced a
quite similar star pattern (though this time without significant extensions
at the setting and nadir points) – (Fig. 13).

odds against winning the lottery are millions to one, somebody
wins the lottery.

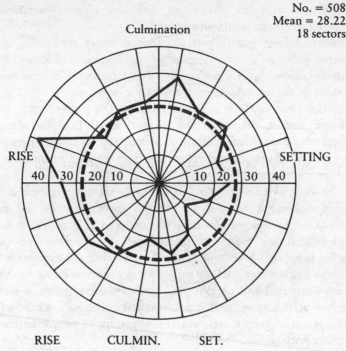

Culmination

RISE

SETTING

40 30 20 10   10 20 30 40

RISE   CULMIN.   SET.

Figure 13. Second group of doctors: Mars

Gauquelin did not discount that possibility. But the pilot study's results stood after all known mitigating factors had been taken into account. And two powerful indicators militated against a high-level fluke. The first was the definite pattern that emerged from the statistics when laid out on a chart, suggesting that a law or orderly process of some sort was involved. The second was the planets involved: Mars and Saturn. These were the two planets that traditional astrology would naturally equate with eminent physicians. The essential now was replication and a control, a test run on a similar sized group of non-physicians with birth-dates roughly corresponding to those of the 576 eminent physicians. In other words, if there was no special significance to the apparent correspondence between Mars/

Saturn and eminent physicians, ordinary citizens would be expected to return similar statistics.

Gauquelin set out to provide the necessary replication and control groups. A new group of 508 eminent doctors was gathered, along with a control group of ordinary citizens with birth-dates corresponding to those of the doctors.

In the charts of the ordinary citizens, the planets were distributed almost exactly at the chance level. But the second group of 508 eminent doctors produced results nearly identical to the original group, with Mars and Saturn again prominent in Sectors 1 and 4 (see Fig. 13).

The same planets appeared in the same sectors with the same highly significant frequency. Though these findings did not correspond to *any* specific current astrological practice, it was evident that the meanings traditionally assigned to the two planets involved (Mars and Saturn) were being substantiated, as was the importance of the 'angles', the cornerstone of houses. Much heartened and happily unaware of the treatment in store for him at the hands of his professional colleagues, Gauquelin now set out to gather data on sizeable groups of people eminent in other professions.

Poring through the French directories, Gauquelin selected the most eminent French figures from sport, acting, writing, journalism, the clergy, the military, science and art. He then proceeded to repeat the process required for the first groups. The letter-writing alone strained his meagre finances to the limit. As the replies came back, the horoscopes were calculated by hand, a laborious enterprise in those pre-computer days, and the results tabulated.

These dramatically substantiated and amplified the figures returned by the eminent medical men in a most intriguing fashion. Profession by profession, specific planets occupied key Sectors 1 and 4 in the Gauquelin charts at highly significant levels. Taken profession by profession, the odds involved ranged from thousands to one against chance to many millions to one against chance. But the planets involved also corresponded in the main to astrological tradition. It was not just any planet in

No. = 570
Mean = 31.67
18 sectors

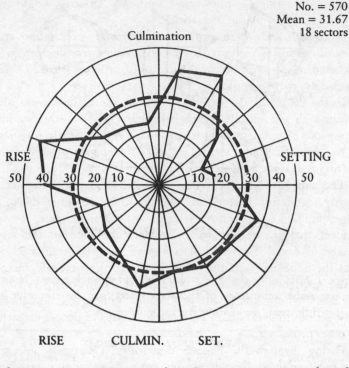

Sectors	1	2	3	4	5	6	7	8	9	10	11	12	13	14	15	16	17	18
Actual	41	47	28	24	23	42	46	27	18	26	37	33	33	32	37	29	25	22
Expected	33	34	33	33	32	31	31	31	30	30	30	30	31	31	32	32	33	33

Results

The diagram and the figures indicate how the positions of Mars at the birth of the 570 champions are distributed. There would be no need for a statistical test to be struck by the remarkable structure of the distribution. It forcefully repeats the observations made with the doctors. Like the Academicians, sports champions are born in large numbers when Mars occupies the zones of the sky which come after its rise, its culmination and to a lesser extent the opposite zones. Statistical analysis confirms that the observed distribution of Mars is significantly different from its theoretical distribution.

Figure 14. Well-known sportsmen: Mars

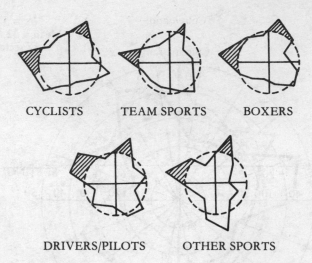

CYCLISTS   TEAM SPORTS   BOXERS

DRIVERS/PILOTS   OTHER SPORTS

Figure 15. Mars in the charts of athletes, broken into sub-groups. Notice the remarkable consistency of the Mars Effect 'star' pattern, with its characteristic strong peaks at the rise and culmination.

SPORTS	EXP. FREQ. 1 + 4	OBS. FREQ. 1 + 4	PROBABILITY
418 cyclists	71	89	1/50
390 team sports	67	87	1/200
307 air pilots and racing drivers	52	63	1/10
207 boxers and wrestlers	35	48	1/50
163 other sports	29	40	1/50

the key sectors but the planet or planets astrologers would expect to find there: Mars/Saturn for the doctors, Mars for the athletes, Mars/Jupiter for the military, the moon for writers, Saturn for the scientists and priests, Jupiter for the actors ... If these were chance results, they were roughly the equivalent of picking nine 100,000 to 1 long-shots in a row (Figs. 14–18).

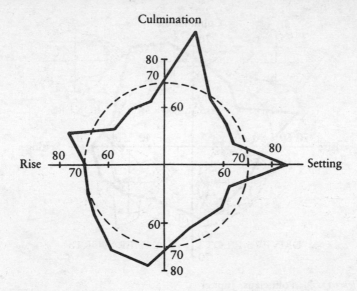

Figure 16. Jupiter in the charts of 1,270 European actors. The odds against chance: 1:500.

Meanwhile, a number of traditional correlations were not borne out. Mercury, traditionally associated with writing/journalism, did not show up above the chance level anywhere, nor did Venus, commonly associated with the arts. (More recent work proves a Venus correspondence, but not associated with a specific profession.) The 'new' planets, beyond the orbit of Saturn – Uranus, Neptune and Pluto also occurred at the chance level throughout.

The astrological significance of these results has been outrageously under-emphasized by Gauquelin's opponents (and, initially, for complex reasons we shall shortly come to, by Gauquelin himself). Nothing was found that did *not* correspond to astrological tradition, nor was anything found that contradicted astrological tradition. There were several surprises that no astrologer would have suspected, but that yet powerfully

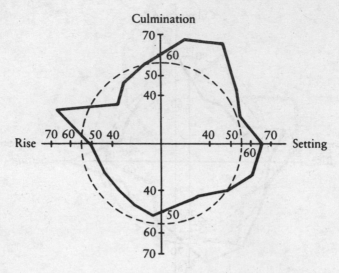

Figure 17. 993 Politicians: Jupiter.

corroborated traditional astrological understanding. For example, planets considered inimical to certain professions, such as Mars and Saturn to writers and artists, Jupiter to doctors and scientists, and the moon to athletes and soldiers were found *absent* from Sectors 1 and 4 (see Fig. 19).

The significance of these results dawned only gradually over the years, but can be summarized in a paragraph. It is not that Mars rising guarantees eminence in sports or the military, but rather that a planet rising or culminating tends to produce a certain personality type that *corresponds* to the requirements of certain professions. This is not to say that there is no such thing as a martial writer, or a moony boxer, but as a general rule, introspection and imagination are advantages in literature and disadvantages in boxing, while the kind of aggression associated with Mars is essential for sports but no great use in writing. So in the charts of eminent writers, Mars seemed to *flee* the angles, as it were, appearing there much *less* often than chance would dictate.

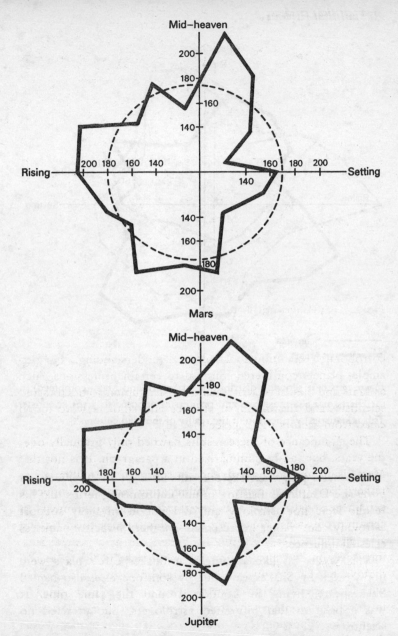

Figure 18. Mars and Jupiter in the charts of 3,142 military leaders.

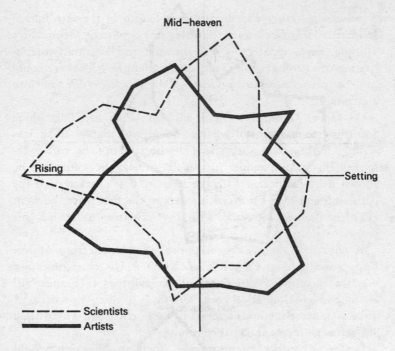

Figure 19. Chart showing distribution of Saturn and Mars (combined) in the charts of 2,048 musicians and painters as opposed to 3,305 scientists. This is statistical verification of the reality of the 'two cultures'.

Gauquelin published these results in 1955 in *L'influence des astres* (Le Dauphin), insisting in uncompromising terms that his results were not astrology and did not in any way support astrology, but rather represented another, hitherto nameless celestial influence.

This was a bit like arguing that Shakespeare's plays were not written by Shakespeare but by someone else, also named Shakespeare, living in London around the same time. It was a position that infuriated astrologers, but attracted no scientists.

The French popular press was moved to extensive coverage.

L'influence des astres was discussed at length in the astrological journals. However much astrologers deplored Gauquelin's attitude, here, apparently, was the first real scientific corroboration of astrology. But Gauquelin's scientific colleagues could not be provoked into reviewing the book, not even into attacking it.

As far as Gauquelin could tell, his work had been done according to the most rigorous modern standards. If he was wrong, if there was some facet of the situation he had overlooked that would render his results invalid, he wanted to be shown it by his peers. With the tenacity that characterized the gathering and calculations of his data in the first place, he went after the '*savants chevronés*' with the expertise to review his work.

Eventually an unwilling response was drawn from Marcel Boll, a well-known French science-writer. His chief objection was that Gauquelin had confined his inquiries to France. All Gauquelin had done, Boll contended, was to discover a national fluke. The same methods applied to other countries would yield altogether different and chance results.

Under any other circumstances, such an objection would have made Boll a laughing stock among his colleagues. The correlations uncovered by Gauquelin were statistically significant at levels of millions to one against chance regarded individually. But the agreement between the significator planet/profession with traditional astrology (Mars/athletes, Saturn/scientists, etc.) increased those odds exponentially. They were no longer proper to the lottery but rather occupied a number realm normally associated with astronomical phenomena or the United States budget deficit.

The fact that the data had been gathered in France was utterly irrelevant. Boll's objection was the statistical equivalent of the reasoning of *Alice in Wonderland*.

Professor Dauvillier, Professor of Cosmic Physics at the Collège de France, responded: 'If there is anything resembling a correlation, it can be nothing but a fluctuation showing that the group was insufficient.' This same savant had written elsewhere, 'those who are even the least advanced in natural philosophy will understand how fortuitous the astronomical and physical causes of our existence have been, and they will *refuse to examine* [italics ours] a link between the solar system and the human race.' (M. Gauquelin, *L'Astrologie devant le science*, Planète, 1966, p. 160).

A Belgian Committee (Le Comité Belge pour l'Investigation Scientifique des Phénomènes Réputés Paranormaux; mercifully referred to as the 'Para Committee' from now on) had been set up in 1949 expressly to objectively examine data purporting to prove the existence of paranormal phenomena. But this committee found itself too busy to study Gauquelin's work, though previously the astronomer Paul Couderc, a vitriolic opponent of astrology, had exulted in the fact that the Committee had been given so little work to do. Finally, Marcel Boll, who was also a Committee member, was goaded by Gauquelin into a reply. 'Your conclusions are nothing but pulp romances, the worst sort of proof, and the issue is without hope, for if you undertook the same inquiry in Great Britain, Germany, the USA and Russia you would come out with nothing but national idiosyncracies.'

Here was Alice again. The odds that Gauquelin's results represented a national fluke were almost incalculable. Even so, such odds were not unknown in science. They were, for example, the kind of odds routinely called into play in support of evolution as a chance process, which in turn creates something of a philosophical and scientific dilemma. It can mean that the realization of such odds does in fact take place in this vast universe of ours and is, indeed, responsible for us human beings being here (see Professor Dauvillier above), or, alternatively, it can mean that scientists will believe anything.

It was, therefore, not absolutely inconceivable that Gauquelin had stumbled across a statistical aberration occurring at almost inconceivable odds against chance. Despite the work involved, Gauquelin had little choice but to answer the challenge.

Gauquelin, now working with his assistant (subsequently his wife, subsequently his ex-wife) Françoise, now took the European countries nearest to hand, and assembled extensive lists of eminent people in the designated professions, following the procedure of the earlier work. Free time and vacations were devoted to travel to Italy, Germany, Belgium and the Netherlands (England did not record the hour of birth at that time and so data could not be collected) poring through the archives for birth certificates – not everybody's idea of spending vacations.

After a few years, the total sample of eminent professionals had grown to over 25,000, spread over nine professions culled from five countries; a massive survey by any recognized statistical standard. The results of this new study very closely matched those of the French groups. The same planets appeared in the same key sectors againt similar odds, but with variations that could genuinely be called reflections of national idiosyncracies.

Humor is as infrequently associated with statistics as is heroism, but there was something droll about the way Gauquelin's statistics reinforced certain stereotypical portraits.

Mars, for example, was prominent in Sectors 1 and 4 in the charts of soldiers, no matter what their nationalities. But Italian soldiers had Mars in the key sectors far more often than did German soldiers. Superficially this might seem counter to expectations. Who would say that the Italians were more warlike than the Germans? (A joke making the rounds not so long ago listed *The Complete Encyclopedia of Italian War Heroes* among the world's shortest books.) The lesson hidden in the figures was that the Germans did not particularly need Mars on the angles to make soldiers of them, while the Italians needed an overdose. Along the same lines, when great women athletes were considered separately from the men, the frequency of Mars in Sectors 1 and 4 was higher – suggesting that the women needed 'more Mars' as it were, to make champion athletes of them.

It is worth stressing the extraordinary regularity and repetitiousness of these results. The same planets invariably showed up in the same sectors for the same professions. It was not just

Mars in Sectors 1 and 4 for athletes most of the time, or in certain countries, but invariably; Saturn invariably showed up in the charts of the scientists. Mars and Saturn invariably *fled* the angles in the charts of actors, painters, writers and journalists. Not one of these results contradicted the most ancient and most basic assertions of astrology. The only unastrological element involved was the lack of significance shown by the sun, Mercury, Venus and the outer planets. The chart below breaks down these planetary significances for the test professional groups.

Here are some of the odds involved:

Planet	Number	Profession	Expected frequency	Actual frequency	Odds against
Mars	3,305	Scientists	565	666	1:500,000
Mars	3,142	Military	535	634	1:1,000,000
Jupiter	3,142	Military	525	644	1:5,000,000
Mars	1,485	Athletes	253	327	1:5,000,000

Not only did the same planets show up associated with the same professions but there was a broad agreement in the level of the odds as well, from country to country. The Mars/athletes correlation was very high everywhere, the moon/writer correlation rather lower. There was a certain common sense element involved in these degrees of significance as well. Of all the professions in the survey, sport is the one with the fewest opportunities for unmerited success. Artists, journalists, politicians, actors and clerics often seem to succeed with little apparent talent for their calling. Famous writers have little in common characterologically except their writing. But there is a real singleness of purpose to athletics (however different the sports themselves) that makes athletes a much more homogeneous group; the same applies to scientists. The Gauquelin figures bore out these common-sense observations.

Though all Gauquelin's planetary correspondences were statistically highly significant, it was the Mars/athlete figures that somehow caught the attention of the public, and this in turn has bestowed a name upon Gauquelin's work in general. To both opponents and supporters, it is called 'The Mars Effect'.

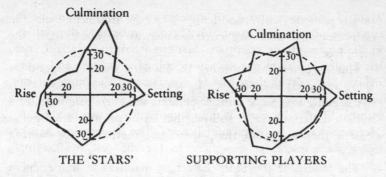

Figure 20. Stars and supporting players. Gauquelin compared the positions of Jupiter in the charts of 604 European 'star'-calibre actors, and 661 lesser-known professionals. The left-hand 'star' chart shows the familiar star pattern with Jupiter strongly prominent in Sectors 1 and 4, following the rise and culmination. One hundred and thirty-four actors were born with Jupiter in these sectors as opposed to the 100.5 predicted by chance, (1:5,000 odds). The peaks have all but disappeared in the right-hand chart (118 times intead of 110.2 – not statistically significant). Effectively identical results were produced with all Gauquelin's professional groups. Only the most eminent displayed the Mars Effect.

Meanwhile, Gauquelin had been running his sample group against control groups of non-specialized people. Invariably, and without any exceptions, the control groups provided data at the chance level.

But when Gauquelin used as a control a sample group of people within a given profession but not eminent, the results were also chance; not even weakly significant. At first glance (see Fig. 20) this seems an extraordinary situation. Critics of Gauquelin's work, desperately looking for some flaw in it that might allow them to retain their Rationalist superstitions, have seized upon this curious circumstance, pretending that in some fashion it nullifies the positive results. Why should the second-stringers and the second-raters not have the same planets in the same sectors, they argue? They are also professionals though run-of-the-mill. If the second-raters don't produce a similar planetary correspondence – goes the argument – that can only mean the planetary correspondences do not exist in the first place.

This argument has nothing to do with science, beyond its being advanced by scientists. Its apparent logic is illusory. It is like arguing that since famous painters sell their paintings for a million dollars apiece, it follows that lesser painters must get at least a thousand, and that, therefore, there are no starving artists.

The failure of the Mars Effect to manifest in non-eminent professionals is actually a spurious curiosity. To begin with, the test is repeatable: the Mars effect only occurs among people eminent in their field, in every field. It can also be explained statistically. It is not that famous athletes show the Mars Effect at odds of millions to one against chance and second-stringers don't show any correlation at all. It's not cut and dried that way, even though the figures make it seem so. The Mars Effect corresponds to eminence, but deciding what constitutes eminence statistically involves a choice. In making his original selections, Gauquelin set up certain objective criteria. His eminent people had to be included in certain yearbooks or directories devoted to the field. Then the top performers were chosen from this large group. In such a process the top represents no problem. The top people are obvious. But there comes a certain point in which a decision must be made between who is 'eminent' and who is not. Gauquelin never found a way to make the decision absolutely clear-cut. This grey area has therefore been used by Gauquelin's opponents to cast doubts upon his methodology.

Göttingen University psychologist Suitbert Ertel recently studied the possibility of unconscious or deliberate selection errors in Gauquelin's work ('Grading the Eminence, or Raising the hurdle for the athletes' Mars Effect', *Journal of Scientific Exploration*, Pergamon, 1988). Ertel found that when the data was subjected to more refined analysis the Mars Effect was powerfully enhanced, and the apparent discrepancy between the eminent and the non-eminent could be explained away (Ertel's study is discussed in detail on pp. 302–8).

The massive European replication of the original French data took up the next five years of the Gauquelins' lives. Though Gauquelin was obliged to pay the printing costs out of his own pocket, the book was published as *Les Hommes et les astres* (Denoël, 1960) and treated to a reception that Gauquelin ultimately learned to anticipate.

After the Mars Effect

Meanwhile, Gauquelin's work was coming to the attention of astrologers outside France. A small number of these had equipped themselves with a thorough grasp of statistics permitting deeper analysis of the voluminous Gauquelin data – available to all who asked. In person, they also found Gauquelin less uncompromising about traditional astrology than he seemed in print. Though they might have preferred less derisive public language, Gauquelin's interest was in astrology as a possible science. Upon that basis he was certainly justified in making the clear distinction between what was proved and what wasn't. What was proved was the 'Mars Effect', a relationship between planets and eminence in certain professions. What was not proved was all the rest of astrology.

But with or without the kiss of scientific approval, Gauquelin's results called for study. It was clear to all knowledgeable astrologers, as well as to Gauquelin himself, that the Mars Effect could not be an isolated or meaningless phenomenon, an orderly glitch in the otherwise random heavens. Less clear was what the statistics signified.

The Gauquelins were led to two chief areas of inquiry: first, determining the nature of the personality traits associated with the planets, and, second, establishing the planetary or astrological basis of heredity. These studies have occupied most of Gauquelin's time the past twenty years; along with his uphill, unflagging, time-consuming and frustrating crusade to get his impeccably prepared results reviewed, critiqued and recognized by his professional peers.

The Planets and Personality

Gauquelin's statistics had incontrovertibly established links between planets and eminence in certain professions. The recurrence of planets in a number of professions (and recurrent negative significance in others) made it clear that this link was a personality factor, not a direct correspondence. In other words, the statistics did not mean that Mars in Sectors 1 or 4 allowed an astrologer to predict that a child born with that configuration would be an Olympic Gold-Medalist or a Four-Star General. Roughly one out of six children is born with Mars in Sectors 1 or 4. What seemed to be indicated was a kind of planetary personality, that, all else being equal and/or propitious, would further or provoke eminence in certain professional fields for certain gifted individuals.

Now this was hardly a new idea. The astrological tradition equates the putative natures or qualities of the planets with the human personality and human affairs. It is a concept so thoroughly imbued in everyday language that we forget its planetary origins – the 'martial' arts, a 'jovial' gathering, a 'saturnine' mien, a 'venereal' disease, a 'mercurial' disposition, a 'lunatic' notion, and so on . . .

Surfacing up through the impersonal numbers of the statistics was a verification of the planetary archeypes: the martial, jovial, saturnine, and lunar (creative/imaginative) personalities. The Mars Effect proved that different planets played statistically significant roles in the specific professions with which traditional astrology associated them. But there was still nothing to really prove that there was a difference between the Mars personality and the Moon personality, or between the Jupiter personality, and the Saturn personality. Universal common sense experience assures us that there is a very real personality difference between writers and athletes (just as everyone knows there is a difference between Swedes and Spaniards), but who can prove it? From the scientific point of view, without proof, there is no difference. Gauquelin was looking for a way to give quantitative expression to the planetary archetypes in such a way that it stood as scientific proof.

Poring through the written accounts of his eminent professionals, Gauquelin was struck by the way in which the same words recurred again and again in the biographical descriptions his data was drawn from. The same athlete would be described over and over as 'iron-willed', 'determined', 'impossible to deter' and so on, while another (atypical) champion might be described as 'easy-going' 'non-competitive' . . .

Language is of course notoriously deceptive, subjective and impossible to quantify on the individual level. Everybody will place a slightly different meaning on practically every word in the language, especially those carrying an emotional message. 'Love' means something different to everyone, and yet everyone is in a kind of general agreement as to what 'love' means. Otherwise, the song-writers would be out of business. So if a dozen different biographers describe a certain eminent doctor as 'generous' they will certainly all place slightly different personal connotations on the word. But it was unlikely that, given a dozen different accounts, six would call the doctor 'generous' while the other six would call him 'stingy'. In reality, what happened was that a few might call him 'generous', a few others 'magnanimous', still others 'benevolent' and still others, perhaps, taking a negative view, 'grandiose' or even 'pompous'.

But out of these written accounts, a definite picture of a whole personality emerged. This rough agreement suggested to Gauquelin it might be possible to undertake a statistical linguistic survey of these written accounts of his eminent professional groups which would then yield the quantitative corroboration he sought; the definitive link between certain types of personality and the individual planets.

Gauquelin decided to focus on the four professions that gave the most clear-cut indications of a single planetary correspondence: atheletes/Mars, scientists/Saturn, actors/Jupiter and writers/moon. If there was anything to his hypothesis, analysis of the biographical detail should provide objective descriptions of the four distinct personality types: martial, jovial, saturnine and lunar.

Gauquelin first set up personality profiles for 'typical' athletes, actors, scientists and writers, drawing from psychological and other studies. Upon the basis of these profiles, 'trait-words' were chosen that best matched the profile. Obviously, given the nature of the study and the subjectivity of language to begin with, there is a certain messiness and overlap to such a procedure. Nevertheless, at a certain point, the sheer weight of numbers begins to tell. (Questions about the objectivity of this process often arise, and cannot be answered briefly. Details of the methodology can be found in Gauquelin's recent book, *Birthtimes* [*The Truth About Astrology in the UK*]. Since Gauquelin's methods have been examined in the minutest detail by opponents determined to debunk him, the failure to fault the methodology of the character-trait study is a fair indication that it cannot be faulted).

To nobody's surprise, 'energy', 'tenacity', 'courage', a 'will of iron' and 'aggression' were descriptive words commonly applied to the great athlete; the great actor turned out to be 'vain', 'talkative', 'funny', 'theatrical', 'expansive', 'elegant', 'outgoing', while the famous scientist was 'scrupulous', 'methodical', 'quiet', 'precise', 'introverted'. The writer was 'sensitive', 'witty', 'subtle', 'impressionable', 'capricious', 'imaginative', 'communicative'.

This method of developing a profile, at once ingenious and yet obvious, had its own built-in system of cross-checks and balances: the anti-profile. What about the 'introspective' actor and the 'gregarious' scientist; the 'aggressive' writer and the 'moony' athlete? If Gauquelin's hypothesis was correct, the 'typical' athelete with the Mars personality would have Mars in Sectors 1 and 4 significantly often, while the atypical athletes would *not* show this correspondence.

Moreover, the planetary types should be detectable whatever their profession. In other words, if the *locus* of trait-words suggested that an eminent actor was not typically Jupiterian but actually Saturnine this should be detectable statistically.

The results precisely bore out these expectations. The athletes whose profiles were typically 'martial' according to the biographical material, had Mars rising or culminating to a highly significant degree; ditto for actors and Jupiter, scientists and Saturn and writers and the moon. By the same token, when the atypical professionals were extracted from the sample and collated in separate groups ('martial' actors, writers and scientists together; 'lunar' actors, athletes and scientists together, etc.), these corresponded statistically to the planetary type revealed by their profiles. The 'martial' actors, writers and scientists had Mars rising or culminating, just as did the martial athletes, and the same correspondences applied to the other planets. In all instances, the odds ran 100,000 : 1 against chance, or better. (Gauquelin also found evidence of a Venus personality, corresponding closely to the traditional Venus qualities. But this Venus type corresponded to no specific profession, making it relatively elusive and difficult to study. From the astrologers' point of view this is important evidence, another of tradition's basic building-blocks corroborated.)

A repetition of the character-trait experiment on famous Americans was carried out in 1980. It produced nearly identical results.

The Planets and Heredity

The character-trait experiments occupied most of the 1970s for the Gauquelins and extended or fleshed-out the earliest work that established relations between planets and professions. We described them in sequence because thematically the one follows from the other.

But, chronologically, most of the 1960s were devoted to another massive astrological experiment with a different focus: a study of possible astrological relationships between parents and children. The result was to prove the reality of 'astral heredity' – a definitive link between the position of planets in the birth-charts of parents and children, a rediscovery with far-reaching implications – not only for astrology. The results were published in Michel Gauquelin's *L'Hérédité planetaire* (Denoël, 1965). An updated English translation was published in 1988 by ACS under the title *Planetary Heredity*. This important publication is Gauquelin's most exhaustive work to date, spelling out in detail both his methodology and his data. The English translation finally overcomes the language barrier for English-speaking readers interested in personally investigating Gauquelin's work.

Like almost everything in astrology, the notion of astral heredity was not new. Astrologers believe astrology is implied in this statement made by Hippocrates 2,500 years ago: 'When the time comes, the baby stirs and breaks the membranes containing it and emerges from its mother's abdomen.' If so, Hippocrates doubtless had that information from earlier sources. Ptolemy, 500 years later, rephrased the idea in incontrovertible astrological language and Kepler believed he could demonstrate it empirically, comparing his own chart to his mother's. Choisnard and Krafft also believed they had established empirical demonstrations of the ancient idea.

Though Gauquelin had earlier exposed the technical errors made by Choisnard and Krafft invalidating conclusions drawn from their experiments, this did not mean the basic idea was wrong, only their procedures. Apart from the intrinsic attraction of astral heredity as a concept, it also seemed to have a methodological advantage from the Gauquelin point of view. There would be no need to scour the countryside tracking down birth certificates of the eminent. A large enough group of ordinary citizens was all that was required. But as it turned out, Gauquelin was not to be let off easily (Gauquelin is never let off easily!). In France, for reasons of privacy, it was not permitted to draw *en masse* from the birth registers. Special authorization had to be obtained, and of course no hint could be given that astrology was involved. 'Demographic research' was the term employed. While the birth-times of children posed no vast problem in principle once permissions were obtained, getting quantities of birth-dates and birth-times for their parents was another matter. But as it happened, since 1923, French law had required recording the birth-dates and birth-times of parents on their children's birth certificates. This was a piece of gratuitous bureaucracy that could probably only occur in France. It is difficult to imagine a rationale behind it – outside of some wondrous, precognitive, karmic link between the forgotten bureaucrat responsible for writing the law into the rulebook and Gauquelin's subsequent research. So, though laborious in the extreme, the research required at least stopped short of masochism.

The fact that the experiment dealt with ordinary citizens added to its attraction. Gauquelin's critics had ridiculed an astrological effect that applied only to the famous. From a true scientific point of view, given Gauquelin's data and flawless methodology, this was criticism on the same *Alice in Wonderland* level as the national fluke objection. Nevertheless, there *was* something emotionally or artistically unsettling about an effect that applied only to the famous.

With 30,000 birth-times collected and 30,000 horoscopes calculated (twice to make sure!) by hand, Gauquelin was ready to start his study. (The computer now makes the computations effortless, of course.) As in the planet/profession experiment, the traditional relationships – sun signs, planets in signs, mutually recurring aspects – were not statistically significant. But when Gauquelin applied the methodology of the planet/personality experiments, strong positive results appeared.

When parents had specific planets in key Sectors 1 and 4, their children tended to be born with the same planets in one of those sectors. When both parents had the same planet there, the chances that the child would have it there as well was doubled. On days following intense solar flares, when the earth's magnetosphere was especially turbulent, the relationships were much stronger. The most significant planet was the moon, followed by Venus and Mars, with Jupiter and Saturn less strong but still statistically significant. The odds against Gauquelin's results being due to chance were more than 1,000,000 : 1.

These statistically significant planetary relationships between parents and children corroborated the spirit if not the letter of Kepler's observations. As with other Gauquelin findings, astrologers were upset to find no evidence corroborating *any* element of the zodiac. But at least a fundamental astrological assumption had been demonstrated, and astrologers were not altogether taken by surprise.

The same cannot be said for geneticists and doctors, though the Gauquelin study provided a certain rationale for a fact that otherwise had no rationale at all. Thirty years ago, the notion that a child chooses its moment of birth was as unthinkable as was the notion of an energetic atom 100 years earlier. Over the past few decades, however, the medical profession has gradually come round to a kind of tacit acceptance of this particular old wives' tale. There is a mysterious timing element to childbirth, and it is the child who chooses when to come out into this world. Birth involves an act of *volition*. In a lifeless, unconscious, purposeless world that is all mechanism and no mechanism-maker, there is little room for unmeasurable, unquantifiable and unrepeatable volition to begin with (except perhaps for the 'will' to discover the objective truth about this meaningless-world). When that volition is shown to be linked to planetary positions in the charts of parents, the bright light cast by this revelation picks out deep fissures in the vaunted smooth façade of the Church of Progress.

There is, clearly, a mechanism involved. Just as Mozart's genius is transmitted mechanically (instruments, sound-waves) and received mechanically (vibrating eardrum activating auditory nerves) and then retranslated – by something that is beyond mechanism – into emotion, so in this instance, there is bound to be some hormonal/nervous physical mechanism that serves as receiver/transmitter of impulses, whatever form these might take. Though as essential as the instruments are to the music, the mechanism is secondary (there would be no flute if there were no music to play on it, while the music can and does exist in the composer's head and heart independent of an instrument). What is most important is what is being transmitted. And what is being transmitted astrologically is, as in Mozart's music, *meaning*.

The discovery of this planetary link to heredity also had its own built-in control. The data suggested that it was the baby who somehow initiated or mediated the process. If that conclusion was correct, then births that were other than natural – by Caesarean section, or drug-induced – should no longer show an astrological affinity to their parents.

This was precisely the case. The charts of babies whose births were induced (by *any* method) no longer showed a correspondence to the charts of their parents. This control was important from the astrological viewpoint, because it was so straightforward. It was not only Gauquelin's opposition who had trouble accepting the earlier findings – when the second-stringers in a given profession showed no planetary correspondence, and the eminent did. Until the Ertel analysis mentioned earlier and discussed later on (see pp. 302–8), astrologers also had trouble accepting and understanding these results. In the heredity experiments the results were clear-cut. Under natural circumstances there was a highly significant statistical correspondence between the birth charts of parents and children. This correspondence disappeared when births were unnatural or induced in any way, in effect proving that the positive data could not have been a fluke.

The heredity data poses intriguing metaphysical, philosophical and medical questions – what is this 'choice' that the fetus makes? On what level of consciousness does it occur? What mechanisms permit the baby to effectively control the complex birth-process? And so on. But Gauquelin's data also poses questions with immediate practical consequences. Since there is a link between planets and personality and also a link between planets and heredity, it is safe to postulate a natural psychological bond between parents and children that is in some real if indefinable sense astrologically determined. Obviously, there are many cases today where the doctor must interfere with the birth process to prevent damage or even death. But when that astrological link is deliberately and unnecessarily broken it would seem bound to result in an estrangement between parents and children. In other words, doctors should not tamper with the birth process if not medically essential.

Science Responds

Astronomer Andrew Fraknoi, of the Astronomical Society of the Pacific, described the Gauquelin experiment in an article entitled 'Scientific tests debunk astrology', a contribution to *Astronomy and Astrology*, a pamphlet distributed by the Astronomical Society of the Pacific.

Since Fraknoi has denied us permission to quote, we must again prevail on the jury to accept on trust our account of his account. According to Fraknoi, Gauquelin examined 3,923 parent–child horoscopes looking for astrological correlations. The study included a variety of astrological factors beyond the familiar 'sun signs'. But the results of Gauquelin's inquiry were wholly negative. There was no correspondence between astrology and heredity, declared Fraknoi.

The Saga of the Data

The credibility of witnesses is often a factor in deciding cases at law. In attacking astrology, the Prosecution commonly prefers opprobrium to evidence: calling astrology's adherents idiots or semi-literate (see pp. 144, 146) or depicting them as timorous, confused individuals who turn to astrology as a refuge from uncertainty and the harsh facts of reality. Since he has no evidence at his disposal, Martin Gardner (pp. 435–7) impugns psychologist H. J. Eysenck's credibility in order to repudiate Gauquelin. In the Fraknoi example above, the scholarly weapon of preference is the bare-faced lie. It is employed with impunity, secure in the knowledge that the scientific community will not object, and the belief that the lay public will not detect it.

Strictly speaking, our case can be presented without descending to such tactics. Leaving all other evidence aside, Gauquelin's evidence speaks for itself. It has been subjected to exhaustive scrutiny by critics determined to discredit it. It has passed every test to date. Until or unless invalidated, it is safe to assert that the premise of astrology stands as proved.

But acceptance of that proof by science and, by extension, the general educated public, presents an altogether different problem.

It is, of course, our own belief that astrology, consciously employed, may play a vital role in individual spiritual development and in the destiny of humanity as a whole. If this is correct, the saga of the Gauquelin data becomes more than a harrowing tale of survival by a determined heretic. Put another way, it doesn't matter a damn to our daily lives, or to our inner emotional state, if there has been Continental Drift or not, or what the age of the universe may be, or for that matter if the earth is round or flat. But if astrology is valid, if it can actually be *used* by those pursuing a spiritual path, then its future becomes a matter of both personal and social significance, and the credibility and integrity of its opponents deserves investigation.

This investigation coincidentally serves to illuminate Culver and Ianna's optimistic assertion that science is unbiased even though scientists are not.

Thirty years after the fact, Gauquelin admits that a 'profound naivety' fueled his expectations of a fair review of his initial results by his peers. Gauquelin believed wholeheartedly that his impeccable credentials and the rigor of his methodology would earn him a hearing. But anyone acquainted with the history of science should have known better. Practically every major scientific advance has been accepted only over the course of time, and over the massed, bitter opposition of defenders of the current dogma, whatever that happens to be. In science this is the rule, not the exception. And this rule is occasionally recognized even by scientists, especially by those who have tried to run a genuinely new idea past their colleagues. As the great physicist Max Planck observed years back: new ideas do not take hold in science because of the weight of the evidence. What happens is that opponents of the old idea eventually die off and a new generation that has grown up with the new idea and is comfortable with it embraces it. Here is a more recent observation of the same phenomenon, in response to an article defending scientific orthodoxy and open-mindedness.

Unorthodox Ideas
Phillip Gething draws a clear distinction between 'well-read scientist with original views' and 'cranks'. ('Calling all cranks', *Forum*, 4,

November). In real life things often may not look that obviously demarcated.

It is important to apprehend the typical difficulties which almost any new idea faces in trying to get published. It is a rather general and deeply rooted phenomenon that a substantial segment of the scientific establishment is at best utterly unreceptive and at worst openly hostile to a profoundly new idea or approach. It happened not in the 'dark Middle Age' but around 1977 that Mitchell Feigenbaum could not publish his epochal ideas on the universality in chaos for a few years because of repetitive rejects from several major physical journals. Similarly, it took me 10 rejects to publish an idea of isotopic fibre-optics as an alternative to the conventional fibre-optics ... There are numerous other examples of the same phenomenon at virtually all levels of scientific significance. It is a popular misconception that the world is overpopulated by all sorts of cranks eager to flood all literature with their crazy ideas. In fact the number of such individuals is amazingly low. The overall per-person impact of these 'cranks' on the scientific progress could, in fact, be well above average for the so-called 'normal' science ...

Alexander A. Berezin, Department of Engineering Physics, McMaster University, Hamilton, Ontario, Canada
(*New Scientist*, 16 December 1989)

This is, of course, a shameful state of affairs in a discipline whose stated interest is the discovery of 'the objective truth'. And even when acknowledged, no one ever seems to ask what is responsible for it. But there is a very simple psychological reason behind it, altogether unrecognized by science and, generally, barely intuited and seldom voiced even by those who regard science with less than the proscribed adulation.

Unless we have successfully passed through a spiritually oriented training designed to teach us to master our egos, that is what controls us: our ego. This is so normal and ordinary that we accept it as the way things are and must be. So the athlete's ego is bound up in winning. When he loses, his inner world comes apart and he's unhappy. The businessman's ego is bound up in success. When he goes broke, it's not just the loss of money that gets at him; it's the loss of face, and he despairs. The scientist pretends that he is interested in the objective truth. But if that were the case, new, even outrageous theories would meet with no emotional opposition. The evidence would be weighed objectively, and if the evidence called for the abandonment of the reigning thinking on the subject, there would be no fuss about it. But the history of science and academia in general proves that this is *never* the case. New theories are accepted only after bitter arguments and acrimony on all sides. Scientists and their apologists find all manner of excuses to account for this, including calling the process 'healthy debate'. But they avoid approaching the real issue.

The scientist and his spiritual blood-brother, the pedant, are not interested in the truth at all; or rather, they are interested in it only in so far as it supports the view they are already committed to. They are interested in being right. Their egos are entirely bound up in their rightness and can brook no opposition. If the scientist is proved wrong, effectively he ceases to exist since he has nothing else to call his own beyond his ego. This is of course the case for the athlete and the businessman as well, and for most of us. The difference is that not all of us are hypocrites about it. The athlete knows he wants to win, and the businessman makes no bones about his need for success. But the scientist pretends it is the truth that motivates his efforts.

Thus science is probably the only major profession in the twentieth century that is hypocritical at its core. And it is this that accounts for the otherwise inexplicable opposition that greets any new theory, even those that do not carry any apparent emotional freight. How, for example, can sane, rational people get excited about whatever it may have been that was responsible for the demise of the dinosaurs? What difference can it possibly make? To anyone? But the headline in the Science Section of the *New York Times* (19 January 1988) reads: 'The Debate Over Dinosaur Extinctions Takes an Unusually Rancorous Turn' – suggesting in turn that rancor is usual, merely heightened over this particular question.

But though rancor may indeed be usual in establishing any

new theory, two unique elements distinguish the Gauquelin saga from other major scientific breakthroughs.

The first is the implications of his evidence, which undermine the very foundations of Rationalism, in a manner even more unmistakable than the New Physics. We shall return to this under Implications (p. 313). The second is the manner in which Gauquelin has carried on his campaign over the years.

A Statistician, He Would A-Wooing Go

There can be no doubt that Gauquelin's lack of respect for most astrologers was and remains real. He has no use for the misty, uncritical, slightly hysterical metaphysics that pervades the typical astrology convention. It is also fair to say that the deeper underlying metaphysics of astrology, that aspect of it that engaged the minds of Plato, Plotinus and Kepler is not his chief interest either – though the implications of his work take him inexorably in that direction as the years go by.

Nevertheless, his fierce attacks upon astrology (as opposed to astrologers) were not entirely straightforward, even from the beginning. Gauquelin now admits that really, behind all his efforts, was the hope that he would find a valid scientific basis to astrology; that the weight of his accumulated evidence would vindicate, at least in principle, astrology as a potential *science*. Yet his early books read as though he had set out specifically to disprove astrology only to stumble across the Mars Effect accidentally. That impression was created deliberately. But this has only complicated the question of recognition; it has not eased it.

Gauquelin describes his initial disenchantment with astrology: 'like being betrayed by a lover'. And there can be no doubt that, early on, Science replaced astrology in Gauquelin's affections. He understood correctly that he could not hope to win favor with his new amour if she suspected any lingering nostalgia for her former rival (lovers are like that), hence the savage denunciations of astrology.

But Gauquelin courted his new flame no less blind to her

true nature. Despite the reception of his first book, in subsequent works he was still addressing Science as though she might be seduced by truth and billets-doux.

> We reject from the onset occult explanations, according to which the planet, at its rising, 'casts a spell' more or less immaterial or symbolic upon the newly-born, a spell which will follow at his feet the duration of his life, and will decide his destiny. Such aphorisms are of no interest, for in science one cannot propose hypotheses except that they be firmly material, limited, and precise.
>
> M. Gauquelin, *L'Astrologie devant le science*,
> Planète, 1966, p. 168

Surely, these should have been sweet words to Science. Yet Science saw right through them, evidently calling upon intuitive powers that, according to her deepest convictions, do not exist.

By whatever name Gauquelin chose to call his rose, Science smelled a rat. The people so fond of shoving the truth down the unwilling throats of others could not be induced into swallowing it themselves, even though it came to them carefully sugar-coated on a spoon.

In retrospect, probably the titles of Gauquelin's books alone were enough to alert Science to his dishonorable intentions. *L'influence des astres, Les Hommes et les astres . . .*! His suspicious, saturnine vestal resisted seduction with the outraged indignation befitting a medieval maiden.

Astrologers, on the other hand, reacted like Rationalists, taking every word at face value, and never questioning Gauquelin's motives. Again, in retrospect, as astrologers, certain subtleties of the situation should have been deducible.

Even if they were unaware of Gauquelin's early astrological interests (never mentioned in his earlier books, but finally revealed in *Cosmic Influences on Human Behavior*; see Confession in the Form of a Prologue, pp. 17–20) they should have been tipped off to his real motives by his birthdate, 13 November 1928.

For here was the archetypal Scorpio at work – no matter that

A. Statistical Evidence

Gauquelin's statistics have thus far failed to verify sun signs, and Gauquelin himself repudiates their validity, at least in print.

> ... there is an unwavering devotion to principles ... the sign is extremely thoroughgoing ... there is usually courage and also energy and capacity for toil in the pursuit of any aim which claims the native's devotion ... They do nothing by halves, and having once selected their course in life, pursue it relentlessly ... *They excel as detectives, inspectors, and investigators of all kinds* ... [italics ours].
>
> C. E. O. Carter,
> *The Principles of Astrology*, p. 75

> Beware of trying to pull the wool over a Scorpio's eyes. The 'Scorpion sting' may be the result ... Scorpios have strong passions which run deep and *often silently* [our italics]. They have strong energies which, when channelled, can give great qualities of endurance ...
>
> Mary Orser, Rick and Glory Brightfield,
> *Instant Astrology*, ACS Publications, p. 12

It would be difficult to find a more typical Scorpio. Gauquelin could be the prototype for the standard description. (Incidentally, it is this kind of correspondence, by no means uncommon, that makes astrologers so loath to abandon their belief in the validity of sun signs and their corresponding astrological archetypes, whatever the statistics show.) In classical, traditional astrology, Scorpios are legendary not only for their determination but also their deviousness. Passionate disclaimers to the contrary, Gauquelin's ultimate aim was to *prove*, not disprove, astrology. Yet, the astrologers failed to see through his typical Scorpio ruse. They took his jibes and insults at face value, in retrospect, justifying the jibes and insults. If the astrologers really could delineate and predict character on the basis of the horoscope, they should have been able to discern Gauquelin's true motive. His time and hour of birth were available. (In our first edition we finished our essay on Gauquelin calling him 'L'Astrologue malgré lui'. He had us fooled, too.)

In the Footsteps of Javert

As detective work, Gauquelin's data (and statistics in general) represent some 90% Javert and only 10% Holmes. The realization that trait-words could be used for statistical verification provides the Holmesian element in Gauquelin's life work, but most of the rest is pure Javert, the relentless pursuit of a quarry. And a lucky thing for astrology! For the same determination that allowed Gauquelin to assemble his data in the first place has allowed him to weather thirty years of massed opposition with rarely ruffled equanimity.

The annals of the Church of Progress are replete with shameful stories. But Gauquelin has been subjected to Inquisitorial procedures extreme even by its normal unprincipled standards. The opposition is not dealing here with an obvious crank like Van Däniken, or a best-selling enthusiast like Velikovsky; Gauquelin's work has been performed meticulously according to universally accepted scientific codes. Yet, Gauquelin's attempts to get his data reviewed, criticized and replicated by his scientific peers, have been met by evasion, abuse, calumny, neglect, deliberate lies and finally, in all probability, fraud. The saga is by no means over. Following are its highlights, or lowlights as the case may be . . .

Gauquelin and the Para Committee

The late Paul Couderc, astronomer at the Paris observatory, and one of astrology's most dedicated opponents, wrote in 1951:

> If the stars are an important factor in the personality of each individual, and played a part, *however small*, in the formation of bodily and spiritual characters, along with all the thousands of other factors which shape his destiny (heredity, environment, chance . . .) then it would be an incalculably valuable property. One could try and apply it for the good of mankind.
>
> Paul Couderc, *L'Astrologie* (PUF, Paris, 1951 edn.)

Couderc claimed that scientists were ready to examine claims of astrological correspondences, but complained that the various commissions set up for that purpose had been given no work to do.

Gauquelin writes,

> Spurred by this challenge, I sent my book to a number of people, including those on the commissions of control, and Paul Couderc himself. None of them replied, and I was to continue to bombard them for months, years even, until eventually I did get a reaction. But Couderc, between 1955 [when Gauquelin's first book was published] and his death in 1980, remained completely silent. The fact that he occasionally pronounced on my works in public was my sole confirmation that he had ever received them . . .

> *Birthtimes*, p. 98

Gauquelin's efforts focused in on the Para Committee, mentioned earlier, whose motto on their coat of arms was encouraging: 'Deny nothing *a priori*, assert nothing without proof'. Less encouraging was the reply he received from Sylvain Arend, astronomer with the Royal Belgian Observatory, and a Committee member, 'Professional astronomers have studied the question *a priori*. For them, planets are nothing but celestial bodies which have cooled down and do little more than reflect the radiation they receive . . .'

Meanwhile, however, the initially hostile Jean Porte, statistician and administrator at the Institut National de la Statistique et des Etudes Economiques, had consented to look into Gauquelin's work, and apart from a few quibbles, could not deny the validity of Gauquelin's methodology. He affirmed as much in the preface to Gauquelin's 1957 book on his method. The Para Committee was unmoved, and Gauquelin let the matter drop as he carried out his experiment with eminent professionals from other countries beside France.

In 1961, having countered the initial (specious) objections of a national fluke, and now backed by Porte's support, he again assaulted the Para Committee. A year passed before a Committee member, engineer Jean Dath, wrote Gauquelin to say that he, too, could find nothing wrong with the methodology. But the

Committee published nothing, and personally conveyed its conviction that subconsciously or otherwise, Gauquelin had selected only those data that might support his claim.

This was welcome criticism. Gauquelin proposed a replication of his experiment with new data. Curiously, the Committee that but recently was languishing for lack of claims to test, suddenly found itself pressed for time. 'We are unfortunately not able to do this, because the difficulties of getting together a new group of births are insurmountable.' In other words, what Gauquelin and his wife had accomplished on their own, on a shoestring, without academic or financial support, and no university affiliations, a funded committee made up of academically connected professionals could not accomplish working together.

But though this particular door had slammed shut, others were slowly, grudgingly opening. Giorgio Piccardi, of the University of Florence, had demonstrated an apparent correlation between celestial phenomena and chemical reactions (see p. 337), and Frank A. Brown, of Northwestern University in Illinois, had demonstrated that animal behavior was in some way linked to celestial bodies, the sun and moon in particular. Though both these scientists were regarded with suspicion by their colleagues, both were sufficiently eminent to command a measure of attention. Also, their work did not directly confirm any specific aspect of astrology. With their help, Gauquelin was invited to read papers at legitimate scientific conferences. Reactions ranged from yawns to skepticism until the time came to publish. Then, suddenly, interest became intense enough to have Gauquelin's papers edited out of the proceedings.

The New European Replication

In 1965 Gauquelin decided to take on the Para Committee once again. He had figured a way out of the 'insurmountable' problem posed by a collection of new data. Because eminence in sport is fleeting, and fame comes early, hundreds of new athletes had risen to prominence in the twelve years elapsed since the initial experiment. This data was readily available.

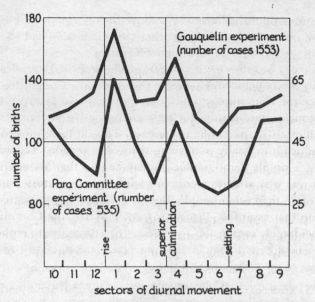

Figure 21. The Mars effect and sports champions: comparison of Gauquelin and Para Committee results.

Procedural details were mutually agreed upon. Gauquelin made certain that no one, including himself (especially himself) would be able to shout 'foul' after the experiment had been run.

The objective was simple: to find out, in the new group of 535 champion athletes, if a statistically significant number were born with Mars in Sectors 1 and 4, following the rise and culmination.

The results precisely matched Gauquelin's original experiment. (See Fig. 21.)

Both sides had taken precautions to ensure that no one could cry 'foul'. But Gauquelin had neglected to take precautions to ensure that someone whispered 'fair'. Rather than publish the results, the Committee now expressed doubts about Gauquelin's method, though they had accepted it six years earlier. A technical dossier of correspondence grew. The Committee carried out other experiments, all vindicating Gauquelin. Professor Koenigsfeld, president of the Committee, explained the Committee's lack of action in publishing its results: 'We have, in fact, verified M. Gauquelin's calculations and we are in agreement with them . . . But what we are not in agreement about are his conclusions, which we cannot accept.'

Since the Committee could not be goaded into presenting its own conclusions, Gauquelin took the initiative and presented them himself at a scientific conference. This, in turn, moved the Committee into finally publishing their own version. According to this, a simple demographic law lay behind the 'Mars Effect' which was why athletes were born with Mars in Sectors 1 and 4 more often than other people. But no evidence was presented to back up that assertion. Professor Luc de Marré, the Committee member largely responsible for forcing the Committee to replicate Gauquelin's experiment in the first place (subsequently an ex-member of the Committee) wrote,

> As a matter of fact, the Committee was unable to discover any mistake or error in M. Gauquelin's calculations or in the results which he claimed . . . The results of these experiments tended to confirm M. Gauquelin's hypothesis. In particular, a sliding of the birth hours, in function of alphabetical order of the champions, showed beyond all dispute that Gauquelin's theoretical (expected) frequencies were correct. In September 1976, the Committee published a 17-page report on its work concerning the research. It was astonishing to see that it did *not* mention any of these counter experiments; on the contrary, it accused M. Gauquelin of imaginary demographic errors . . .
>
> Luc de Marré, *Zetetic Scholar*, #9, p. 71

In 1967, in his book, *L'Astrologie*, Courderc was still saying, 'M. Gauquelin's results are without value, his methods are confused, and no scientist worthy of the name would accept them.' But in 1974, he devoted fourteen grudging pages to 'The Case of M.G.' (coyly refraining from mentioning Gauquelin's name this time), and cited without further comment the verification of Gauquelin's data by the Committee. But in 1978, in an updated version of his book, he was happy to have the Committee's recently published report as a new, authoritative reference.

M.G. has certainly underestimated the complexity of astronomical questions which he thought to represent accurately in elementary formulae. The astronomers and statisticians of the Committee Para, after a conscientious examination, have declared these formulae to be inadequate. This conclusion will reassure all those whom M.G.'s propositions have alarmed.

'Le cas M.G.' in *L'Astrologie* (PUF, Paris, 1978 edn.)

To the true defender of the unfaith, imaginary demographic errors are quite as good as demographic errors. Professor Couderc is equally untroubled by the contradictions involved in his latter sentence. Why should seekers after objective truth get 'alarmed' in the first place? Why should they require 'reassurance'? The truth is the truth, simple, unvarnished, carrying no emotional freight . . . at least that is what is written into the credo of the Church of Progress.

Front and Center: Keystone CSICOPS

(We are deeply and permanently indebted to astronomer Dennis Rawlins [see pp. 281–91] for these 'Keystone CSICOPS'.)

In 1975, in the magazine, the *Humanist*, Bart Bok and Lawrence Jerome published the famous manifesto, signed by 186 eminent scientists, along with the anti-astrology articles that subsequently became the book, *Objections to Astrology*. Jerome, a non-statistician, attacked Gauquelin's work so ignorantly and egregiously that initially Gauquelin contemplated legal action. Instead, he settled for a published reply in the *Humanist*, describing the replication of his results by the Para Committee. Paul Kurtz, editor of the *Humanist*, and (subsequent to its establishment in 1976) director of the American equivalent of the Para Committee, the Committee for the Scientific Investigation of Claims of the Paranormal (CSICOP), sought opinions from his own committee members on the controversy. Marvin Zelen, professor of Statistical Science at Harvard, confirmed that Jerome's mathematical arguments were inept and undeserving of serious consideration (a fact overlooked by the 186 eminent scientists putting their names to the manifesto). But since Zelen was neither demographer nor astronomer, he could not confirm or deny the Para Committee's objections along those lines.

However, he proposed an experiment of his own. If an unrecognized demographic factor was indeed involved, then the 'Mars Effect' would also show up in the charts of ordinary citizens born on the same day, and in the same general area as the champion athletes. In other words, on those days, there should be a statistically significant number of ordinary people (that is, non-champions from all walks of life) *also* born with Mars prominent in Sectors 1 and 4. UCLA astronomer (the late) George Abell joined Kurtz and Zelen on the team, and the wheels were set in motion.

The Zelen test was proclaimed 'definitive' – though over the objections of astronomer Dennis Rawlins, a co-founder of CSICOP, and a passionate and professed skeptic in the CSICOP mold. Rawlins was as convinced as the others that Gauquelin was wrong, but his own preliminary study of the Gauquelin data convinced him that no demographic error had been committed; that the Para Committee's objections were a smokescreen. Rawlins was betting on flawed selection of data (i.e. cheating). But he warned that calling the Zelen test 'definitive' would put the Committee in deep trouble.

This initial difference of opinion escalated into several years of acrimony, in-fighting, and sporadic attempts at co-operation on Rawlins's part to salvage the project. It finished with Rawlins excommunicated, which in turn led to his detailed exposé of the behind-the-scenes science according to CSICOP, a docu-drama worth examining in some detail here, even though breaking the strict chronology of the unfolding saga.

'sTARBABY'

Rawlins's account of the CSICOP/Gauquelin debacle, 'sTAR-BABY', was published in the October 1981 issue of *Fate* magazine. (A reprint is available for $1 from *Fate*, 500 Hyacinth

Place, Highland Park, Illinois 60035. Readers unacquainted with *Fate* should not be put off by its title, its format or even by its embarrassing ads – which represent the psychic/occult/self-development movement at its least attractive [a sample: EXTRA TERRESTIALS ... What are they trying to teach us? THE HYPNO-DISK: Have you tried to obtain one? ... THIS WOMAN'S PROPHECIES COME TRUE ... WIN $1,000 at any racetrack ... and ANDREIK THE WITCH: 'Tell me what you want and I will cast a spell for you' – $10.00]. Despite such ads, *Fate* runs serious articles on subjects related to the paranormal. Its subhead reads: 'The World's Mysteries Explored' which is what it does, at times in depth. Unlike the *Skeptical Inquirer*, which might otherwise be considered the other side of the same coin, *Fate* does not hesitate to expose charlatans within its ranks, or to admit its mistakes; nor does it have an inviolable party-line.)

'sTARBABY' is written in undisguised anger and disgust. Initially a manuscript 250 pages long, it had to be cut to its present 32 pages to make it suitable for magazine publication. There is no doubt that readers are better off for having been spared the lengthy personal attacks. And much of the minutiae of the CSICOP in-fighting would be of interest only to those deeply concerned with this particular CSICOP/Gauquelin episode. But the severe cutting (or perhaps the episode's intrinsic convoluted nature) has made it less than a model of clarity. Nevertheless, its main points are unmistakable. *Fate* sums them up in its own editorial heading: 'They call themselves the Committee for the Scientific Investigation of Claims of the Paranormal. In fact they are a group of would-be debunkers who bungled their major investigation, falsified the results, covered up their errors and gave the boot to a colleague who threatened to tell the truth.'

Despite 'sTARBABY''s extreme tone, its truth has been confirmed by independent sources, including CSICOP members, and ex-CSICOP members. The late Richard Kammann, the highly respected co-author of *The Psychology of the Psychic* (a skeptical study of psychics), first looked into the

Rawlins account convinced that Rawlins had to be wrong; that he could not be (as he maintained) the one just man in a council that included such public figures as Martin Gardner and the conjuror, James ('the Amazing') Randi.

After seven months of careful research Kammann concluded that Rawlins was justified in every regard. He could not even accuse Rawlins of exaggeration. Kammann quit CSICOP in disgust and sent in his report to Marcello Truzzi, at the *Zetetic Scholar*. Truzzi, himself a former editor of the *Skeptical Inquirer*, had left CSICOP some years earlier when it became clear that the Committee for Scientific Investigation was not interested in scientific investigation, only in debunking, and set up the *Zetetic Scholar* to make good the lack – which it does admirably. Kammann's report concluded, 'CSICOP has progressively trapped itself, degree by irreversible degree, into an anti-Rawlins propaganda campaign, into suppression of the evidence, and into stonewalling against other critics.'

Historian of Science, Patrick Curry, commissioned by Truzzi to investigate the entire story, was no less emphatic. Since his twenty-page report was published prior to the appearance of 'sTARBABY', and since Curry had no axe to grind, his conclusions are particularly interesting.

> I don't think I need to stress how badly the committee has handled the investigation of the Mars effect; the facts above speak for themselves. Their work could now best function as a model and a warning of how *not* to conduct such an investigation. Given the ample internal (Rawlins) and external (Gauquelin) warnings that went suppressed or ignored it is even difficult to accept protestations of 'good faith' and 'naivete' (Abell). Rawlins and Gauquelin are in fact the only two major figures to emerge with scientific credibility intact. It seems to me that this situation must call into question any further (unrefereed, at least) CSICOP involvement in research on the Mars effect, and possibly other 'paranormal' areas.
>
> *Zetetic Scholar* #9, 1982, p. 49

Meanwhile, back at CSICOP's Precinct Headquarters . . .

The Zelen Test

Rawlins's warning went unheeded, and the Zelen test challenge was put to Gauquelin. With Luc de Marré, he assembled the charts of 16,756 ordinary people (non-champion athletes) born on the same day and in the same general area as his champion athletes. Though the original Gauquelin group of champions included 2,088 names, matching control data was not readily available for all. The 16,756 people matched the data for a group of 303 champion athletes born in major population centers.

The planet Mars was distributed over the charts of this enormous control group of 16,756 at the chance level of 16.4%, virtually identical to the level Gauquelin had found in his other control groups. (16.7% was the theoretical frequency predicted by his calculations.) In one swoop the Zelen test proved the *absence* of the imaginary demographic factor concocted by the Para Committee, and also silenced any doubts (deliberately cast by the Committee) about the legitimacy of the level Gauquelin claimed represented chance.

Though the Zelen test totally vindicated Gauquelin, the fears expressed by Rawlins were unfounded. CSICOP was not in deep trouble after all, and would not be to this day were it not for Rawlins himself. In print CSICOP revealed themselves perfectly unembarrassed. For in that winter wonderland where unbiased science and biased scientists enjoy a symbiotic relationship, there is no obligation to report experiments that do not live up to rational expectations.

CSICOP neglected to announce that the test supported Gauquelin (that is, the Mars Effect did *not* apply to ordinary citizens with charts similar to those of the champion athletes). Though initially proclaimed 'definitive' in *The Humanist*, the Zelen test no longer merited serious consideration once the results were in.

Since it had not won the game, CSICOP changed the rules. The experiment itself was now transformed into a re-examination of the Mars Effect on champions; the 303 against whom the control group was matched. This group, which clearly demonstrated the Mars Effect (22% of champions born in key sectors as opposed to 16.7%), was then broken down into small sub-samples obscuring the effect, while violating all accepted statistical procedures.

These now-meaningless results were then trotted out to show how delicate and fragile a science statistics was; how just a few charts with Mars in a key sector gave the illusion of statistically significant results – when, really, the results were merely chance! But this argument in fact applied only to the Kurtz/Zelen/Abell (henceforth KZA) doctored version of Gauquelin's data; it did not apply to Gauquelin's data. As Rawlins writes,

> . . . KZA tried to obscure the clear success Gauquelin had scored. The Control Test had entailed analyzing 16,756 nonchampions born near (in time and space) 303 champions (a subsample of the original 2088 champions). KZA had believed that they too would score at 22% in key sectors (1 & 4) thus establishing that the champions' 22% hit rate was 'natural'. Instead the nonchampions scored at exactly the chance-level (17%) that Gauquelin and I had predicted from our Mars/dawn-corrected expectation-curve analysis.
>
> Faced with this disaster, KZA pulled a bait-and-switch. (Thus the report will hereafter be called the BS report.) Suddenly converting their *non*champions test into a *champions* test, they attacked the subsample of 303 champions! The subsample had of course been chosen simply as a means *en route* to testing the point KZA had proposed the Control Test Challenge for in the first place, namely, was chance level 17% or 22%? Since the 303 had scored at 22% (like the full 2088) the only ploy left was to protest that *this* 22% (of the 303) was not *strongly* statistically significant (not as strong as the 2088). Now, anyone familiar with statistics knows that no sample of 303 *can* produce strongly significant results if one is trying to measure 22% versus 17% rates . . .
>
> To sum up: the whole purpose of the Control Test – of collecting nearly 17,000 nonchampions (the control group) – had been to test whether Gauquelin's champions' 22% hit-rate was just a 'natural' (nonastrological) function of the time and place of birth. Had the

nonchampions control group shown at the 22% rate also, the 'natural' hypothesis would have been confirmed and Gauquelin's neoastrology would have been disconfirmed.

However, the opposite occurred. The nonchampions' rate turned out to be 17%, establishing the 22% rate as a real, *highly* significant above-chance result.

. . . Lawrence Jerome . . . 'congratulated' CSICOP . . . Incredibly, Jerome was claiming confirmation by the Zelen–Abell test, of his (and their) belief that astronomical/demographic biases explained Gauquelin's 22% rate. 'The [Control] test proved no such thing,' I wrote Kurtz. 'To the contrary, [Zelen and Abell] *confirmed* Gauquelin's expectation values . . . showing that there was indeed about a 17% probability for being in sectors 1 & 4 for nonchampions . . . If I believed the European champion sample was clean (which I don't) I would count the [Control] test as a major proof in support of Gauquelin.'

. . . Years later I learned that Abell (as well as Kurtz) had known the awful truth all along. In 1980 I obtained a copy of the smokiest Smoking Gun in this case, a letter written by Abell to Kurtz . . . The Smoking Gun letter to Kurtz reveals that KZA knew they were in trouble. But as Abell learned pronto, Kurtz wasn't about to publish any letter that admitted Gauquelin had won the Control Test. He was going to pretend that nothing had gone wrong.

'sTARBABY', pp. 11–12

The published report (*The Humanist*, Nov/Dec 1977) was couched in language designed to obscure and mislead. The implications of Gauquelin's work as a whole were ignored. The report hedged around making a clear statement of the objectives of the original Zelen test, nor did it give reasons for failing to examine in detail its results. KZA evidently hoped that the sweet smell of fudge would disguise the unmistakable reek of red-herring beneath.

But Rawlins apart, others, even within the CSICOP ranks, found the combination unpalatable. Professor Elizabeth Scott, a statistician at the University of California at Berkeley, had already complained that the KZA report 'may be misleading'.

She subsequently quit CSICOP when her professional criticisms of the handling of the experiment were simply ignored.

Nevertheless, further evasive culinary action was deemed necessary. Having glossed over the vindication of Gauquelin by the Zelen test; having illicitly broken down the legitimate 303-champion sub-sample into further, meaningless sub-sub-samples, the published report concluded that what was *really* necessary (to prove Gauquelin had not cheated) was a replication of the experiment using American athletes, with a sample gathered by someone other than Gauquelin.

Gauquelin agreed. This was what he had been trying to force his opponents to do for twenty years! In personal meetings with KZA he detailed the exact procedure he had followed in his own selection process; in particular the criteria for deciding who was eminent and who was not. These steps, obviously, had to be followed exactly; otherwise it would not be a replication of the experiment. Caution was doubly important in this case due to the (now no longer) mysterious fact that the Mars Effect disappeared in groups of professional but lesser athletes.

CSICOP undertook the gathering of data and it was at this point, according to Rawlins, 'that the handling of the Gauquelin problem was transformed from mere bungling to deliberate cover-up' ('sTARBABY', p. 9).

The Mars Effect Test in America

Astronomer George Abell had been delegated to do the calculations but found himself pre-occupied with other projects. Despite already strained relations, Paul Kurtz prevailed upon Rawlins to do them. Rawlins writes,

> Kurtz started receiving the American birth data as early as September (1976). Stung by his private knowledge that he'd lost the Control Test (as he confessed aloud at least once), he was frantic to get on with the diversion of retesting (using the American sample) as quickly as possible . . . Kurtz told me that this time he wanted an advance look at the results, to see what was going to happen. He

stressed that his sneak peek was to be strictly confidential . . . In succeeding weeks Kurtz mailed me further birth data as well as unsolicited cash. At one point (after 120 names) I told him by phone (he preferred hearing the accumulated score instantly, without waiting the few days the mail took) that the key-sector score was now at 22%). He groaned. I emphasized that the sample size was too small for the result to be statistically meaningful. He drew no comfort from this remark. I asked him if he were *sure* this was a clean sample. He was, so I assured him that the score was bound to revert to roughly 17% as the sample got larger – unless astrological claims were true, which I certainly didn't believe . . .

In mid-April Kurtz visited California and we saw quite a bit of each other. He couldn't stop talking about the Gauquelin business. In the middle of conversations on other matters he would grow silent and go back to discussing some possible 'out'.

During this visit and subsequent phone conversations Kurtz tried out various schemes for getting off the hook. My favorite was the notion that Gauquelin fudged the *non*champions to force the score *down* to 17%.* Hilarious. First, if fraud or bias was involved, it would be lots easier to work it on the smaller original champion sample. Second, it was ridiculous to suspect fraud simply because the nonchampions came out at the very level chance would predict!

This is the 'scientific investigation', which CSICOP claims as its middle name?

. . . The next morning, June 8, all 325 athlete's sector-positions were computed, tabulated and dropped in the mail to Kurtz.

No sooner was this task finished and the American test supposedly completed than Kurtz phoned me up and said oops, we accidentally missed a lot of names . . .

. . . The last 82 names came in at summer's end.

I ran off the final data at SDSU. The cumulative score was not 22% or 17% but only 13½% – strongly anti-Gauquelin . . .

Abell couldn't believe that my calculations were correct because

---

* KZA publicly: 'Nowhere did we wish to suggest that Gauquelin "cheated" and we regret any such implication.' *Skeptical Inquirer*, Summer, 1980, p. 67.

the score had come out at 13½% instead of 22%. He wondered if I had tampered with the sample. I replied the sample had come from Kurtz . . .

'sTARBABY', p. 12 ff.

Assessing the American Mars Effect Test: or 'Oops, We Accidentally Missed a Lot of Names'

When the results of the American test were published (*Skeptical Inquirer*, Winter, 1979–80) Rawlins agreed they did not confirm Gauquelin. But he pursues the matter of this unique progressively deliquescing sample no further. This is understandable. As a scientist with an unusually delicate constitution, he could not stomach red-herring à la KZA with its generous fudge topping. But he had often and stridently (e.g. *Zetetic Scholar*, 1977) voiced his desire to see Gauquelin's results repudiated. Rawlins may be excommunicated, but he is not a lapsed CSICOP. Kurtz provided the sample, Rawlins asked no embarrassing questions. But we do not feel that discretion necessarily serves the interests of objective truth.

The first 120 champion athletes displayed the Mars Effect at the strongly significant (and common) rate of 22%. As the sample was simultaneously increased (and watered down without Gauquelin's knowledge) by sub-samples made up of lesser athletes, the Mars Effect diminished dramatically. Only 12% for the second sub-sample of 325, and 7% for the final Oops-we-accidentally-missed-a-lot-of-names sub-sample of 82. A 12% Mars Effect is well below what chance would predict, but the figure is not statistically significant. However, the 7% Mars Effect produced by the final 'Oops!' sub-sample is a statistically significant *low* result.

Given CSICOP's disregard for established scientific protocol throughout, this anomaly is treated with admirable restraint by those adversely affected. Eysenck and Nias politely call it 'a mystery', and go on to other matters. Curry discreetly brings to the attention of readers the fact that the last sub-sample was statistically significant at the .02 level and lets them draw their own conclusions. Gauquelin himself makes clear his suspicions. 'We have to find out an explanation for the striking statistical difference between the 22% score of the first data and the 7% score of the remaining 'accidentally missed' 82 names. Gauquelin's letter to Kurtz was not answered, yet Gauquelin does not elaborate further.'

Not everyone will know what the .02 level means. In plain language it means that the odds are 50–1 *against* this 7% Mars Effect being due to chance.

Gauquelin Replies

Rawlins had counseled against CSICOP involving itself in collecting the sample without rules in advance in writing, and impartial judges. Gauquelin, still caught up in that 'incredible naivety' that characterized his attitude to science thirty years earlier, made no such stipulation, believing a gentlemen's agreement would suffice. Two main requirements were stressed by Gauquelin as essential and inviolable:

1. degrees of eminence had to be maintained, and this was possible through objective criteria (amount of space allotted in sports dictionaries, Olympic Gold Medals, etc.), and,
2. the sample had to comprise only natural births. His methodology was conveyed in detail in person to KZA in Paris, whom he then left to get on with the arduous task of collecting the sample back in America.

Neither stipulation was adhered to. Collecting accurate birth data is, for a variety of reasons, more difficult in the USA than in Europe. KZA were unable to obtain a large enough sample of qualifying champions to make up an adequate sample group. Perhaps more to the point, as Rawlins notes, Kurtz was secretly monitoring the results as they came in, and he was aware that the Mars Effect was present in the first group of champions. In any event, instead of looking for other ways of collecting a proper sample, and without consulting Gauquelin, Kurtz proceeded to collect his remarkable sample, with its unique and progressively diminishing Mars Effect, according to rules of his own devising. No effort was made to distinguish between natural and induced births.

Publication of the American results provoked a lengthy and increasingly labyrinthine correspondence between KZA, Gauquelin and other interested parties. This was selectively aired in the *Skeptical Inquirer*, with the *Inquirer* exercising full editorial control over what was published, what was not, and what was subject to editorial change. (This did not apply only to Gauquelin, but to dissenters within the CSICOP fold as well. One of Rawlins's most bitter complaints was that, having done all the calculations for the experiment, he was not permitted to publicly voice his dissent over the manner in which the experiment had been conducted. Kendrick Frazier, editor of the *Inquirer*, restricted him to a brief statement and then edited that to his own satisfaction, according to Rawlins.) KZA were invariably awarded the right of final reply.

The Curry and Kammann Reports

The controversy raging *post hoc* over the KZA American Mars Effect experiment has been reported in objective detail by Patrick Curry, an English historian of science ('Research on the Mars Effect' by Patrick Curry, *Zetetic Scholar*, #9, 1982), and others. Its complexity is such that there is no way to satisfactorily convey the conflicting separate elements involved without reproducing long documents from both sides. This is outside the scope of our book. The main points of Curry's assessment may be summed up succinctly enough, however. KZA have never directly attempted to refute them, though there has been considerable evasive action.

1. Because a different and idiosyncratic methodology was employed in gathering data, the American Athlete Experiment does *not* constitute a legitimate replication of Gauquelin's experiments. It cannot stand as a disconfirmation as KZA claim.

2. Forced to argue *post hoc*, Gauquelin's case is indubitably weakened in this instance, but in this instance only. Nevertheless, for the sub-sample that represents a replication of his own methodology (athletes of true championship caliber) he is justified in insisting the Mars Effect is present. In other words, when the smokescreen deliberately set up by KZA is blown away, and the genuine complexities attending the experiment are unravelled in so far as this can be done, the American athletes show the Mars Effect present. Thus, even this bungled and deliberately watered-down experiment confirms Gauquelin, though less decisively than those undertaken by himself.

3. KZA's handling of the entire experiment is, given the benefit of every possible doubt, amateur; indefensible as science on any level. This view is shared by Rawlins, of course, but also by all other independent scientifically qualified investigators, some of whom are (or were) CSICOP members themselves (cf. *Zetetic Scholar*, #'s 9 and 10).

Richard Kammann, Associate Professor of Psychology at the University of Otago in New Zealand, co-author of *The Psychology of the Psychic*, a CSICOP member and staunch supporter prior to the Mars Effect episode, was even more scathing. Nearly a year of research into the controversy culminated in a lengthy, two-part article, 'The True Disbelievers: Mars Effect Drives Skeptics to Irrationality'. The article was initially sent to *Psychology Today*, *The Humanist* and the *Skeptical Inquirer*. Each of these magazines had allotted considerable space to the CSICOP version of events in earlier issues. All declined to publish Kammann's article. It ultimately found a home in the *Zetetic Scholar* (#10).

Kammann wrote:

> In recent years psychologists have become increasingly fascinated by the versatility of the true believer in finding reasons to go on believing in spite of clear evidence to the contrary. These belief-preserving maneuvers are most readily seen in everyday aberrations like racial prejudice, superstition, religion [sic] and the slogans of politicians, but it is now recognized that they also occur in the

very halls of science from which 'truth' is supposed to be broadcast with dispassionate, value-free ojectivity . . .

This article is a case study in which a small group of antipseudo-science skeptics fall back on a remarkable line of illogic and defensiveness when confronted by intractable data suggesting that the position of Mars in the sky when one is born has an effect on the likelihood of becoming a sports champion . . . Abell, along with Professor Paul Kurtz, the chairman of CSICOP and former editor of the *The Humanist*, and Professor Marvin Zelen, statistician at Harvard University and fellow of CSICOP, have persisted in offering the public a set of demonstrably false statistical arguments against the Mars Effect in spite of four years of continuous and steadily mounting criticisms of their illogic.

This is a tragedy since the major criticism against the CSICOP's handling of the affair has not come from allies of Gauquelin but from fellow rationalists who are in fact skeptical of the validity of the Mars Effect. In short, the CSICOP has been – in my view – guilty of the very pathological science that they were set up to attack. Instead of exemplifying a rational approach to an anomalous claim, CSICOP has descended into protecting orthodoxy and its own reputation as a goal more important than finding the truth. The inquirers have indeed become the Inquisitors that some feared they might.

(pp. 50–80)

Patrick Curry and most of the other critics of CSICOP's handling of the controversy steer clear of accusing CSICOP of deliberate fraud in the many instances where it may seem indicated. Kammann, however, finds himelf unable to attribute all CSICOP errors to mere incompetence and blind prejudice. He shies clear of specific accusations, and so do we. Still, we ask the jury to particularly bear in mind that 'oops-we-accidentally-missed-a-lot-of-names' sub-sample with its significantly low Mars Effect at the .02 level. Professors Eysenck and Nias genteelly consider this result a 'mystery'. But given Paul Kurtz's failure to reply to Gauquelin's request for an explanation we think the solution may not require calling in Sherlock Holmes to solve it.* The jury may well find itself similarly unbaffled.

The Gauquelin Challenge: A New European Replication

Because KZA had incorrectly carried out the American replication, then misrepresented its results, Gauquelin felt obliged to issue a challenge of his own.

Birth data is easier to gather in Europe than America. Fifteen years had elapsed since the last group of athletes was gathered for the Para Committee experiment. It was now possible to gather a new large sample of champion athletes. Gauquelin therefore proposed a European replication, to be carried out under the complete control of CSICOP but with rules written out in advance, agreed-upon impartial referees, and an airtight verification treaty (letter to Paul Kurtz, 10 November 1978).

But Kurtz had evidently lost interest. There was no reply, nor to a second letter repeating the offer.

Rather than let CSICOP go on claiming that its botched (and probably fudged) American 'replication' constituted disproof of the Mars Effect, Gauquelin went ahead and carried out a European experiment on his own. A sample of 432 new champion European athletes, gathered from seven countries, according to his established objective criteria, demonstrated a Mars Effect of 24%, statistically significant at the .001 level (1,000–1 odds against chance). A control of 432 ordinary athletes showed no Mars Effect.

Suddenly, KZA were interested. Since they had declined to agree to the conditions of the test beforehand, they were now in a position to attack those conditions after the fact. Operating the smoke machine with one hand, and fishing into the red-herring barrel with the other, a number of new objections were

---

* If fraud is involved, it is an easy fiddle. Add or drop a few hours from the recorded birth-times and positively significant results become negatively significant.

raised, most of them concerning the method of selection (*Skeptical Inquirer*, Winter, 1979–80, pp. 57–9).

However, as Gauquelin now reminded them in his rejoinder, (*Skeptical Inquirer*, 1980, pp. 58–62) CSICOP had been given two opportunities to control the selection, and indeed, the whole experiment, themselves. The method of selection was identical to that used so often before, and the control group of ordinary athletes (selected according to the same objective criteria of ordinariness employed in former tests) displayed no Mars Effect. KZA were also thoroughly familiar with the selection procedure from detailed personal conferences with Gauquelin and had never raised objections to it before. Kurtz had stated as much earlier. He admitted he had 'inspected the Gauquelins' archives and was impressed by the meticulous care with which the data had been collected' (*The Humanist*, Nov/Dec 1977). Later, he would insist that this imprimatur concerned only the meticulousness of the methodology, not its freedom from bias – as if the question of bias would never have occurred to him initially.

As with the American 'replication', the *post hoc* combination of obfuscation and evasion makes it difficult to convey to the jury the extent of KZA's distortion and misrepresentation – without reprinting *in toto* their objections, the Gauquelin rejoinders, rejoinders to the rejoinders and so on. This in turn cannot not help but bewilder and/or exhaust even knowledgeable and interested parties; an effect unlikely to be fortuitous.

If enough people can be forced into eventually crying 'enough', the Mars Effect can be dropped into the oubliette reserved by the Church of Progress for inconvenient facts, and forgotten.

As military strategy, evasion and delay may be very effective (especially when the *Skeptical Inquirer* controls communiqués from the battlefront to the mainstream media). But as science it is indefensible – as is the incessant, idiotic talk of 'victory' and 'defeat', the terminology consistently employed by CSICOP throughout – as recorded by Rawlins. Science is supposed to be carried out, as CSICOP itself insists (see p. 164), in a spirit of dispassionate inquiry.

A. Statistical Evidence

Remembering that KZA were twice offered the opportunity to control the replication before work was undertaken, that they should object at all is simple effrontery. The level on which this takes place is best illustrated by a representative 'objection'.

In their 'Rejoinder' (*Skeptical Inquirer*, 1980) to Gauquelin's reply to their initial objections, KZA claim that the 31 Olympic Gold-Medalists in the 432 European champions sample do not in fact display the Mars Effect. Since Olympic Gold-Medalists represent the *crème de la crème* among amateur athletes, according to Gauquelin, this stands as a disconfirmation of the Mars Effect, according to KZA.

There are two problems with this objection:

1. The European Replication is *not* a test of Olympic champions. The Mars Effect is valid because it shows itself consistently, indeed, invariably, in samples of champion athletes large enough to provide statistically significant results. Therefore, the level at which the Mars Effect shows itself in any sample of 31 Gold-Medalists is irrelevant as an argument, pro or con. A sample of 31 of *anybody* is meaningless as far as statistics is concerned. KZA were well aware of this. (Nevertheless, it *was* true that prior experience would have led Gauquelin to expect that any group of Olympic Gold-Medalists would, indeed, display the Mars Effect. They had always done so before. *Et, voila!* . . .

2. The European replication did *not* include 31 Olympic champions as KZA claimed; it included 55. (Oops! we accidentally missed 24 more names!) Of these 24 Gold-Medalists somehow not included by KZA, 11 (46%) displayed the Mars Effect. The score for Olympic Gold-Medalists in the European replication was not, therefore, 4 out of 31, or 12.9% as claimed by KZA, but 15 out of 55, or 27.2%, a highly significant figure, and typical of that found by Gauquelin when dealing with groups of Olympic Gold-Medalists.

Gauquelin's letter, pointing out the curious omission of these 24 missing Gold-Medalists, was not published by the *Skeptical Inquirer*.

'*sTARBABY*''*s Fallout*

When the story of the dissolution of the Church of Progress is written, the Gauquelin saga and the CSICOP cover-up will provide a key chapter. In that chapter, it will be possible to trace the genesis of the scandal to a single, seemingly innocuous decision: George Abell's refusal to perform the calculations for the American replication of the Mars Effect experiment.

By calling on Dennis Rawlins, with his thin skin, delicate stomach, and shrill voice, CSICOP placed themselves in a position from which there is now no escape.

For were it not for Rawlins and his central role in the proceedings from beginning to end, the inside story of KZA's handling of the Zelen test, the subsequent cover-up, the camouflage daubed over the cover-up (the so-called American replication), and the final smokescreen thrown up to obscure the camouflaged cover-up ('A Reappraisal'), CSICOP's handling of the experiment would never have come to light. Gauquelin might have complained. Astrological journals, unread outside of the astrological community, might have discussed the injustice at length, even knowledgeably. None of this would have bothered CSICOP at all. As Rawlins records, 'The following May [1977] I was startled to see an identical attack [to his own attack of KZA's bungling] by Eric Tarkington in *Phenomena*. When I phoned Kurtz in shock at the embarrassment of having correct analyses published in the proastrology journal while CSICOP was publishing crap, his reply was, "Nobody reads [*Phenomena*]"' ('sTARBABY', p. 12).

Even if the bungled science had become known, it would have been sloughed off as an unfortunate but minor error, at least by the CSICOP faithful. Truzzi and his skeptical but responsible colleagues who abandoned CSICOP to begin the *Zetetic Scholar*, might have done so under any circumstances. But without Rawlins, they would never have suspected the squalid shenanigans behind the bogus science; Kurtz's determination to conceal the truth at any cost, and the enthusiastic complicity of CSICOP's chief public figures, Martin Gardner and James ('the

Amazing') Randi. With its circulation of 600, and its low profile, it is unlikely the *Zetetic Scholar* analysis would have found its way to the general public, either. Even as it stands, CSICOP has been relatively successful at keeping the truth hidden, a situation that is about to change dramatically.

'*A Reappraisal*', or: *Larry, Curly and Moe Eat Crow — with Fudge Topping*

Unable to live down the uproar set off by Rawlins, KZA published 'A Reappraisal' (*Skeptical Inquirer*, Spring 1983) intended to clear the air and own up to certain errors. But this reappraisal is actually not a reappraisal at all; it is an attempt by KZA to plea-bargain their way out of an undefendable position.

Thus they admit to varying (minor) degrees of carelessness but evade all the more serious charges of fraud, dishonesty and deliberate misrepresentation. They confess they had failed to acknowledge that the Zelen test results actually *confirmed* Gauquelin's calculations of the chance level in a sample of non-champions; that is, the *absence* of the Mars Effect. But they fail to discuss the significance of that confirmation in the face of the *presence* of the Mars Effect in samples of champions. They also claimed that the pressures of their other work made them neglect 'to examine the manuscript with sufficient care'. But this amounts to still another sock at old 'sTARBABY'.

'*What Did They Know and When Did They Know It?*': *The Road to CSICOPgate*

Thanks to Rawlins we all now know that Abell had examined the manuscript very closely at the onset. He knew that it categorically supported Gauquelin and he had communicated that knowledge to Kurtz. Thus, KZA knew Gauquelin had 'won', and they knew it from the beginning. The claim that pressure of work had kept them from examining the manuscript closely is therefore a deliberate lie. All of this is documented by Rawlins (see above).

Yet what KZA may lack in integrity, they make up for with *chutzpah*. Demonstrably guilty of academic crimes that would have had them thrown out of their universities were the subject at issue anything other than astrology, they call Gauquelin's honesty into question: 'we should add that there is no clear evidence that the Gauquelins intentionally biased the sample . . .'

'No *clear* evidence', indeed! There is no evidence at all – that the sample is biased, or that it is biased intentionally. Nor has there ever been such evidence. Apart from the minute, easily corrected discrepancies discovered by Jean Porte back in the 1950s, the *only* valid objection found to Gauquelin's selection method has been that his criteria for determining degrees of eminence, though objective, was not entirely consistent from experiment to experiment. For example, in one experiment he used only Olympic Gold-Medalists, and in another he included Olympic Gold, Silver and Bronze-Medalists. But this is a quibble. Those who raised the quibble (KZA, 'The Contradictions in Gauquelin's Research', *Skeptical Inquirer*, 1980) were aware that it did not affect the overall results. In fact, as Ertel has shown (see below), the inclusion of lesser athletes invariably *weakened* the Mars Effect. This single quibble aside, the evidence overwhelmingly indicated the sample is not biased. But if it is, then it is up to opponents to find the ways in which bias has entered in, and to then show, if possible, that the bias is intentional. Innuendo and character-assassination are not supposed to play a role in the search for objective truth.

Interested parties have always been welcome to examine and criticize the criteria used by Gauquelin in setting up his categories of eminence. Equally, interested parties have at their disposal the birth data that came back to him from the registries throughout the world in the original documents. The material is available in its entirety, as it should be in science. As we have seen, Paul Kurtz had examined it in detail in Gauquelin's own laboratory and acknowledged that fact in writing (Account of the Meeting of Paul Kurtz with Michel and Françoise Gauquelin in Paris, 24 June 1977, private correspondence).

The following passage, both illustrative and typical, comes from the 'Concluding Comments', in 'A Reappraisal' with numbers in parenthesis indicating items upon which we will comment in turn.

> While we are more than willing to acknowledge our mistakes and shortcomings as we become aware of them, [1] we do not want to leave the impression that the Mars effect is in any sense confirmed [2]. We believe that the results of the Zelen test suggest [3] that Gauquelin adequately allowed for demographic and astronomical factors in predicting the expected distribution of Mars sectors for birth times in the general population. On the other hand, such a highly unexpected phenomenon as the Mars effect must, in our judgement, be confirmed independently and under strict controls [4, 4a] to rule out data bias or manipulation. This has not been done either in the Gauquelin's studies or in the negative [5, 6] test on U.S. athletes.
>
> (*Skeptical Inquirer*, Spring, 1983, p. 82)

We trust the jury will be sufficiently aware of the facts by now to discern for themselves the circumlocutions, distortions and evasions packed into this short paragraph. But just in case anyone has been drowsing, here are the more important.

1. KZA are not 'more than willing to acknowledge [their] mistakes and shortcomings as [they] become aware of them'. They were aware of them six years prior to acknowledging them. Rawlins pointed out the mistakes and shortcomings in the most unmistakable language imaginable. It was only the uproar set off by 'sTARBABY' that drove them to acknowledge even minor mistakes and shortcomings.
2. The Mars Effect had been in practically *every* sense confirmed at the time 'A Reappraisal' was written, since none of its critics were able to cast legitimate doubts upon it.
3. The Zelen test does not 'suggest' Gauquelin was right about the chance levels in samples of non-champions; it *proves* it.

4. KZA turned down the opportunity to carry out the European replication under strict controls, and therefore disqualify themselves from making slanderous remarks about the lack of strict controls.

4a. The controls on the European tests (Gauquelin's) *were* strict – because Gauquelin controlled them, not KZA. KZA examined the data themselves, and could not fault it.

5. The US test was not 'negative'; it was bungled, and its results misrepresented. At the very worst, it might be termed 'indecisive', but this is giving KZA the benefit of every doubt, a courtesy uncommitted observers may feel they do not deserve.

6. It *is* true (the only unequivocally true statement in the passage) that strict controls were *not* in place to rule out data bias and manipulation in the test on US athletes. Nor is the complete data available to check for possible bias and manipulation. This is hardly surprising. The American test was carried out by Paul Kurtz, Marvin Zelen and George Abell, not by Michel Gauquelin.

But our own favorite passage (and we hope it will be the jury's) in 'A Reappraisal' appears under 'Point 3' on the preceding page.

> . . . Before conducting our test, we did discuss with Gauquelin how an American test might be carried out and what directories might possibly be [read *'definitely had to be'*] used, but there were no written agreements . . . Although we wish we had proceeded according to point 3 above, we wish to emphasize that we were under no scientific or moral obligation to do so.

> (p.81)

Ecce homines!

Gauquelin was not permitted a rejoinder in the *Skeptical Inquirer*.

'A Reappraisal' was largely ignored by the mainstream press, but happily accepted at face value by the scientific press, when the occasion arose to refer to it (*Science 84*, October).

A. Statistical Evidence

'Grading the Eminence': The Ertel Report

The refusal by CSICOP to acknowledge that the Mars Effect has been confirmed is closely equivalent to refusing to admit the world is round, prior to satellite photos.

All the evidence available points to confirmation; *no* evidence points to disconfirmation. In science that is generally the criterion used to consider a question proved true – until or unless proved false.

Following CSICOPgate, for diehard opponents of astrology – which means the very considerable congregation of the Church of Progress – only one possible legitimate hope remained to disprove the Mars Effect. This was to demonstrate that, despite all apparent evidence to the contrary, some undetected element within the selection process (unconscious or otherwise) enabled Gauquelin to show a Mars Effect when in fact there was none (and a Jupiter Effect, a Moon Effect, and a Saturn Effect for just those professions astrologers had always associated with these planets).

The jury will be astonished to learn that no one within CSICOP was rushing to undertake this final, decisive investigation. It was left to an unaffiliated psychologist, Dr Suitbert Ertel, present chairman of the psychology department at Göttingen University. Dr Ertel is not an astrologer, but became interested in Gauquelin's work after reading the chapter on terrestrial/celestial relationships in Gauquelin's book, *Cosmic Clocks* (Paladin, 1973).

In 'Grading the Eminence, Or: Raising the Hurdle for the Athletes' Mars Effect', Professor Ertel describes two equally valid methods for uncovering hidden selection factors. The first is of course a major new replication of a Gauquelin experiment using all-new data. The second is an independent examination of the Gauquelin data, designed to reveal any biases in selection, '. . . the crux and perhaps the Achilles' heel of the "Mars Effect" dispute', according to KZA ('A Reappraisal', p. 88).

Ertel chose to re-examine Gauquelin's data in search of such an Achilles' Heel. His starting point was his agreement with the single valid KZA objection: that Gauquelin's selection method was not entirely consistent from one experiment to another (only Gold-Medalists in one test, Gold, Silver and Bronze-Medalists in another, etc.).

This lack of absolute rigor, in Ertel's view, might be concealing the elusive hidden variable critics had not been able to detect. What was therefore required was an absolutely objective method for determining degrees of eminence; that is to say, for deciding who should be included in the sample and who should not. If Gauquelin's own sampling method could be shown to contain some selective bias it would tend to negate or at least cast serious doubts upon his thirty years of unremitting labor. On the other hand, if no bias could be found, in Ertel's opinion, it would be very difficult to go on pretending that both Gauquelin's key assertions had not been confirmed:

1. Champion athletes tend to be born with Mars in Sectors 1 and 4 more often than ordinary people.
2. The more eminent the athlete, the more likely he (or she) is to be born with Mars in one of the key sectors.

Confirming Assertion (1) involved showing that in making up his samples, champion athletes showing *no* Mars Effect had not been excluded. This was a straightforward process. All Ertel had to do was to check the biographical sources used by Gauquelin in putting his sample together to see if top athletes had been excluded for reasons other than an inability to acquire accurate birth data. Ertel found no suspicious exclusions.

Confirming Assertion (2) was more complex. Ertel reasoned that if Gauquelin was right; if the very top athletes showed a much higher Mars Effect than lesser but still eminent athletes, a study that graded athletes according to eminence should reflect that contention. In other words, a sample of superstars extracted from the total sample would show the highest effect of all; star athletes would show less, and so on down the line to the lowest level included in the sample. Though Gauquelin had noted this

eminence factor in his work, he had never systematically ex-
ploited it.

Ertel's method for determining eminence amounted to a
systematization of Gauquelin's. He reasoned the more eminent
the athlete the more frequently he (or she) would be cited in the
various sport encyclopedias and reference works from the
various countries. Only the very top would be listed in international directories spanning the range of sports, and these
would also be listed in all national directories as well as all
directories devoted to an individual sport. The next rank of
athlete would not make the international all-sport directories,
but would deserve national all-sport mention, as well as international mention in directories devoted to the particular sport
. . . and so on down the line to athletes noted only nationally in
reference works devoted to their particular sport.

Thus, the most eminent athletes would be cited most often in
sports directories, and the number of citations would provide
an absolutely rigorous and objective method of grading eminence. It could be applied to the total Gauquelin sample of
4,291 athletes. It functioned independently of Gauquelin's own
method, and over-rode the minor differences in the criteria
applied by Gauquelin. This in turn (particularly in sport where
there is relatively little opportunity to achieve eminence except
via excellence) provided an absolutely objective method of
testing the Gauquelin hypothesis that related strength of Mars
Effect to degrees of eminence. In other words, superstar athletes,
those cited most often, should show the most pronounced Mars
Effect, and the Mars Effect should gradually diminish as eminence diminished. Anything but a steady decrease in the Mars
Effect from superstar to first-string, hard-working pro would
cast doubt upon its validity.

Ertel used a total of 18 screening sources, 9 devoted to a
single sport. He found it practical to set up five degrees of
eminence corresponding to the number of citations. When the
athletes had been graded into these five degrees of eminence,
Ertel found Gauquelin's hypothesis precisely confirmed (see
Fig. 21). The superstars (Grade 5) showed a Mars Effect of

32.3%, the stars (Grade 4) 30% and so on down to Grade 1, 24.4%, still above the chance level of 22.2%.*

The Included and the Disincluded

Going through Gauquelin's data, Ertel was able to settle the question of possible bias in selection once and for all. Virtually all athletes of the upper three ranks had been included. It was only in the lower two ranks that Gauquelin had made decisions as to who to include or not include. But these decisions had not been made on the basis of prior knowledge of the Mars position of any given chart (KZA's insinuation). Rather, Gauquelin had applied his own criteria for eminence on the basis of performance within the given sport. Formerly a ranking French tennis-player himself, Gauquelin had the kind of overall knowledge of sport that allowed him to make such judgements with confidence. As Ertel himself admits, though his own system for grading eminence was absolutely objective (on the basis of number of citations in sports directories), Gauquelin's system though in a sense subjective on these lower levels, was almost certainly more accurate when it came to deciding, out of a number of lesser athletes with similar credentials on paper, which deserved to be called 'eminent' and which not.

But the essential finding was that when those athletes who had *not* been included by Gauquelin (because they had not met his own criteria for eminence) were added to the sample, the Mars Effect was still apparent for the group as a whole (24.4% as

---

* Noting that the Mars Effect is pronounced just *before* the rise and culmination as well as after, Ertel used a slightly different zoning system than Gauquelin so as not to lose those athletes born in those sectors – which the Gauquelin system omitted. These 'Gauquelin Plus Zones' added to Sector 1 the latter third of Sector 12 (the portion closest to the rise), and added to Sector 4 the latter third of Sector 3 (closest to the culmination). Using enlarged zones raises the percentage attributable to chance to 22% instead of 16.7%. Significant results were obtained using the standard Gauquelin Sectors 1 and 4 but the Plus Zones gave more consistent and still more significant results.

opposed to 22% at the chance level). Thus, any doubts that may have remained regarding bias in the selection process may be considered dispelled once and for all. *As long as a sample is made up of athletes above a certain level of eminence, the Mars Effect will be present.*

Ertel's study confirmed the reality of the Mars Effect. It put Gauquelin's observation that the Mars Effect increased with eminence on an objective basis. It also vitiated another spurious objection.

Gauquelin opponents honest enough to admit they could not fault the statistics, had often taken refuge in the relative weakness of the Mars Effect, claiming that while statistically highly significant, it was not powerful enough to give credence to astrology as a whole in any substantive sense. The argument was that since 16.7% of ordinary citizens would be born with Mars in the key sectors to begin with, a percentage of around 24% for athletes did not really prove anything (earlier scientific thinkers tried to discount the moons of Jupiter on this basis; if they could not be seen by the naked eye they were unimportant, and if unimportant, they did not exist). As science, of course, this is a non-argument, but grading the levels of eminence further reduces its impact. As we see, the highest level of champion athletes show a Mars Effect of 35% which certainly cannot be dismissed (Fig. 22).

As Ertel observed, the exigencies of statistical studies had to a large extent forced Gauquelin to minimize his own results. In order to make up samples large enough to qualify for statistical significance, he had been forced to include large numbers of lesser athletes. Had he been able to make up large enough samples of superstar and star quality athletes (eminence grades 5 and 4) the Mars Effect would have been that much more pronounced, over 30% as opposed to c. 24%.

Grading the Eminence: Conclusion

In scrutinizing Gauquelin's methodological procedure Ertel found certain inconsistencies and a lack of formal rigor in the

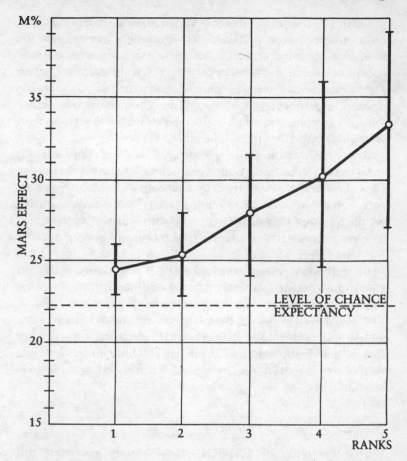

Solid line: Mars Key Sector percentage (m%) for athletes of five ranks (5 = highest rank) based on citation frequencies (N = 4391).

The Mars effect increases when the citation frequencies increase (for details see text).

The vertical bars show the ranges of possible chance variation for p = 0.95. (The ranges of confidence increase with ranks, which is due to decreasing numbers of individuals (see text)).

(from Ertel, 1988)

Figure 22. The eminence effect for Mars among athletes vindicated by Prof. Ertel's experiment

sense that Gauquelin's method varied somewhat from experiment to experiment (a result of Gauquelin's own search for foolproof objective criteria). But these inconsistencies did not constitute bias in any sense whatsoever. On the contrary, when the inconsistencies were eliminated, and when all Gauquelin's separate experiments were merged into one enormous (4,291 athletes) sample, the Mars Effect figures cited by Gauquelin were enhanced rather than diminished.

Apart from settling the question of bias once and for all, Ertel's study confirmed both Gauquelin's chief hypotheses: (1) Champion athletes will tend to be born with Mars rising or culminating (key sectors 1 and 4) more often than ordinary people (or indeed, professional but undistinguished athletes). (2) The more eminent the athletes, the more pronounced will be the Mars Effect.

By extension, these conclusions will necessarily apply to Gauquelin's other planetary correspondences: Jupiter/actors, Moon/writers, Saturn/scientists, and so on (Fig. 23).*

Those correspondences precisely confirm the oldest and most widespread of astrological beliefs, that one aspect of astrology that is universally acknowledged from culture to culture: the relationship between the individual planets and specific personality types.

Meanwhile, Back at Precinct HQ

Within the ranks of CSICOP, Ertel's study generated still further Gauquelin controversy. A number of previously skeptical members, basing their skepticism on the (remote) possibility of bias, have acknowledged the apparent soundness of the Ertel report, and in increasingly strongly worded terms, have urged

---

* Those crucial further independent replications of the Mars Effect are beginning to trickle in. A study of 1,000 eminent German physicians has been done by the German psychologist. Professor Arno Mueller. The results were statistically significant at levels similar to those obtained by Gauquelin. They will be published in *Der Zeitschrift für Parapsychologie und Grenzegebiete der Psychologie*.

857 scientists
belonging to the Académie de
Médecine *or* the Académie
des Sciences

361 MINOR painters

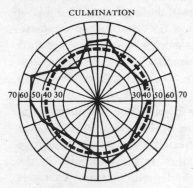

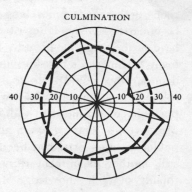

68 scientists
belonging to both
Academies *at the same time*

236 FAMOUS painters

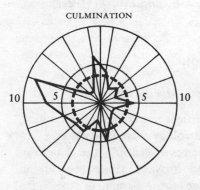

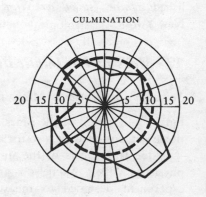

Figure 23. Two examples of the eminence effect with the planet Saturn. In the examples to the left, the Mars Effect is clearly visible in the upper chart. However, when the most eminent individuals are culled from the list, the effect is dramatically enhanced. The same applies in reverse fashion in the right-hand charts. Saturn retreats from the angles in the charts of the lesser-known painters, but flees headlong in the charts of the renowned.

the *Skeptical Inquirer* to publish and discuss it, suitably refereed. To no avail.

The *Skeptical Inquirer* has declined, claiming that its readership has become wearied of the Gauquelin controversy, and also claiming that the technical language of the Ertel report would not be understood. This latter objection is curious, since the masthead of the magazine proudly lists among its official supporters many of America's best-known scientists, philosophers and academics, who would seem to have the qualifications needed to follow the argument. They will now be deprived of the opportunity of reading and judging Ertel's study for themselves. Moreover, a long two-part article by Dr Geoffrey Dean was published after Ertel had been rejected. This article concerned still another experiment designed to test astrologers on the totality of their knowledge in blind prediction and character analysis. The results were negative. The jury may find it odd that the *Skeptical Inquirer* should publish Dean, but not Ertel. However, a review of 'Grading the Eminence' has been published by the *Journal for Scientific Exploration*, #3 (Pergamon, New York).

The Mars Effect: Implications

Scientific Implications: Michelson–Morley Revisited

Final confirmation of the Mars Effect has far-reaching implications: but, curiously, less so for astrology than for science.

In the latter years of the nineteenth century, the American physicists Albert Michelson and Edward Morley set up an experiment designed to measure the velocity of the earth through the luminiferous ether by measuring the effect such velocity would have upon the velocity of light. To their surprise, the velocity of light was unaffected. Careful replications of the experiment produced identical results, and it became necessary to abandon the theory of the ether, that imaginary and most rarefied of materials, accepted axiomatically by Victorian scientists. For the ether was an absolutely essential component in building the then-reigning theories of Newtonian physics. The proven absence of the ether destroyed the foundations of Victorian physics in a single blow, paving the way for relativity theory.

So, while the Michelson–Morley experiment was not in itself an epochal discovery, all modern physics follows from it.

We think it likely that the science of the twenty-first century will look back at Gauquelin and the Mars Effect in a similar but even brighter light.

Like the Michelson–Morley experiment, the Mars Effect renders untenable a number of axiomatically held scientific convictions. It overthrows the belief that the planets are no more than cooled rocks that exercise no influence in earthly matters. Confirmation of the Mars Effect paves the way to a more profound and more realistic science: one in which meaning certainly (and consciousness probably) cannot be excluded.

But unlike the Michelson–Morley experiment, Gauquelin's work is not so much a breakthrough into something new. Rather it is a corroboration of one of the oldest beliefs there is (actually, so was the Michelson–Morley experiment, when ancient science is correctly understood. The energetic nature of matter was known from earliest antiquity).

But this is a point that, to date, only astrologers have chosen to acknowledge. Even those very few scientists (Eysenck, Geoffrey Dean, Dr Percy Seymour and a handful of others) honest enough to acknowledge the reality of the Mars Effect minimize its relationship to traditional astrology (a position endorsed by Gauquelin himself in his early years). But facts are facts, and the fact is that Gauquelin's vast labors have not uncovered one single new planetary relationship (planets 'fleeing' the angles in professions 'inimical' to the personality type typified by that planet [Mars for writers and artists; the moon for scientists and athletes], amounting to a new way of looking at traditional relationships). Beyond that, *all* Gauquelin's positive evidence simply corroborates correspondences astrologers have worked with for as long as there has been astrology. And, as we have seen, there can be little doubt that astrology antedates recorded history.

A. Statistical Evidence

This is not intended to minimize Gauquelin's prodigious labors in any way. Rather it is intended to underscore both the validity and the antiquity of the ancient astrological doctrine; to impress in the jury's mind that what Gauquelin has proven is *astrology*, by whatever name it may be called.

Geocosmic Astropsychological Stellarbiotics

Assuming that those presently inconceivable valid objections to Gauquelin's work remain inconceived, a new branch of science may well take root and flourish in its wake. But it may well insist upon calling itself Cosmobiology or Astrobiology or Geocosmics or Psychocelestial Mechanics, or some other such acceptable twentieth-century periphrasis – anything but 'Astrology' (astrologers seeking scientific approval are no less guilty of such sins of nomenclature).

Psychologically, it is crucially important for the priesthood of the Church of Progress to maintain its belief in progress itself; in its conceit of a barbarous past leading inevitably to the enlightened present. But confirmation of the Mars Effect proves the Church was scooped – perhaps some twenty thousand years ago or so – by scientists at least as sophisticated and infinitely wiser and more sensitive than themselves. Equally important, the recourse to jargon will be part of a desperate campaign to pretend that the Rationalist foundations of the Church of Progress can support even this unwelcome annex.

It cannot. By whatever name it goes by, what they will be studying is astrology; nothing but astrology: the proven relationship between the position of planets at birth and the human personality. Gauquelin's work amounts to the *scientific* vindication of the ancient metaphysical doctrine of the Harmony of the Spheres; that doctrine that recognizes the planets and stars as both embodiments and transmitters of Divine or Cosmic Principles.

Now it is just possible that through a leap of scientific imagination as bold and as wrong as Darwin's, a way will be found to incorporate the Mars Effect into the Materialist cosmology. This would involve extending the accidental mechanisms allegedly responsible for life on earth to the solar system – in such a way that Mars rising just happens to foster a personality that wins Gold Medals at the Olympics while Jupiter rising is fortuitously conducive to an Academy Award under the right circumstances. While such a hypothesis is clearly not impossible, it would appear difficult for even Rationalists to put forward with a straight face. To accept as valid the basic astrological premise is, effectively, to disavow the basic premise of Rationalism: that matter precedes mind, and that we human beings are but accidental occurrences, evolutionary aggregates in a universe that is fundamentally unconscious, meaningless and barren. A valid astrology presupposes a precisely contrary cosmogony and cosmology and in this metaphysical Wild West, there is no room for both philosophies. One will have to go. The confirmation of the Mars Effect, Gauquelin's life work, makes it absolutely certain which one this shall be – hence CSICOP's bitter animosity, the cover-up, the all-too-probable fraud, and the willingness of 186 eminent scientists to abandon their principles and sign a futile document based upon shoddy and outdated science. The Mars Effect is to Rationalism what Michelson–Morley was to the luminiferous ether.*

Astrological Implications

It is ironic that Gauquelin's work, the single body of evidence that stands as scientific confirmation of astrology's most basic premise, has very clear implications for science, for philosophy and for metaphysics, but much less clear implications for astrology itself.

---

* Actually, the theory put forward by astronomer Dr Percy Seymour (see pp. 369–92), scrupulously leaves these metaphysical questions unaddressed. It is strictly concerned with the manner by which proven astrological effects might be *physically* transmitted, via resonance, from the planets to the earth. But the scientific community seemed to suspect a threat to its biological survival. Evidently unable to bear up under the intense selection pressure, it responded with the kind of hostility the jury will now recognize as both typical and inevitable.

Unlike Michelson–Morley, the Gauquelin work is not an end in itself. As Ertel and other researchers have already discovered, the enormous meticulously documented files represent a mine for the further scientific investigation of astrology. Certain avenues have already been opened; others, as yet unenvisaged, will depend upon the insight and ingenuity of future researchers. The material is there and waiting. But the ultimate effects upon astrology as it is now understood and practiced are anybody's guess.

For astrologers, these practical and theoretical effects are of paramount importance. But they are not central to building our case for astrology; particularly since we are much more concerned with establishing and defending the validity of astrology's premise than its practice. Nevertheless, it is the practice of astrology – specifically the horoscope and its interpretation – that *is* astrology to the general public, and to most astrologers. So, for whatever it may be worth (more, we personally believe, than the scientific data may indicate up to now) it is in order to develop, at least in broad outline, the major implications the Mars Effect poses for astrological practice.

Most astrological interpretation takes as its starting point the signs of the zodiac and the positions of planets within the signs – precisely that which adamantly declines to declare itself (directly) valid through Gauquelin's or anyone else's statistics to date.

Apart from the normal human dislike of being proved wrong, astrologers are loath to relinquish their beliefs without alternative or better interpretive tools at their disposal. The proven validity of the Mars Effect, and of the astrological premise in turn, does not quite justify (as a necessary corollary) the ability to interpret and predict. On the other hand, that proven 'influence' or correspondence between planets and personality at birth, certainly does mean the connection does not cease at birth. But we stress again, Gauquelin's negative statistics, and the negative statistics compiled by other researchers do not *dis*prove the validity of the zodiacal signs, either, as opponents pretend. Perhaps the fairest assessment would be to consider the validity of the signs of the zodiac emphatically *un*proven.

And this puts astrologers in a quandary. Powerful as it may

be statistically, the Mars Effect does not teach astrologers much; practically or conceptually. It suggests that they should perhaps take into account the positions of planets relative to the angles before anything else. Planets rising or culminating (or, alternatively, fleeing the angles) may well be the chief astrological key to personality, not the sun sign or Rising sign.

On the other hand, this conclusion does not *necessarily* follow from Gauquelin's findings.

Roughly 25% of champion athletes have Mars rising or culminating (35% of superstar athletes), statistically an overwhelmingly significant result. But practically, this still means that 75% of athletes no less eminent do *not* have Mars rising or culminating. Thus, the proven Mars Effect tells astrologers nothing they did not know before, while doubts have been cast upon much they thought they knew.

Some of the questions raised might be answered by more concerted and sophisticated raids upon Gauquelin's own data, but the outcome is impossible to predict. It is possible that astrologers may ultimately have to face further unproof of many of their most cherished beliefs. But for the moment they are quite within their rights to insist that unproof is not tantamount to disproof.

Quantifying the Unquantifiable

Even if more sophisticated experiments do come up negative, escape routes remain. *In extremis*, astrologers can *always* take refuge in the argument that these aspects of astrology defy quantification. Depending upon the nature of the unproof, this argument could be valid. After all, though scientists can blow up the world at the touch of a button, or poison it irrevocably with toxic waste, or destroy all of humanity with some ingenious new bug or gas, they still cannot find significant differences between Spaniards and Swedes, nor prove that Beethoven's Quartet in C Minor is a better piece of music than 'The Star-Spangled Banner' or 'God Save the Queen'. Astrologers may with some justification insist that the questions being asked of astrology are of this latter order, and therefore outside the scope and competence of modern scientific inquiry. But this does not make them any less real or valid.

In short, it is possible that astrologers have failed tests because, to date, these tests have seldom been designed to test what astrologers actually do. The tests are blind, which may be necessary from the scientific point of view, but blind tests run absolutely contrary to normal astrological practice. Expecting an astrologer to delineate character blind, is like expecting a physician to diagnose an illness with the patient absent.

The Genius Factor

And finally, no matter what the accumulated unproof may seem to imply, there is always the possibility that astrologers fail tests simply because they are not good enough astrologers. Any practice largely devoted to interpretation is, and must be, more art than science. Seeing what is involved in astrology, it is not inconceivable that statistically consistent successful interpretation may require a higher degree of personal spiritual development than most modern astrologers have reached. Tell a thousand college students to write a poem about a nightingale and it is unlikely they will produce one worth printing. But if one of those students happens to be John Keats, the whole experiment is turned round. At a certain point the qualitative will impinge upon and obviate the quantitative.

There is even some evidence this 'genius' factor may be less rare in astrology than in poetry. Dean (*Recent Advances*, p. 137) cites a number of instances where people can guess the sun signs strangers were born under with accuracy ranging between 60–80%. Dean describes the odds against chance at this level as 'astronomical'.

In another sign-guessing experiment run by a British newspaper (ibid., p. 136) four leading British astrologers were presented with twelve unknown subjects (one for each sign). Strict rules applied. The astrologers were permitted up to two five-minute interviews (which they did not always require) with each subject, and were allowed to ask them anything except their birth-date. The subjects had no knowledge of astrology or interest in it, and gave away as little information as possible. A decision was reached by the panel together.

A chance result would give the astrologers one correct sun-sign guess out of twelve. The panel got eight right: odds of a million to one against chance. Dean writes, 'Judgement was based on the whole person and no characteristic was used consistently more than another.' The jury may find it odd that, having written this latter sentence, elsewhere Dr Dean should deride the argument that the chart must be judged as a whole, and liken it to 'saying that overeating won't make you fat' (see p. 236).

Dean continues, 'The brief clues given with each verdict appear trivial out of context but illustrate the wide range of characteristics considered.'

Aries	Right	His active restless behaviour, thin-faced looks.
Taurus	Wrong	One said Taurus because she wanted a mink coat bought by someone else, the rest could not agree.
Gemini	Wrong	One said Gemini because of her lively face.
Cancer	Wrong	Panel did not agree, settled for Libra.
Leo	Wrong	Panel were homing in on Taurus.
Virgo	Right	His tidyness. A typical Virgo.
Libra	Right	His self-deprecation and charm.
Scorpio	Right	She felt she had power over people.
Sagittarius	Right	Her optimism, luck and love of gambling.
Capricorn	Right	Thin mouth, expressive hands.
Aquarius	Right	Clear, candid eyes, calm manner and detachment. Panel reached a decision almost immediately.
Pisces	Right	Her self-honesty.

Dean continues, 'The possibility of telepathy means that the correct guessing of Sun signs does not necessarily support the validity of signs.'

Of course, from the point of view of the Church of Progress, telepathy is no more acceptable than astrology. But if appropriate safeguards against telepathy were taken, and astrologers were successful at guessing the sun signs of strangers, it would go a long way towards validating this difficult and elusive but crucial element in traditional astrological practice. In effect, it would mean that the astrological tools available are good enough to allow astrologers to judge subjects as a whole, on the basis of just a few minutes with them, and to deduce their sun signs on that basis. In effect, the astrologers know from their brief interveiws who will pick up the stick and who will not notice it has been dropped, and will relate that *locus* of personality traits to the appropriate sign.

Demonstrations such as the above put astrologers on less shaky ground *vis-à-vis* the unproven elements in astrology than the evidence would otherwise suggest. Apart from the intrinsic problems involved in subjecting astrology to decisive quantitative scientific tests (a situation invariably minimized by opponents), there is always this wild-card possibility of a single astrologer or a few astrologers subverting the carefully compiled negative results of a thousand others.

In any event, thanks to Michel Gauquelin, astrologers now *know* that in principle astrology is justified. Astrological practice may well be in need of revision and rethinking, and astrologers who are not absolutely tradition-bound and averse to any contact with science, look for ways to incorporate or wed the powerful quantitative methods of science to the essentially qualitative art of astrological interpretation. Perhaps the most promising avenue is the work in harmonics initiated by John Addey.

Harmonics: The Work of John Addey

A harmonic is a wave superimposed upon a fundamental wave with a frequency that is a whole-number multiple (or fraction) of the fundamental frequency. If a string is vibrating at 100 vibrations per second, its second harmonic will vibrate at 200 vibrations per second, its third at 300 and so on.

The word 'harmonics' of course conjures up the image of music, but over the past few decades, the concept has been vastly extended. As modern physics has finally discovered (actually, rediscovered), the physical world in its entirety is made up of energy, manifesting itself in wave forms (the Egyptian glyph for water, from which all creation arose is ∿∿, a wave form). Under certain conditions and in certain states, these wave forms are interpreted through the human sensory apparatus as 'matter'. But all is, ultimately, energy, manifesting in wave form. The study of harmonics, expanded to take in the relationships between these infinitely various wave forms, thus becomes a universal study. Harmonic relationships are formalized in the various theories of resonance – which are now applied to the physical, nuclear, and chemical realms ... while the operation of harmonics in the world of our common experience are legion: the soprano hits a particular note and the crystal wine-glass shatters; French acoustic researchers generate powerful sound waves below the threshold of hearing and destroy their lab and their own insides; sand sprinkled on a metal plate attached to a violin forms a lovely geometric pattern as a certain note is reached; the pattern dissolves into chaos as the pitch of the note is changed and then forms another, different, but related pattern as a *harmonic* of the original note is sounded. An early Israeli acoustical researcher, Joshua, reputedly brought down Jericho through an understanding of the resonant properties of its walls, while Plato explained astrology as a result of the Harmony of the Spheres.

Like most valid knowledge, the knowledge of harmony and resonance (and the Number Symbolism that ultimately underpins and gives meaning to both) is very, very old. In fact, the pioneering work of Schwaller and like-minded scholars has given rise to a criterion that may be applied with a high degree of confidence to knowledge and ideas in general: if an idea is old enough (pre-Greek), it is probably right even if presently unproved; if it is new, distrust it until the proof is ironclad – think twice before you reject reincarnation, more than twice before you accept black holes, superstrings, ten-dimensional space or the concept of Progress.

Behind the banal, often silly, and indubitably unscientific terminology commonly employed by pop astrologers (Saturn is a 'cold, reserved' planet, while Jupiter is, well, 'jovial' and Venus 'loving and tender') there is a complex system based upon an understanding of Number Symbolism, resonance and harmony. Artists, philosophers, mystics, and serious astrologers have never lost sight of this fact – while their Rationalist opponents have never paid attention to it, though harmonics and resonance are now understood as fundamental scientific principles underlying all material creation, and their application to celestial correspondences follows logically from what is known about them in other physical domains.

The late John Addey was a founder and long-time president of the Astrological Association of Great Britain, an organization set up expressly to further research into astrology; particularly to explore those aspects of astrology amenable to scientific inquiry. In effect, the Astrological Association was, and is, concerned with distinguishing between baby and bathwater.

Addey began his researches around the same time as Gauquelin, in the mid-1950s, but did not become closely acquainted with the Mars Effect for another ten years. Though no less interested than Gauquelin in finding a scientific basis for astrology through statistical inquiry, Addey's approach was along a different path. It was astrology's metaphysical verity that was his chief interest; astrology as a paradigm of divine order. This was, of course, the allure of astrology for its most eminent adherents past and present.

Addey was convinced (as are so many of us) that astrology 'works' – up to a point. But as a practicing astrologer with a keen critical sense (not the most common combination in the world of astrology), that conviction was much hedged round with reservations (see p. 227). For that point, up to which astrology 'works', is elusive to say the least. In part this was unavoidable in a practice in which interpretation played a central role, but also, Addey was convinced, it was because astrology had gradually lost its integrity over the centuries as it lost touch with its underlying metaphysical and Pythagorean principles. Aware of the significance of harmonics and resonance in the breakthrough physical theories of the twentieth century, Addey perceived a potential link between the old sacred tradition and the new secular science (that so obstinately refuses to recognize its own necessary metaphysical foundation in Consciousness).

That astrology was based upon a fundamental understanding of harmonics was undeniable. It is the interaction of Number, through the polarities, modes, elements that gives meaning to the signs of the zodiac – not some imaginary resemblance to animals, virgins and water-bearers; while the astrological aspects each represent a whole-number fraction, or harmonic (the opposition, second harmonic; trine, third harmonic; square, fourth harmonic; and so on).

While Gauquelin sought a confirmation of astrology without particular regard to the soundness of any theory, Addey was looking for some physical harmonic manifestation of what he considered unarguable metaphysical truth.

His scientific starting point was different than Gauquelin's, but analogous. Addey initially decided to look for significant correlations in groups of people sharing some very specific quality or trait, rather than a common profession. Addey chose first a group of 970 nonagenarians, taken inclusively from *Who Was Who*.

He first checked for significant deviation in the sun signs. (Capricorns are reputedly long-lived. Are they? Pisceans, according to the text-books, tend to be short-lived. Is there any truth in this?) Addey's figures corroborated what is now becoming a statistical commonplace: the sun in the various signs seems to play no detectable role in whatever it is that is undergoing statistical analysis. Addey found as many nonagenarian Pisceans as Capricorns, and so on around the zodiac, just as Gauquelin had found as many soldiers born under allegedly peace-loving Libra as he had under the 'martial' signs, Aries and Scorpio.

Nor could Addey find statistical evidence for any of the other traditional astrological pointers of longevity. And while one may rationalize and say that nonagenarians have nothing in common, really, except their longevity, it seemed to Addey that this alone was enough to merit a connection in some fashion. And it is at this point, incidentally, that an important difference may arise in two equally scientific experiments. The opponent of astrology, seeking to disprove it, would have cheerfully abandoned the experiment after the more obvious statistical avenues had been explored (as in the various examples cited on pp. 225–6), while the astrologer, convinced through experience that a correlation must exist, will keep looking. And ultimately Addey did find at least one significant factor.

Astrologers have long recognized a qualitative difference between an aspect that is 'applying' and one that is 'separating'. For example, if, in a horoscope, the sun is in ten degrees Aries, and Saturn, a slow-moving planet, is in twelve degrees Aries, that aspect is said to be 'applying'; the sun closing in, as it were, upon Saturn. If the positions were reversed, then the aspect would be 'separating'. Analogically, astrology would compare the process to the Doppler effect: when 'applying', the aspect breeds tension, excitement, action; when 'separating', it signifies a release, an extension, a dilation, passivity. Addey discovered an impressively significant preponderance of separating aspects in the charts of his 970 nonagenarians. And though no one had thought of it before, a preponderance of separating aspects made astrological sense; nonagenarians might typically be expected to share an ability and propensity to conserve energy, not to waste or play havoc with their physical resources. This might well be an effect related to the separating aspect according to astrological tradition.

So, looking for a correlation of one sort, Addey found another one altogether; less conclusive and satisfying, certainly, than a pronounced preponderance of nonagenarian Capricorns would have been, but an astrological correlation none the less. This in turn led to a still more interesting (and ultimately important) experiment.

It was still possible, despite the high level of significance obtained, and the accord with astrological tradition, that the results were a high-level fluke, and Addey therefore determined to test a group of people from whom the opposite – a preponderance of 'applying' aspects – might be expected.

A polio victim himself, and a teacher in a polio hospital, Addey had a built-in test group of particular interest from this astrological viewpoint. It is a medical fact that polio victims conform closely to a recognizable 'type' – bright, nervous, active. Dull, plodding types rarely contract polio.

Addey reasoned that if nonagenarians showed a preponderance of separating aspects, then polio victims, characterologically opposed, might be expected to show a preponderance of applying aspects.

This hypothesis was borne out with a high degree of significance. A group was analyzed and applying aspects were found to occur significantly more frequently than separating aspects; in gratifying contradistinction to the nonagenarians.

In studying the wave forms of his charts, Addey was struck by their recurrent nature. He realized that these forms were susceptible to the statistical technique called 'wave analysis', in which data are broken down into their component harmonics. This method is currently being applied to the study of natural cycles, 'biological clocks', and a variety of other phenomena directly correlated to celestial and planetary cycles.

Though the Music or Harmony of the Spheres had been explicitly a part of astrological language since Pythagoras (and implicitly since astrology's origins), and many of the greatest astrologers had attempted to correlate music and astrological theory, none before John Addey had looked into studying astrological data in terms of wave forms. Through wave analysis, Addey believed that ultimately the widely mistrusted traditional genethliacal astrology could be brought into line and interpreted – at least in part – in a manner consistent with the rigorous quantitative demands of modern disciplines, yet without sacrificing or distorting astrology's Pythagorean principles.

Immediately, a number of otherwise baffling astrological problems became comprehensible. Addey's polio victims were clearly linked by astrological factors – the statistics could not conceivably all be flukes. But these factors were common to no known astrological tradition. No interpretation in terms of the usual twelve-sign zodiac, or any other sign-zodiac made sense. It was the *recurrence* that was significant. The regular recurrence created a wave form. This wave form corresponded to a harmonic – in this case of a year, which corresponded to the fundamental.*

Re-interpreting the data in terms of sun signs, Addey now found that while the traditional divisions into Aries, Taurus, Gemini, etc., yielded nothing, if one neglected these preconceived divisions and watched for wave forms, distinct patterns emerged. Polio victims tended to be born according to the twelfth harmonic, and, most strongly of all, according to the 120th harmonic. Taken out of statistical language, Addey's chart suggests that a child born every third degree (irrespective of the zodiacal division) is 37% more liable to contract polio than a child born in the two intermediary degrees (or was, in the pre-polio vaccine days). The odds against Addey's figures being chance are 1:1,000. A control group of non-polio children selected at random yielded chance results.

What do Addey's statistics mean? No one as yet is sure. They do not mean that an astrologer can, from birth data alone, tell which child will contract polio and which will not. But they do mean that Addey has isolated at least two astrological factors – applying aspects, and the 120th harmonic – in the susceptibility to polio.

Other early studies by Addey into such diverse test groups as clergymen, doctors and red-heads yielded similar results. Different, statistically significant wave forms representing a number

---

* To visualize this, draw – or imagine – a straight line representing a year. Divide it into 360 parts, each representing a degree of the zodiac. Now note at each degree how many polio patients were born with the sun in that degree. Relatively high numbers appear at every third degree, still higher numbers every thirtieth degree, (120th and 12th harmonic respectively), while relatively low numbers were born in the degrees between. Now consider that the original straight line of 360 degrees represents an average or chance number of births. Superimpose the higher or lower numbers of births at each degree in points above and below the horizontal, connect those points and a wave form reveals itself.

of harmonics characterized Addey's sample groups selected for some common factor (susceptibility to a specific disease, a specific profession, a physical trait).

Apart from proving an overall astrological correspondence, Addey's work may perhaps provide insight into the scientific study of the role played by the sun in the birth chart. Though generally considered by astrologers the most important 'planet' in the horoscope, the sun to date has declined to co-operate with tests designed to reveal its influence. This, in turn, has furnished the Prosecution with most of its ammunition. Addey's work in harmonics proves that the sun does, indeed, play a role, albeit one apparently outside the pale of traditional astrology. But since the zodiac itself is harmonically determined (30 degrees per sign is a division of the zodiacal circle according to the 12th harmonic), further research may yet forge an accord between the new harmonics and age-old tradition.

Harmonics Applied to the Mars Effect

Addey had been developing his harmonic theories for a decade before he became aware of the commanding figures and rigorous methodology supporting the Mars Effect. A glance at Gauquelin's charts, particularly those devoted to Saturn and Mars, was enough to show him a harmonic phenomenon was responsible for the diagrams. The pronounced clear peaks at the rise and culmination (lesser, but equally clear peaks at the setting and nadir) provided dramatic confirmation of a harmonic configuration of astrological correspondences; far more dramatic than that emerging from his own data. Much of Addey's energies from that moment on were devoted to applying his theories to Gauquelin's massive files.

The Mars Effect data proves the validity of the astrological premise. But it is Addey's work that gives it a firm theoretical basis. The nature of Addey's harmonic discoveries is such that it is very difficult to convey a sense of their significance without a very detailed and technical discussion that is outside the scope of the present work. Here, it will suffice to say that Addey's work upon the Gauquelin files strongly corroborates the significance of the third and fourth harmonics, which in turn support (in principle) the importance astrologers have always extended to the major aspects, the square (fourth harmonic) and trine (third harmonic). Mars and Saturn, the 'strict' planets, manifest powerfully in the fourth harmonic in the samples of scientists and soldiers, and four is the number of 'material' (the four 'elements'), of concretization. The third harmonic becomes prominent in groups of writers and artists. Three is traditionally the number of 'relationship', the synthesizing faculty, that which reconciles opposites.

Though Addey, like Gauquelin and everyone else, was unable to find any scientific justification for the validity of sun signs, or any significance for planets in signs, his analyses and extension of Gauquelin's work promises to give astrologers the tools to redefine and improve astrology, starting with its basic principles, that is to say, the interplay of Number. Some astrologers are already experimenting with purely harmonic charts that ignore sun signs and that zero in on the given horoscope's harmonic content.

At the moment, it is impossible to predict if Addey's work will really pull the plug on the bathwater once and for all, and allow astrologers to improve the *practice* of astrology to the point where it, in turn, has enough scientific validity to pass realistic tests set to it.

As it stands, it is fair to say that Addey's careful and brilliant analysis and interpretation of his own and Gauquelin's data provides astrologers with a working conceptual framework from which to proceed. Though it does not and will not provide critics with the physical mechanism they insist on before they will legitimize astrology as a 'science', this is, as we have argued at length, no more than a last-ditch subterfuge, a final attempt to shore up a doomed metaphysical position, masquerading as 'Science'.

At the frontiers of *all* the physical sciences of the latter twentieth century, where 'matter' shades off into energy, or, as in genetics, into 'information', there is a similar lack of physical causative mechanism. When an appropriate model is used to investigate astrology (the concert hall, rather than the hammer-and-nail), Addey's work provides a methodology for studying quantitative and qualitative factors simultaneously without detriment to either.

Addey's work demonstrates that many of the chief elements of traditional astrology (excepting, alas, the chiefest of all, the zodiac!) – aspects, the angles, the significance of specific degree areas, the position of planets relative to the angles – are based upon realities, and that these realities are, to a certain extent, amenable to a statistical approach.

His harmonic studies build a sturdy theoretical framework that should permit all but the most obdurate and obtuse to realize that there is nothing 'supernatural' or 'paranormal' behind Gauquelin's Mars Effect, or other astrologically significant data, or behind astrology. It is rather a matter of science extending its myopic horizons to the point where these proven phenomena are understood as natural; inevitable consequences of a universe that is, before all else, an act of Divine Intention and in which humanity plays a role.

B. Cosmic Influences Upon Living Organisms

Obviously, if planetary effects are real, they must influence or regulate other forms of life, other physical phenomena, not just humans. While these effects obviously do not and cannot prove the validity of astrology as a means for delineating character or making predictions, planetary effects in the physical world provide a further powerful argument for the validity of the astrological premise. That is to say, if other forms of life, other physical phenomena, are influenced by celestial cycles, it follows inescapably that human beings must be influenced as well. There is an abundance of such evidence, well recognized in various branches of science. Here are some of the more striking.

Frank A. Brown

Virtually every living organism lives according to set, predetermined rhythms. For many years, the nature of the mechanism responsible for the regulation has been disputed. One school of thought believed the organism responded to changes in air ionization. Another school postulated an internal 'biological clock'. But it was impossible to explain how or why air ionization should cause the apparently purposeful and intelligent – though unconscious – behaviour of the organisms under consideration, while it was equally impossible to locate any physical mechanism capable of serving as a 'clock' – yet every cell in the body was responsive to the rhythm; the elusive 'clock' was at once everywhere and nowhere.

Ultimately, a truce was declared between the opposing factions. It was shown that air ionization and biological clocks were not mutually exclusive. The difficulty, however, remained. Even when offering mutual support, the combined theories could not account for the phenomenon.

Frank A. Brown, Professor of Biology at Northwestern University, disagreed with both prevailing hypotheses, and with a team of workers, after ten years of experimentation, offered impressive evidence supporting an alternative theory attributing the 'biological clock' to celestial rhythms, obviating the need for an internal physical mechanism.

In a well known article in *Science* (4 December 1959), Brown described these experiments. Brown and his co-workers ran long series of tests on the nocturnal movements of beans (Bean Sleep Movement), on the amount of running performed by rats during the course of the day (Rat Running);* the variations in the color of fiddler crabs (Crab Color Change) and the sleep patterns of flies (Fly Emergence). Brown discovered that all followed a definite, recognizable, and similar cycle, though the shape of the curve differed from one species to another. These tests were performed under strictly controlled conditions, and it was clear that these rhythms must be due, not to external climatic changes, but to influences of a pervasive and cosmic nature. The principal and the most obvious factors involved were the sun and moon.

Organisms as dissimilar as the potato and the fiddler crab showed unmistakable yearly (solar) and monthly (lunar) periodicities. These rhythms were characteristically most depressed at the new moon, and most active at the full moon; they were indifferent to temperature, and even to drugs. A rat, under control conditions, in a darkened cage, was twice as active when the moon was over the horizon than when it was beneath it; thus bearing out insistent testimony of all those generations of old wives and gardeners.

But perhaps most impressive of all was Brown's experiment

---

* Not to be confused with the 'Rat Race', a sociological phenomenon and manifestation of much longer, subtler astrological rhythms.

with oysters. Oysters open and close their shells in a distinct rhythm, attuned to the tides. And it had been assumed that the physical action of the tides, not the effects of the moon, was responsible. Brown, however, took oysters in light-proof containers from New Haven, Connecticut to Evanston, Illinois, and placed them in specially prepared pans of salt water in a dark room.

Within two weeks the oysters had adjusted their opening and closing rhythms to the lunar phases of Evanston; that is, to what would have been the tidal rhythm of Evanston, had there been tides there, proving that it was the moon and not the actual action of water which provoked the periodicity.

This discovery led to a massive study of a vast variety of living organisms, from algae to flowering plants, from invertebrate to vertebrate animals. It was found that the metabolic rates of all were quite independent of the immediate external conditions. 'It has now become quite clear that under such constant conditions all living things have continuously imposed upon them from the environment metabolic rhythms of exactly the nature of geophysical frequencies,' Brown wrote. An astrologer, however, would dispute the use of 'imposed', and would maintain simply that Brown's natural geophysical frequencies were but the Harmony of the Spheres making itself manifest.

As a scientist, Brown naturally steered clear of metaphysics. Yet, in his attempt to explain the action of the solar and lunar rhythms revealed by his experiments, he inadvertently draws close to an explanation that verges on the symbolic. Having dispensed with the need for the hypothetical 'clock', Brown had to account for the manner in which minute differences in the energy level can bring about such dramatic changes in the entire organism. He postulated a 'trigger mechanism', whereby a minute application of energy upon the 'trigger' (which is, incidentally, as physically hypothetical as the 'clock') sets off a chain reaction culminating in the relatively vast amount of energy expended by the organism.

As an analogy Brown cites a train schedule, in which the

complex processes of the railway are set in motion by the schedule, which is its 'trigger'.

This analogy is more revealing than Brown intended. For a train schedule does not just 'happen'; the actual physical schedule (information rather than energy, in fact) is the manifestation of the decision to operate trains at such and such a time. This decision is a mental event. It is invisible. And it is undemonstrable. We cannot prove that a decision has been made. But, since it has been made by people, we know from our own experience that a train schedule could not be made without this original idea, or decision.

Rats and potatoes operate on a schedule far subtler than our railways. And we have had no part in the organization of their schedules. But it is quite unwarranted, and in fact unscientific (because contrary to experience) to imagine that our schedules require thought, but that Nature's schedules just happen.

While Professor Brown did not draw these conclusions from his analogy, they are implicit in it, legitimate, and difficult to avoid.

Brown also learned that if he kept various organisms in the dark, they maintained their normal night–day rhythms despite the absence of light. However, if an unnatural rhythm of artificial night and day was imposed upon them, the organisms could be forced into obedience. They could be made to respond to a 'day' that was less or more than the usual twenty-four hours. But, interestingly enough, outside interference would be tolerated only up to a point. Beyond that point – about a thirty or an eighteen-hour day – the organism would stand for it no longer, and would 'break away', reverting to its natural rhythm no matter what schedule was imposed upon it. Viewed theologically, this would seem to imply that hope is built into the very molecules of the fiddler crab. It will tolerate only so much interference with its preordained rhythms. And if this is the case with the fiddler crab, why should it be otherwise with us. We personally believe the resurgence of astrology and the burgeoning 'New Age' movement represents a massed, instinctive reaction by human beings to the inhuman rhythms and mores imposed upon us by the reigning Church of Progress.

B. Cosmic Influences Upon Living Organisms

Leonard J. Ravitz

Dr Leonard J. Ravitz of Duke University, plotting changes in electrical potential emitted by the body in normal and insane people, found marked changes, coinciding with the phases of the moon, and with the seasons. The more disturbed the patients were, the more they were affected.

On the basis of his findings, Ravitz was able to predict successfully the emotional states of his patients, and he ratified the ancient belief that there was more unrest among the insane when the moon was full. Ravitz asserted: 'Whatever else we may be we are all electric machines. Thus energy reserves may be mobilized by periodic factors (such as the forces behind the moon) which tend to aggravate maladjustments and conflicts already present.'

Other Positive exPeriments

Because there is no recognized organization working to follow up the implications of experiments such as Brown's and Ravitz's, it is impossible to say if, or in what way these and related findings will corroborate or contradict traditional astrological beliefs.

In *L'Astrologie devant la science*, published in 1967 (Peter Davis, London), Michel Gauquelin was already able to list bibliographical references to forty-two scientific papers and books exploring celestial/terrestrial relationships. That number has been growing steadily over the succeeding years, and it is worth describing briefly a few of the experiments, old and new, that swell the file of quantitative evidence. Not all are equally conclusive; some have not been replicated independently. And since all (excepting those of the Anthroposophists) were carried out in the absence of any unifying philosophy or theme, any summary of them makes for fragmentary reading. It is their cumulative weight that is impressive as evidence; the proof that, from a wide range of disciplines, the physical and the celestial worlds are inextricably linked.

In 1938, in Japan, Yamahaki studied the frequency of 33,000

births and found a significant frequency occurring at the full and new moon; the least frequency occurred one or two days before the first and last quarter. Meneker, an American gynaecologist, confirmed this from a study of half a million births.

Gutman and Oswald, studying 10,000 cases of menstruation over a period of fourteen years, found a definite maximum at the full and new moons. Arrhenius, earlier in the century, had come to a similar conclusion from the study of over 11,000 cases. But other researchers have not been able to isolate such a rhythm.

After reading of the experiments carried out by the Italian chemist, Giorgio Piccardi (see p. 337), Dr Abram Hoffer, Director of Psychiatric Research at University Hospital, Saskatchewan, Canada, decided to see if mental patients under his care were subject to the same external influences as were the chemical precipitates of Piccardi.

He found that depressives reacted strongly, their worst periods falling unmistakably in March. Neurotics, on the other hand, showed periodicities, but of another nature altogether, with peaks of neurosis in January or July, while schizophrenics showed themselves remarkably insensitive to any form of outside influence. Hoffer made the interesting observation that, since neurotics were the most nearly normal, it might be worth looking into January and July as psychologically significant among the population at large.

Dr Edson Andrews, an American physician, was told by his nurse that patients were haemorrhaging significantly more frequently at certain times than at others. Andrews at first scoffed at the idea, but a rough test seemed to confirm it. A more elaborate and organized inquiry revealed that in 1,000 cases of tonsillectomies, 82% of the bleeding crises occurred between the moon's first and third quarters. This disproportion was even greater than it appeared, Andrews claimed, since fewer patients were admitted near the full moon. A re-check by another doctor yielded similar results.

B. Cosmic Influences Upon Living Organisms

Experiments of the Anthroposophists

Rudolf Steiner (1861–1925), philosopher and noted authority on Goethe, was leader of the German section of the Theosophist movement. But having quarrelled with Annie Besant, Mme Blavatsky's successor, Steiner broke away and established a school of his own, practicing 'Anthroposophy' or 'Wisdom of Humanity', with headquarters in Switzerland.

The Anthroposophical movement incorporates a number of recognizable features common to all traditions, but with its distinctly Germanic cast, and following the lead of Steiner – with his own deep regard for Goethe – the movement has placed considerable emphasis upon modern science, and includes among its members a number of qualified scientists. Many years of organized, directed research have produced positive results, in many fields relevant to astrology. But this work rarely finds its way into the popular press, to say nothing of the scientific journals.

The scientific work of the Anthroposophists seems to be carried out under control conditions as strict as those prevailing elsewhere. Anthroposophical publications invite inspection by outsiders. And, while it is true that Anthroposophical research is based upon the premise of a coherent and meaningful universe, this does not make the science less exacting than a science based upon a contrary premise.

A long series of experiments carried out by Mme Lily Kolisko culminated in her book, *The Moon and Plant Growth* (Anthroposophical Publishing Company, 1938). Following thousands of laboratory experiments, Mme Kolisko concluded that there is a very definite relationship between the rate plants grow and the phase of the moon they were planted under. In general, it was found that vegetables grew best when planted shortly before a full moon and slower when planted under the waning moon. These findings have been elaborated and refined by many anthroposophical researchers since that time (leafy vegetables grow best planted under the full moon, root vegetables best planted under the waning or new moon), initiating a revolutionary but exacting agricultural program called 'Bio-dynamic Programming' that produces miraculously rich organic crops for the farmers committed to practicing it.

Despite an airy dismissal by Eisler back in 1946, based upon conclusions reached after a single incomplete experiment by Maby and Franklin, joint authors of a remarkable book, *The Physics of the Divining Rod* (G. Bell & Sons, London, 1939), the findings of Frank Brown and many others enhance the possibility that Mme Kolisko's results after twelve years of research are no fluke, and that her data was not cooked to fit into a preconceived plan.

In theory, of course, experiments such as these can – and ought to – be performed by disinterested outsiders before conclusions are reached. But the experience of the Anthroposophists indicates that in this case 'theory' sometimes chooses to be uncooperative. Some of the most interesting and ostensibly most convincing experiments seem to depend upon who performs them. This is to say that, 'unscientific' though it may appear, the gardener's proverbial 'green thumb' is probably no myth, and disinterested outsiders are not so easily come by, either. Most experiments are run by people who, for one reason or another, are personally and emotionally involved in their outcome, either pro or con, and when the experiment involves organic life, this emotional involvement may influence the outcome.

Today, this idea sounds less superstitious than it did fifty years ago. An article in the March 1987 *Discover*, a magazine normally rigorously committed to broadcasting Church of Progress orthodoxy, talked about the proven effect of 'attitude' in healing. Though *Discover* did not acknowledge it (and might well have killed the story if this necessary conclusion had been drawn to their attention), this admission is tantamount to recognizing faith healing, since all the healer must do is change the patient's 'attitude' to initiate a cure in certain instances. If recalcitrant cells can be brought back into line through emotion, an emotional bond, positive or negative, between plant and planter is hardly far-fetched – particularly since it conforms to common experience anyway. There are those with 'green thumbs' and those without. Since yogis have known for at least three thousand years that mind can influence matter – an article in the equally hard-headed *New Scientist* back in February 1969 (p. 343) acknowledges this ability – its belated 'discovery' by science hardly rates as revelation. But orthodox science has no satisfactory theory to account for 'mind', nor one to account for 'matter', so the connection, between attitude and healing, and between plant and planter, is far more of a mystery than is let on. All esoteric traditions, however, insist that both 'mind' and 'matter' are but manifestions of the same Higher Consciousness. To this way of thinking the power of 'mind' over 'matter' is but an expression of the natural hierarchy; a scientific mystery certainly, but in no way a philosophical problem or paradox. There can be little doubt that, having scientifically established the link between attitude and healing, untold numbers of laboratory animals will now die painful deaths as scientists look for the 'mechanism' that allows 'mind' to act upon 'matter'.

In any case, Mme Kolisko's experiments appear to provide dramatic proof of the influence of the moon over plant growth. (Apart from the Maby and Bedford experiment, carried out prior to the outbreak of World War II, it would appear that no one has directly replicated her work.) Equally interesting results were obtained from another Anthroposophical experiment described in *Moon and Plant* by Agnes Fyfe. In other experiments, Nick Kollerstrom and Maria Thun planted potatoes and other root vegetables in controlled experiments and claimed they grew best when planted while the moon was in an earth sign, worst when in a water sign – one of the very few experiments that seem to validate zodiacal signs. Kollerstrom has also carried out a long series of experiments in which metal salts are precipitated on filter paper. He claims to have found some significant correspondences between the rates of precipitation and conjunctions of the planets to which those metals are traditionally connected: Saturn/lead, Jupiter/tin, Venus/copper and Mars/iron.

Rudolf Steiner maintained that it was possible to prepare a

remedy for cancer from mistletoe, but that the effectiveness of the remedy would depend upon the time the plant was picked.

Accordingly, when a cancer research laboratory was set up in 1949, Anthroposophists decided to test mistletoe to see if these supposed variations in its potency could be measured. Its toxicity on white mice was tested regularly and its pH value (degree of acidity) measured.

The sap of the mistletoe was also put through a process called capillary dynamolysis, in which the sap is allowed to rise in a piece of filter paper. This forms a pattern which, when stained, can be photographed. And over the course of time the photographs can be compared for changes in pattern.

After 70,000 such experiments had been performed, definite, complex harmonic wave-patterns were established, both long-term and short-term. The patterns were quite insensitive to the immediate weather conditions, but violently affected by extra-terrestrial factors, eclipses in particular. Without jumping to any conclusions as to the effectiveness of mistletoe in cancer treat-ment, it is nevertheless reasonable enough to suppose that changing patterns formed by the mistletoe sap may well represent a change in its medicinal properties – whatever these may be.

Given these results, the ancient Egyptian insistence upon the time that remedies are both prepared and administered appears quite reasonable, at least in theory. R. A. Schwaller de Lubicz gives personal testimony for an unguent that worked almost miraculously when prepared according to a traditional ritual, and that was actually poisonous when prepared otherwise.

The Anthroposophists' work in these areas is extensive and there is a considerable literature devoted to it. But since most of it is sensibly directed towards practical application in medicine or agriculture, rather than 'proof', we cannot begin to do justice to it in these pages.

The 'Piccardi Effect': Extraterrestrial Influences in Inorganic Chemistry

Of all the fields of science, none appears so devoid of mystery as inorganic chemistry where X will always combine with Y at a given rate in a given ratio to form XY. Or so we learn at school.

But in fact the matter is not quite so simple. There are skeletons in the inorganic chemist's closet. Colloids and precipitates in particular refuse to conform to chemical standards of behavior, and water, the commonest of liquids, is also the most mysterious, exhibiting any number of embarrassing aberrations. Though long known to chemists, this wayward behavior has generally been overlooked, ascribed to faulty equipment or laboratory mistakes, or frankly put down to 'freaks of nature' and ignored.

However, an Italian chemist, Professor Giorgio Piccardi of Florence University, became interested in these matters in the 1930s and after long and persistent experimentation has shown that these chemical anomalies are caused by extraterrestrial factors.

Most impressive of Piccardi's experiments was one beginning in 1951 and extending through 1958, performed as a contribution to the International Geophysical Year.

Using specified, pre-arranged methods, following a pre-arranged plan, Piccardi and other scientists in laboratories around the world prepared a precipitate of bismuth oxychloride in water, under strictly controlled laboratory conditions.

It was discovered that the rate of precipitation varied from day to day. The possibility of quirks in equipment had been eliminated, as had the possibility of carelessness in organizing the experiments. When a copper sheet was placed over the experimental vessels, the precipitate formed at a constant rate meaning that the copper voided the effects of whatever it was that caused the fluctuations.* Over the course of seven years, more than 200,000 separate experiments were performed.

Piccardi found that the rates of precipitation followed a definite and predictable cyclical pattern throughout the year,

---

* In other experiments, sheets of different kinds of metals placed over the experimental vessel altered the chemical reactions within *in different ways*. It is but a short step from these results to the beliefs held by primitive and superstitious peoples in the magical properties of certain precious stones and metals.

with a minimum in March. He also found variations according to latitude – interesting in view of cycles research which indicates that biological, ecological and even economic cycles follow similar patterns; corresponding not only to latitude but to the earth's magnetic field as well. The cyclical pattern was shattered violently whenever there were sharp magnetic disturbances in the atmosphere. And the yearly cycle was 'enveloped' in the familiar 11.1 year sun-spot cycle. All of this corroborated cyclical data from a number of fields, with the exception of the sharp yearly fluctuation in March. This fluctuation could not be accounted for in terms of earthly phenomena, nor even in terms of known phenomena within the confines of the solar system, and Piccardi boldly hypothesized that the March fluctuations were due to factors that are galactic in origin.

The earth revolves about the sun, which in turn races towards the constellation of Hercules, meaning that the earth describes in space not a flat orbit, but a complex spiral, whose action in March is unique.

The old idea of 'empty space' has of course been discarded, and in its place science now talks of 'fields of force'. While denying any connection to astrology, Piccardi theorizes that the singular displacement of the earth within the galactic field of force during the month of March results in the curious fluctuation in the speed of the chemical reaction during that month.

Piccardi's chemical experiments have for many years been accompanied by research into the anomalies of water. He has shown that water is particularly sensitive to outside influences between temperatures of 30 degrees and 40 degrees Centigrade and that colloids, subsequently, share in this strange sensitivity. 'There is no need to underline the importance of this fact,' Piccardi asserts;

> it is well known that life takes place in an aqueous and colloidal system.*

---

* 'By far the most important molecule to living organisms is water. No water, no life anywhere in the universe. I think water is also the strangest molecule in the

> Water is sensitive to extremely delicate influence and is capable of adapting itself to the most varying circumstances to a degree attained by no other liquid. It may be that it is this infinity of possibilities that makes the existence of life possible ... electromagnetic fields of low frequency and therefore of *very little energy* [our italics] are capable of acting upon water.

See the objection raised by astronomer George Abell (p. 147) where he attempts to dismiss this factor as relevant to astrology.

Piccardi has found that results were most striking in VLF (Very Low Frequency) wavelengths. Experiments in other fields have also found that VLF waves caused marked biological changes.

> Electromagnetic radiations and field variations ... strike the entire mass of a body, and thus of an organism, and provoke the oscillations, or excitation or, at any rate, the resonance, so to speak, of all the structural elements capable of responding to their stimulus wherever they are found. *Their action is ... total* [our italics].
>
> ...these elements which, depending on their geometric form and their internal energetic relationships, are able to respond to radiations of approximate frequencies, are the structural elements ... there can be no resonance without structure.
>
> *The Chemical Basis of Medical Climatology*,
> Thomas, Springfield, Illinois, 1962

This latter would ring familiar in the ears of the medieval astrologer; and in those of the architects of the cathedrals and of the temples of Egypt, as well. For the structures they built were designed consciously to provoke just that desired resonance within the hearts and heads of the beholders. It may seem

---

whole of chemistry, and its strangest property is that *ice floats*. If ice did not float I doubt that life would exist in the universe.'

George Wald, Nobel Laureate and Harvard Professor Emeritus in Biology, in *Noetic Sciences Review*, Spring, 1989, p. 12.

strange that Piccardi, among all these experimenters, should publicly decry traditional astrology. But this could be circumspection as much as conviction. After all, his renowned countryman, confronted by an equally unenlightened religious establishment 300 years ago, denied the earth moved round the sun, all the while knowing better.

Further 'Piccardi Effect' Experiments

Japanese haematologist Maki Takata developed an index designed to measure the level of albumen in the blood. Albumen is an organic colloid that helps blood to clot. He discovered that the albumen level in blood varied widely for reasons that were not apparent. Eventually he was able to tie this worldwide variation in albumen level to sun-spot activity, leading him to conclude that fluctuations in solar radiation profoundly affected this particular quality in the blood. The index went up during periods of heightened sun-spot activity, and also, on a regular basis, just before sunrise. Since the physiological and the psychological are linked (Church of Progress unfaithful are always trying to explain psychology as a fortuitous consequence of chemistry), it is interesting to speculate on the level of knowledge underlying ceremonies carried out just at sunrise by so many religious traditions . . . but probably they were just greeting the sun, releasing them from their primitive fear of the dark. (See *Helvetica Medica Acta*, vol. 17, 1950, pp. 254–74.)

There is a certain amount of evidence linking the incidence of heart attacks and strokes to sun-spot activity, and a Soviet haematologist, Schultz, found that the level of white blood cells in people with certain types of blood was highly susceptible to sun-spot activity.

A. Rothen studied immunologic reactions, which are the basis of tests for antigens. These tests involved a certain type of activated, nickel-coated slide, whose level of activation fluctuated widely, following a 24-hour rhythm.

The slides were fully active at night but gradually *lost* their activity as the day went on, starting at sunrise. The effect was regularly observed throughout the year, but was voided if the experiment was carried out deep underground or beneath a lead shield. (See *Journal of Interdisciplinary Cycle Research*, vol. 7, 1973, pp. 173–82.)

Having ruled out magnetism as the motivating factor, Rothen concluded that solar radiation was responsible. Among the many puzzling aspects of these experiments was the fact that the sun *in*activated the slides, while activating so much else in the cosmos. But for astrology perhaps the main point was that the amount of energy involved in triggering these changes in inactivity was negligible, while the effect produced was dramatic. Opponents of astrology never stop insisting that celestial forces are too small to produce effects on earth. The experiments of Piccardi, Takata and Rothen incontrovertibly prove the opposite: that in science there are instances where tiny celestial forces do indeed produce major measurable effects, and astrological effects are no more unlikely than these. Astrology's opponents are well aware of these experiments but decline to acknowledge their obvious relevance to the controversy.

It remains only to demonstrate the existence of the kind of tiny forces that might plausibly serve to trigger such proven effects.

Dr Jose Delgado and the Mind Fields

Dr Jose Delgado is a world-famous Spanish neuroscientist whose decades of experimentation leave no doubt about the sensitivity of living organisms to tiny electro-magnetic forces.

Dr Delgado is often described as 'controversial' but that controversy does not concern his results which are acknowledged valid. It is the implications of those results that provoke the controversy, along with Dr Delgado's methods of attracting attention.

Dr Delgado is a showman. His demonstrations are spectacular. His earlier research concerned specific functions of the different parts of the brain, generally involving drastic surgical procedures. Some years ago, to illustrate the effects of stimulating certain brain areas of experimental animals, Delgado faced a charging bull that had had electrodes implanted in its brain. As the bull charged, Delgado activated the electrode, instantly calming it and bringing it to a halt at his feet.

It is the flash that his colleagues mainly object to. The practice of implanting electrodes into the brains of animals doesn't appear to trouble them at all.

Delgado's later work has been marginally less repugnant but, as far as astrology is concerned, more important. Working with a large staff at a state-of-the-art Madrid hospital, Dr Delgado has carried out an enormous number of experiments on a wide variety of animals, birds and fish. All species proved sensitive to tiny fluctuations of electro-magnetic fields (EMFs). Delgado uses fields as low as 1/50th the earth's own magnetic field (less energy than you would be subjected to standing under a fluorescent bulb).

Delgado finds that when the field is tuned to *certain precise frequencies*, all organic life dances to the tune. Animals may become hyperactive at one frequency, and doze off at another; other frequencies speed the healing of bone fractures in rats, still others impede the growth of bacteria in cultures. Chick embryos hatched in magnetic fields become grossly deformed, an ominous result that has even Church of Progress initiates expressing concern since the fields that produced the genetic mutations in chicks are very similar to those emitted by microwave ovens, video display terminals and a host of other modern electronic devices. Meanwhile, the military ponders, as the military will, the possible ways in which these findings might be used to kill or disable the enemy. Since it is well known that the Russians have devoted far more time and energy to the study of EMFs, there is talk that subtle, space-age, undetectable EMF weapons are already being developed or deployed; possibly to induce paranoia in the military.

This is, of course, the sort of stuff that provokes learned conventions, the modern equivalent of those earlier synods that debated the Arian heresy or predestination: it is what inspired

Omni magazine to devote a major article to Delgado and the equally telling corroborative experiments of a growing host of co-workers in EMFs ('The Mind Fields', Kathleen McAuliffe, *Omni*, February 1985, p. 44). The relationship of this work to astrology goes unrecognized but it is profound.

These dramatic effects, brought about by infinitessimal changes in energy levels, categorically refute the endlessly reiterated objection that 'astrology demands the existence of unimaginable unknown forces' and fatuities such as 'a book placed three feet from the newly born baby exerts more tidal force on it than a planet'.

The point is that we respond to tiny *fluctuations* in the force fields in which we are forever immersed, just as we respond to the solo flute in the concert hall, while that amount of sound in any other context would not affect us at all. 'Unimaginable forces' are not needed.

These experiments also provide possible models for that 'plausible mechanism' that Culver, Ianna and their colleagues insist is absent. The experiments of Frank Brown, Piccardi and others prove incontestably that organic and inorganic realms are affected by celestial phenomena. To date, no one seems to have been able to measure just what it is that responds or what it is that changes in the environment that provokes the response. Delgado's work provides a possible clue to the latter mystery at a probable level of amplitude. The universe is electro-magnetic through and through. If living organisms respond to minute fluctuations in EMFs under laboratory conditions, if such changes even produce dramatic genetic mutations, it is surely reasonable to suggest that in the greater laboratory of the planet earth, organic and inorganic life responds to similar tiny fluctuations in the electro-magnetic or geomagnetic or gravitational environment.

Proof is conclusive that terrestrial/celestial correlations exist, and the Mars Effect proves that the human personality itself responds. What has not yet been conclusively established is a formal planetary role in dictating fluctuations in the pervasive electro- and geomagnetic environment. But it is possible that it has, in fact, been found. And even if the most promising current leads turn out to be unjustified (a number of earlier hypotheses did not stand closer scrutiny) researchers have a good idea where to look: into the sun-spot cycle.

Cycles and Sun Spots

Sun spots are intense magnetic storms which show up as darkened areas on the sun's surface. The cause of sun spots is still not known, but their nature and their effects have been studied extensively. They emit huge amounts of radiation; they send out charged particles and they increase the strength of the 'solar wind', the stream of ionized gas emitted by the sun. There are periods when sun-spot activity is minimal, and other times when it is intense. The life of individual sun spots is variable and unpredictable. They appear and disappear on the sun according to an irregular schedule that nevertheless fits within an overall cycle lasting 11.1 years on average. The cycle appears to recur with great regularity.

The connection between the sun-spot cycle and earthly phenomena was first noticed in 1801 by Herschel, the discoverer of Uranus. The prices of wheat seemed inexplicably to follow the 11.1 year cycle of sun-spot frequency. Throughout the nineteenth century intermittent efforts were made to isolate cycles and utilize them – principally as they related to business. But it was not until this century that systematic research was begun.

The Russian historian A. L. Chiszhevsky looked back into history for cycles, studying data from seventy-two countries and dating back to 600 BC. He found an extraordinary periodicity to social upheavals, mass migrations, revolutions and epidemics – and was packed off to Siberia for these efforts by Stalin, presumably for suggesting that forces other than the class struggle and dialectical materialism were responsible for such epochal events. Though re-instated into favor towards the end of his life by Khrushchev, Chizhevsky's inspired research has still not been explored in depth.

Around the same time, at Harvard, a team of workers under

Professor Ellsworth Huntington discovered inexplicable cyclical data everywhere they looked. A number of books ensued that provoked considerable scientific head-scratching, whoops of delight from astrologers, and an irate disclaimer from Huntington himself: 'All this may suggest astrology ... The relation of this book to astrology, however, is like that of modern chemistry to alchemy ... Nevertheless the cold fact as to millions of births leaves no doubt that on the average people born in February or March differ decidedly from those born in June and July.'*

And the still colder fact was that nothing known to orthodox science could explain this discrepancy, or any of the other cyclical phenomena that Huntington and his team were uncovering. After decades of work, Huntington, without actually mentioning the forbidden word, as much as left the door open: 'The evidence is sufficient to warrant the working hypothesis that atmospheric electricity, due presumably to the sun, but perhaps also to the whole solar system, is a cyclic factor closely associated with psychological rhythms.'

Cycles had been found operating in biological, economic, meteorological, geophysical, human, animal, and virtually every other sphere. It is a truism of statistics that if you juggle the numbers long enough, something is going to turn up that looks unrandom. But cycles research found unrandomness everywhere.

Though subsequent research has cast doubt upon or discredited a number of individual cycles, the correspondence of many important cycles with the overall Sun-Spot Cycle is accepted as a fact. As we have seen, some of astrology's opponents (p. 144) claim that this is the *only* bit of real evidence astrologers have to support their beliefs, and that this represents too slender a

---

* Though Huntington's later work focused on the importance of the sun-spot cycle, these yearly winter/summer distinctions do not correspond to the sun-spot cycle but would seem rather to correspond directly to the sun, the only celestial body that occupies the same place in the heavens on a month-by-month basis year after year.

foundation. So it does, when taken by itself. But when it is seen as a piece in a much larger puzzle, it takes on greater evidential stature.

Cycles were shown to be highly un-random. Certain definite periodicities showed up time and again, while others never occurred at all. For example, a 9.6-year cycle manifests itself in a variety of phenomena from the size of salmon catches in Canada to tree-ring widths, and cotton prices in the USA, but nothing has been found that follows a 10.6-year cycle. That the distribution was non-random and due to factors other than chance was demonstrated when cycles turned up again on schedule.

As a further demonstration, the cycles usually manifested themselves harmonically, that is, in double and treble progressions, but never in fives or sevens. Thus there are three distinct 15-year cycles enveloped in a greater cycle of 45 years, etc.

Cycles were a fact. They could be accounted for by nothing on earth. The logical place to look was the heavens but this cycles-researchers declined to do. And, meanwhile, the astrologers, though pleased with the new cycles data, could not account for it in terms of traditional astrology.

Huntington's cycles fell into astrologically awkward time-slots – 41 months, 9.6 years, 11.2 years, 18 years. None coincided with the speeds of the major planets in orbit seen geocentrically. Astrologers would have liked to see neat 12-year cycles corresponding to Jupiter; 28-year cycles corresponding to Saturn, and so on.

In 1950, in America, the Foundation for the Study of Cycles was inaugurated, in affiliation with the University of Pittsburgh.

This foundation, which has now grown to ten thousand subscribing members, though observing due caution in openly discussing astrology, has never been inimical to it. Indeed, among the Board of Directors is Lieutenant-Commander David Williams, a well-known astrologer and author of numerous articles for astrological magazines, who evidently makes no effort to conceal his astrological interests. Over the years, as the circumstantial evidence for astrology piled up, the Foundation has leaned further and further towards an open interest in the subject. Edward R. Dewey, President of the Foundation, declared in 1967:

> The really important aspect of the comparative cycle study is the possibility that it will lead to the discovery of *hitherto unknown* [our italics] environmental forces that affect life, weather and many other terrestrial phenomena ... What could these external forces be? Unfortunately, we do not yet know, but it seems clear that they are something ... If such forces are real, as we said in the beginning, it is a matter of utmost significance to mankind. The proof of the existence of such forces will push back the frontiers of knowledge as much as any single discovery I can think of.

In September 1968, in *Cycles*, Professor Dewey published an article entitled 'A Key to Sunspot–Planetary Relationship'. Dewey wrote that while many cycles-researchers had felt that the planets were in some way bound up with sun spots, and therefore with the whole complex of cyclical phenomena, no one had been able to discover what this relationship was. But it had been remarked that, though sun-spot frequency followed the familiar 11.1-year cycle, this was not a true cycle. Sun spots are magnetized and normally occur in pairs. In one 11.1-year cycle north spots lead and south spots follow, and in the next cycle south spots lead and north spots follow. Therefore, Dewey reasoned, a true cycle would be 22.22 years.

Having established 22.22 years as the true sun-spot cycle periodicity, a number of attempts have been made to find some regular combination of planetary configurations, some recurrent pattern meshed to the sun-spot cycle, that might serve as the postulated planetary 'trigger'. Though critics insist the mass of the planets combined is too small compared to the sun to provide this motivating force, the experiments of Piccardi, Delgado and others prove that energy in the minutest amounts applied to systems at critical resonant frequencies can produce dramatic effects, effects exponentially greater than any simple cause/effect relationship would predicate. As we have stressed repeatedly, much of the dispute over astrology, and astrology-related phenomena, arises because opponents inadvertently or otherwise use an inappropriate model as the basis of their argument.

Dr Geoffrey Dean, a bitter opponent of astrology as a predictive or analytic tool and of astrology as an expression of metaphysical verities, nevertheless argues that negligible though the mass of the planets may be, they store 98% of the solar system's angular momentum. This, given the results of Piccardi, Delgado and others, makes it reasonable to go on looking into the movements of the planets as a plausible motivating source for the sun-spot cycle.

But however plausible, it has proved elusive to date, and difficult to extract from the 'noise' of so many planets simultaneously in orbit. A number of early attempts proved unsatisfactory, but Dr Dean, himself, has devoted considerable time to the problem and believes he has found the key or cardinal cycle that meets the necessary requirements: it must synchronize with the solar equator because sun-spot formation is symmetrical about the equator, and it must synchronize with the sun-spot cycle itself. He claims the Jupiter/Neptune cycle does this and his analysis of the other planetary cycles shows them corresponding to harmonics of the Jupiter/Neptune cycle. (See *Recent Advances in Natal Astrology*, pp. 510–14.)

Unfortunately, Dean's hypothesis has elicited relatively little independent attention, and it is impossible to say if the Jupiter/Neptune cycle is in fact the key to the sun-spot cycle or if it is merely another apparent correlation (there have been others in the long search for the secret to cycles) that disappears when seen from a fresh angle or through more penetrating eyes. In general, Dr Dean places little confidence in experiments supporting astrology that have not been replicated. Ironically, until independently verified, his work on the Jupiter/Neptune cycle must be regarded with similar caution.

To date, Dr Dean's suggested astronomical rationale for the hypothesis (Jupiter is the largest planet and Neptune, third largest) has provoked little enthusiasm among astronomers or other cycles-researchers, perhaps because it is somehow inelegant and emotionally anticlimactic rather than because it is scientifically implausible. Astrologers are equally lukewarm for related reasons: there is nothing in the traditional astrological canon that would place such singular importance on a Jupiter/ Neptune cycle. Given the bulk of evidence *against* so much traditional astrology such conservatism may appear unwarranted. Yet for all the negative astrological results, whenever positive results *do* appear, they verify some major tenet of classical astrology (Mars/athletes, Jupiter/actors, Saturn/scientists, etc. . . .). So on the basis of this experience, astrologers may have earned the right to their gut unenthusiasm for the Jupiter/Neptune cycle as *the* key to sun-spot periodicity.

In any event, the correlation between sun-spot cycles and terrestrial phenomena is a fact. Dr Dean may or may not have pinpointed the planetary 'trigger'. At present it is subject to the same reservation that he so commonly applies to promising research by others: lack of independent replication and/or confirmation. But even if his hypothesis should be ultimately disconfirmed, the planets remain favorite candidates for the role.

From the point of view of our 'Case' this key to cycles is less important than the existence of cycles in the first place. Cycles have been demonstrated over the spectrum of physical experience: salmon catches and lynx pelts follow a cyclical pattern. Tree-ring widths are cyclical, as is the acreage planted in wheat and wheat prices; there are weather cycles, war cycles, disease cycles, psychological cycles and economic cycles. Admittedly, some of the data is shadowy and different experiments have returned contradictory results. But much is ironclad, verified independently by different researchers and extending over decades and centuries of accumulated records. So for our purposes there is no need to discuss the controversies over individual cycles or their possible causes (see Eysenck and Nias, *Astrology: Science or Superstition?*, pp. 114–42, for a clear layman's exposition of the pros and cons and problems involved in cycles research). For us, it is enough to say that if cycles are a fact (and they are), if cycles are in some way linked to sun spots (and they are), if celestial and terrestrial phenomena are shown to be inextricably linked (and they have been), then it follows necessarily that the basic premise of astrology is validated from still another physical angle.

Events in the heavens correspond in some way to events on earth: this is the fundamental premise of astrology on its cosmic (rather than its human) level.

Summary and Conclusions

So, even if the body of physical and statistical evidence does not fit together neatly, it does, as compensation, cover a wide field of interests, many of which touch directly upon various traditional astrological precepts. Gauquelin's work is direct corroboration of the correspondence between the planets and personality; cycles study seems to imply that on a huge scale human and animal psychology and physiology is affected by cyclical factors which in turn depend upon the solar system, and so on.

In presenting our evidence, we have repeatedly used music as a metaphor or model; as music 'works' on the earthly plane, so does astrology on the celestial.

Certainly astrologers would feel much more comfortable were they able to provide unequivocal physical evidence proving *how* astrology works. But this is not absolutely essential in arguing our case. Scientists and engineers were making use of electricity for a century before they understood how it worked. Celestial influence in many areas is a fact. And we think that 'plausible physical explanation' is near at hand.

C. Proof of the Pudding?

We have cited a number of prominent astrologers expressing deep concern over the state of astrology – as a practice. But despite their reservations it is seldom that an astrologer gives up astrology in disgust or despair. Is there then enough validity, even in present-day astrology, to justify the time spent on it by otherwise lucid individuals? Or are they, along with their clients, all, without exception, deluding themselves? Is it possible, as Dr Geoffrey Dean and the extreme science-oriented wing of astrology contend, that while cosmic 'influence' is an incontestable fact, the whole of the astrological edifice is superstition?

As is so often the case with astrology, such questions cannot be answered categorically yes or no. Nor is it possible to attribute the intrinsic ambiguity to semantics – proposing that the problem lies in an improper phrasing of the questions. It is the subject itself, astrology, that is too complex, multileveled and subtle to yield to over-simplified scientific treatment or strictly logical yes-and-no questions. As it stands, opponents blow up the negative evidence as though it represented clear disproof of astrology. With the enthusiastic collusion of the media (see pp. 416–40), it is this view that prevails officially, while, as everyone now knows, the highest government officials themselves routinely ignore their own church's edicts and anathemas and covertly seek out the advice of their astrologers.

But neither the bluster of the opposition nor the political and economic eminence of the astrologers' list of clients addresses this secondary question the jury is to pass judgement upon: the validity or lack of validity of astrology as a *practice*. If the jury is genuinely open-minded and conscientious it will not find the judgement easy to make.

The truth is that it is exceedingly difficult to devise methods of putting astrology, and astrologers in particular, to tests that satisfy scientific requirements without forcing astrologers to distort their methods in order to comply with the test – at which point of course it is no longer astrology or astrologers that are being tested, but some aspect of it that may or may not prove amenable to testing. The widely publicized Carlson experiment (pp. 209–12) is a casebook study in bungling the job, from both the scientific *and* the astrological point of view. At this stage, Gauquelin's statistics must be accepted as conclusive. They are absolutely objective in the sense that, once the factors that determine selection are agreed upon, personal interpretation plays no part in the experiment. But *all* tests designed to test astrological interpretation must, by their nature, contain subjective elements.

We have repeatedly stressed that this interpretive aspect of astrology is actually tangential to our case. Despite the volume of negative evidence to date, it is not difficult to argue that most of it stems from over-reliance on the validity of the same set of basic – and universal – astrological assumptions (signs of the zodiac, planets within the signs and houses) as determining factors for *specific* results (suicides, choice of profession, etc.). We have argued that signs, the zodiac, and perhaps even houses in some formulation may ultimately be proved valid (see pp. 227–39) but the persistence with which they return negative results when put to scientific examination suggests either that their importance has been over-rated or that astrologers interested in convincing science of their claims must devise better ways to test validity.

Apart from the relationship between planets and professions, none of the other astrological generalizations have been borne out. Obviously, a piecemeal approach based on these generalizations, though the easiest to devise, is not a promising approach to pursue. But we repeat, though embarrassing to astrologers (and to a lesser extent to us), these negative results are effectively irrelevant to our case.

On the other hand, at least a few of the scientific experiments devised to test astrologers on the *totality* of their knowledge, rather than specifics, have come out positive. Obviously, these, if they can be substantiated and replicated, strengthen our case, and they also complicate it unduly.

But because it is this interpretive aspect of astrology that is the principal concern of astrologers themselves, and of the public, of businessmen, of the President of the United States, of the Russians and of astrology's opponents, we cannot in fairness leave the subject unaddressed. So let us look at a few significant, representative tests.

Vernon Clark

The first is a series of experiments devised by the late Vernon Clark, an American psychologist who became interested in astrology – initially because for a supposedly extinct superstition it seemed to be showing remarkable vitality.

Without having contact with astrologers themselves, Clark noticed, in the early 1950s, a number of purely scientific findings (cycles research, etc.) which seemed to bear upon the astrological premise.

His interest piqued, Clark then took the rare step of actually studying the subject for himself. That is, instead of spending years minutely examining the works of 'authorities' on astrology, all of whom are convinced *a priori* of its fallacy, Clark began casting horoscopes. Like so many who take that step, he was soon convinced that somewhere, somehow, there was something to the business. He decided to devise a test to see if his newly acquired conviction could be put on an acceptable scientific basis, or at least a statistical one.

Clark first decided to test the astrologers' claim that, from the data provided for the moment of birth, future talents and capabilities could be predicted.

He contacted a number of the most highly regarded astrologers in England and America, of whom twenty-three agreed to co-operate, though one dropped out *en route*. In the end it was determined to take as test results only the answers of the first twenty to reply.

Clark then selected the horoscopes of ten people on the basis of participation in some well defined profession, five male, five female. The group included a herpetologist, musician, bookkeeper, veterinarian, art teacher, art critic, puppeteer, librarian, prostitute and pediatrician.

These horoscopes were chosen on a first-come, first-served basis. No attempt was made to select 'casebook' horoscopes – which co-operatively obey all the rules – or 'problem' horoscopes – which obey none of the rules. But the following stipulations were made:

1. The Native (astrological terminology for the subject of the horoscope) must have followed his or her profession for a considerable length of time – people who had switched jobs often were ruled out.

2. Professions had to be distinctly defined, though no attempt was made to prevent overlapping functions, as with the veterinarian and herpetologist, or with the art critic and the prostitute.

3. Natives had to be between forty-five and sixty-five years of age. This rules out implicit hints; for example, had a senator been included in the selection and had several of the horoscopes belonged to Natives in their twenties, astrologers would have known that these could not belong to a senator.

4. Birth in the USA was made a condition to eliminate the possibility of geographical hints: a chef who satisfied all other conditions was eliminated because he had been born in France.

5. The hour of birth was determined as precisely as was possible.
Finding Natives who complied with all these requirements was, Clark found, rather less easy than he had thought. But with the task accomplished, the horoscopes were erected and sent off to the participating astrologers.

The astrologers were told only the nature of the professions. Their test was to match up the professions with the horoscopes, according to their order of likelihood, i.e. the astrologer was to select the horoscope most likely to be that of the art critic, next most likely, and so on, down to the fifth most likely.

As a counter-experiment, Clark gave exactly the same test to a control group of non-astrologers – professional psychologists and social workers – who were to make blind selections. This group yielded a chance return.

The astrologers did considerably better, returning answers at a .01 level of significance above chance, according to Clark's calculations. That is: the odds were 100 to 1 against the astrologers' answers being attributable to chance.

And going further into the data (since statistics are open to a number of refinements and subtleties), it was discovered that the results would have been even better had the newest and most advanced statistical methods been employed. But these remained unofficial, not because of the astrologers, but because orthodox statisticians tended to distrust these methods.

Clark found that using his original scoring technique, sixteen out of the twenty astrologers scored above the chance level. But using a bull's-eye-only technique of scoring, seventeen out of twenty were above chance. And by adding the scores of the two astrologers who had been last to answer – and who therefore had been omitted from the test – the results also would have been improved.

From this test, then, it was possible to conclude tentatively that the characters of individuals are influenced by or determined by the position of the planets at birth, and that, using birth data alone, astrologers could distinguish and delineate character.

Still the conclusion was tentative. Hundred-to-one shots do come in. And the experiment was criticized on a number of minor counts, chief among them that possibly the astrologers had achieved their results through ESP. As we've pointed out on a number of occasions elsewhere, from the Rationalist point of view, such a conclusion would be no less unwelcome, but it could not be used as evidence for a strictly astrological argument.

So both possibilities had to be tested. An even more difficult test was devised. Test I showed only that astrologers could distinguish. Test II was set up to see if they could also predict.

The astrologers were given ten pairs of horoscopes. Each pair had an attested history attached, with dates of important events in the life (honors bestowed, crucial journeys, deaths, etc.). The astrologers were told that one of the pair belonged to the history while the other belonged to someone of about the same age and sex, born in the same vicinity, but whose history was different. (Actually, the false horoscope was a spurious one, 'cooked' at random for a time and place near the true chart: the astrologers of course did not know this.)

Since it was impossible for Clark to have any information on the (hypothetical) people corresponding to the cooked charts, the possibility of ESP was minimized, though not obviated (it is almost impossible to exclude the possibility altogether). The new experiment would test the ability to predict, at least in retrospect – if an astrologer could tell on the basis of birth data alone that an accident or a marriage or award belonged to horoscope A rather than horoscope B, it meant that in theory at least the astrologer could have predicted an event of this nature before the fact.

In this test, the astrologers again scored above the .01 level of significance. The returns of all twenty-three co-operating astrologers were utilized this time. Three had matched up all ten horoscopes with the histories, eighteen scored above chance, two scored chance.

Two 100-to-1 long-shots in a row is a rarity (the odds are 10,000–1 against it). But Clark decided to test still further. It had been demonstrated that astrologers, on the basis of birth data alone, could distinguish and predict. It was now decided to see if they could categorize. The possibility of ESP between Clark and the participating astrologers still remained a factor.

On this new test, Clark did only the organizing. The task of selecting the Natives was performed by a board of physicians and psychologists, and the charts were erected by an outside astrologer who was not told what the charts were supposed to divulge, this time effectively ruling out the possibility of ESP between Clark and the astrologers, though not between the astrologers and the unknown psychologists who did the organizing.

Again the test was set up in pairs. This time, one of each pair was a victim of cerebral palsy, while the other was someone with a quite similar chart who was above average in intelligence and in some way or other exceptionally gifted.

The astrologers had no case histories to go on, no dates of important events, no personal information whatsoever beyond that one chart of each pair belonged to a victim of cerebral palsy. Their task was to determine which.

Again the astrologers scored above the .01 level of significance. As every horse player knows, three 100-to-1 shots in a row makes a good day at the races (odds: 1,000,000–1 against chance). Though Clark could not say that, test by test, his astrologers were returning scores at the Gauquelin level of significance, they were being tested on the *totality* of their knowledge, in a manner far more demanding than anything that would ordinarily arise in a professional capacity.

Clark, however, trained to science, and attempting to win approval for astrology, bent over backwards to minimize the significance of his tests. He pointed out meticulously that his tests did not 'prove' astrology, but that they 'failed to disprove it'.

> With years of experience behind them in working with this hypothesis, they [the astrologers] are hardly in need of proof that mankind is indeed reactive to his planetary environment. But our scientific friends must still, for a while, be treated with the ceremony due to parlor guests; we must be careful, as hosts, to address them in their own language, and offer entertainment which we know ahead of time will be to their liking.

Clark's experiment was scrutinized by statisticians and could not be faulted. Throughout the course of the experiment, unusual precautions had been taken to ensure proctoring by non-astrologers to forestall accusations of fraud.

'Never again,' Clark insisted, 'will it be possible to dismiss the astrological technique as a vague, spooky, and mystical business – or as the plaything of undisciplined psychics – or as merely the profitable device of unscrupulous quacks. Those who, out of prejudice, wish to do so will have to remain silent, or repeat these experiments for themselves.'

But Clark's scientific friends were not entertained. His results were reported in no scientific journals. Only *Cosmopolitan*, a magazine with a limited scientific following, saw fit to give Clark's work a public airing. No scientist repeated the experiment.

But, years later, when close variations of the experiments finally were repeated by astrologers (exact replication was of course impossible), two corroborated Clark's findings, while two did not. Dr Geoffrey Dean spells out and analyzes the details of these tests in *Recent Advances* (pp. 547–53).

Tests from Recent Advances in Natal Astrology

ASTROLOGY NOW: In 1976, the American magazine *Astrology Now* repeated Clark's second test – distinguishing between genuine and spurious horoscopes – using new data. In this test 49 astrologers participated, 23 with more than five years' experience, 26 with less. The less experienced did equally well, and the composite score bore out Clark's initial result. Astrologers, given a brief individual case-history, and two horoscopes to choose from, one genuine and one spurious, were able to select the genuine one at a statistically significant level. In this case, the odds were roughly 250–1 against chance.

DEAN AND EDWARDS: A particularly rigorous test was run by Geoffrey Dean and R. A. Edwards, designed to test astrologers' ability to determine personality traits in blind trials.

According to Dean, the problem with Clark's and related tests was that they were not designed to test directly the astrologers' claim that they could delineate the entire character as a whole, or *Gestalt*, on the basis of the horoscope alone – which is perhaps the most deeply cherished conviction held by practicing astrologers. But, as Dean and Edwards realized, the problem with the problem was establishing 'character' in the first place: what the individual's 'character' is really like, as opposed to what he or she imagines it to be like (which also involved eliminating spurious or self-affirming judgements made on the basis of illicit or universal assumptions. For example: you are to fill out a personality questionnaire. You are born under Cancer. You know that Cancers are supposed to be moody, introspective, home-loving, poetic. So you fill out your questionnaire accordingly).

Dean writes:

> One solution is to use traits quantified by personality inventory. It can be argued that inventory indications are still basically subjective and that a person can be everything at one time or another. However by using only subjects with conspicuous traits on which the assessments by self, friends, and personality inventory all agree, any uncertainty can be largely eliminated. [This is precisely what the Carlson experiment did *not* do.] Furthermore, by rejecting doubtful or ambiguous traits and those for which the astrological significators are not yet established, and all cases without accurate birth data, the trial can be made as astrologically acceptable as possible.

Dean and Edwards assessed four separate personality inventories and selected the Eysenck and the Dynamic Inventories as the most suitable. From these a number of traits compatible with astrological delineation were selected, each with its polar opposite. For example, Introvert–Extrovert, Conventional–Unconventional, Easy-going–Disciplinarian, Prudish–Sensual, Shy/inadequate–Assertive/confident, etc.

The tests were then administered to volunteer university students. Before the inventory test results were disclosed, the volunteers were asked to evaluate themselves on each pair of traits according to a ten-point scale. Dean then chose the twelve subjects with the most accurate birth-times and the best agreement between personal assessments and inventory results. In other words, those who scored introverted, shy, self-effacing (or whatever) according to their own evaluation as well as on the tests were used in the experiment.

The birth charts were then computer-calculated and given blind to participating astrologers. The astrologers had to evaluate the different traits on a ten-point scale from their reading of the individual horoscopes.

Without going into the complex statistical methodology used by Dean and Edwards to evaluate the replies, and the niceties involved when the replies were subjected to different kinds of detailed analysis, the overriding result was that astrologers' evaluations on the trait scale agreed with the personality assessments made by the volunteers and the inventory assessments at high levels of significance-ranging from 1,000–1 against chance to 10,000–1 against chance. Dean and Edwards conclude: 'The results show a signficant ability to make correct judgements.'

On the negative side, in 1975, R. A. Joseph repeated a version of Clark's third experiment (gifted vs. palsied) using new data. Twenty-three outstanding astrologers selected by three different astrological associations participated. They were to distinguish between pairs of charts, one of which was that of a severely retarded child and the other that of a highly gifted child. The cases were selected by an independent pediatrician personally familiar with all the subjects. But the astrologers were unable to distinguish between the charts of the gifted and the retarded child beyond the chance level.

Negative results were produced by Press et al., in 1976, with a test somewhat similar to Clark's second test (see p. 356). In the Press experiment, astrologers were to distinguish between the charts of suicides, and a chart chosen randomly of someone still living, born the same year as the suicide. They returned results at the chance level.

In the 'Discussion' (*Recent Advances*, pp. 553–4), following the account of these blind trials, Dean and Mather comment:

> The first three (Clark, *Astrology Now*, Dean and Edwards) produced significant results: overall, a total of 127 astrologers made a total of 2,046 judgements and were correct 1,254 times or 61%. By chi-squared this is significant at the p 10^{-25} level. [That is, 10,000,000,000,000,000,000,000,000:1 against chance – long odds.]
>
> The other two produced non-significant results ... If the last two are excluded on the reasonable grounds that relevant diagnostic criteria have yet to be established (even though this conflicts with the results of Clark's third test) the results appear to provide

convincing support for astrology. In fact, however, this conclusion is not justified:

The survey of intuition on pages 16–20 provide ample support for the hypothesis that the results could be due to intuition and not astrology. Thus in Clark's double-blind trial, Lee deliberately applied intuition and after spending only 2 minutes on each chart got 7 out of 10 right (see page 20). In *Astrology Now*'s test the two highest scoring astrologers (one a student, the other a professional) had studied astrology for only two years and both indicated that intuition played a role in their judgement. It may not be irrelevant that the levels of accuracy of the three significant studies were very similar – all about 60%.

On the other hand, if intuition is responsible for success and not astrology, this does not explain the merely chance results of Joseph and Press et al. Intuition may be individually erratic but is unlikely to be collectively erratic.

Whatever the explanation, it is clear that the significant blind trials have not demonstrated that astrology works but only that astrologers work.

Summary

But this conclusion – that it is the astrologers who 'work' rather than astrology – does not follow from those results, either. Intuition, whatever that may be, and however it may be defined, cannot be extracted from *any* interpretive enterprise. The composer works with an infinity of possible combinations of notes before him, and it is his inspiration or genius (which might be called 'informed intuition') that selects the music out from the noise. So, in the tests described above, astrologers, working with (effectively) an infinity of astrological factors, determined those relevant to the tests at statistically significant levels. True, it may be 'intuition' that triggers the selection, but it is the astrological training and the astrological doctrine (wooly and imprecise though that may be) that informs the intuition in the first place (just as it is the currently reigning musical tradition that allows the composer to successfully 'choose' the music;

without that training and tradition, the music would not happen).

Dean's criticism is unwarranted. Moreover, since it is the astrologers that are being tested in these particular experiments, not astrology as such, the criticism is also irrelevant.

To prove that astrology 'works', not just astrologers, it is only necessary to refer back to Gauquelin – whose work proves the validity of one central tenet of astrology, the correspondence between specific planets and specific personality types. As we have seen, Gauquelin's work does not directly apply to astrological interpretation of the individual chart (beyond suggesting perhaps that astrologers pay more attention to the position of the planets relative to the angles and less to the zodiacal signs in general). But its value as science is paramount, since no intuition is or can be involved.

So if Dean and Mather are willing to acknowledge that 'astrologers work' on the basis of successful tests carried out by Clark and the others, it's hard to see how they can avoid concluding that astrology also works, since the Gauquelin data supports at least one fundamental tenet of the doctrine upon which the successful astrologers base their 'intuition', and Dean and Mather accept the Gauquelin work as valid. In other words, *something* legitimate must be behind the astrologers' ability to delineate and predict successfully (since the same tests carried out by controls ignorant of astrology invariably return chance results). That something can only be astrology. Intuition alone is not enough. So the only question remaining, really, is: how does it work? What is the agency through which, or by which, proven astrological effects manifest themselves? Throughout this book, we have been suggesting that astrology can be explained in terms of resonance. Let us now look closely at this phenomenon and the manner in which it applies to astrology.

D. The Question: How?

Cymatics: The Study of Wave Forms

Cymatics is the name given by its founder, Hans Jenny, to the study of wave forms and the way in which wave forms influence matter.

Essentially, Jenny's work is but a vast refinement of a phenomenon examined by the eighteenth-century German physicist, Ernst Chladni, who discovered that when sand was scattered over a plate attached to a violin, and different notes played on the violin, the sand arranged itself in a variety of beautiful patterns, which changed according to the note played. In science these figures are well known as 'Chladni figures'.

Chladni's methods were crude and permitted few refinements, materials were limited, and the frequencies difficult to control or to alter in the course of the experiment. But the conclusion was clear: form was in some way a function of the frequency of vibration.

Jenny, an Anthroposophist, artist and scientist, decided to investigate this phenomenon. He developed equipment which would allow him to subject a wide range of materials to a wide range of frequencies, all under a flexible control system. Sands, powders and liquids were spread on metal plates, or placed in receptacles and vibrated at different sound frequencies, producing a spectacular array of forms and patterns. One series of experiments merits particular attention from our point of view.

Among Jenny's inventions is the 'tonoscope', a device designed to convert the vibrations of the human voice, and of sound in general, into visual terms. When the human voice was directed into the tonoscope, photographs of the shape of the sounds were obtained, and it was found, for example, that the spoken letter 'O' produced a perfectly spherical photograph.

Of all the ancient and primitive beliefs, few have been more universally ridiculed by modern critics than the notion that words and names were imbued with magical or other properties beyond the arbitrary act of inventing a word or name to stand for a thing or person.

> In ancient Egypt precautions were taken to prevent the extinction of the eighth or Name-soul . . . In the pyramid texts we find mentioned a God called Khern, i.e. Word: the Word having a personality like that of a human being. The Creation of the World was due to the interpretation in words by Thoth of the will of the deity . . .
>
> Children are often similarly anxious to conceal their names; and just as children always demand what the name of a thing is (never if it has a name) and regard the name as a valuable acquisition, so we know that the stars all have names . . .
>
> In some way the twentieth century suffers more grievously than any previous age from the ravages of such verbal superstitions . . .
>
> The persistence of the primitive linguistic outlook not only throughout the whole religious world, but in the work of the profoundest thinkers, is indeed one of the most curious features of modern thought.
>
> Ogden and Richards,
> *The Meaning of Meaning*
> (Routledge & Kegan Paul, 1956), pp. 27–9

The rational mind is immune to such nonsense; and the Rationalist knows that had, say, Vladimir Nabokov elected to name Lolita, his famous nymphet, Edna or Joan it would have made no difference. Yet Jenny's photograph of the vowel 'O' stands there, permanently thumbing its nose at reason. For unless Ogden and Richards are prepared to dispense with all art, literature, poetry, music and architecture, as the purely 'emotive' residues of primitive superstition, it would appear that in this instance, as in so many others, the Egyptians and other ancient civilizations were dealing in realities. Art affects us by its structure, by the sensory vibrations which it sets up, and which are afterwards interpreted by our aesthetic faculties – whatever these may be.

Jenny's tonoscope is designed so that sound vibrations act upon inert material whose action can be photographed. 'O' not only sounds like 'O', it looks like 'O'. By merely pronouncing the vowel, inert material can be made to conform to what might be called the 'Law of O'. 'It may be said that the sounds of the human voice have specific effects on various materials in various media, producing what might be called corresponding vocal figures,' says Jenny. The Egyptians and so-called primitives look ever less superstitious and primitive: science has already admitted that sound waves can influence the growth of plants; it is but a short and logical step to the admission that the repetition of sacred formulae and chants (sound waves) can objectively cure diseases. If music can affect plants, why should viruses and bacteria be immune?

We have already discussed the Law of Three, the Law of Relationship – symbolic traditionally of 'Spirit' – which insists that for anything to happen in the universe three forces, not two are necessary. But this third force is ineffable. Jenny's Cymatics is essentially the study of this elusive third force which so steadfastly remains immune to our reason: it is the 'idea' between the sculptor and the block of wood; the 'desire' that mediates between man and woman; the Holy Spirit of the Christian Trinity.

The importance of Cymatics lies in its ability to reveal this third force, and to allow scientists to study its manifestations quantitatively. But it must be stressed that this does not mean the third force has been explained. It is as mysterious as ever. Power is applied to matter through the mediating agency of 'vibration'; but this 'vibration', like Professor Brown's train schedule, is the manifestation of a conscious decision. It is neither matter nor energy. It refuses to be pinned down linguistically. Yet without it Jenny would have no patterns, Professor Brown no train schedule.

To repeat: form is impossible without frequency, and frequency is inexplicable. As one early enlightened scientist put it: 'In the beginning was the Word'. Still earlier scientists in Egypt credited Thoth with Creation for his interpretation in words of the Divine Will. Jenny's work opens an important approach to the physical aspect of astrology – and the physical aspect of astrology is of course the only aspect to which the scientific method can be applied.

Cymatics makes it clear that the ancient concept of the Harmony of the Spheres must be taken *literally*. The medieval analogy of resonance, long discarded as impossible in a Newtonian mechanical universe in which planets whirled about in empty space, now returns as demonstrable fact.

The solar system is a coherent, vibrating whole. To our senses, the planets move slowly in orbit. But to a being who considered a hundred thousand years as a second, the solar system would be invisible, but audible (provided such a being's senses were attuned to magnetic and electro-magnetic and not merely atmospheric disturbances). Like every other vibrating system, the solar system is bound to produce a multitude of interacting harmonics, the effects of which constitute the research we have been describing.

Jenny's experiments show that form depends not only upon the frequency of vibration, but also upon the nature of the material being vibrated. Different materials vibrated at the same speed produced different patterns. This is a visual demonstration of qualitative difference. And to attempt to explain it away in terms of the atomic structure of the materials is simply to beg the issue; the apparently simple arithmetical addition of electrons also results in qualitative differences between the basic elements. And in music the same note played on a violin and on an oboe affects us differently. It is no good maintaining that there is no 'real' difference in the notes beyond the sum total of the respective harmonics: the difference in effect is as 'real' as the calculations.

As we have been arguing throughout this book, the situation in the solar system is analogous to an orchestra. The planets (instruments) are composed of diverse materials, and they differ hugely as to mass and density, they orbit (vibrate) at a variety of speeds, and these speeds are ceaselessly changing in relation to each other, and also in the distances and angles at which they interact. It is now accepted that the planets are all magnetically and electrically charged; Jupiter and the earth, at least, are known to emit radio waves, and it is obvious that we are only beginning to learn the true physical natures of the planets.

Given the Gauquelin work, it seems incontestable that the 'influences' of the planets vary widely; it is no mistake that Saturn, not Venus, turns up in charts of scientists in the statistics, Mars in the charts of athletes, etc. And the work of Piccardi, Dewey and the others makes it equally incontestable that every atom of every molecule of the earth has no choice but to respond to this cosmic tune.

Sperm unites with ovum; the so-called 'genetic code' determines out of the infinity of possibilities what the fetus shall inherit from its parents. But what is the genetic code? What is the precise nature of the 'message' the messenger RNA carries to the DNA before the latter can operate? It is not the genes themselves, but their arrangement: in other words, it is not a thing, it is the result of an act, which in itself is neither matter, nor energy. In Jenny's experiments, arrangement (form) is contingent upon frequency. Is it not possible that the genetic code is the response of united sperm and ovum to the complex of cosmic frequencies prevailing at the moment?

Though couched in different terminology, astrologers have been contending that this was the case since history began.

More important, they have contended that, as far as character is concerned, the moment of birth, not of conception, is the determining factor. This has now been proved in general, statistical terms by Gauquelin's and Addey's work.

But to account for this fact in physical terms may well be impossible. And this book is not the place for a dissertation on the nature of the 'soul' or even for a résumé of traditional teachings on the subject. (See the Bibliography for further reading on this esoteric aspect of astrology.)

It is, however, safe to say that the sum of frequencies,

tonalities, rhythms and harmonies of a piece of music does not constitute the *meaning* of the music. Yet the secret of meaning is locked into the interplay of these factors, and the genius of a Mozart, a Bach or a Beethoven unlocks it.

So we may measure all the alpha, theta and other rhythms of the brain of the man calculating a train schedule. It tells us nothing of the meaning of his efforts, nor of the decision that motivates him in the first place.

The harmony of the spheres, then, is no fanciful figure of speech, but reality. Yet we must guard against the too-facile conclusion that we are 'influenced' by the music of the spheres. We are not 'influenced'. In some subtle but ineluctable fashion, we *are* that music. And astrology is, or should be, the discipline, part art, part science, dedicated to the interpretation of its meaning.

Dr Percy Seymour's Theory

Our explanation of The Question: How, based upon Jenny's Cymatic's, is analogical, and unabashedly so. For all of so-called 'hard science' is analogical at its core. Its 'facts' are no more than analogies drawn on human experience which is reality seen through the prism of the senses. Difficult as it is to live with, the table that we put our plates on is fundamentally a whirr of energetic particles. That is its real 'reality' according to science. We, however, see it as 'table' because it corresponds to a particular state of our own perceptual faculties, themselves based ultimately upon energetic particles. In other words, because our faculties are designed as they are, we perceive the table as table, not as energy. The table is therefore a specific kind of analogy, it is a form of likeness or correspondence.

So, drawing upon our experience of music, Jenny's Cymatics and the correspondence or likeness of the vibratory system that prevails in the concert hall with the vibratory system prevailing in the solar system, we could offer a plausible modus operandi for the proven astrological correspondences. Just as the interplay of frequencies at a given moment in time of a piece of music represents the musical 'meaning' of that moment of music, so the interplay of planetary frequencies at a given moment in time represents the astrological 'meaning' of that moment of celestial music. And a child born at that moment and coming to consciousness outside its mother's womb for the first time is indelibly stamped by, imbued with, that meaning. That is the astrological signature of the soul. He or she carries that impress through life, and when the planets in their orbits hit specific notes or chords related to that signature the child will resonate accordingly – though the precise manner in which the resonance will manifest depends upon a multiplicity of factors, not least of which is what that person has done with his or her life up to that point.

What was missing from our theory was that 'plausible physical explanation' that science insists upon before it will put its imprimatur upon a given phenomenon.* Given the known existence of geomagnetic fields of the earth, the proven sensitivity of living organisms to fluctuations of the geomagnetic field, and the no less proven existence of solar and planetary magnetic and electro-magnetic fields, we could with some assurance maintain that interconnections had to exist between these solar, planetary and, no doubt, galactic fields. In some way the earth's field was 'tuned' to the celestial fields producing those successive astrological 'moments' whose results were borne out incontrovertibly by Gauquelin's statistics and accounted for harmonically by John Addey. Only we lacked the scientific background that might allow us to make a testable theory out of the hypothesis.

It is possible that this missing major piece to the puzzle has been provided by Dr Percy Seymour, an astronomer and an authority on cosmic and planetary magnetism.

---

* As we have seen, in science that insistence is conditional. If the phenomenon in question does not directly violate the religious tenets of Church of Progress dogma, as with electricity or Continental Drift, the phenomenon is allowed to exist independently of that 'plausible physical explanation', which may come later.

Dr Seymour's theory was developed without knowledge of our own argument via Cymatics put forward twenty years ago. We therefore find it particularly gratifying that he uses nearly identical analogical reasoning, based upon the universal properties of resonance, and the now-physically-justifiable concept of the Harmony of the Spheres as his starting point.* He also independently seconds our hypothesis that the moment of fertilization astrologically determines the 'information' encoded in the DNA of the newly fertilized ovum. And he proposes an important detailed hypothesis of the manner in which astrologically determined genetic inheritance attracts its proper astrologically determined personality.

The Magnetic Universe

Dr Seymour's theory rests upon the established magnetic properties of the earth, moon and planets and the no less established ability of organic life to respond to magnetic stimuli via the nervous system.

> The magnetic field of the Earth vibrates with a wide range of natural frequencies. According to my theory some of these frequencies are almost exactly the same as those associated with the weak tidal forces of the planets, and these tidal forces, though weak,

---

* The argument from resonance between the necessarily interacting parts of the unity represented by the solar system and, indeed, the entire universe, has been the basis of all the theories put forward by those few other scientists willing to look seriously into the astrological question, How? At a conference called 'Astrology and Science' held at New York University in 1973 the mathematician and cyberneticist, Dr Theodor Landscheidt, explained astrological correspondences by drawing analogies to information theory and the manner in which information is transmitted and stored by living systems. He proposed that the faint gravitational waves coming from the galaxy would be received by the solar system, acting as a giant antenna, or resonance system, that amplified and then transmitted these waves – the planets in their orbits providing specific frequencies or stations. The 'messages' would then in turn be picked up and amplified by the human receiver, tuned to the cosmic transmitter. Warren Weaver, before he died, was entertaining related possibilities.

are able to make the natural frequencies keep in step with them or, to use the normal language of science, the natural frequencies become phase-locked to the tidal frequencies. In other words, some of the natural frequencies are tuned to some of the planets . . .'

This (magnetic) field extends far into space in all directions. In the direction of the Sun it extends to about five times the diameter of the Earth, and in the opposite direction it extends to about twenty-five times this diameter. The sheer size of the magnetosphere also serves to amplify the weak tidal forces of the planets, even if we use equilibrium tidal theory. Since the magnetosphere on a magnetically quiet day is at least ten times the size of Earth, the tidal range of a particular planet is ten thousand times greater in the outer parts of the magnetosphere than it is near the surface of the earth. Trapped in this extended magnetic field are a number of charged particles which form what is known as a plasma. The magnetic field forms a series of bays, estuaries and canals which can amplify the tidal forces of the planets on the plasma. The situation is further improved by the fact that the magnetic field itself can be pictured as a series of elastic bands, stretching into space, which have their own natural frequencies, and some of these are in time with the tidal pull of some of the planets.

The interaction between magnetic bays and plasmas has been investigated in terrestrial laboratories. These investigations show us that it is very easy to start magnetic vibrations in magnetic fields . . . The Solar Wind . . . distorts the magnetosphere, rather as an ordinary wind would distort a windsock at an airfield. It is the gusting of the Solar Wind that gives rise to magnetic storms of the extended magnetic field of Earth. According to my researches the sunspot's cycle is linked to the positions and motions of the planets as seen from the Sun, and this part of my theory provides a further link with some ancient concepts in astrology.

Astrology: The Evidence of Science,
pp. 116–18.

Dr Seymour develops his theory in detail in language that is scientific but non-technical. It can be followed by anyone capable of reading a popular science magazine such as *Discover* or the

New Scientist. But to illustrate graphically how his theory might work, Seymour also uses an analogy. He compares the solar system to a huge transmitter of cosmic music. The planets, sun and moon are its broadcasting 'stations', each sending out signals of a specific frequency. The music is received and amplified by the earth's magnetosphere, and picked up by human beings through their individual antennae – which have been astrologically preset through genetics and through birth to respond more powerfully to certain 'stations' than to others. Thus Seymour's theory closely resembles our own analogical thinking based on Jenny's Cymatics and the concert hall model of reality – but his comes armed with scientific teeth.

Though Seymour's theory is not easy to condense in such a way that the evidence remains in place and comprehensible while the argument continues to flow, the Prosecution itself has provided us with a splendid solution to the impasse. Dr Seymour's book was greeted by the scientific establishment with few tidings of gladness and joy. The London *Sunday Telegraph* and the widely read and prestigious science journal, the *New Scientist*, responded to it with the unbridled acrimony more commonly associated with the *Skeptical Inquirer* or a speech by the Ayatollah Khomeini. Dr Seymour wrote detailed rebuttals to their criticisms. And we find that by reading the reviews and Dr Seymour's defense in tandem, the scientific plausibility of his theory is made clearer than it would be through any attempt of ours to condense and summarize it. At the same time the jury will be treated to still further useful insights into Prosecution tactics. Though long, we felt this correspondence too important to our case to relegate it to an appendix.

Stellar by Starlight

This is a shameful book. One would have hoped that Percy Seymour's lectureship in astronomy at Plymouth Polytechnic and his directorship of a planetarium would have persuaded him to defend orthodox science. Instead he has done the opposite; like Ronald Reagan, he has embraced astrology.

D. *The Question: How?*

It is bad enough when a leading statesman like Mr Reagan allows himself to be guided by pseudoscience; but it is far more alarming when the same offence is perpetrated by an academic astronomer. Indeed it is hard to exaggerate the culpability of a professional scientist in the twentieth century, one responsible for guiding the young, who claims that we can tell our fortunes by the stars. He can only do so by ignoring the mathematics of scale, which tells us that the planets are too small and far away to affect our personalities at birth. And this Dr Seymour has done.

His 'theory' is that the orbits of the planets cause changes in the Earth's magnetic field, which in turn interferes with electrical activity in the developing human foetus. This interference helps to determine personality. It would be idle to complain that he fails to present any convincing evidence, for the simple reason that there isn't any. He writes at length about gravitation and tides (which seems irrelevant to his premiss), and then calls passionately for the 'tolerance of new ideas'. Most of us are in favour of tolerating scientific dissent, but an actual denial of science, which would require the rejection of established knowledge, is surely intolerable.

Adrian Berry, *Sunday Telegraph*,
16 July 1988

Dr Seymour responds:

Sir,
In his review of my book, Adrian Berry seems to be advocating a witchhunt for academics who have non-orthodox views. There are university professors who support parts of astrology, others who believe in the paranormal, a few who believe epidemics are related to cometary visitations, and professors of divinity who question the divinity of Christ and the virgin birth. Perhaps Berry would like to see the whole lot burnt at the stake – or is this to be reserved only for those of us who dare to take an interest in astrology?

Adrian Berry claims that I have ignored the 'mathematics of scale' in my theory. In fact I make it abundantly clear in my book and in my paper of 1986 (*A Causal Mechanism for Gauquelin's Planetary Effect*), that I made use of the concepts and mathematics of resonance in constructing my theory. Resonance between the tidal tug (due to gravity) of the planets on the gases trapped in the magnetic fields of the Sun and Earth, and resonance between the resulting fluctuations of the Earth's field and the neural network of the foetus. Resonance makes it possible for a radio telescope to tune into specific vibrations of hydrogen atoms in the Andromeda Galaxy (14 million million million miles away), for us to listen to a specific radio station as we drive along in our cars, for the Moon to shift 100 billion tons of water out of the Bay of Fundy in Canada twice a day and for moderate winds to have caused the collapse of a suspension bridge in the USA in 1940. In all these cases the naive 'mathematics of scale' gives the wrong answer! Many examples of resonance exist in the universe; from the scale of the nuclei of atoms, through engineering structures, right up to the scale of the Solar System. Indeed the universe as we know it could not exist if it were not for resonance, yet all the calculations carried out by scientists to show that cosmic effects on humans are far too small, have, until I did my work, ignored this possibility.

The necessity to question received opinion is an essential part of all academic training. Students are taught how to access the scientific literature in order to learn the alternative points of view and be able to make up their own minds. A much more serious threat to the dissemination of ideas arises from some science writers who distort the nature and contents of science in their evangelical zeal to maintain the current dogma as 'absolute truth'. The major access to current thinking for many people is via the media. If science writers misrepresent information because they are uncomfortable with the uncertainties or do not understand the subtleties of a subject, they run the risk of applying a censorship based on their own prejudices and limitations.

Dr P. A. H. Seymour

Nigel Henbest in the *New Scientist* (12 May 1988) writes

In 1975, the American magazine. *The Humanist*, published a statement that declared: 'We, the undersigned – astronomers, astrophysicists and scientists in other fields – wish to caution the public against the unquestioning acceptance of the predictions and advice given privately and publicly by astrologers ...' It was signed by 186 scientists, including 18 Nobel laureates. You don't need to be an astrologer to predict the effect of this pompous and patronising statement on the public's acceptance of astrology: absolutely zilch. Since then, astrologers have become, if anything, more prominent: more people read their daily horoscopes and consult astrologers, including, it seems, President Reagan.

Meanwhile, scientists continue to 'refute' astrology by saying, in effect: astrology can't work, and therefore it doesn't. Most have never even read a serious astrological work, so their dogmatic attitude is indefensible. It is also thoroughly unscientific. Astrology is testable, as a scientific hypothesis, because it makes specific predictions. If you were born at a certain place, at a certain time, then you will have certain, quite predictable character traits.

Scientists should also beware of dismissing astrology just because they can't think of a way in which the stars and planets can affect us. This attitude led, for example, to the wrongful rejection of continental drift back in the 1920s.

Onto the stage leaps a book titillatingly subtitled 'The evidence of science'. The author, Percy Seymour, has trained as a scientist; he has a PhD in astrophysics from Manchester University. He now lectures in astronomy at Plymouth Polytechnic. Seymour believes that astrologers will hail his book as providing the scientific validation of their subject, so it is important – in the context of the continuing debate between science and pseudoscience – to look carefully at what Seymour has, and has not, established.

First, that subtitle. A careful read through this sometimes confusing book establishes that Seymour in fact presents no new empirical findings. The evidence consists solely of the results already published by the French psychologist Michel Gauquelin. Seymour actually sets out to provide a *mechanism* that can explain Gauquelin's results.

This limits what Seymour is attempting to explain. The front cover blurb tells us: 'Orthodox science has always held that astrology cannot work. Now, for the first time, a scientist argues that it does.' This statement may lead the casual reader to believe that Seymour is supporting traditional astrology: 'I was born under Taurus, so I'm boring and mercenary' – right? Wrong. When you winkle out the relevant part of the text, Seymour admits '[Gauquelin] found that there was no evidence for . . . claims involving Sunsigns.' The French researcher also found that the positions of the planets among the stars made no difference to people's personalities – so dismissing altogether any influence of the famous constellations of the Zodiac.

In addition, Seymour accepts Gauquelin's conclusion that half the planets (Mercury, Uranus, Neptune and Pluto) play no role at all. Add to this the fact that Gauquelin finds positive evidence for celestial influences only in the case of 'eminent people', and what Seymour sets off to 'prove' turns out to be something very different from what you or I would call astrology.

Gauquelin's claim is that eminent people in certain professions were born when the Moon and a few planets – Venus, Mars, Jupiter and Saturn – were at certain positions in the sky. Generally, they were either rising or at their highest point; sometimes they were setting, or at their lowest points.

Seymour's explanation goes like this. The gravity of the Moon and the nearer planets cause 'tides' in the Earth's magnetosphere. These produce electric currents which alter the Earth's magnetic field in a regularly repeating pattern. Because each planet moves around the sky at a different rate, there are distinct frequencies (with overtones) associated with each planet. Certain neural circuits in the brain of human embryos can resonate with these frequencies. An embryo that is destined to become a world-leader, for example, has circuits that resonate with Jupiter's influence. So this embryo chooses to be born when Jupiter is rising in the sky.

Could this very plausible-sounding mechanism actually work? Seymour leads strongly enough, with an undisputed fact: that the Moon affects the Earth's magnetism. The Moon raises tides in the Earth's magnetosphere, which cause a compass needle to swing northward when the Moon rises. Might this prompt the birth of 'lunar-type' personality?

Let's first put the lunar magnetic effect into proportion. The compass needle does not swing wildly at moonrise; its position changes by about one-hundredth of a degree. It's such a small effect that you can only detect it with sensitive magnetometers sited well away from electromagnetic interference. Even then, the effect is masked on most days by changes in the magnetosphere that are caused by the buffeting of the solar wind.

A pregnant woman in a modern household will experience much stronger magnetic fluctuations from the washing machine and the food processor. The regular rhythm of the storage heaters will swamp the weak lunar signal.

Seymour's 'hypothesis' degenerates further, into a string of unsupported speculations, founded neither on known facts nor on physical calculations. He says that the planets, too, should raise tides in the Earth's magnetosphere, and so should cause similar magnetic fluctuations. In principle, yes – but then, in principle, someone rhythmically dabbling their toes in the sea in Miami should affect the waves in Cornwall.

Seymour himself acknowledges that the planetary tides would be extremely weak. Nothing daunted, he heads down the path of analogy. The Earth's ocean tides can be amplified as they travel up an estuary, so perhaps there are 'magnetic bays' in the Earth's magnetosphere. Perhaps. But the magnetosphere is extremely squishy, and as far as we know it contains no permanent features that could amplify anything in this way. Indeed, if there are effects that the fetus can perceive, why do they not show on magnetometer traces?

Finally, comes the weakest link of all. The embryo's neurons are supposed to pick out the regular rhythms of the different planets. The magnetic tides repeat roughly once a day as the Earth turns, but the planets are moving at different speeds, and so the period of repetition is different for each.

Jupiter's 'signal', for example, recurs every 23 hours 56 minutes and 24 seconds, and Saturn's every 23 hours 56 minutes and 12 seconds. Are all human embryos so similar that each can pick out the longer period as the signal for a world leader?

These supposed resonances in fact provide the final rocks on which Seymour's hypothesis founders. Seymour nowhere tells the reader one vital fact. As seen from the Earth, the planets do not move across the sky at a constant rate: from time to time they seem to slow down, stop and reverse their motion. So the period from planet-rise to planet-rise is not constant. The values I've given above are averages: the period between Jupiter-rises, for example, changes by 92 seconds during the year, and for Saturn by 36 seconds.

When a fetus is near the point of birth, Jupiter could well have a period of only 23 hours 55 minutes and 30 seconds, while Saturn could be rising at intervals equal to Jupiter's average rate. How is the poor fetus to know which planet causes the latter signal?

Unfortunately, not many readers will have the patience, or the knowledge, to unravel and refute Seymour's circuitous text. I suspect that astrologers will, as usual, latch uncritically onto the book's claims. Dogmatic 'scientists' may, with a clear conscience, ignore this astrological work.

Dr Seymour replies:

A Critical Analysis of Nigel Henbest's Review of my Book: *Astrology: The Evidence of Science*
Nigel Henbest, writing in the *New Scientist* magazine on 12 May 1988, ended his review of my book with the words, ' "Dogmatic" scientists may, with a clear conscience, ignore this astrological work.' Henbest's appraisal of my book, is, to me, just another in a long series of rebuffals which my work has received from orthodox scientists. In 1985, Dr Magnus Pyke, talking to a reporter of a Sunday national newspaper, had this to say of an earlier version of my work: 'This man is dangerous, and the work non-sense.'

I feel it is necessary, for several reasons, to examine Nigel Henbest's review in some detail to establish the factual content of what he has to say. Henbest is the astronomy consultant of *New Scientist*, which is the only magazine of its kind in England, and his comments can be seen as the only 'official' response to my book, to date. Also, he has a degree in physics and astronomy from Leicester University and an MSc. in radio astronomy from Cambridge, so many other scientists and science writers not well versed in these matters may well give a great deal of weight to what he has to say. The wording of his review carries the distinctive characteristic often evident in statements made by science writers who get a great deal of media exposure, i.e., his pronouncements sound very much as if they are undisputed facts and revealed wisdom. The most important reason is that his review highlights the very nature of science, the dissemination of scientific ideas and the methods used by the supporters of orthodox science to attack those who do not always toe the party line.

Before launching into the attack, Henbest quotes from the now famous (or infamous, depending on your point of view) manifesto against astrology which was signed by 186 leading scientists, including 19 Nobel Prize-winners. He describes this statement as 'pompous and patronizing'. Then Henbest sets out to discredit me. Any scientist who takes an interest in astrology must, of necessity, be either mad, a fool, or in it for the money, so it is the duty of the science writer, who is the guardian of 'scientific truth', to discredit him. He says that 'Seymour believes that astrologers will hail this book as providing the scientific validation of their subject ...' Since I have never discussed the matter with Henbest I am not sure what evidence he has used to reach this conclusion. I have been to several astrological meetings and conferences, and I have addressed and argued with many astrologers, so I was well aware long before I actually wrote the book that the last thing the majority of astrologers wanted was scientific validation of what they do. At most a handful consider my work of value to astrology, a few more have a passing interest in some small parts of my work, and many more will listen tolerantly to what I have to say. Anyone who has spoken to an astrologer of some standing in the astrological community (as distinct from media astrologers) will realize that most astrologers have their own vision of reality, which to them is greater than the view offered by present-day orthodox science. In fact anyone who has heard me talk at an astrological meeting knows that I am not there to agree with the astrologers, but to make the point that although my work provides an understanding of some aspects of astrology, I think much of astrology is a belief system, based on some scientific principles, which has become highly embroidered with time. At several points in my book I make this point clear. This is the first indication, of many, that Henbest did not trouble to read my book thoroughly. The fact that I was well aware of how astrologers felt about my work is very clear from an article, entitled 'Unwelcome Ally for the Horoscope Brigade' by Diana Hutchinson, which appeared in the *Daily Mail* on 21 November 1987. In that article I was correctly quoted as saying: 'A lot of astrology is on very shaky ground, and it is for the scientists to sort out the wheat from the chaff. Astrologers are digging their heels in because they fear they will be left naked by the attacks of conventional science.' My book was also rejected by many publishers on the grounds that it did not provide astrologers with the type of justification which they wanted. Henbest thus makes his claim about my belief with no evidence at all, purely in an attempt to discredit me, but later on he is rather sanctimonious about evidence.

Next he sets out to show that I am trying to mislead readers by the subtitle of my book: The Evidence of Science. He says that the evidence consists solely of the results of the French psychologist Michel Gauquelin. There are several ways in which this statement of his is grossly misleading, and factually untrue. I also introduce some of the evidence collected by the late John Addey and the more recent work of Professor Peter Roberts, formerly professor of systems science at the City University London, which has only appeared in *Correlation* – the research journal of astrology. The whole point about formulating theories is that they bring together in a meaningful way a great deal of evidence from many different areas of experience. The additional evidence is then relevant within the context of the theory. Thus my book also discusses a great deal of other evidence from Solar Physics, Space Science, Geophysics and Biology, which is relevant to the theory I have developed.

Further along the road of his attempts to show that I am trying to mislead he says that what I am considering '. . . turns out to be something different from what you and I would call astrology'. With this statement he is showing his own appalling ignorance of the wide spectrum of beliefs that go under the name of astrology, and he is seeking public support for his ignorance. Just as all Christians do not hold the same set of beliefs (although they would all say they believe in Christianity), so astrologers do not have the same consensus opinion on many fundamental topics. The one thing that unites all astrologers is the conviction that there are links between the extra-terrestrial universe and life on Earth, so this is really the fundamental tenet of astrology. At the one end of the very wide spectrum of beliefs we have those that believe that everything on Earth is controlled by the Sun, Moon, planets and stars, and at the other end of the spectrum we have the supporters of the new astrology of harmonics. Thus astrologers differ widely in the fundamental techniques they use, and even in the importance and role of the zodiac. For the last thirty years Gauquelin has been showing that the signs of the zodiac do not have the influence they are supposed to have, and his work has been added to in recent years by Eysenck and Nias, from the Institute of Psychiatry of London University, and also by Dean and Mather (in *Recent Advances in Natal Astrology*), two professional scientists with an interest in astrology. In many of the modern developments in astrology, and astrology has changed very much in recent years, the angular relationships between the planets are much more important than their positions along the zodiac – which plays the role of a reference system. It is only in Sun-sign astrology – the type of astrology used in newspapers – that the zodiac is of prime import-ance, and most serious astrologers do not consider this type of astrology to be of much importance. In fact my book includes the following quotation from Dr Lyall Watson: 'For a start, we can disregard the popular newspaper version of astrology altogether. Glib, all embracing predictions ... have nothing to do with as-trology. They are held in well deserved contempt both by as-trologers and their critics.' Henbest then makes it quite clear that his understanding of astrology is really based on newspaper as-trology, and that he has never read a serious book on modern statistical research methods as applied to astrology, in his life. I am sure he would take a dim view of anyone who based their view of science purely on what they read in newspapers.

One can forgive Henbest for his misunderstanding of astrology – he is after all a trained scientist, a science writer and the author of popular books on astronomy – but his complete misunderstanding of some very basic principles of science, and of the methodology of science is less easy to overlook in someone with these credentials. Quite often people accuse others of those faults that they themselves are guilty of, and in the technical sections of his review we see Henbest at his misinformed and misleading best.

His most important fault is that he does not understand resonance – which is the cornerstone of my theory. Although the space surrounding Earth is full of radio waves from many radio and television stations, household and industrial equipment and naturally produced disturbances, we are still able to tune into the television station of our choice and make sense of the resulting information we receive, because of resonance between the transmitter and the receiver. An essential feature of resonance is that frequency is more important than the strength of the signal, and that small disturbances can have effects which are out of all proportion to their strengths, if they are in tune with the natural frequencies of a system. The normal methods of calculating the response of a system to external influences break down when resonance conditions apply. Thus a single violin string vibrating at the right frequency can shatter a wine glass, while the full might of the orchestra will leave it untouched. All scientists are aware of the power of resonance. If the nucleus of the carbon atom did not have a certain resonance condition then life as we know it on this planet would not exist. Atoms and molecules only respond to radiation of the right frequency. On the 7 November 1940, in 'moderate winds', the Tacoma Narrows Bridge in the USA developed a very large oscillation because the gusting of the wind was in resonance with the natural oscillations of the bridge, and after seventy minutes the central span collapsed. This incident provides us with one of the most spectacular examples of the power of resonance.

Because of the importance of resonance in many areas of physics there exists a well-developed framework of mathematics to explore the consequences of resonance in other areas. All the calculations used by scientists to show that cosmic forces are too weak to affect life on Earth have ignored the possibility of resonance. I have used the mathematics of resonance to construct my theory. I am suggesting that a foetus with a given set of inherited characteristics has a nervous system genetically tuned to receiving specific fluctuations of the geomagnetic field, and that it will not respond to others of greater strength to which it is not tuned. The work of Professor Frank Brown, a biologist from Northwestern University, has shown that many organisms have two biological clocks; one that can respond to the solar magnetic variation, and another that can respond, independently, to the lunar daily magnetic variation (which is only 15 % of that of the solar variation), even in the high technological environment of a modern biology laboratory. These results, together with many others carried out by various scientists, were the subject of a BBC Horizon programme entitled 'Magnet Earth', which explored very thoroughly the biological consequences of living on a planet that possessed a magnetic field. Several of the experiments discussed on this programme, especially those of Professor Brown, show that Henbest's claim that the lunar daily magnetic variation is masked on most days, by the buffeting of the magnetosphere by the solar wind, is without experimental support. In fact, Henbest's dogmatic statement is merely ill-informed opinion.

Henbest further claims that 'A pregnant woman in a modern household will experience much stronger magnetic fluctuations from the washing machine and the food processor. The regular rhythm of the storage heaters will swamp the lunar signal'. Once again, he shows that he has not understood the basic concepts of resonance. The magnetic fields of household equipment have a basic frequency of 50 cycles per second, whereas the lunar variation has a frequency of 2 cycles per lunar day, so the magnetic fields due to household equipment are far from being in resonance with the internal biological clock of a foetus with a lunar-type personality. However, it is worth noting that even in terms of the strengths of the fields due to electrical equipment in the home, Henbest has not done his homework. In March of this year the World Health Organization issued a booklet, *Environmental Health Criteria 69: Magnetic Fields.* This booklet showed that the 60-cycles-per-second fields produced by equipment in the American homes got weaker very rapidly the further one got from the source. For most ordinary equipment, like washing machines and refrigerators, the field more than 2 metres from the source was smaller than that of the lunar daily magnetic variation. The worst offenders were electrical can-openers and hair dryers, which had fields greater in strength, and which had to be used at close quarters. However as already stated, they have the wrong frequency, and even if they had some effect the exposure times are limited. Few pregnant mothers spend more than a few minutes using these pieces of equipment in one day, whereas they are exposed to the lunar daily magnetic variation for 24 hours per day! Henbest cannot even claim originality with this particular criticism, since it was the first one presented to me by people who were not scientists. He can, however, be accused of arrogance for believing that I would not have investigated this criticism during my own investigations. In fact, this particular criticism is discussed on page 123 of my book, showing once again that Henbest did not read the book properly.

Earlier on he said of the lunar daily magnetic variation: 'It's such a small effect that you can only detect it with sensitive magneto-meters sited well away from electromagnetic interference.' The reason why geomagnetic observatories are sited away from urban environments is because geophysicists are interested in the full range of the variations in the field, including those of very short duration, which can be swamped by the rapidly fluctuating fields of electrical equipment. The equipment used to record the changes in the geomagnetic field also records all the fluctuations without any selective tuning. Because of the points already made about domestic equipment, they were not considered a major threat to geomagnetic observatories. The most important threat to the recording of high-frequency fluctuations (of the order of a few minutes or less) came from the electrification of the railways. This was why the magnetic observatory moved from Greenwich to Abinger in 1925. The continuing extension of the electrification programme led the Astronomer Royal, Sir Harold Spencer Jones, to write in 1939, 'As a safeguard against the probable extension of railway electrification in the future the essential condition for a new site is that it should be at least ten miles from any railway.' This is because the magnetic field associated with a long straight conductor becomes weaker with distance much more slowly than the fields associated with domestic sources and equipment. In any case, the frequency is still far removed from the resonance frequency associated with biological clocks to which I am referring. Thus, Henbest's comments show his limited understanding of geomagnetism and the techniques used in its investigation.

Henbest then accuses me of going along the road of speculation. I make no apologies for this, and his comment shows a very deep misunderstanding of the fundamental nature of theoretical science. It is the task of the theoretical scientist to bring together a host of evidence and from this to produce a theory that not only explains the available evidence, but offers a framework for testable speculations that lie beyond the limits of the available evidence. The prestigious scientific journal *Nature* once rejected a paper by the famous Italian physicist Enrico Fermi, in which he proposed the existence of a sub-atomic particle called a neutrino, on the ground that it was too speculative. The existence of this particle has been demonstrated over and over again, so Fermi was right. In fact, Henbest's attitude towards theory does not seem to be far removed from that of a movement which existed in Germany in the 1920s. This movement was led by Johannes Stark who firmly believed that physics should be strictly based on empirical data only, and who went on to attack quantum theory and relativity as being too speculative and a creation of the Jews.

Speculation is an essential and positive aspect of science as is clear from the following quotation of Karl Popper: 'The essence of a good mathematical model is that it should embody the bold ideas, unjustified assumptions and speculations which are our only means of interpreting nature' (quoted on page 177 of my book).

Henbest then attacks the part of my theory that argues that the planets can affect, by their gravitational tidal tug, the vibrations of the Earth's magnetic field. Here he stoops to ridicule: 'In principle, yes – but then, in principle, someone rhythmically dabbling their toes in Miami should affect the waves in Cornwall.' He omits to mention that in another chapter in my book I discuss how the tidal tug of the planets affect the magnetic field of the Sun, and here I comment on two books written by John Gribbin (the physics consultant to *New Scientist*) and Stephen Plagemann, in which they highlighted the vast literature on the subject. Over the years many scientific journals have carried articles discussing the tidal effects of the planets on the solar cycle, including the very prestigious journal, *Nature*, until some work by Professor John Eddy seemed to kill off the theory and subsequent papers. Thus the idea of the coupling between the magnetic field of Earth and the tidal tug of the planets is not without a respectable precedent. In fact, I have formulated a theory for the solar cycle, based on the tidal effects of the planets on the Sun, which overcomes all the objections levelled against previous theories. One of my students at Plymouth Polytechnic did a project based on this theory, in which he carried out a series of calculations on our computer, demonstrating the viability of the principles involved ('Planetary Influences on the Solar Cycle' by A. Turner, April 1987). I am now working on the extension of this theory to more complex models of the solar cycle, and I have also extended the basic principles of the theory to include a discussion of planetary effects on the magnetosphere of Earth.

In *Geomagnetism*, vol. 1 (edited by Prof. J. A. Jacobs, Academic Press, 1987), R. A. Langel discussed much of the recent work on the effect of the solar cycle on the magnetosphere of Earth, and this work shows very clearly that there are fluctuations of the magnetosphere related to the 22-year and 11-year periods of the solar cycle and their harmonics (with periods of about 7, 5.5, 4.3, 3.7, 2.4, 2.27 and 2.11). Since, according to my theory (which cannot be rejected on the basis of available evidence), the solar cycle already contains information on the relative positions of the planets (including Earth), these investigations provide evidence to show that the fluctuations of the magnetic field of Earth also contains this information. This work, however, refers to the annual averages. In the Harold Jeffreys Lecture delivered by the late Sir Edward Bullard (one of the greatest geophysicists of this century) he said: 'The amplitude of the terms (connected with the solar daily magnetic variation) varies with the season of the year and with the sunspot cycle; it might, perhaps, be more convenient to regard these changes not as changes in the amplitude of a term with a single frequency but as beats between a group of terms with slightly different frequencies; for example, the group near the daily frequency would have a line with the exact daily solar period flanked by lines with periods ($1 \pm \frac{1}{365}$) of a day which would given an annual fluctuation in amplitude.' I am proposing that because of what Henbest calls the squishyness of the magnetosphere responds to the harmonics of the solar cycle, and that some of the frequencies near one-half of a solar day will be the same as those of the planetary tidal periods and hence they will become phase-locked to those periods. In this section, Henbest also asks why these periods have not been detected by sensitive magnetometers. I can best answer this question by quoting again from Sir Edward Bullard. 'It is curious that no attempts seems to have been made to resolve this fine structure by the methods of power spectrum analysis.' Although this statement was made in 1965, I have not been able to find evidence, by searching the more recent literature, that such an analysis has been carried out since then, so this part of my theory will have to wait further research, but then this is in the nature of the general progress of science. This is one of the many examples in his review where Henbest is actually being anti-science. Also in this section Henbest accuses me of heading down the path of analogy. Once again he misunderstands the role of analogy in science. It is perfectly valid, and a method used by many working scientists, to use analogy because of the mathematical similarities between many different types of physical system. In fact, the mathematical theory of neurons is based on the mathematics of analogous electrical circuits (see, for example, *An Introduction to the Mathematics of Neurons* by F. C. Hoppensteadt, one of the references which I quote in my book).

His last point begins to show that he is at least beginning to understand something about my use of resonance in the theory. He rightly points out that Jupiter and Saturn have different average times that they take to go around the Earth, which are very close to each other. He also points out that the periods do vary over the year, and that sometimes it is possible for Jupiter to have the average speed of Saturn, while Saturn has a different speed, and vice versa. He then asks the question: 'How is the poor fetus to know which planet causes the latter signal?' In my theory, as stated many times in my book, specific fluctuations of the geomagnetic field affect the foetus over a considerable part of the nine months of pregnancy, and the geomagnetic effects are not confined to the time of birth. I am proposing that the foetus has a very stable biological clock that can oscillate freely for several days without receiving the signal of the 'right' frequency all the time (biological clocks, like pendulums, do have this property) but since this free oscillation is equal to the average magnetic tidal periods of a particular planet, it will become locked-in to the apparent movements of that planet as seen from Earth. If Jupiter has the average period of Saturn (while Saturn has a different period) at the time of birth, and the two planets are within a few degrees of each other, or they are separated by almost 180 degrees, no problem will arise, since the magnetic tides of the two planets will be in phase with each other. However, if a Saturn-type personality becomes locked to the average period of Saturn sometime during pregnancy and then later on Saturn has a slightly different period, but Jupiter has the average period of Saturn, but this time they are separated by a large angle at birth, the foetus will not suddenly shift from following Saturn's tide to following Jupiter's tide. This is because biological clocks (like pendulums) have their own 'momentum' and cannot undertake sudden shifts of phase. This has been shown to be the case for all internal biological clocks and indeed it gives rise to the jet-lag problem which is experienced by people when they cross time zones. This means that in a statistical sample of babies with Saturn-type personalities more are likely to be born with Saturn in particular parts of the sky, but not all will necessarily do so. It is a common fallacy to suppose that a few exceptions undermine a theory that has been proposed to explain statistical evidence, for example: 'My grandfather lived to 86 although he smoked 20 cigarettes per day, so smoking has no link with lung cancer.' Henbest fell into this trap! It is also worth pointing out that even within its own terms the review contains a glaring logical flaw. If he uses the theory of resonance circuits to try to demolish this part of my theory, then the same resonance circuits would not respond to the 50 cycles associated with household equipment and circuits tuned to receiving the lunar daily magnetic variation and would not respond to the buffeting of the magnetosphere by the solar wind. Henbest cannot have it both ways!

His review provides a great deal of evidence to show that his understanding of resonance is extremely confused, his knowledge of geomagnetism very limited, his awareness of the extensive work on the biological effects of magnetic fields and biological clocks virtually non-existent, and his understanding of the role of specula- tion and analogy in science exhibits an appalling ignorance of the history and philosophy of science. My own literary searches un- dertaken in the course of my own research, show that Henbest has not produced any scientific papers of note in the area of magnetic fields in astronomy. Between 1964 and 1967 I pioneered the applica- tion of the mathematical techniques used in geomagnetism to the study of the magnetic fields of the Milky Way. This was the basis of my MSc. and PhD. theses, and since then I have published scientific papers on the subject, so it was necessary for me to become acquainted with the physical and mathematical principles of geomagnetic phenomena. In 1985, I wrote an introduction to magnetic fields in astronomy, called *Cosmic Magnetism* (published by the Institute of Physics), for amateur astronomers and un- dergraduate students doing general courses in astronomy, and once again I came across no important papers written by Henbest, in this area. The philosopher of science, Paul Feyerabend, said about the manifesto against astrology: 'It shows the extent to which scientists are prepared to assert their authority even in areas in which they have no knowledge whatsoever.' Henbest ends his review with these words: 'unfortunately, not many readers will have the patience, or the knowledge, to unravel or refute Seymour's circuitous text.' To me, this statement sounds 'pompous and patronizing'!

For none of the dogmatic statements which he made in the review did he quote from specialists in the appropriate areas of research, neither did he quote any relevant measurements to back up his assertions. He does not seem to have checked out any of the 77 references given at the end of my book. In other words the whole review is based on his own personal ill-informed opinions, which he is asking people to accept because of the authority vested in him by the editor of *New Scientist*. In his desire to discredit me and my theory Henbest compromised his scientific integrity and his craft as a science writer. Instead he stooped to those journalistic practices which one normally associates with the least respectable parts of the British press. I would not presume to say that Henbest believes this or that, but my own feeling is that he felt he could 'get away' with such a shoddy and contemptible piece of writing in *New Scientist*, because he was writing about astrology. Most of the readers (and the editor, it seems) would be only too pleased to agree with his 'knocking' of astrology. Those with enough know-ledge of resonance, biological clocks and geomagnetism to see the gaps in Henbest's knowledge and the glaring flaws in his arguments would just say to themselves: 'We will not lift a pen to defend an astronomer (with a specialist knowledge of magnetic fields and tidally induced phenomena) stupid enough to get involved with as-trology.'

On 18 June I wrote a letter to the Editor of *New Scientist* pointing out some of the factual errors which occurred in Henbest's review, and which I asked him to consider for publication. Since then two letters have been published in *New Scientist* which com-mented on the Henbest review. The first letter merely took the review as an excuse to put forward a theory to explain Sun-sign astrology, for which there is as yet no scientific evidence, and completely ignored the contents of the review and the contents of my book, as outlined in the review. A more recent letter was from one of the signatories of a manifesto against astrology defending why he signed the manifesto and making a few general comments on astrology. Once again it completely ignored the details of the review and the details of the book as outlined by Henbest. My own letter has not yet appeared. Is the Editor reluctant to impugn the authority of his own astrology consultant?

I find the response of the Editor surprising in this respect, especially since he, very bravely, gave a great deal of support to Rupert Sheldrake when he proposed his theory of morphic reso-nance to explain how organisms develop, learn and adapt. This theory is even more speculative than mine, in that it proposes the existence of fields that lie outside the currently accepted framework of science and his theory is not backed (as is mine) by a mathematical model. There are two other instances which highlight the in-consistency of the attitude of the editorial board of this magazine to my theory. On 19 March 1987, *NS* carried an article on dowsing by Tom Williamson. Here Williamson had this to say: 'To detect underground features, the dowser needs a quite extraordinary degree of magnetic sensitivity – almost on a par with that of the best magnetometers.' This is not the only implication of the theory on dowsing which was being discussed by Williamson. It also implies that the dowser is able to distinguish between the very small fluctuations associated with these underground features and the natural fluctuations of the geomagnetic field. The ability to respond selectively to different fluctuations of the Earth's magnetic field, through tuning and resonance, is an essential feature of the theory of astrology discussed in my book. In *New Scientist* on 24 April 1986, there was a small item on 'Magnetic Fields Speed Reaction Rates'. This item pointed out that scientists were wrong to just dismiss the idea that magnetic fields could affect chemical reaction rates, and that evidence was being accumulated which showed that even weak fields could alter the ordering of a chemical system and thus they could also affect reaction rates. However, it does seem that when it comes to astrology, anything is acceptable when it comes to dismissing it and that as far as their attitude to this subject is concerned, it is but old wine in *New Scientist* bottles.

Percy Seymour, Reply to Nigel Henbest's review in
New Scientist, 12 May 1987 (unpublished)

Summary and Conclusions

The scientific evidence supporting astrology comes from many fields. Some of it is direct, some indirect. But when the evidence is compiled, and examined both as science and in relation to the astrological doctrine as whole, the verdict is unmistakable. Both aspects of the fundamental premise of astrology have been established beyond any possibility of doubt:

1. There is a correspondence between events in the heavens and events on earth.
2. There is a correlation between the position of the planets at birth and the human personality.

Less certain is the practice of astrology. The Clark experiments, and those derived from it are less 'hard' than those of Brown, Piccardi, Delgado or Gauquelin, and they are less conclusive. They involve human variables and are therefore subject to more mysterious, more capricious laws. On the other hand they were designed to test the astrologers on their own ground, and the astrologers passed those tests often enough for even the hypercritical Dean and Mather to conclude that the 'astrologers work'.

Caution is surely in order and more research essential. Nevertheless, at the moment, on balance, the evidence is in favor of, *not against* the astrologers' claims. If these positive results are eventually replicated and vindicated, and then viewed in the light of the Gauquelin data, and the indisputable indirect 'hard' evidence proving celestial/terrestrial correspondences over a wide spectrum of fields, there will then be no doubt at all that astrology also works; imperfectly no doubt, but well enough for astrologers to produce significant results in tests far more difficult than anything they would encounter in the normal practice of their profession.

The only really major point still at issue is the reality of the zodiac. Honorable critics (if such exist) may rightly insist that its validity is unproven, not disproved. Adherents may argue with some justification that the proven ability of astrologers to successfully delineate and predict character on the basis of the horoscope amounts to indirect support of the zodiac – since the astrologers all used the zodiac in making their statistically significant interpretations.

Not only is the factual evidence supporting astrology commanding, but it is also now possible to develop a plausible theory for the manner in which astrological effects manifest themselves within the framework of the known physical world. Modern physics and astronomy both make it clear that the ancient concept of the Harmony of the Spheres is no longer a poetic metaphor but a legitimate analogy drawn upon a unified solar system in which each part affects every other part via the well understood phenomenon of resonance.

D. The Question: How?

A number of major figures in science have agreed that there is nothing implausible about astrology *in principle*, given what we now know about the physical universe. Dr Seymour's theory may or not prove to be the correct description of astrology's *modus operandi*. But as far as our case is concerned, it is enough to know that an expert in cosmic and planetary magnetism finds it possible, within the framework of known and acknowledged laws, to put forward a testable scientific theory to account for evidence that cannot be denied. And those effects take place, in the main, according to a time-honored astrological tradition whose origins are lost in pre-history.

Under such circumstances it would appear difficult to avoid concluding (and pointless, given the behavior of the Prosecution, to employ more diplomatic language) that, on the subject of astrology, Pythagoras, Plato, Plotinus, Ptolemy, St Thomas Aquinas, Albertus Magnus, Johann Kepler, Goethe, Ralph Waldo Emerson and Carl Jung were right, and all of modern science wrong.

IV.

HERESY IN THE CHURCH OF PROGRESS

Adrian Berry, in the *Sunday Telegraph*, concerned about the tender sensibilities of children, advocates overt scientific McCarthyism to keep them safe from anti-Rationalist ideas. Nigel Henbest's review in the *New Scientist* looks authoritative but, examined closely, has no more factual integrity than a pre-glasnost *Pravda* article. A protracted campaign by Dr Seymour to have his rejoinder printed by the *New Scientist* was unsuccessful.

This emotional reaction to Dr Seymour's sober book,* in conjunction with the unprincipled handling of the Gauquelin data all along, underscores the need to discuss several further issues — issues not directly affecting the volume and quality of astrological evidence, but germane to our case. Among them: how is it possible for self-described 'Rationalists' to behave so irrationally the moment evidence seems to favor an unwelcome idea? And what is it about astrology in particular that elicits this reaction?

The answer to the first question lies in understanding the true nature of 'Rationalism', one of history's more egregious misnomers. For Rationalism is not, as its adherents would have us believe, a considered, intellectual response (and the only possible response) to the physical facts revealed by science.

---

* The sole exception to date: a detailed, thoughtful and well-written feature article in the December 1989 issue of *OMNI* magazine by Dava Sobel on Dr Seymour and his theory.

Is the Church of Progress a Church?

The Fundamentalist Christian Right commonly accuses its athe-
tistic opposition (under its various names of 'Secular Humanism', 'Materialism' or 'Rationalism') of being a religion in
its own right, and it is tempting to discount *any* claim made by
the Fundamentalist Right (to paraphrase the old joke: with
Fundamentalists for enemies, Rationalists hardly need friends).
Predictably, the accusation is both ridiculed and denied by
Rationalists, Materialists and Secular Humanists. They point to
the lack of any official, written dogma and of any central
authority vested with the power to enforce dogma; they emphasize the absence of a belief in any sort of transcendent reality
(the essence of all other religions), they disavow both faith and
personal experience as valid means for accessing truth, and they
insist upon empirical proof as the sole criterion for the establishment of truth.

This may sound legitimate enough but it is no more than
evasive action. Rationalists know perfectly well that the accusation does not concern these issues.

It is the alleged religious, or quasi-religious nature of scientific
belief that is behind the charge, and this has been leveled by sources
far more reputable and better informed than the Fundamentalist
Right. Philosopher of Science Paul Feyerabend has spelled out the
similarities in detail (*Science in a Free Society*, Schocken, New York,
1978), and earlier in the century the eminent mathematician and
philospher Alfred North Whitehead wrote:

> The certainties of science are a delusion. They are hedged round
> with unexplored limitations. Our handling of scientific doctrines is
> controlled by the *diffused metaphysical concepts of our epoch* [italics
> ours]. Even so, we are continually led into errors of expectation.
> Also, whenever some new mode of observational experience is
> obtained the doctrines crumble into a fog of inaccuracies.
>
> *Adventure in Ideas*,
> Cambridge University Press, 1933, p. 198.

In building our case for astrology, we have pointed out many instances where our opponents have failed to distinguish between the physical facts of science and unwarranted metaphysical conclusions drawn upon those facts. Once these metaphysical conclusions are accepted as axiomatic and institutions grow up around them dedicated to proselytizing them and preserving them from attack, the similarities to religion (as we know it in the West, especially) become obvious.

But religion is a vast subject, with metaphysical, psychological, sociological and political sides to it. To fairly judge whether Rationalism is a religion or not, it is first essential to specify which aspect of religion we are judging and then to define that aspect, ideally in terms agreeable to the opposition.

If, as a starting point, we concentrate on religion's primary metaphysical function and call it 'a system of undemonstrable beliefs held without reference to physical evidence', theologians might not like it very much but we think it unlikely that Rationalists would object. Yet they subscribe to just such a system of undemonstrable beliefs.

The Atheology of the Church of Progress

Its unofficial, unwritten, but universally accepted credo goes something like this: the universe is an accident; matter precedes mind; consciousness is a kind of spin-off of matter;* human life,

---

* J. B. S. Haldane, with characteristic bluntness, set out the premises upon which his materialism was founded: (1) 'That there was material before there was mind'. (2) 'That there were events before there were any minds to perceive those events'. These perfectly undemonstrable and metaphysical notions were set out in a book entitled: *Science and Life: Essays of a Rationalist*. A geneticist, Darwinist and Rationalist, Haldane was also a staunch, life-long Communist. Most of the members of the committee that is CSICOP's French equivalent, the Comité Français pour l'Étude des Phénomènes Paranormaux, are also Communists. On the other hand, most of CSICOP's most vocal members are extreme right-wing conservatives. Philip Klass, CSICOP's chief UFO-debunker, has even suggested that those who maintained the US government was covering up information proving the existence of UFOs, were, if not actually part of a Communist plot, at least guilty of deliberately aiding the Soviets by making Americans doubt the veracity of their own government. Called to

indeed, all life, serves no higher purpose. Spirituality is another name for superstition. There is no consciousness higher than our own (at least not on this planet) and no possible transformation of the material into the spiritual. There is only Progress, hope defrayed into the future. Jacob's ladder no longer bridges the gulf between heaven and earth. It has been laid flat along the ground. Given enough time, science and technology will establish their version of heaven right here on earth. All we have to do is continue implementing those proven rational values that have brought our planet to its present state. At a certain point (perhaps around the time when the biased scientists disappear and unbiased science prevails) Progress will automatically take over and everyone will live happily ever after.

This is a system of beliefs, a credo. Call it the atheology of the Church of Progress. Only it is not acknowledged as a credo. It is called 'reason' and it is said to follow from the facts of science. But it has nothing to do with science. Its several chief elements are in no sense necessary corollaries of the actual scientifically validated facts of the physical world – as its faithful pretend.*

This credo has dispensed with the usual reliance upon a divine, transcendent, indivisible god. Instead, it is held together by the Krazy Glue of Neo-Darwinian evolution. But there is nothing rational or scientific about that either (see the bibliography for a selection of scientific literature effectively disproving the possibility of life arising through accident).

Rationalists claim that the inability to prove divine intention proves the lack of intention; that the inability to prove purpose,

---

account on this extreme position, the Editor of the *Skeptical Inquirer* saw nothing to amend. We find it intriguing that the philosophy calling itself Rationalism should be able to count among its members adherents of both the extreme left and the extreme right. Surely, following the logic recommended by Martin Gardner and Bertrand Russell (see pp. 146, 151) only one of these groups can be Rationalists.

* There is a vast literature, much of it written by eminent, if marginally heretical, scientists and philosophers proving this point from many different angles. (See the Bibliography for a selected list.)

proves purposelessness. This is obvious sophistry. We cannot physically prove intention or purpose on the human level, much less the divine, yet we would have precious little science without it. If you cannot prove you have been faithful to your wife, does this mean you have been unfaithful?

Moreover, to qualify as science, following the Rationalists' own precepts, that very lack of intention and purposelessness must itself be demonstrable, measurable, predictable and replicable.

Of course it is not, nor can it be, for the simple reason that these criteria are value judgements, by definition beyond the pale of both experimental and theoretical science.* So the insistence upon accident and purposelessness, and upon reason in turn, is metaphysics in its own right, a set of unprovable assumptions, no more and no less metaphysical than the acknowledged metaphysical systems of other religions; distinguished from them only in that the assumptions are wholly negative.

The credo is neither science nor reason; it is merely what most scientists happen to believe.

And once it is understood as a religion, that passionate defense of dispassion ('I'm trying to bring society around to a Rationalist point of view . . . I'm fighting a battle here, and I have a lot of troops on my side') becomes comprehensible if no less comic. Judging by the antics of self-proclaimed Rationalists, the belief in nothing must be defended with the same zealotry normally associated with the defence of a belief in something – leading to the conclusion that at heart, belief in something and belief in nothing have more in common than meets the eye.

---

* Demonstrability, replicability, etc. represent *decisions*; decisions made by the priesthood to distinguish between what deserves inclusion in the 'real world' and what does not. But following definitions laid down by Church atheologians themselves, a decision, any decision, cannot help but be a value judgement. Since values are purely subjective (according to the Church of Progress but not according to most other religions), they have no objective reality, and therefore play no part in the 'real world'. Thus, ironically, according to its own standards, this Church is as subjectively based as those it disavows. And therefore it, like the others, is rooted irrevocably in unreality. As Lawrence E. Jerome might put it: 'it is purely a product of the human mind. It has no physical basis in fact.'

Politics in the Church of Progress

Seen as a system of undemonstrable belief Rationalism stands exposed as a religion. However, when Rationalism is commonly criticized as a religion, its critics are not so much referring to a doctrine, a corpus of beliefs, as to a corrupt and tyrannical institution set up to preserve those beliefs from heresy or other forms of attack. In other words, these critics are drawing parallels to the political rather than the philosophical aspect of the church.

This accusation is equally valid, and it has been leveled often, even from within its own priesthood (see Richard Kammann, p. 292). The parallels between this modern-day Church of Progress and the organized Church of Rome at its worst are legion.

CSICOP stands as obvious, self-appointed Chamber of the Inquisition in the US (other countries have similar Chambers). When discussing CSICOP it's admittedly difficult to refrain from exaggeration. Lest the jury suspect we've succumbed, here is CSICOP donning the Inquisitorial robes in its own words: 'Our society has opted for a complete free-for-all of conflicting theories. But if it is this chaotic, who will ensure that there is law and order? Who will guard the truth? The answer is: CSICOP will!' (exclamation point theirs) wrote Douglas R. Hofstadter in *Scientific American* (February 1982).

CSICOP's handling of the Gauquelin case obviates the need for further elaboration on this point. Happily, our modern Inquisitors have no access to the rack, thumbscrew, or heated iron jackboot. Though they and their supporters may try to stop 'otherwise reputable publishers' from publishing heretical works, or call for periodic bookburning,* they lack (in the West at any rate) the authority to order an *auto-da-fé*. They are relatively few in number, and it is tempting to dismiss them as a

---

* The influential English science journal *Nature* called Rupert Sheldrake's book, *A New Science of Life*, 'the best candidate for burning there has been for many years'. Sheldrake's theory of morphic resonance challenged a number of cherished evolutionary ideas and opened the possibility of an intelligent as opposed to accidental origin to life.

little band of manifestly twisted hypocrites – the dispassionate rationalist is about as common as the Fundamentalist Christian who loves his enemies.* †

But like their sinsister forerunners, our modern Inquisitors wield an influence beyond their numbers, and it would be a mistake to ignore them. Though the Inquisitorial dirty work is done by CSICOP henchmen – professional debunkers, conjurers and scientists otherwise without distinction in their fields – CSICOP boasts among its Fellows (via the *Skeptical Inquirer*) an impressive list of well-known scientists, science writers and scholars: Steven Jay Gould, Francis Crick, Carl Sagan, Isaac Asimov, L. Sprague de Camp, Sidney Hook, W. V. Quine, Bernard Dixon and Antony Flew among them.

Following the 'sTARBABY' scandal and the investigation by Kammann and Curry, a private letter to all Fellows was circulated by Professor Ron Westrum, an associate editor of the *Zetetic Scholar*, informing them of the activities being carried out under their unwitting aegis (none could have suspected the true state of affairs from reading the *Skeptical Inquirer*). But there was almost no reaction to this circular. Few Fellows bothered to voice objections; still fewer resigned. The message was unmistakable. Any means were acceptable as long as the end was served. A major heresy such as astrology could not be allowed to prevail. So, while most of *SI*'s Fellows play no active personal role in CSICOP, their names on the *Skeptical Inquirer* masthead stand as powerful personal testimonials to its practices, and an imprimatur of its policies. With such backing, it is not surprising that CSICOP has been relatively successful in keeping the truth from the general public.

---

* To satisfy themselves on this point, members of the jury might find it useful to carefully read through a few copies of the *Skeptical Inquirer* and *The Humanist*.

† Those familiar with the Gospels may have noticed that Jesus makes salvation or redemption available to just about everyone – prostitutes, publicans, Roman centurions, thieves, even the rich, under certain conditions – but not to hypocrites. Hypocrites believe themselves already redeemed. Thus hypocrisy may be the one vice or psychological condition that is actually beyond redemption.

Again, like their counterparts, our modern Inquisitors are charged with defending the faith (in this case, perhaps the unfaith) and punishing heretics. Though they wield their power with considerable autonomy, they are none the less themselves empowered, as were their progenitors, by the greater organization responsible for formulating and propagating dogma. And it is here that the close parallel to the earlier Church diverges and diffuses somewhat. The relatively clear-cut roles of Pope and College of Cardinals no longer exist. There is no formal hierarchical structure to lay down the law. Excepting occasional anathemas like *Objections to Astrology*, the Church of Progress eschews bulls, edicts and encyclicals. Though no less pervasive and invasive to society as a whole, it extends its influence on a tacit, consensus basis through its three separate but complementary orders of Jesuits.

Jesuits of the Church of Progress: Science, Education and the Press

For two centuries, these have been the forces or institutions that have shaped Western society, and consequently the rest of the world. While their power is universally recognized, they are seldom examined within their rightful religious context: as guardians and proselytizers of the Church of Progress. Though we are of course mainly concerned here with their relationship to astrology, a brief digression into their broader socio-religious roles is essential to make that relationship comprehensible to the jury.

In a nutshell, Science calls the tune, Education plays it, the Press gives it rave reviews.

For over two centuries the three have worked closely hand in hand. But that spirit of co-operation is not quite what it used to be.

The Jesuit Order of Science

Though the Church of Progress insists its dogma is based upon science, this is not true, and has not been true for almost a century. The energetic rather than material nature of matter contravenes the Church's simple-minded materialism while its fundamental premise of a mechanical, accidental universe has been challenged from within its own ranks by at least a few of its own most eminent physicists and biologists. As bookstores add metaphysical sections to cater to the exponentially growing interest, there is often a separate shelf devoted to titles exploring the relationships between metaphysics and the expanding frontiers of science. We discussed some of these ideas dealing with the objections to astrology. The important point to make here is that the latest findings of science not only fail to support the basic materialist dogma of the Church of Progress, but in many instances, particularly in physics and biology, they contravene it.

Most of these ideas have not yet made significant inroads into education or the press. They are too complex, too remote and too philosophically abstruse to unsettle the rank and file of Church unfaithful. On the other hand, the hero-worship science enjoyed through all of the nineteenth and most of the twentieth century is no longer unconditional. Over the past few years, a number of heavily funded glossy magazines intended to make the wonders of science intelligible to the educated lay reader have foundered. Editorials in those that survive repeatedly stress the difficulty of attracting high-level students to science. The authors imagine it is the science programs that are to blame, but actually it is science itself, this secular, earth-bound science that even on its highest and purest level, concerns itself with practically nothing that matters to human life.* Science still commands considerable popular respect, but some of the glamor has gone, and much of the trust.

The lead editorial in the *New Scientist* (20–30 December 1989), summing up the decade for science, expresses a wistful

---

* On rare occasions this crucial point is recognized by scientists themselves and published in scientific magazines. 'The point is we have backed ourselves up an intellectual cul-de-sac where feelings and emotions are downgraded (thereby denying our totality as human beings), leaving us squarely on our own. Exciting as the scientific endeavour undoubtedly is, its vision of the Universe is ultimately devoid of inner meaning. It lies in pieces at our feet and is, in essence, dead.' (Lionel Milgrom, *New Scientist*, 19 August 1989)

imperative: 'Somehow, scientists have to regain some of the ground they have lost since the 1950s, when people listened to researchers when they wanted to know about scientific subjects.'

As if to underscore the tempered view of science developed throughout this book, the editorial continues,

> This is not to say that scientists are the only ones who should get a hearing, just that they are worth listening to, a point that seems to have escaped many of the more rabid doom-mongers.
>
> Perhaps in the 1990s science can settle into a middle way. But first we have to do something about that dreadful cliché, the demographic time-bomb, or there won't be enough scientists around. If the greening of politics in the late 1980s does anything to counter the 'greeding' that prevailed throughout most of the 1980s, we might just be able to persuade youngsters that science is entertaining, important and rewarding.
>
> It does not help the scientists' case that the 1980s saw the growth of what not long ago would have been frowned on as shady practices. The stinginess of governments around the world may have forced scientists to fight for a living, but do they really have to indulge in unseemly battles for patents and glory like those that surrounded high-temperature superconductors, for example? The 'publication by fax' engendered by that particular nine days' wonder was at least of mostly sound science: the same cannot be said of this year's media hype, cold fusion.
>
> Too much has already been written about that farce to warrant disinterring the corpse yet again, but when the world of particle physics gets sucked into the circus, as it did with squabbles between the European Centre for Particle Research (CERN) and the Stanford Linear Collider, the time has surely come to separate the children and call for a little decorum. Behave like spivs and the world will treat you accordingly.

But 'the point' has not escaped the rabid doom-mongers. They simply note the role played by science and science-based technology in virtually every one of the major disaster areas facing the planet – global warming, toxic and nuclear wastes, environmental degradation, pollution of the earth, sea and skies, destruction of the rainforests, nuclear weaponry and nuclear power, bacteriological and chemical warfare stockpiles, food additives and contaminants . . . all without exception have their roots in science and could not have happened were it not for science, and the universal acceptance of the Church of Progress credo that has vested science with so much prestige and authority. Moreover, scientists were generally among the last to acknowledge the reality of these catastrophes. To this day they but rarely admit to their rightful lion's share of the guilt. It is the 'greedy industrialists' and 'power-hungry politicians' (who are of course responsible for their paychecks in the first place) who have misused the results of the scientists' dispassionate search for objective truth. Under such circumstances, the most rabid of rabid doom-mongers may be largely justified in thinking that scientists may well be among the last people worth listening to on these matters.

The remainder of the editorial powerfully buttresses that conviction. It is the 'stinginess of governments' that has 'forced scientists to fight for a living', and provoked the unprincipled behavior. Presumably artists, writers, politicians, athletes, businessmen and, needless to say, 'astrological charlatans' don't have to fight for a living. The world of particle physics bears no responsibility for its actions. It was 'sucked into the circus', unwilling victim of the vortex. Cold fusion advocates are neither 'cranks' nor 'scientific charlatans'. They are the victims of 'media hype', poor souls.

Since it is unlikely that an editorial slap on the wrist from auntie *New Scientist* will dissuade scientists from behaving like spivs, it is equally unlikely that the world will be dissuaded from treating them any differently.

It therefore falls largely upon education and the press to inculcate, foster and maintain the unfaith among the general public.

The Jesuit Order of Education

What is called Education is not education in any meaningful sense of the word (derived from *educere*, to lead forth). In reality it is no more than a vast seminary program, designed to select and develop candidates for the Church of Progress priesthood, while producing a docile, unquestioning laity.

The original Jesuits used to boast, 'Give us the child until he's seven years old and he'll be ours for life,' (or words to that effect). In principle, the Jesuits of today's Church of Progress educational programs would seem to wield even more decisive influence. They have us in their power for at least twelve years, often for sixteen or more, and during the first twelve we have the various elements of the church credo drummed into our heads without respite. Neo-Darwinian evolution (evolution as a chance process) is taught as though it were fact. Progress is taught as though it were manifest destiny. All past civilizations are presented as though they were but misconceived dry runs for the technological age that superseded them. All that is not science is presented as superstition, with the possible exception of Western secular art and literature – which enjoy a certain status as harmless diversions from the ongoing serious business of science/technology. No hint is ever given that other points of view exist, and may be held even within the Church itself. While Progress is supposed to be furthered through the free interchange of ideas, our extended introduction to Progress, through education, is as thorough a form of brainwashing as anything devised by those earlier Jesuits, or for that matter anything existing under oppressive ideological political systems that make no pretense of open-mindedness. Even so, the advantage enjoyed by modern educators over these others is more apparent than real.

Like all religious institutions, this Church is viable only in so far as its truths appear immutable, and the philosophy based upon its truths coincides with real or perceived human needs. To survive and prosper the Church (any church) must inspire allegiance, devotion, faith – coercion will take it only so far. But there are psychological as well as logical problems confronting a Church forced by its own atheology to demand a fervent belief in disbelief (in everything save Reason of course, and the various elements of the credo).

As is so often the case with this religion that calls itself 'Rationalism', a deceptive nomenclature confuses what would otherwise be much clearer. A belief in something is called 'credulity'. Credulity retains its hold through 'faith' which must play no part in the life of the rational human being. On the other hand, the no less passionate and equally undemonstrable belief in nothing is called Reason. Reason is sustained through the diligent exercise of 'skepticism'. But the role skepticism plays in a society dominated by the Church of Progress is rarely recognized for what it is and it looms large in the attitude towards astrology.

A Skeptical Look at Skepticism

According to Culver and Ianna: 'The scientist, and every rational being, must be the eternal skeptic, for he knows only too well how easy it is to be wrong.' (*Gemini Syndrome*, p. 35)

As is their wont, Culver and Ianna express personal opinion as an imperative. But there is no obligation to subscribe to this enthusiastic but quite unskeptical endorsement of skepticism; devoid as it is of scientific or philosophical content. The eminent mathematician, Edward Witten, developer of the controversial 'superstring theory' declared, 'It's extremely important *to believe in what you're doing* [italics ours] . . . One lesson you can learn is don't make mistakes. But that's not very useful. Another lesson is don't give up on right ideas . . .' ('A Theory of Everything' by K. C. Cole, *New York Times* Magazine, 18 October 1987). Ralph Waldo Emerson took a still more skeptical view of skepticism. He called it 'slow suicide'.

At the risk of descending into the irrational, we, personally, would rather be wrong once in a while than go through life as 'eternal skeptics', distrusting everything and everyone all the time. Pretty bluntly, 'eternal skepticism' seems a horrible emotional state to live with day in and day out. Nor is it an effective guard against error. Eternal skepticism did nothing to prevent Culver and Ianna from offering three different, mutually contradictory assessments of science and the scientific method within the space of a single page. Dedicated born-again religious fundamentalists do no worse.

Skepticism: Environmentally or Genetically Determined?

Obviously, in the practice of science, (or art, cooking, baseball and, for that matter, serious religion) a keen critical sense is indispensable. It is essential to be able to distinguish between right and wrong, better and worse in any given situation. But this has absolutely nothing to do with skepticism, or with maintaining an eternally skeptical attitude.

Culver and Ianna's skeptic believes the defendant guilty until proven innocent. This is a sorry enough philosophy in principle, but in practice it's even worse. For when the skeptic becomes an 'eternal skeptic' (and most do) he continues to believe the defendant guilty *after* proven innocent, since he has arrogated to himself the right to disbelieve or ignore the proof – even when set out according to rules laid down by himself.

Just as Rationalism is a euphemism for negative religion, so skepticism, as extolled by Culver, Ianna and their colleagues at the *Skeptical Inquirer*, is a euphemism for negative credulity. It has nothing whatever to do with a keen critical sense – which is perhaps the last quality the Jesuits of Education care to inculcate. For a keen critical sense along with knowledge of the metaphysical and historical alternatives to the Church of Progress credo would lead swiftly to mass defections. As it stands, CSICOP-style cynicism is certainly a frequent corollary of a modern upbringing. But it is far from universal.

That renaissance of interest in spiritual matters in which astrology plays a leading role (the 'tide of irrationality' bemoaned by *SI*'s flyer) gathers strength in direct defiance of Church indoctrination. This amounts to heresy, and is treated accordingly, as we have seen. But meanwhile, even the on-going campaign carried out by Education, designed to inculcate negative credulity, produces wide-scale unexpected effects, effects that are not specifically heretical but nevertheless counter-productive to Church goals.

The intellectually incurious respond to the Church in any case only on its bread-and-circuses level: the cheap thrill of technology. For this majority, church allegiance is maintained only through perpetually re-stimulated enthusiasm (the space program, for example, is the psychological equivalent of selling indulgences and the easy remission of sins that the corrupt Church of Rome resorted to when it was losing its grip). But it is accompanied by little passionate unfaith. Indeed, many at this level of comprehension accept material C. of P. benefits and, ingrates that they are, violently reject its metaphysics and embrace the mindless evangelical religion that is the other side of the same counterfeit coin.

Most of the intellectually better-equipped also resist deep indoctrination. Some vestige of good sense, or perhaps merely an instinct for self-preservation combined with insensitivity, allows them to direct their energies towards ambition or success. They live out their lives, perhaps aware that something is awry but yet not sufficiently disturbed to track it to its spiritual source. It is this that Thoreau had in mind when he said 'most men lead lives of quiet desperation'. By more contemporary thinkers, and especially by politicians, a life lived according to such values is often called 'the pursuit of the American Dream'.

The chief victims of an education that deifies skepticism are, of course, the sensitive. For the only legitimate emotional response to the negative metaphysics of Rationalism is despair (the Existentialists were quite right on this point, wrong only in the direction they took to find a solution). Despair takes many forms among the young, not all of them commonly recognized as despair. The rapid increase in teenage suicide is the most dramatic; drugs are the most obvious; with apathy, rebellion, violence, and an aimless, frenetic hedonism close behind. All happen because of, not in spite of, modern education.*

---

* If proof of this sweeping assertion is required, the jury need only look at what happens when the Church of Progress converts a tribal, or so-called 'primitive' society to its values, or even when it supersedes a highly sophisticated and intellectual

Modern education is to the mind what AIDS is to the immune system. Prolonged, repeated exposure enhances the danger. And all of us, without exception, are called to skepticism (who can avoid going to school?). Yet, miraculously, not that many are chosen. Susceptibility varies widely, and seems mainly restricted to a certain psychological type (we'll expand upon this shortly).

Happily for the future of humanity, skeptics cannot be produced at will through education; not in the kind of numbers that ensure the continued hegemony of the Church. While none escape unscathed, many escape. The creative, the courageous and the lucky do not cave in under the strain. They zero in, more or less swiftly, more or less accurately on the problem, locate its source and look elsewhere – often into the philosophy and art of the past – for those true, spiritual values that alone can produce and sustain normal functioning human beings.

The restoration and restatement of those values in acceptable contemporary form is the real challenge facing humanity. The various catastrophes threatening our planet are all, without exception, results, not causes. All follow naturally, inescapably from adherence to the debased, joyless, negative metaphysics espoused by the Church of Progress in the name of Reason. When and if different values prevail, different results will follow from them. In the effort to restore and restate those values, astrology may well play a significant and unique role (we'll return to this point in more detail soon). Therefore, the battle to have it generally acknowledged as valid has profound implications. It is not just a question of the astrologers being right, and the skeptics being wrong. The very virulence of the opposition is a tip-off that something vital is at issue.

---

but non-technological society. The results are invariable: suicide, drugs, apathy, violence, rebellion and an aimless, frenetic hedonism. See the telling indictment in anthropologist John H. Bodley's *Victims of Progress* (Benjamin Cummings, 1982).

The Jesuit Order of the Press

We do not stay in school for ever. The press (a term we use interchangeably with the media world as a whole) is more autonomous and at the same time less coercive than education. It has to be, since it cannot be forced upon people.

In our free (more accurately: chaotic) world of the West we must go to school, but we are not obliged to watch television or read *Time* magazine. The media, in the West at any rate, must keep a keen ear tuned to the market-place or it goes out of business. The vast percentage of its profit of course still comes from peddling violence, loveless sex, scandal and titillation. Read the headlines of any mainstream daily paper, including the 'serious' ones, or look through the shelves of your video store and you will see what is being sold, and obviously, what is being bought. These remain attractive largely because of the continued hegemony of the Church of Progress. People who know no better take whatever is easiest and nearest to hand to fill the inescapable emotional inner void produced by embracing its values. When this ingestion of psychic poison is carried out in the name of 'keeping abreast of current events' or 'maintaining a lively interest in the arts' the malaise that necessarily follows becomes still more difficult to diagnose accurately. Nevertheless, there are signs of improvement.

We derive no sustenance from the misery of others once our own lives become creative and fulfilling. We lose the desire to fill our heads and hearts with murder, rape, famine, espionage and the rest once we have found a purpose of our own. In other words, there is a growing market for heresy. Newspapers and magazines have sprung to life to fill that need, some reaching wide, informed, prosperous, even influential audiences. *Parabola*, *Rolling Stone*, the *East West Journal* and *Utne Reader* are a few of the magazines largely devoted to 'New Age' ideas, while the growing ecological and back-to-the-land movement often has a spiritual or sacred content. More and more people are taking a profound, sympathetic interest in the knowledge and traditions of Native Americans, Australian Aborigines, Eskimos and other peoples hitherto castigated as 'primitive' by the Church of Progress. This interest is no longer empty academic curiosity, the detailed study of the quaint customs of lesser breeds without the credo. Rather, it is focused on what we in the West have to learn from these people; what we have lost and they have retained (until they and their way of life are totally obliterated by C. of P. missionaries). The current has been picked up by Hollywood – always sending out interesting signals *vis-à-vis* the reigning *Zeitgeist*. The recurrent imbecilities of *Rambo*, *Rocky* and their clones are surely offset if not altogether negated by the Spielberg films and theirs – which often project the values of esoteric understanding into a comic-book context, yet without quite destroying their integrity or their power. Moreover, the image of the objective scientist-as-God that prevailed in dozens of mass-audience films from the 1930s through the 1960s is now a rarity. Hollywood these days is more likely to portray the scientist as an insensitive, egotistic boor, deeply interested in his reputation but much less so in the truth. 'Reputable' book publishers are publishing more, not fewer books on all those subjects blacklisted by the *Skeptical Inquirer*. The boom in New Age books (for lack of a better term) has been the subject of lead articles in the publishing trade journals, *American Bookseller* and *Publishers Weekly*. Major commercial publishers are busy developing separate 'New Age' imprints.

Astrology as Significator

It would be wrong to single out astrology as the most important element in this broad-based disavowal of Church of Progress values and rekindled pursuit of the spiritual values of the past (including a keen interest in the inner spiritual significance of the traditional religions, which, on the surface, appear to have very little spiritual left to them). But astrology plays, or could play, depending on how matters develop, a unique and significant role in hastening the downfall of the Church of Progress, providing an opportunity for the re-establishment of civilization – absolutely unthinkable as long as the C. of P. is in control.*

While it is easy to expose the flaws in an erroneous metaphysical system such as Rationalism, the history of philosophy and theology from Plato onwards suggests that it is impossible to categorically prove the truth of a correct system – in such a way that opponents are compelled to accept it. For there is no way in which to categorically establish the truth of the premises upon which the system rests. In metaphysics, evidently, there is no shoving the truth down unwilling throats. No amount of purely speculative, considered and *rational* (in the correct sense of that much abused word) argument can overcome the resistance provoked by a lifetime of unacknowledged negative experience. And since positive personal experience is automatically discounted under Church of Progress rules, there is no point citing the recorded testimony of the saints, masters, yogis, shamans, mystics and the great artists of the various traditions all over the world (as collected in William James's classic *Varieties of Religious Experience*, for example). Culver and Ianna and their colleagues will go on insisting, 'only empirical evidence counts'.

It is here that astrology takes on its unique importance. For astrology is perhaps that component of the universal, spiritually

---

* This, incidentally, does not mean the abolition of technology. Whenever the suggestion is made that science and technology ought perhaps to exercise some measure of restraint in their normal untrammeled rush to do whatever is do-able, without thought of the consequences, the priesthood reacts like the NRA when the suggestion is made that perhaps handguns should not be given away as prizes at McDonald's . . . curtailment of Freedom! Violation of the Constitution! . . . What is required is not an alternative or even an appropriate technology, but a *selective* technology. We don't throw away our dentists' drills. But technology becomes subservient to an altogether different set of values – with results that cannot really be predicted beyond saying that we would *not* poison the earth, seas and skies, we would *not* deprive the mass of men and women from using their creative faculties in earning their living (technology's most malignant, and most unacknowledged consequence), and we would respect the life of the planet and the right of other creatures to live upon it.

based, metaphysical doctrine that best lends itself to scientific validation following standard ground rules. As we have pointed out, there is much in astrology that does *not* lend itself to scientific validation; much that must always remain interpretational and subjective, and there is plenty of rubbish, fantasy and hysteria attached to its modern manifestation. Nevertheless, compared to the problems encountered by those attempting to put, say, ESP or channeling (trance mediumship in earlier Theosophical terminology) into a scientific framework, those confronting astrology are relatively minor. More important, given the evidence already at our disposal, many have already been overcome.

The proven correspondence between position of the planets at birth, and the proven correspondence between specific planets, and specific psychological types invests the planets with *meaning*. There would seem to be no other possible interpretation of these demonstrations. And if the planets have meaning it would be as difficult to ascribe those meanings to accident as it would be to maintain that accident is responsible for the development and design of our musical instruments. Once the premise of astrology is acknowledged valid, the house of cards that is Rationalist atheology is toppled once and for all.

Though never mentioned by astrology's opponents in so many words; probably not even formulated by them in so many words, it is the gut recognition of the threat posed by astrology that accounts for the rabid opposition; for that extraordinary willingness to resort to any means, no matter how unprincipled, to distort or suppress the facts. If the premise of astrology is valid (the practice doesn't matter in this context), Rationalism is invalid. The priests of the Church of Progress are fighting for their lives. It is as simple as that.

With this at stake, the jury will appreciate the importance of responsible coverage by the press. Not much can be expected from science as an institution. The willingness of so many of its leading figures to endorse CSICOP's bad science and worse principles reveals its attitude towards truth. On the other hand, unbiased *individual* scientists are much less rare than the unified scientific front would indicate.*

At any given time there may well be individuals qualified in their fields and with impeccable scientific credentials (for example, Warren Weaver, Percy Seymour, and H. J. Eysenck) willing to look at evidence that challenges pet beliefs and courageous enough to publicly support that evidence when they find it persuasive. But to prove effective, that support must be made public. To date, the scientific press has been able to suppress or misrepresent those dissident voices, and Science as an institution can be expected to defend the Church of Progress credo to the bitter end.

Even less can be expected from Education. Taking its cue from Science above, and from the vague, inchoate desires of the general public below, Education incorporates change very slowly indeed. Again, within Education, particularly at the college level, all manner of heretical opinions flourish and are freely expressed by individuals. Much of the correspondence generated by the original *Case for Astrology* came from people involved in the educational system. But it will certainly be many years before grade-school students studying ancient history for the first time are told that astrology was not a misguided superstition dreamed up by dreaming Chaldeans on watchtowers; before

---

* The similarity to organized religion imposes itself here in a rare positive context. The Christian Church as an institution has been a catastrophe from its earliest days. However, over its long, bloodthirsty history a number of individuals managed to put the precepts of Christ into practice and actually became Christians. And it was undoubtedly the influence of these individuals, the realized and radiant spirituality of the great saints and, on the local level, of the humble, unsung but loving village priests, and the healing sisters of mercy that made Christianity credible for two thousand years. In other words, the Church stayed alive *in spite of*, not because of its dogmatism and its grotesque intolerance.

The situation in science is to some extent analogous – though modern science almost by definition excludes a spiritual element (which is not to say that individual scientists do not occasionally profess spiritual beliefs and practices). The great advances in science tend to be made by scientists who are mavericks if not downright heretics.

high school students become acquainted with Michel Gauquelin along with Michelson and Morley.

So it is up to the press to spread the word.

The Press and the New Age

Prior to the explosive awakening of interest in all things spiritual, exotic and environmental that characterized the 1960s (but that actually gathered most of its momentum and crested well into the 1970s) the media had paid little attention to astrology. What attention there was was negative. Astronomers and other 'authorities' leveled occasional *ex cathedra* anathemas indicting astrology as a bogus science and ancient superstition. The quotes opening Part II, Objections to Astrology are typical.

But the dramatic resurgence of interest in astrology in the late 1960s produced a somewhat different climate. Whatever interested the counterculture automatically became news. Extensive articles now appeared in major magazines and newspapers all over the Western world (among them: the London *Observer*, *Time*, the *New York Times*, *New York*, and *Life*). They ranged in tone from polite disavowal by the *New York Times* to an extended, derisive sneer in *Time* Magazine. Although these articles were uniformly uninformed as well as negative, the sheer, quantitative extent of the coverage meant that astrology had been brought to the attention of the mainstream of the Western world.

Given the notorious power of the press to make or break movements and reputations, we examined several of these articles in depth in the original *Case for Astrology*, leaving open the question of the aftermath.

More than twenty years have now passed. In retrospect, the negative attention had little visible effect. Obviously, it did not stem the tide of interest in astrology at its popular level. Jerome, Bok and the 186 eminent signers of their manifesto considered themselves on the defensive; self-styled little Davids of Reason battling the Hydra-headed Goliath of superstition. Nor was their manifesto effective. The inner contradictions and slipshod science went unnoticed. It was greeted with unqualified praise by the mainstream press and given worldwide coverage. Yet it has sold only 30,000 copies to date. Bookstores seldom stock it. 'Otherwise reputable publishers' ignore its recommendations. As do high-powered business leaders, eminent politicians, and of course, during the Reagan administration, the President and First Lady themselves.

Nevertheless, there can be little doubt that the slanted press produces effects on more insidious levels. Intellectually alert people routinely question the Establishment's view on the whole range of sensitive political issues (foreign policy, covert operations, the FBI, the CIA [and their equivalents throughout the Western world], the environment, nuclear power, Star Wars, etc., etc.). They demand investigative reporting; they want to hear all sides of the issues. Yet when it comes to astrology, or any other subject that is spiritually rather than politically sensitive, the same people accept the Establishment's version, unaware that party-line science is as biased as party-line politics – indeed, for the most part they are unaware that it is party-line science they are being fed. It is here that the Church of Progress still exercises power. Nothing these politically wary people have ever read, nothing they have encountered at school or university has led them to suspect that there is and has always been a serious astrology; that since the 1950s, strong scientific evidence existed – Gauquelin's in particular – that justified reconsidering it; that at least a few brave, otherwise respected scientists have acknowledged that evidence as valid.

The question now facing astrology is: can the press bring itself to accurately report the situation? There are reasons for both hope and doubt.

News journalism by its nature tends to attract skeptics; individuals who have accepted the credo of the Church and who believe they are rational beings because they are able to describe without emotion the horrific, tragic or catastrophic events that make up their normal daily assignments. A couple of years of this and they become 'eternal skeptics'.

At the other extreme, the film and television industries attract people who either failed to absorb the credo at school, or who simply find it irrelevant to their aims or inimical to their beliefs and/or experience. Often that disallegiance is flaunted publicly. When these people happen to be celebrities they cannot be ignored, and a delectable situation commonly arises: the eternal skeptics are obliged to acknowledge at length opponents they privately dismiss as flakes or worse. The best they can do is to attempt to discredit or sabotage them, but even this has its limits. The public will accept only so much character-assassination when its idols are at issue.

So while reporters feel free to be as vitriolic, as derisive and as biased about the subject of astrology as ever, an avowed interest in astrology by any given celebrity must be handled with a measure of restraint. Obviously, the public espousal of astrology by an Einstein would do more to establish its credibility than endorsement by a film star or business leader or even by a popular president. But, even as it stands, the coverage seems to have a cumulative effect; at least on the popular or social level. Over the course of twenty years, it's possible to follow the way in which this widespread public interest has begun, gradually, to filter down into the mainstream media.

A leading series of articles in the respectable English *Guardian* followed in detail an astrological study (result mostly inconclusive but not necessarily negative) on the relationship between sun signs and personality run by sociologist Professor Alan Smithers. It included a serious commentary by Dr Smithers on the subject. Twenty years ago few professors would have owned up to an interest in astrology and held on to their jobs ... And no major journal would have run an article taking astrology as a potentially serious subject. The article in the *New York Sunday Times* Financial Section cited earlier ('What's New in Parapsychology') focused on the interest in paranormal methods of forecasting business trends. A later piece by Jennifer Stoffel (*New York Times*, 9 October 1988), covered 'What's New In New-Age Marketing'. Though light-hearted in tone, both were notably smirkless. This gradual shift in attitude, detectable through a careful reading of signals described above, was dramatically emphasized in the uproar generated by the disclosure that astrology played a role in the White House under the Reagan administration.

Given astrology's potential importance in the civilization of the future, and the importance of the press in fostering or impeding that role, we think the jury may be interested in examining in some depth and comparing a few typical articles from major mainstream sources; two, putatively solidly researched, from the late 1960s, covering the newly resurgent astrology of the era, the others rescued from the flood of instant journalism generated by the Reagan story.

Astrology and the Press: Then . . .

Is there anything at all to the claims of astrology? As recently as a decade ago the verdict would probably have been a flat and unanimous 'no'. The few experiments and statistical analyses that had been performed, the best known by Carl Jung, who became interested in the archetypal symbols of astrology, had proved negative or at best inconclusive. Astrologers lack the objectivity or the academic training to do acceptable research. Science has more pressing tasks. 'Life is short and there is a lot to do,' said Professor Gibson Reaves of the Department of Astronomy and of the University of Southern California, who has studied astrology because of its roots with astronomy, 'I can either work on something that I know will be useful or on astrology. Some people say they don't see how astrology could work,' he went on, 'but nobody has ever proved finally that it doesn't. The only really useful question is whether or not it does work, and I see very little evidence that it does. It's the social scientists, I think, who are missing a bet by not looking into its influences.

While no serious scientist appears to regard the casting of horoscopes and predictions of the future as more than arcane flapdoodle, there are at least a couple who think the electro-magnetic fields of the sun, moon and the planets closest to the earth may influence life here in many still unrecognized ways. Experiments carried out by Dr Frank A. Brown, Jr., Morrison Professor of Biology at Northwestern University, have led him to believe that organisms may be exquisitely sensitive receivers of even the weakest of these impulses, although their specific effects have only just begun to be investigated.

Tom Buckley, *New York Times* magazine, 15 December 1968

This single column is the only one, out of twenty, devoted to the serious and experimental side of astrology. Now, in Buckley's defense, the very nature of journalism encourages the inadequacy of such articles. Short of commissioning a literate astrologer to do the job, or at least of finding a journalist to some degree informed on the subject, these articles are written by staff reporters who have taken a few days and made a few phone calls to 'research' it out. As the jury now realizes, the subject is complex and delicate. And since most reporters are eternal skeptics to begin with, it is hardly surprising if they find ways to avoid acknowledging challenges to their skepticism.

So with Mr Buckley: up to 1950, statistical inquiries had proved negative or inconclusive. But since 1950, at least a few had proved positive and suspiciously conclusive. Buckley does not mention the work of Gauquelin, Addey or Vernon Clark. Was he unaware of them? An interview with any knowledgeable astrologer would have been enough to apprise him of the existence of these positive statistical inquiries. It goes without saying that an honest paragraph or two on Gauquelin in the *New York Times* in 1968 would not have gone unnoticed. Still, Mr Buckley's sins, though grave, are mainly those of omission.

Foolish Daughter Meets the Real Pros: Astrology and Time Magazine

The institutionalized performance of *Time* magazine creates quite another category.*

* Aware of its responsibility to the public, *Time* made a special effort to assign the story to a writer whose interests qualified him for the job; Associate Editor Douglas Auchincloss, 'interested in the occult ever since a family maid told his fortune from

Language Inaudible to Man

It is the interpretation of a given chart that determines whether an astrologer is adjudged good, mediocre or bad. And it is here that astrology's scientific pretensions are tested, and fail. [1] If astrology works in any way other than intuition on one side and faith plus hope on the other, the key question for modern man is 'how?' The how of things seldom bothered the Babylonians, for whom a mountain might fly through the air or the sun stand still. Later it was assumed that some kind of emanations issued from the heavenly bodies to affect the characters and destinies of men. When scientists found no emanations powerful enough, sophisticated astrologers abandoned causality altogether and eagerly embraced Jung's theory of 'synchronicity' – that everything in the universe at any given moment participates through that moment with everything else that shares the same unit of time. [3]

These days, though, the emanations may be staging a comeback. Some astrology apologists [2] point to the fact that experimental oysters transported from Long Island to Evanston, Illinois, and shielded from light and temperature change, gradually altered their rhythm of opening and closing from the tidal cycle of Long Island to what it would have been in Evanston – if Evanston had a tide. Apparently, the moon was communicating with the oysters in some language as yet inaudible to man. Japanese Dr Maki Takata found that the composition of human blood changes in relation to the eleven-year sunspot cycle, to solar flares and sunrise and during eclipses. French science writer, Michel Gauguelin, [4] foresees a new science of astrobiology, which could vindicate the intuited conclusion of the scientists that extraterrestrial forces affect human life, and at the same time explode the anachronistic conglomeration of myth and magic cluttering up modern astrology.

---

tea leaves when he was a young boy'. Moreover, *Time* tells us, in pursuit of the assignment, not only did Auchincloss have a pair of horoscopes cast, but he also consulted a palm-reader and interviewed a clairvoyant. So much for the doctrine to which the best minds throughout the ages have devoted lifetimes.

Lucky Break
In the meantime, astrologers must continue to uphold the fancy [5]
that particular planets influence particular facets of human
personality or specific events . . .

'Astrology, Fad and Phenomenon', *Time*, 21 March 1969, pp. 11, 47–56

1. The statement 'it is here that astrology's scientific pretensions
are tested, and fail' is of course an outright lie. The only tests
designed to test the astrologers' pretensions at the time that
article was written were Vernon Clark's, and those appeared to
prove that astrologers *could* back up their pretensions well above
chance level.

2. It is curious that those who cite Brown's experiments are
'apologists'. Why 'apologists'? Either the moon affects oysters or it
does not. If it affects oysters then there is every reason to believe
that it could affect other forms of life, including our own.

3. Sophisticated astrologers never abandoned causality theories for
Jung's synchronicity. Sophisticated astrologers attributed the
operation of astrology to 'synchronicity' long before Jung applied
that particular name to it. It was only the unsophisticated
astrologers who attempted to account for astrology in causal terms.

4. This brief, backhanded allusion to Gauquelin is perhaps the
most telling instance of *Time*'s sleek genius for blending mis-
information, disinformation, half-truths and untruths and passing the result off as 'journalism'.

In one deft verbal manoeuvre, not only has Gauquelin had
his name mis-spelled but he has been innuendoed into insignificance. According to *Time*, he is not 'Sorbonne-trained psychologist and statistician, Michel Gauquelin', who has carried
out twenty years of intensive research; he is 'science writer,
Michel Gauguelin', merely expressing a personal opinion.

Those twenty years of research go absolutely unmentioned;
not a word about Gauquelin's massive test group of 25,000
eminent professionals; about the Mars Effect proving beyond
possible doubt that particular planets do indeed correspond to
specific human personality types, and that those correspondences
corroborate traditional astrological doctrine.

5. As a parting effrontery, it is precisely that demonstrated correspondence that is singled out and sloughed off by *Time*'s mystics-in-residence as 'a fancy'.

That the journalists responsible for the article were aware of the evidence is self-evident. *Time* could scarcely refer to Gauquelin without knowing the results of his work, and of the failure of opponents to discredit those results. Moreover, we know from personal contacts that *Time* interviewed officers of American and English astrological associations at length, yet ultimately declined to use *any* of the information furnished by them.

The jury may want to pay particular attention to the treatment of astrology by *Time*. For *Time*'s extraordinary success, extending over fifty years, proves the efficacy of its journalistic approach.

By treating religion like sport, sport like art, art like business and business like religion, *Time* has tapped into something essential within the American psyche, possibly justifying the magazine's grandiose view of itself as mainstream America's bell-wether (and as America goes, so goes the world).

But this guiding role is not without its problems. The American sheep is a product of the melting pot. Despite its many homogenized features, the dominant McDonald's/Disneyland strain resists final standardization; sports, freaks, throwbacks and just plain black sheep abound. Pastoral pressure from Science or Education above seems incapable of selecting out a strong initial injection of goat. In short, Americans don't always go where *Time* wants to lead them (placidly munching their way round and round the shopping mall). So when *Time* senses an inclination to stray, perhaps on to that perilous road that may actually lead somewhere, it will take whatever journalistic measures it deems necessary to make the status quo grass look greener.

That failing, *Time* may subtly shift its own direction (in such a way that it looks as though that was the intention all along). Thus, minor shifts in *Time*'s attitude may reflect major shifts in the country as a whole. With this understanding it is instructive to see the way astrology was handled twenty years later – first, peripherally, in a cover story (7 December 1987) devoted to various manifestations of the New Age (Shirley MacLaine on the cover, and the copy: 'Om ... THE NEW AGE Starring Shirley MacLaine, faith healers, channelers, space travelers and crystals galore') and, second, when *Time* scooped the world (16 May 1988) by obtaining an exclusive to excerpts from Donald Regan's memoirs, *For the Record*, and broke the Reagan/astrology story (cover copy: 'Astrology in the White House').

Time, *the Stars and the Superstars*

In the first, 'New Age Harmonies ... A strange mix of spirituality and superstition is sweeping across the country', there are significant lapses in the sustained mockery *Time* normally reserves for such subject matter. A social scientist who 'invokes Zen, yoga and tarot cards when he teaches his course Creativity in Business at the Stanford Graduate School of Business', is quoted without further editorial comment. Two straightfaced paragraphs are devoted to a description of New York's Open Center 'which enrolls 3,000 students a month for a range of 250 one- and two-day workshops and such courses as Aspects of Zen Practice, Internal Kung Fu and Jungian Symbolism in Astrology'. Director Ralph White is quoted at some length, after which *Time* comments: 'This relatively level-headed approach to spirituality has its attractions in the world of commerce, particularly in the important area of management training.' (In all likelihood, it is the attention paid to these matters by business that impressed *Time* and provoked the tempered coverage.) A practitioner of therapeutic touch is described as 'a slight, intelligent, no-nonsense woman', and Mason Sexton, a graduate of Harvard Business School, is allowed to describe his stock-market forecasting service that combines the Fibonacci Series with astrology without editorial interference or further comment. (Sexton was one of a number of astrologers who correctly forecast the October 1987 stock-market crash, obviously enhancing his credibility.)

Astrology and the Press: Now . . . Time *and Reagangate*

Time exercised a similar restraint in dealing with the Reagan story. Donald Regan's book was simply excerpted. The excerpts themselves were more personal attacks upon Nancy Reagan than a condemnation of astrology, though Regan made his own distaste for the subject self-evident. In particular, he expresses irritation at having to adjust the President's schedule to suit an astrologer's recommendations. And he emphasizes the importance of the President's schedule:

> As I discovered in my turn, there was no choice *but* to humor the First Lady in this matter. Still, the President's schedule is the single most potent tool in the White House, because it determines what the most powerful man in the world is going to do and when he is going to do it. By humoring Mrs Reagan, we gave her this tool – or, more accurately, gave it to an unknown woman in San Francisco who believed that the zodiac controls events and human behavior and that she could read the secrets of the future in the movements of the planets. When the Geneva summit was held in 1985, I couldn't resist reflecting that a heavy burden must have been placed upon the poor woman. She was called upon not only to choose auspicious moments for meetings between the two most powerful men on our planet but also to draw up horoscopes that presumably provided clues to the character and probable behavior of Gorbachev . . . I had never dealt with anything like this in nearly 45 years of working life. 'Maybe your friend is wrong,' I would suggest to Mrs Reagan. She did not think so: her Friend had not only predicted the assassination attempt nearly to the day but had foreseen the explosion of a bomb planted in a TWA plane that was damaged over Greece in 1986, and had been right about other things, including a premonition of 'dire events' in November and December 1986 – that is, the Iran–*Contra* scandal.

Earlier (p. 146), we quoted the geneticist J. B. S. Haldane, scoffing at astrological predictions, unimpressed by 'a few lucky hits'. We would suggest that a qualitative factor must be taken into account. When the 'few lucky hits' happen to be assassination attempts the intended victim may perhaps be forgiven an inclination to overlook other, inaccurate but perhaps less portentous forecasts, even if the latter should ultimately prove more numerous than the correct ones. (If your astrologer picks you nine wrong horses in a row and then picks the lottery right, how do you assess your astrologer? If you are an eternal skeptic presumably you dismiss her for not attaining even the 11% accuracy of Culver and Ianna's newspaper astrologers (p. 199). And of course you would not have bought a ticket. On the other hand, if you are sufficiently ignorant, irrational and superstitious, you cash in your ticket, cancel your subscription to the *Skeptical Inquirer* and spend the rest of your days calculating interest rates instead of statistical probabilities.)

Ronald Reagan's uncanny ability to survive successive crises, any one of which would have brought down and even had impeached another president is of course legendary. There cannot be the slightest doubt that timing played a major role in that on-going success story. And that timing was, by the admission of the White House itself, to a greater or lesser extent astrologically determined. Neither Donald Regan, nor *Time*, nor anyone else has ever been foolhardy enough to fault the President *post facto* on his timing. And *Time* wisely refrains from further direct comment on astrology, contenting itself, at the end of the page devoted to Joan Quigley, the Reagans' astrologer, to the observation: 'No matter how much stock the First Lady put in Quigley's advice, the astrologer is certainly fallible.' * Presumably *Time* is not?

This is feeble stuff for the magazine that twenty years earlier

---

* *Time* continues: 'According to a friend, Quigley had been predicting for months that a major earthquake would rock San Francisco on May 5. She was out of the city on that day, which may or may not show that she takes her own forecasts seriously. But May 5 came and went with nary a tremble – except perhaps on Quigley's personal Richter scale. That was the last day of blissful anonymity for the First Lady's astrologer. (The story broke on May 5, 1987, prompting one New York astrologer to say "The Age of Aquarius began on May 5, 1987".)'

rode rough-shod over the entire subject; misinforming, misrepresenting, ignoring evidence and reducing Michel Gauquelin to the status of 'science writer'. Only in the essay by Lance Morrow, 'The Five-and-Dime Charms of Astrology', does *Time* show something of its old spirit. But this, relegated to the end of the issue, and by definition, as essay, merely expressing personal opinion, exerts little of the influence of the regular *Time* imprimatur.

> The pedigree of astrology in ancient times had a certain splendor. But astrology has been intellectually weightless since Isaac Newton. [1] Yet it accomplished a miraculous revival around the turn of the century. King Edward VII (Scorpio) and Enrico Caruso (Pisces) consulted astrologers. The '60s, the dawning of the Age of Aquarius, brought in the great age of astral tourism.
>
> . . . Astrology is harmless, it is an entertainment. Whatever its former glories, it seems now a five-and-dime glimpse of the cosmos. Still astrology has a certain sidelong, irrational prestige. Life is more interesting when the horoscope arouses the mind for a moment with a promise or a warning, [2] when it seems that a universal order is at work that one can manipulate fate by reading the signs. Of course, as the astronomer Carl Sagan points out, in a reduction to absurdity, the gravitational pull of the obstetrician would have far greater influence at a child's birth than the tug of a planet. [3] Still, one hungers for the mystic connection, the enveloping weave of synchronicities . . .'

'The enveloping weave of synchronicities' indeed! The jury by now may prefer astrology's five-and-dime charms to this fancy dress rationalist flummery. Certainly, it will be able to judge the intellectual weight of Mr Morrow (1) and Carl Sagan (3) for themselves. However, we do find ourselves inadvertently agreeing with Mr Morrow at (2). Life is definitely more interesting when the horoscope presages a warning, the would-be assassin fires, and the would-be assassinee has managed to manipulate fate and is not in the line of the bullet . . . Perhaps it's this sort of thing that gives astrology its 'sidelong, irrational prestige'.

... *and Around the Nation*

Generally speaking, in America and elsewhere the reaction to the White House astrologer was circumspect. Astrology itself was but rarely attacked. Journalists could have turned to CSICOP, to the *Skeptical Inquirer*, to any one of the 186 signers of the famous manifesto for scathing, misinformed, authoritative opinions. Few did. Financial papers tended to give extended, straightforward coverage to correct astrologically determined market forecasting. In general, the press was bemused rather than outraged, perhaps intuiting that the President's (and astrology's) popularity combined with his long track-record of flawless timing made an awkward subject for a hatchet job?

In most instances, the headlines tell the tale. Here are some typical examples and a few selected excerpts.

White House confirms Reagans Follow Astrology, Up to a Point

Steven V. Roberts, *New York Times*, 4 May 1988

NANCY – I'LL STILL WISH UPON A STAR
City's astrologers see a starry future

Eli Teiber, Mary Papenfuss, *New York Post*, 6 May 1987

Seeing Dollar Signs in Searching the Stars: From the White House to Wall Street, astrology has never been more popular.

N. R. Kleinfield, *New York Times*, 15 May 1987

ASTROLOGER RAN THE WHITE HOUSE

New York Post, 9 May 1987

In the Stars: a 400 Dow

New York Times, 15 May 1987

It's in the stars: Reagan takes the way way out
Astrology is more than detractors claim, less than some adherents would like

Donna Warner, *The Atlanta Constitution*, 4, 11 May 1987

(Miss Warner is a practicing astrologer)

From Don Regan, Wall Street's gift to Washington, the world learned last week that Ronald Reagan has been watching his horoscope. So we checked in with Wall Street's best known astrologer (a title for which competition is not brisk), Arch Crawford, and were told the revelation was old news, 'He was always looking at his chart when he was an actor,' Crawford said, adding that in later years, 'we could see that if there was any leeway in making a speech, he would choose the most astrologically favorable date.'

Crawford, once a technical analyst for Merrill Lynch, is about to celebrate the 11th anniversary of his New York based newsletter, Crawford Perspectives. He's been more than a bit annoyed that we haven't mentioned the fact that he forecast, from planetary movements, a major market top for last Aug. 24, a day early, and was suitably bearish going into the crash, saying not to buy after Oct. 22. That was two days after the bottom. 'Nobody did better in print,' he says.

His record, alas, is not perfect. He also forecast a crash in February, albeit with a bit more hedging than he displayed last fall . . .

Crawford now thinks the Dow will go down, up and then way down from here. The near-term low, at or below 1925, should be near May 22 or on June 7, when a variety of planets are in formations he deems interesting. Then comes a reversal to send prices up to 2200 or so by late June or early July. 'From there, we expect the crash to continue,' he says, 'bottoming on Nov. 13, 1989 with the Dow under 800.'

Floyd Norris, The Trader, *Barron's Market Week*, 9 May 1987

Has Reagan become lost in the stars?

Cal Thomas, *New York Daily News*, 9 May 1987

THAT BOOK! *Nancy's weekly confab with astrologer led to bizarre daily schedule*

Daily News, 9 May 1987

ASTROLOGY HAS NO SCIENTIFIC FANS

David L. Chandler, *Detroit Free Press*, 17 May 1987

THE FIRST LADY'S STARRING ROLE

They have been consulting the stars at the White House.

Thus speaks Donald Regan, the latest former loyalist to put a shiv into the Ronald Reagans in book form. But not the least. For the image of the First Lady, vetting everything from presidential travel to the signing of a summit treaty in conformity with astrological charts is likely to remain for a while. Granted it may yield the first ripple of pro-Reagan sympathy ever known among the counterculture/New Age types – and similar devotees of the irrational. Still it was not for the Reagans, a propitious star that saw this story launched. Nor did it require a reading of tea leaves to know that we would find an astrologer – of the most respectable type of course, no jewels in the nose or funny hairdo – weighing in on 'Nightline'.

As there was, one Dr Caroline Casey, who proceeded to talk lengthily about planetary order and 'fixed future models' and not least about that problem haunting to so many great minds of this sort: 'How to grow as a human being' . . .

Dorothy Rabinowitz, *New York Post*, 6 May 1987

Of the dozens of stories provoked by Donald Regan's disclosures, the last two best illustrate the major problems faced by astrology in its attempt to get a fair hearing from the media.

Devotees of the Irrational

Assailing 'devotees of the irrational' from the pages of the *New York Post*, of all places, is an unenviable strategic position. It is unlikely that a von Clausewitz or a George Patton would recommend it; and Miss Rabinowitz's derivative, hard-boiled style inspires little confidence – she seems to be marketing herself as a discount Dorothy Parker. News of the White House astrologer provoked no Reagan sympathy among 'devotees of the irrational'; mostly it embarrassed them – like discovering that your sworn, bitter enemy is also a passionate reader of Shakespeare's sonnets and shares your admiration for Beethoven's Late Quartets. And the ungenerous assessment of astrologer Caroline Casey's performance on 'Nightline' would certainly be contested by many who watched the show. Confronted by Richard Berendzen, a signer of the original anti-astrology manifesto, Dr Casey at least kept her composure in the face of a typical CSICOP cross-examination: part Church of Progress atheology, part bullying, part fake science. Dr Casey's occasional lapses into New Age platitude were certainly less grave violations of standard debating practice than those committed by her opponent. Some typical Berendzen arguments: '100% hokum'; 'It's just gibberish'; 'No validity'; 'Tested and tested, it's absolute lies'. Presumably, Miss Rabinowitz sees in such apoplectic splutter a cogent defense of the rational?

What Dr Casey did *not* do was respond to Berendzen's fake science with real science. To allow an opponent to get away with saying that astrology has been tested and tested and come up short is to miss a golden opportunity. A thorough familiarity with the Gauquelin work alone would be enough to send an opponent of this caliber scuttling for cover. And the ability to expose Rationalism as the shoddy and fraudulent metaphysical system it is should be a part of every working astrologer's arsenal.

But Dr Casey did not take advantage of it and neither did any of the other astrologers who took part in the major television exposure following the Reagan story. Giraldo Rivera, Ted Koppel, Morton Downey, and the MacNeill/Lehrer Report all devoted shows to the subject. Most pitted astrologers against skeptical opponents, all of whom used versions of the same old, untenable arguments to put down astrology (infinitessimal gravitational pull, the Carlson experiment, no sun-sign evidence, and so on).

Certainly, the astrologers were at an opening disadvantage. Their hosts were obviously eager to see them shot down in flames. But the audience was not. When it seemed as though the astrologers might be turning the tables, measures were taken to bring the show back to the 'entertainment' level – which the astrologers accepted, evidently satisfied to be allowed to make predictions on network television. (On Giraldo Rivera's show, all four astrologers predicted a Dukakis victory. Maybe they'll get the lottery numbers right next time and all will be forgiven?)

Without exception, the astrologers failed to engage the opposition on the level of science; insisting upon a kind of separate but equal status for astrology. Given the limitations of science, this is legitimate, but it is not the strongest argument; nor one that makes an immediate impact on an audience trained from childhood to accept the authority of science. Even though the game was handicapped, the astrologers were given a grand chance to undo a couple of centuries' worth of incomprehension, misrepresentation and insult. They failed to take advantage of it.

That inability is reflected by David Chandler, whose headline is cited above, the one journalist who tried to do his homework and learn something about the subject. This is the only article out of the dozens provoked by the Reagan scandal that mentions Gauquelin and that cites Dr Geoffrey Dean. Unfortunately, in gathering information Chandler went no further than the *Skeptical Inquirer* and Andrew Fraknoi of the Astronomical Society of the Pacific. Thus Chandler in good faith repeats the exploded claim that the Belgian Para Committee discovered fatal flaws in Gauquelin's statistical methods, and he quotes Fraknoi: 'Cosmobiology (Gauquelin's original name for the Mars Effect) has exactly one practitioner and one believer. That is Gauquelin himself', a statement that, if not actually libellous under current law, should at least add inches to the length of Fraknoi's nose.

Chandler goes on to mention studies that show astrology has proved useful as a psychological tool in therapy. But his headline sums up the tenor of the article: 'Astrology has no Scientific Fans'. 'Few Scientific Fans' would have made it strictly accurate, but this is a quibble. The important point is that 'no scientific fans' and 'no scientific basis' are two totally different matters, and should not be confused.

Astrology and the Science Press

We trust the jury will now accept the fact that there is ample scientific support for the astrological premise. We have shown that the various agencies of the Church of Progress have stopped at nothing to subvert and suppress that evidence. They have been successful to the extent that the dozens of reporters assigned to the Reagan story did not even think to look for scientific evidence, and the one who did look, didn't find it. (Astrologers have contributed to the situation through their overall lack of scientific interest and/or training, their specific unfamiliarity with the evidence at their disposal, their resounding professional success despite the opprobrium of science, and their inability to gain access to the media in a serious context.)

There is no longer the slightest chance that the Church of Progress will succeed in stopping people from consulting astrologers or from believing in astrology. The most it can do is impede its spread. Its ability to do that rests in its continuing ability to bury the evidence supporting it. This in turn depends upon its success in keeping that evidence out of the media.

The Gauquelin data represents the single most compelling body of evidence supporting astrology. We have discussed at great length the saga of the data in the hands of CSICOP and similar Inquisitorial agencies. But it is the treatment of the Gauquelin story by the popular press that determines its exposure to the general public. In this sense, the coverage of Gauquelin's work may serve as a pretty reliable standard for judging the status of astrology with the media.

Given its revolutionary implications (see p. 313), Gauquelin's work deserves the kind of mainstream press coverage currently bestowed upon the new breakthrough work in superconductivity, or any new major revelation in physics or biology. But no such media blitz has taken place. A handful of more or less specialized magazines and newspapers and a few general interest publications on both sides of the Atlantic have reported on his findings (*Psychology Today*, the English *Observer* and the French *Science et Vie* among them). He was the subject of a serious BBC inquiry on the popular science series, 'Horizon'. (A footnote: the producer, Tony Edwards, came at the subject highly skeptical but finished very much convinced that Gauquelin had to be right. A second footnote: the Gauquelin episode was the only one *not* picked up by American television when it bought the series; an indication of the very real power still wielded by the Church of Progress. Television stations know perfectly well the popularity of astrology among the general public. But evidently they were still more concerned, even in the 1980s, about the flak they would get back from indignant Church members.)

To date, then, astrology's scientific opponents have been largely successful in keeping news of Gauquelin's work from the general public. This has been accomplished partly by ignoring it, partly by misrepresenting it in its own media agency: the scientific press.

This last policy is of crucial importance. For the scientific press represents the interface between new developments in science and the mainstream media world. Science correspondents of the major newspapers and television stations attend but few scientific conferences. No one individual can keep abreast of even the major new developments in science reported in the innumerable highly specialized scientific journals. Journalists must often rely upon general science publications intended for scientists and the scientifically oriented layman to filter out the most important news (*Nature*, *Science News*, the *New Scientist*, *Scientific American* and *Discover* among them). These provide the leads to the science stories that will ultimately find their way into the mainstream media.

Gauquelin's work has not been directly covered in any of the above. But it was indirectly addressed at some length in *Discover* in 1982, by the widely read science writer and expert in mathematical games, Martin Gardner, reviewing the book by psychologists H. J. Eysenck and D. K. Nias, *Astrology: Science or Superstition?* He later expanded this in his book *Order and Surprise*.

We feel certain the jury accepts the validity of the exposé of CSICOP's unprincipled tactics – as described by Dennis Rawlins, the *Zetetic Scholar* and other sources. But doubt may still attend our own further efforts to extend culpability to the rest of the scientific community. Mr Gardner's essay should dispel these doubts. We reprint it in its entirety.

Eysenck's Folly

Imagine you are reading a book, by an eminent British astronomer, called *Flat Earth: Science or Superstition?* You find that the first three fourths of the volume marshals impressive evidence against flatness, then the rest proves that the earth is shaped like the Great Pyramid. Would you not be incredulous?

That was precisely how I felt when I finished Hans Eysenck's latest and most controversial book, *Astrology: Science or Superstition?* (St Martin's, 1982) written with D. K. B. Nias, an associate at the London University Institute of Psychiatry, where Eysenck is a professor. The first nine chapters give all the reasons why traditional astrology is humbug. The remaining two chapters vigorously champion a strange new astrology concocted about thirty years ago by a French psychologist, Michel Gauquelin.

The chapters attacking classical astrology are admirable. There are crisp accounts of flawed efforts by believers to confirm astrology, reports of carefully controlled tests by skeptics that failed to support it, and strong general reasons for disbelief. For example, China and India have ancient astrological traditions just as impressive as the West's, yet based on entirely different star patterns. If one tradition is right, the other two are wrong. If birth charts can give subtle insights into personality and destiny, why are they unable to tell a person's sex, intelligence or race, or recognize the criminally insane? Why is there no clustering of birth dates of thousands who are killed in a single earthquake?

What about people born in northern countries where some astrological signs never rise? Why do astrologers not adjust for changes in the zodiac caused by precession of the earth's axis? As Eysenck and Nias write, 'In the time of Ptolemy, the sun was in the constellation Aries on the day of the spring equinox . . . today it is in Pisces.'

After demolishing traditional astrology, the authors turn to the work of Gauquelin, done in conjunction with his wife, Françoise. As a young man, Gauquelin was a passionate believer in astrology. His faith wavered when he tried to prove its worth. In the course of his efforts, which convinced him that astrology had no merit, he uncovered what he became convinced were mysterious correlations between personality traits and the positions of certain planets at the moment of birth.

Among his findings: Famous doctors are more likely to be born when Mars or Saturn is in one of two 'critical zones' – having just risen or having just passed its highest point. Military leaders tend to be born with Mars or Jupiter in a critical zone. Top athletes with 'iron wills' correlate with Mars, those 'weak wills' correlate negatively. Extroverts incline to births 'under' Mars or Jupiter, introverts under Saturn. Soldiers and musicians have different planetary patterns, but musicians specializing in military music fall midway between the two groups!

The authors reproduce Gauquelin's table of eighty personality traits that are linked to Mars, Jupiter, Saturn or the moon. Recent research, they solemnly tell us, has found traits associated with Venus, but none that relate to the sun, Mercury or the distant planets. Correlations are hereditary. Children tend to be born under the same planets as one parent. If both parents were born under the same sign, the effect on the child doubles in intensity.

Gauquelinology has other bizarre aspects. Correlations with planets do not hold for ordinary professionals, only for the most eminent. They fail completely for drug-induced births. This suggests to Eysenck and Nias that the planets 'are somehow acting as celestial midwives. Some kind of signal emanating from the planet may somehow interact with the fetus in the womb, stimulating it to struggle into birth at a certain time.' These authors answer many questions but ignore the most crucial. How trustworthy are Gauquelin's raw data? [1] To determine their accuracy, a skeptical statistician would have to check the tens of thousands of birth records, that Gauquelin used in his numerous studies. Such records, especially the old ones, are often vague. Only a slight amount of selectivity, an unconscious 'experimenter effect' in deciding what records to use and what to disregard as unreliable, can produce a strong overall bias.

Most scientists think Gauquelin's challenge is too crazy and flimsy to justify the time, cost and labor of having a skeptical outsider verify his data or attempt a major replication [2]. More likely, there will continue to be minor efforts to repeat his tests, with believers getting positive results, doubters negative results, and each side accusing the other of sloppy controls. Meanwhile, astrology buffs will loudly proclaim that Gauquelin's popular books somehow support astrology, when all they support is Gauquelinology [3]. As for Eysenck's own competence as a statistician, it is worthwhile to recall his maverick record [4]. For instance, he has long infuriated colleagues by insisting there is no good evidence that I.Q. differences between races are not genetic. In another field of inquiry, Eysenck snagged a quarter of a million dollars in research grants from the tobacco industry (*Discover*, March 1981) and later published his findings: no good evidence of any causal link between lung cancer and smoking.

For these and many other reasons you don't have to believe Eysenck when he claims that Gauquelin's work 'compares favorably with the best that has been done in psychology, psychiatry, sociology, or any of the social sciences', much less when he asserts that 'the time has come to state unequivocally that a new science is in the process of being born.'

Postscript

A portion of a letter from Gauquelin was published in *Discover* (January 1983):

> In his article 'Eysenck's Folly', Martin Gardner asks, 'How trustworthy are Gauquelin's raw data?' It is very easy to check the accuracy of my data for everyone who really wants to do so. Actually, *all* my birth data were published in eighteen volumes by my Laboratoire d'Étude des Relations entre Rythmes Cosmiques et Psychophysiologiques. Every volume provides complete information explaining how my samples were drawn. I never discarded any birth record, and I am keeping all of them in the files of my laboratory. Several people have inspected them. Nobody found them faulty.

To which I replied:

> Few doubt that Gauquelin's documents support his data. But did unconscious selection bias the gathering and preservation of that

data? Only a costly investigation by a top statistician could answer this question.

In scientific circles, the horse-laugh and the sneer are reckoned wit, and Martin Gardner has acquired a reputation as the Oscar Wilde of Rationalism. Discerning readers are no doubt still chuckling over the deft parallel drawn between support of the flat earth and support of astrology.* Those with their own rational faculties intact, however, will realize that casting aspersions on Gauquelin's methodology (1) is a long way from disproving it, and they may also have noticed that the hatchet job on Eysenck's credibility is performed with a double-bladed axe. Gardner commends the first nine chapters of Eysenck's book, which 'give all the reasons why traditional astrology is humbug'. But if Eysenck is not to be trusted, as Gardner insists (4), why should these chapters be accepted as valid? Just because they corroborate Gardner's opinions? Following rigorous Gardnerian logic (as in the contention that only one system of star patterns can be correct) it follows that if Eysenck and Nias are wrong about Gauquelin, they must also be wrong elsewhere – in which case those chapters showing why traditional astrology is humbug must also be wrong, and traditional astrology stands vindicated.

Gauquelin's work needs no further elaboration. The point at issue here is the treatment of astrology by the scientific press.

In responsible journalism, it is universal practice to give controversial books out to review to people with some pretense to impartiality. When not playing the mathematical games that are his speciality, Martin Gardner has largely devoted his life to debunking the work of all those whose beliefs happen to differ from his own.†

---

* The earth/Great Pyramid image cited by Gardner is inadvertently defter still and keeps the comedy going. For while the earth is not shaped like the Great Pyramid, it is an absolutely undisputable fact that the Great Pyramid is a very precise projection of the dimensions of the earth on to the pyramid shape. See *Secrets of the Great Pyramid*, Peter Tompkins (Harper & Row, 1971), especially the long appendix by metrologist, the late Professor Livio Stecchini.

† See *Fads and Fallacies in the Name of Science* (Dover, 1957) and *Science: Good, Bad and Bogus* (Prometheus Books, 1981).

Some of his targets were undeniably cranks, and a few may have been charlatans. But others were serious scholars of some stature, who may well have been wrong (so, without exception, were all respectable physicists prior to Einstein who pronounced judgement on the structure of matter) but whose work was the result of painstaking scholarship.

Gardner's method is to scrupulously make no distinction between the obvious cranks and the others, ignore those aspects in the work of the latter that do not yield to instant disproof, apply his trademark horse-laugh to the lot, and sit back as scientific colleagues praise him for wit and brilliance.

Here, the treatment of Gauquelin's statistics deliberately fails to mention Gardner's own long relationship with them. As a founding father of the *Skeptical Inquirer* and its spin-off CSICOP he knows full well that Gauquelin's data has been checked and rechecked by skeptics as determined as himself, his own colleagues among them. He therefore knows the entire body of work has never been faulted beyond a few tiny discrepancies, easily rectified by Gauquelin. He also knows that to make the requisite check is a very simple matter, and not at all expensive. All that is required is a representative sample to determine if 'experimenter effect' is involved. Since the entire basis of Rationalist science is at stake if Gauquelin cannot be overthrown, the excuse that the challenge is 'too crazy and flimsy' (2) for scientists to bother with seems more than a bit crazy and flimsy in its own right. Moreover, when Gardner's review was written, the major elements of the CSICOP/Gauquelin débâcle were already in place. Gardner knew that the Committee Para in Belgium as well as his own organization had replicated Gauquelin's experiment, that both were major, not 'minor' efforts, and that CSICOP had fudged its own data when it began to be clear that Gauquelin's results would be vindicated. The Dennis Rawlins exposé had already appeared in *Fate*. Gardner, and everyone else connected with the affair, knew that the account released to the press by CSICOP was a concoction of lies and misrepresentations that fairly reeked at a distance. But editors at the science desks of the mainstream press evidently lacked the basic olfactory equipment to detect the telltale odor of red herring and fudge. The CSICOP version of the story was printed without question.

Gardner also knew that his wittily turned phrase 'Gauquelinology' does not serve to disassociate it from astrology (3). By whatever name, Gauquelinology is directly, irremediably and inextricably connected to classical, traditional astrology. The individual planets (excepting Mercury and the 'new' planets) correspond to precisely those professions traditional astrology assigns them to. Even if all else in the astrological canon should prove wrong, the Gauquelin data, until or unless disproved, substantiates the astrological premise at its most basic and its most crucial. There *is* a relationship between the position of planets at birth and the human personality. The planets have meaning. This is the nub of the Eysenck/Nias thesis, and Gardner knows it.

In a civilized society, academic malpractice would be a crime. Mr Gardner would not be walking around free, and *Discover*'s editor would be charged as an accessory. At face value, Gardner's review seems an exercise in calculated dishonesty. If not that, then it is an instance of the propagandist caught up in his own party-line hallucinations. Either way, it is indefensible as journalism and it is also 100% predictable. Given Gardner's well publicized biases, asking him to review a book favorable to astrology is like asking Goebbels to review a book called *Great Jews*.

Understood as a last-ditch stand by devotees of a threatened and undermined religion, this tacit collusion between Science, Education and the Press to suppress evidence finally becomes comprehensible.

We have argued that the Church of Progress is a religion in every pejorative sense attached to that word. But before the defense can rest, it remains to clarify the one crucial sense in which the Church of Progress is *not* a religion, which in turn involves a brief examination of the curious attraction of Rationalism in the first place.

The Call to the Unfaith

There is only one really important philosophical question: are we human beings on earth for a purpose or are we not? The rest of philosophy (with all its complexities), ethics, morality, art and architecture, ultimately even science,* flows inescapably from the answer we give to that question. Historically, the answer determined the form, the 'soul' as it were, of any given society or civilization.

To date no one has found a way to prove directly and categorically the correctness of either Yes or No.†

Most ancient civilizations (Rome, and post-Platonic Greece excepted), and most traditional 'primitive' societies, answered with a resounding Yes: all proceeded from the premise that we human beings have been put on earth for a purpose. The art, architecture, rituals and ceremonies of these civilizations and societies were all directed toward that one aim: which was (and

---

* The relationship to science is not immediately apparent but examined closely it is no less dependent upon philosophy than are morality or art. If we believe the universe is an accident, then we are accidental beings ourselves and have neither obligations nor responsibilities. Obviously, if we poison the planet so that organic life can no longer live on it, this will prove biologically disadvantageous to us, so at least a few scientists are beginning to think about the consequences of their activities, or at any rate, are being forced to do so by a concerned populace. But this is a purely pragmatic position. We owe the planet nothing, and if we feel like destroying the rest of organic life, or rearranging the ecology to make sure that our hamburgers are inexpensive and our shopping malls are sited exactly where we want them; if we torture animals in laboratories to 'advance knowledge'; if we keep other animals in cages too small to turn round in, in order to eat cheap so that we have money left over to finance Star Wars, why, this is as ethically defensible a position as any other. Alternatively, if we believe we play a role in the cosmic scheme, then, depending upon what that role is, it follows that we have certain responsibilities and obligations, and the kind of science we do will follow accordingly.

† It is, however, possible to prove that organization (of a plant or animal, for example) is inconceivable through the agency of chance alone; that will or intention must be involved; that therefore purpose must be written into the universal scheme, and that, by extension, humanity must partake in that purpose in some fashion. In other words, it is possible to disprove 'no', which would seem to leave 'yes' as the only alternative. See the Bibliography.

is) to re-connect humanity to its Creator, the Source. All religions, without exception (no matter what travesties so many of them became subsequently) were initially set up as systems for realizing that ultimate purpose. However arbitrary their innumerable precepts, restrictions and injunctions may appear in retrospect, or to outsiders, they constituted the rules to a game that involves lifelong, personal commitment. That the rules differed, often drastically, from one religion to another does not, as Bertrand Russell and his uncomprehending colleagues imagine (see p. 151), invalidate them. If you agree to play baseball you cannot suddenly apply the rules of football. They are different games, that is all. And the validity of one does not invalidate the others. But however different the forms, the goal was always the same. (Games, in fact, originally, served consciously as spiritual analogies, in which the two sides represented the fundamental cosmic antagonism between the forces of light and the forces of darkness.) Thus, a properly functioning religion, contrary to reigning Rationalist misconceptions, is the most *practical* of human institutions. Understood in this sense, building a cathedral is a strictly functional activity, while building a superhighway is a frivolity. A working religion is not something people merely believe in, it is something people *do*. And what they do is attempt to claim their birthright, which is both a unique human privilege and a unique human obligation: the return to the divine, immaterial Source.

It is of course the denial of that source, and of that or any purpose, that distinguishes the Church of Progress from all other religions.* In the Church of Progress there is no source, no purpose, and therefore no rules, since there is nothing to be done. In this sense, but only in this sense, the Rationalists, Humanists, Materialists or whatever they choose to call themselves, are quite right to deny that their philosophy constitutes a religion.†

* 'The systematic denial or purpose is the cornerstone of the scientific method.' Jacques Monod, quoted by Huston Smith in the Institute of Noetic Sciences *Special Report*, 1988.

† Strictly speaking, there are or can be important philosophical differences between

But for the rest, it is their fervent belief in denial and purposelessness that turns Rationalism into a religion in the negative sense; a religion that has degenerated from the school of organized spiritually directed action it once was to an authoritarian institution mainly concerned with enforcing belief. The only difference is that the Church of Progress was invalid at its inception, and therefore cannot degenerate still further.

Because we have all been brought up under the hegemony of this Church we seldom question its foundations. But as we have seen, once questioned, those foundations are easily exposed as philosophically unsound, intellectually barren and in no way supported by the science that is invariably cited as the rock upon which the entire edifice is built. It becomes clear then, that like other religions, the appeal of the Church of Progress has to be fundamentally emotional – even though its adherents pretend (and actually believe) they have substituted Reason for faith.

But to whom does it appeal? Who are these passionate crusaders for dispassion; these faithful guardians of the unfaith – who take pride in their eternal skepticism; and who evidently derive pleasure from the conviction that their lives are without meaning or purpose?

Anatomy of the Rationalist

To hear them tell it, they are the straight-shooters; intellectual Clint Eastwoods sitting tall in the saddle of truth; unsmiling, flinty-eyed, unafraid to face 'the harsh facts of reality'. In their view, religion, the very notion of spirituality, is a kind of evolutionary defense mechanism; initiated perhaps when our particular human form of consciousness turned out to have a selective advantage and people realized that sooner or later they

---

the beliefs of people calling themselves Rationalists, Materialists and Humanists. But within the Church of Progress itself, the terms are generally used loosely and interchangeably and we follow that example.

would die (hard to see the selective advantage in that realization!). Unable to face this harshest of all reality's harsh facts, and afeared of dyin', them lily-livered varmints, our ancestors, invented religion. As for the religious experience itself, as recorded by spiritual leaders throughout history, by great artists and by apparently ordinary people who for one reason or another (some call it the Grace of God) were allowed an insight into the life of the Spirit, well, all these people were deluding themselves; hallucinating probably. Robert Eisler provides a rational explanation for the mystic's vision that the jury may consider illuminating in its own right.

> But some people are so 'fascinated' by looking at a random, irregular apparently senseless pattern, or, for the matter of that, by staring for any length of time into an inkwell or into a crystal sphere, that their normal attention is 'dispersed' or unloosened and a flow of day-dream is started. The 'rapture' is increased if the darkness of the black mirror in the inkwell is combined with a dazzling splendour, such as the light reflected from a crystal or from a diamond. Indeed, the contemplating subject may fall into what is called a 'trance', a 'sober drunkenness' as the ancient mystics described the state of the soul induced by the contemplation of the splendid pattern of variously coloured glittering points of light on the velvety black or deep blue of the heavenly sphere.
>
> Robert Eisler, *The Royal Art of Astrology*, p. 54

And so at last the mystery is solved! For failing to understand that the Kingdom of Heaven resided, not 'within', but within His inkwell, Christ died upon the cross. Ignorant of the power of optical illusions, Buddha, Lao Tsu, Zoroaster, the Hindu rishis and the Sufis of Islam preached a lifetime of contemplation and relentless inner work in order to set will above the chaos of fleeting sense impressions that is humanity's ordinary condition. Poor saps! All they had to do was buy a crystal ball. The unapprised Zen master toils for years to subdue his personality so that, in one magical instant, hand, brush and mountain fuse and become one upon paper. All folly. All he has to do is stare long enough into his inkwell. Since history began, sages have meditated, monks have prayed, dervishes have whirled; temples, cathedrals, mosques and pagodas have been built, and sacred art, music and poetry developed . . . all absolutely needlessly; all because our primitive, semi-conscious ancestors persisted in believing that there had to be a significant, qualitative difference between the lucid ecstasy of the saint, and the incoherent reveries of the self-hypnotized Rationalist.

That revealing Eisler passage holds the key to both Rationalism's curious appeal, and the attitude of Rationalists to astrology (and all else based upon the premise that coherence and meaning are written into this universe of ours from above).

Though philosophy and intellectual argument may be used to support a religion (or to attack it), they are never, ever, responsible for its genesis. All, according to their founders, are derived from *experience*. And Rationalism, despite its pretensions to the contrary, is no different. It is also the result of experience, but a very different order of experience.

Rationalists have never built a cathedral, danced a dervish dance or meditated for half an hour. Direct mystical experience is absolutely alien to them. Rarely are they creative artists, even in the modern, Western, secular understanding of art.*

* Contemporary art represents a special case within the Church of Progress. If a poll were taken, it is probable that a majority of today's writers, artists and composers would profess themselves atheists or agnostics, though perhaps not eternal skeptics. But it is the modern artists, not the scientists, educators and academics, who have actually had the courage to face those harsh facts of reality spelled out for them by the Church. It is the artists who have explored their grim consequences. That is why most serious contemporary art is little more than orchestrated despair. Which, in turn, is one reason why it enjoys the grudging imprimatur of the Church of Progress. The ability to organize, even exalt, negation seems to legitimize it – misery loves company. On the other hand, artistic creation presupposes synthesis (putting together, as opposed to analysis: tearing apart) and celebration; it is and must be and can only be an act of love, a process of gestation culminating in the miracle of new birth – even if it is Frankenstein's monster who is born. So the artist who has not seen through Church of Progress atheology is placed in a paradoxical situation; consumed by the holy desire to create (hence a potential

For the most part they are even incapable of responding to the great sacred art and architecture bequeathed us from the past – all designed by masters to make their own direct knowledge and experience of the numinous accessible to those who had not yet traversed their arduous path.

Rationalists call these works 'monuments to superstition', and Rationalism is the name they apply to their inability to respond; or to trust anything beyond that which can be measured, predicted and replicated in the laboratory. But there is nothing 'reasonable' about this incapacity. It is not rational (in the sense that it is the considered result of weighing alternative philosophical possibilities); it is no more than the rationalization, by eternal skeptics, of a few moments of insight into their own inner condition.

Rationalism is the religion of the emotionally defective and the spiritually dyslexic; the religion of those who have lost the ability to experience wonder, awe, gratitude and, above all, reverence. Unable to find meaning or purpose to their own existence they try to project that personal sense of emptiness and disorder on to the universe as its 'essential precondition.*

---

threat to the Church) but unable to discover anything to exercise that creativity upon beyond futility, impotence, confusion, apathy, violence and the ultimate pointlessness of death.

It is no accident that glamor and romance (and no little envy) attach to art, even at this level, since the sacred nature of creation itself is recognized on some gut-level by all but card-carrying members of the Church of Progress. On the other hand, the artists reap few benefits. More often than not they are torn apart by the intolerable paradox of their lives. They respond by drinking too much, doing drugs, and leading the generally unstable and tormented lives for which they are justly renowned.

*That man is the product of causes which had no prevision of the end they were achieving; that his origin, his growth, his hopes and fears, his loves and beliefs, are but the outcome of accidental collisions of atoms; that no fire, no heroism, no intensity of thought and feeling, can preserve an individual life beyond the grave; that all the labours of the ages, all the devotion, all the inspiration, all the noonday brightness of human genius, are destined to extinction in the vast death of the solar system; and that the whole temple of Man's achievement must inevitably be buried beneath the debris of a universe in ruins – all these things, if not quite beyond

Egypt called these people 'the enemies of Re', 'those who had been rejected by the light'.

Their incomprehension of metaphysical principles and their hostility to true religion and to astrology (both based upon the premise of universal meaning and order) follow inescapably. Who is surprised when the eunuchs snigger behind the sultan's back and deride his passions? But when they transform their tragic disability into a virtue, call it 'reason', and take over the palace, the empire is doomed.

---

dispute, are yet so nearly certain, that no philosophy which rejects them can hope to stand. Only within the scaffolding of these truths, only on the firm foundation of unyielding despair, can the soul's habitation henceforth be built.
Bertrand Russell, quoted in E. A. Burtt, *The Metaphysical Foundations of Modern Physical Science* (London, 1932), p. 9
Man must at last wake out of his millenary dream and discover his total solitude, his fundamental isolation. He must realize that, like a gypsy, he lives on the boundary of an alien world; a world that is deaf to his music, and as indifferent to his hopes as it is to his sufferings and his crimes.
Jacques Monod, *Chance and Necessity* (London, 1972), p. 6

V.

USES AND ABUSES OF ASTROLOGY

The Many Faces of Astrology

We have touched upon various aspects and implications of both the astrological premise and its practice whenever these were relevant to our argument. But it is worth developing certain points mentioned only in passing, and systematizing and recapitulating others so that the jury will have a clearer idea of astrology's importance in the past, its potential role in a civilization of the future, and its present strengths and weaknesses. It is also useful to touch upon the questions of level and free will, both relevant to astrology, and both widely misunderstood.

The Soothsayer and the Specialist: Pop Astrology

The mass interest in astrological predictions is the inevitable historical corollary of a society in the last throes of decline and degeneration. The only surprise is that two centuries of materialism, rationalism, and technology should have proved so unconvincing and emotionally unsatisfactory: the same people who sit enthralled watching a space shuttle launch, switch off the set when the show is over and turn to their daily newspaper horoscope to see what is in store. Actually, this may be a hopeful sign. It does not mean that people are more or less superstitious than they have ever been. But it docs mean that it is far more difficult than the Jesuits of the Church of Progress believed to impose their own form of superstition upon humanity to the exclusion of all others.

Newspaper astrology is, of course, the most familiar form of astrological prediction. It pretends to tell all Geminis, all Cancers, all Leos, etc., what the week or month holds in store for them.

Interpretation of the individual horoscope is a complex and delicate business involving a multitude of variables. At its best, modern astrology leaves much to be desired, and prediction is its weakest card. The only astrological factor out of dozens that all Geminis, all Cancers, all Leos share, is their sun sign. Newspaper predictions are mostly made on the basis of the changing daily position of the moon and major planetary transits and the relationships these form to the different zodiacal signs. Since these relationships have different meanings for each individual horoscope, such blanket predictions are devoid of value (and would be even if astrological prediction were reliable as an art or a science – which it isn't). Nobody pretends otherwise, including the people who do it – many of whom are professional astrologers (with plenty of educated, professional people among their clients) making a bit of money on the side. Newspaper astrology does not aspire to do more than titillate. Polls indicate that few take it seriously. The only damage done is to astrology itself. Opponents choose to see no difference between newspaper astrology and the astrology endorsed by Pythagoras, Kepler and Jung; just as they choose to see no difference between the Sermon on the Mount and the fulminating of the Fundamentalists. Were a ban placed on newspaper astrology, the empty columns would only be filled with still more murder and cataclysm. Seen this way it might even be possible to count it a minor blessing.

More interesting are the individual services offered by the fairly large community of hard-sell professional astrologers.

YOU KNOW YOUR BIRTH SIGN BUT WHAT IS YOUR RISING-SIGN?
(it's what can rule your Luck, Love & Happiness)
Most people know their birth-sign in the Zodiac ... Aries ... Capricorn, Cancer, Leo ... whatever it is. But very few indeed know their rising-sign, the sign of the Ascendant on their birthdate. This is the secret part of a horoscope ... the secret part that

must be researched INDIVIDUALLY ... PERSONALLY ... for a man or woman. And· it's usually a costly business for which astrologers charge a highish fee. BUT NOT NOW! Once again I am first with a vital, new and unique astrological advance for the ordinary man or woman who can't spend high fees on Horoscopes. I can not only tell you YOUR Rising-Sign, BUT TELL YOU WHAT IT HAS MEANT IN YOUR LIFE IN THE PAST ... AND WHAT IT CAN MEAN IN THE FUTURE!

You can learn about this great new service FREE if you are over 18. Just send 8d in stamps to cover postage, and tell me your FULL name, FULL address and FULL birth-date (without FULL birth-date I cannot help you) and I will send you a NEW, gay, gorgeous astrological Reading, Star-Linked to YOUR Luck, Love and Happiness.

FIRST & BEST ... ALWAYS

> Madame X
> Oxford Street Observatory, London, W.1.

It is questionable if Imhotep, Chief of the Observers for the Pharaoh Zoser, would have found much worth observing at the Oxford Street Observatory.

An American astrologer, George Cardinal Legros, elaborates considerably upon a similar theme:

> Be in harmony with events. Know what important events are shaping up in your life ... know what action to take and when ... it can make a great difference in your affairs ... all the difference between drifting aimlessly and profitlessly and moving toward contentment and abundance.
>
> Be in harmony with yourself. Know the physical and psychological you ... master your hidden talents and traits, your undiscovered potentials. It can make a difference to your personal life ... in your business and social progress.
>
> But first of all know your astrologer. The Science of Astrology can light your path to a fuller and happier life ONLY if its practitioner is one who has mastered it both as a Science and an Art ... one who has not only the skilled accuracy of long

2 Penn Plaza • New York, NY 10121

Don't be surprised if this turns out to be the most important letter you have ever received.

I, Norvell, have been astrologer and advisor to the world's most famous people— winning their everlasting gratitude.

Now I will predict—then help you shape **your** future. So it brings you all the good things in life you're entitled to.

All the money, the love, the glamor, the success, the romance, the security, the joy, the happiness you should have

And I'll give you a Guarantee to this effect. **Notarized** and **legally binding**.

Norvell

NOTARY PUBLIC OF NEW JERSEY
My Commission Expires August 15, 1988

Dear Friend,

Someone said to me,

"Norvell, you perform magic with people's lives. Famous people, ordinary people. How do you do it?"

I said, "Astrology isn't magic."

"It's the oldest Science in the world."

And yet I had to admit it: Even though it is a Science, Astrology can help put you in control of your future. So you can lead a happier life.

For instance, once I was asked to help a beauty shop attendant who was "down on her luck."

She was very depressed. Living alone. No man, no money. Nothing but a drab routine to face day-in and day-out. She'd daydream away her empty life. "Tuning out" her grey existence.

She hungered after life as it was lived in magazines she read and movies she saw. A happy life - in Technicolor.

A life that was beyond possibility for her.

F4

Or was it?

She asked me to study her Astrological background. I did. And immediately I found the key - that would "unlock" a life of happiness for her.

I told her things about herself (about a wonderful hidden potential and about exciting possibilties) that she never imagined were part of her.

But they were part of her.

They were all "written" in the stars. They had left a mathematical imprint upon her as unique and precise as her own set of fingerprints.

I gave this woman advice about her future.

She took it - and here's what happened -

Almost at once she attracted to her the Man of Her Dreams. A charming multimillionaire. A man who swept her off her feet and headed her straight for the altar - and a Marriage Made in Heaven.

Her hopes had been fulfilled. (As I knew they would.)

Incredible?

Let me give you another example - a farmer from the Midwest.

Also down on his luck. Also depressed. Also penniless.

I gave this man advice about his future. Advice that could profoundly change the course of his life. I saw he didn't have to be a penniless farmer. Didn't have to be in a depressed state. Didn't have to live an unlucky life.

I was right.

He followed my advice. Today, this man - this former penniless farmer - has become one of Hollywood's most successful Movie Producers - with one smash box-office hit after another. A man who thrills hundreds of thousands of people with every film he makes. While earning millions of dollars.

And he gives the credit for his good fortune to me. As his Astrologer and Advisor, I guided his steps across the boundaries of the future - into the unknown. He entered a life of wealth and happiness beyond imagination.

But not beyond my imagination.

I expect success for any person I work with. Because I can bring every individual's "Sleeping Powers" to life.

I can bring YOUR sleeping Powers to life right now.

I've done this for so many people through the years. People you're familiar with. (I was the one who advised a young Bob Hope. A young Bing Crosby. Elvis Presley. Bette Davis. James Stewart. Etc., etc.)

I've advised and guided U.S. Presidents. Business magnates. Government leaders. Television celebrities. As well as would-be magnates, leaders, celebrities.

But they were no longer "would-be's" after they met me.

I counseled them. I charted their paths. Step-by-step. I gave them the right numbers. I even told them which 3 to 5 days each month "they could do no wrong." These were the hot days for big decisions that spelled success. Achievement. Joy. Happiness.

These people were able to get the very things in life they desired.

But let's talk about you.

I'm going to be frank. Nothing would be more satisfying for me than to help someone who really needs my help.

I can make the rich people of this world richer. The lucky ones luckier. But when you're already very successful in life, how much can it matter - to anyone?

And then there's you.

I've contacted you because helping you would make a difference. I'd like to see you get the things you desire. All the good things you've been entitled to from the day you were born.

Do you have strong desires for money? Personal love? Lasting friendship? A successful career? A really happy life?

Don't dismiss such desires as foolish daydreams.

I want to turn your "daydreams" into reality. With my Astrological powers for helping people. (I've used them thousands of times - for thousands of people.)

Now it's your turn.

If you need money, let me lead you to it.

If you need a better job or new career, let me lead you to it.

If you need deeper relationships, more friends and greater popularity, let me lead you to them.

If you need to love people and have people love you, let me lead you to all this.

Here's how we begin.

You tell me a little about yourself: Where and when you were born.

And immediately I'll begin improving and upgrading your life. (I need about a week to ten days after hearing from you. Then wait until you see what you receive: The same kind of material...guidance...advice...and "readings" I provide Movie Stars and the Power Elite.)

First: You will receive from me your
own detailed Astrological Reading.

This elaborately "plotted" Report will grow out of my dissection of your life from interpreting your birthdate information. (I will take intricate readings of the planets as they move through the houses of life in your personal chart.) Revealed here will be your hidden gifts. Your strengths. Your untapped potential - your "Sleeping Powers." All the surprising influences at work right from the day you were born. A wonderful improvement can then happen in your life, because you'll be <u>in control</u> of your future.

Which brings me to the next thing I'll do:
I'll develop a <u>Day-to-Day Charting of your Future</u>.

Yes. I mean it. Based on direct birthdate information, I'm going to send you an actual <u>Day-by-Day</u> Charting of your <u>future</u>. It can be awesome to see your future unfold before you. Your upcoming days mapped out in detail. Imagine waking up every morning and knowing just what to do - in your personal relationships. Your business affairs. Your every future plan.

When I work with you I want to see Money
in your future. So you'll get my <u>Money-Alert Report</u>.

I'm going to show you how to attract money. How to become wealthy. From the information I have of you, I'll help guide you to success in contests, investments, even your own business. Over the years I've created a "Millionaire's Explosion." <u>And I'd like to make you part of it</u>.

You need your own Special <u>Lucky Number Combinations</u>.
I will calculate them for you.

Yes, I will actually compute your <u>very own</u> Lucky Number Combinations - designed to make you one of life's winners. Others who have gotten this "Lucky Numger Power" from me have found the magic touch they'd been searching for. And it can happen for you. Picture yourself winning at the Lottery, track, casinos, cards, Bingo, Sweepstakes <u>again and again</u>.

And I'm going to do more for you...

<u>I am going to assign you your own Individual Mantra</u>. My special word "Mediation Chant" can instantly put you at peace with yourself and with the world. With your own Mantra, <u>you can relax whenever you desire</u>. (That's one reason people pay up to hundreds of dollars for their Mantra.)

<u>I am going to give you your own Complete Biorhythm Chart</u>. This unique "map" of your Energy Cycle tells you when your best days are due. (When "you're hot" and can't miss at whatever you do.) Your Biorhythm Chart gives you the extra edge for winning <u>really big</u> in life.

You may wonder why I'm doing this for you.

You see, I believe you should have the same chance for happiness as people living a privileged life.

I'm ready to help you. <u>I mean to see that you get every good thing in life coming to you</u>. <u>Because you're entitled.</u>

That's why there's a Privilege Form attached with my letter.

For 40 years I've helped the rich and famous live out their dreams.

Now it's your turn.

With sincerest best wishes,

Norvell

Norvell has helped U.S. Presidents, European Royalty and Hollywood's Movie Greats gain incredible success. Incredible happiness. Incredible personal fulfillment.

Can he do the same for you?

YES.

Norvell can bring you incredible success.
Incredible happiness. Incredible personal fulfillment.

How can he make these miracles happen for you?

Because of his far-seeing intelligence and pinpoint-accurate judgment of the destinies of people he works with.

Norvell knows how to put people *in control of* their lives. Awaken their "sleeping Powers." Lead them to REAL happiness.

It's no wonder he commands a worldwide reputation as the leading Astrologer-Advisor of our time.

But Norvell says: "I don't want my services limited to the rich (seeking even more money) and the famous (seeking more fame).

"I want to help people who really *need* my help. Who want to be much happier than they are. It's only right that 'ordinary' people—who aren't rich and famous—*also* get the good things entitled to them. *Every good thing earmarked for them from birth.*"

That is the purpose of this mailing.

If you feel you deserve more out of life than you're getting now, return the Privilege Form. You can then benefit from the astrological skills of this extraordinary seer and advisor.

Norvell can bring anyone's sleeping Powers to life. That's why he expects success for *every* person he works with.

A RARE PERSONAL SERVICE BY NORVELL.
A DREAM COME TRUE FOR *YOU.*

Right now for a limited number of people, Norvell is offering a special opportunity: *His services.* The same kind of astrological services he has provided top Movie Stars and world leaders.

You are one of these people picked for this opportunity.

Respond during the "Privilege Period"—and you will be able to have Norvell at your side as your Personal Astrologer and Advisor.

NVYL4

thousands upon thousands of people.

he famous people he's helped.

to the best Astrologer – no second-best Astrologer would do.)

L NOW

J

JRN FOR
ERVICES

millionaire. Thanks to Norvell, the manicurist is now one of the happiest and wealthiest women in California. *Norvell had put her in control of her future . . . and made her dreams come true.*

There was a health food store clerk. He dreamed of writing songs. Of fame and fortune. After having nothing but bad luck, he came to Norvell. With Norvell's help he became one of America's most popular song-writers. Enjoying all the money and fame he desired. *Norvell had put him in control of his future . . . and made his dreams come true.*

There was a certain ambitious housewife. With practically no business experience nor money. (Ambition was what she had. Period.) Desperate, she sought Norvell's advice. Then she followed his advice. Within a short time she became a business tycoon. Happy as could be. *Norvell had put her in control of her future . . . and made her dreams come true.*

There was the war veteran who "would never say die." Crippled for life, he was physically helpless. But he wanted to become a writer—even though his injury blocked him. Norvell told the veteran he could succeed. With Norvell's help the veteran wrote a book. Published it and sold the movie rights for thousands upon thousands of dollars. Here was a man with all the "odds stacked against him" making it in a glamorous new career . . . happy and satisfied. *Norvell had put him in control of his future . . . and made his dreams come true.*

Success stories like these pour in from women and men

everywhere who turn to Norvell for help *and come away with wealth. Love. Happiness, Security. Well-being. Contentment. Power. Political glory. Personal fulfillment.*

No wonder distinguished national leaders and influential achievers come to Norvell for consultation without regard to cost. They are gladly willing to travel across the country (or across the ocean) and spend hundreds of dollars or more for Norvell's personal attention.

Now, Norvell is interested in YOU.

You are very fortunate to have received this invitation.

Return the Privilege Form right now and Norvell will work with you. Do for you what he has done for others who now lead happiness-filled lives. Norvell will *predict*—and then help you *shape* your future. In his special guidance will come the Answers to the Big Questions about your intimate needs. Your secret ambitions. Your frustrations. Your social aspirations. Your love life. Your urgent desires.

The day Norvell starts helping you will mark a turning point in your life.

And with each passing day, it will become clearer to you what the future will bring . . . *and what you can do about it IN ADVANCE!*

WHEN HE RECEIVES YOUR PRIVILEGE FORM,

1 Norvell will send you your own detailed <u>*Astrological Reading*</u>.

This elaborately "plotted" Report will be based entirely on Norvell's very own interpretation of your birthdate. *From intricate readings of the planets as they move through the various houses of life in your personal chart.* It will consist of thousands of words about you. (Your personality, your mentality, your secret nature, your impulses, your raw instincts.) *Revealing to you your hidden gifts. Your strengths. Your undiscovered potential—your sleeping Powers for happiness and success.*

2 Norvell will develop and send you your own <u>*Day-by-Day Charting of your Future.*</u>

Based on direct birthdate information, you're going to receive from Norvell the most important guidance imaginable: An actual *Day-to-Day* Charting of your *future. The same kind of information given by Norvell to world leaders and celebrities.* Like them, you'll see your future unfold before you. Your upcoming days mapped out. Your possibilities examined. Your opportunities spelled out for you. (*Note: You do not want to risk any important decision or even face the next day without consulting this Report.*)

3 Norvell will calculate and send you your own <u>*Lucky Number Combinations.*</u>

Your *very own* Lucky Number Combinations will be *calculated* by Norvell himself. These Combinations are designed to make you a winner. Others who have gotten this "Lucky Number Power" from Norvell have found the magic touch they'd been searching for. This can happen for you. (Expect to become a *consistent* Big-Time Winner in the lottery, at the casino tables, track, bingo, card games, even sweepstakes contests!)

4 To help you become rich, Norvell will send you your own <u>*Money-Alert Report.*</u>

Norvell has probably helped more people make more money than anyone else alive. Millions upon millions of dollars. From the information Norvell has of you, this personal Money-Alert Astrogram will be dispatched—so you can enjoy true financial success. Norvell will show you how to attract money. Accumulate money. Make fabulous investments. Even make it big in your own business.

5 Norvell will assign you your own <u>*Meditation Mantra.*</u>

Hundreds of thousands of people pay $125 to $300 to receive Mantras from experts. The reason is, a Mantra or "Meditation Chant" can give you *instant* peace of mind. Allow you to relax *anytime.* Norvell wants you to have every possible power, so he will give you your personal Mantra *free of charge.* (Imagine receiving your individual Mantra from the greatest expert of all, the world's #1 Astrologer. Coming from Norvell, your special word Mantra will be charged with a unique "psychic" Energy. that can lead to miraculous happenings.)

6 <u>*Norvell will also send you your own Complete Biorhythm Chart.*</u>

The value of a good Biorhythm Chart is incalculable. Almost every top celebrity and top athlete have had their Biorhythm Charts worked out for them.

Just like these celebrities and athletes, you will have *your* own Biorhythm Chart—based on your astrological information. *Right from Norvell himself.* This Chart will become one of your most prized possessions. Like an unfailingly accurate clock, it will actually lay out for you your Energy Cycle. You'll know when to expect your "Up Days" and "Down Days." And you can make your moves—or lie low—accordingly. *You will always know well in advance when your best days—3–5 per month—are due!* (*Your Biorhythm Chart will prove so valuable and give you such a Winning Edge in life, you may wonder how you ever got along without it!*)

Your Personal Guarantee from Norvell

You will receive so much help BENEFITING YOU YEAR AFTER YEAR AFTER YEAR from the Day-By-Day Charting of your Future . . . your Astrological Reading . . . Personal Lucky Number Combinations . . . Special Money-Alert Report . . . Special Meditation Mantra . . . Special Personal Color . . . Complete Biorhythm Chart . . . you should expect major improvement and upscaling in every area of your life. Starting at once. If for any reason you do not experience total satisfaction, simply notify me through the Astrology Research Center and you'll receive an immediate refund of any money you pay. Furthermore, if you're interested in the Lottery, track, Bingo, cards and/or Sweepstakes, you are guaranteed to win at least $10,000.00 within 90 days. **OR DOUBLE YOUR MONEY BACK.**

experience, but the talent and sensitivity to perceive the subtleties and nuances that make your horoscope unique and different from all others.

Birth Horoscope Analysis $250.00. Forecast for one year $300.00. Horary Chart $25.00. Consultation or private lesson (one hour) $25.00. Correction of birth time $50.00.

We used both these ads in our earlier *Case for Astrology*. Here are a couple of more recent examples.

Miss Jillson's ad is taken from *Fate* Magazine (December 1989): Norvell's is an industrial-strength direct mail package. Both may provoke a measure of sympathy for the Prosecution's case. But even here the jury might hesitate before jumping to conclusions.

Obviously, false modesty is not an affliction of either of these astrologers, and Norvell may have an overdose of disharmonious Jupiter aspects in his chart, or else his PR agency does. The self-assumed title of 'The World's Greatest Astrologer' – emblazoned on his envelopes – in particular rings hollow since there are no astrological Olympics where such a gold medal is bestowed; nor even a Nobel Prize for it. On the other hand, the claims of science are no less extravagant and equally groundless. The language is more circumspect (only to be expected with Saturn rising or culminating, after all). In *The Art of the Soluble*, the Nobel Prize-winning immunologist, P. B. Medawar declared, 'humility is not a state of mind conducive to the advancement of learning', and also, 'Science is a very great work, perhaps the greatest of all the works of man.' By extension, this must mean that scientists are the very greatest of men. We have discussed Culver and Ianna's contention that science is both the best and the *only* means for arriving at truth, a contention both wrong and illogical.

Ignoring the hyped-up language, the astrologers' sins are actually less grievous, since they make no claims to logic or dispassion. Both Jillson and Norvell err, of course, in calling astrology a 'science'. Miss Jillson invites prospective clients to participate in a 'Research Project' that, given the questions

asked, seems unlikely to provide startling scientific confirmation
of astrology. Norvell operates out of 'The Astrological Research
Center'.

According to Miss Jillson in the reprinted article by Gary
Waid (provenance not provided), 'In the past 20 years, the
world of astrology has undergone great changes. Now all the
math necessary to interpret a chart is done by computer. Jillson
tells the students at her astrological school, that they can now
forget about the math and concentrate on the humanity of astrology.'

This is something of an extended *non sequitur*. Actually, not
that much has changed in the world of astrology. The computer
saves the astrologer half an hour or so of time. The math is
elementary and personal interpretation of the horoscope presents
the same problems it always did. Addey's harmonics, the
German midpoint school and Gauquelin's findings, among other
recent developments, give adventurous astrologers more tools
to work with, making astrology more rather than less complex.

However, the computer can now supply more than the math.
Astrological software has become sophisticated. A number of
the most highly regarded astrologers within the astrological
community have worked with computer experts to develop
programs that take into account the vast array of major and
minor astrological combinations and permutations and are not
dissatisfied with the results (perhaps akin to those computerized
chess programs that can defeat all but Grand Masters?). The
computerized reading may then serve as a basis for still more
refined personal interpretation.

In those pre-computer days, all you could get for nothing
plus the postage (from the Oxford St Observatory) was your
'secret rising-sign' (sixty seconds' worth of calculation even
back then: the result is then looked up in the printed ephemeris)
and the promise of a gay gorgeous horoscope. Today the
computer can churn out quite detailed interpretations, not just
charts, in minutes, at minimal expense (Jillson – $1, Norvell –
$15). Astrology may therefore be one of the few areas of modern
life where prices have actually gone down. Even the prices

charged for personal consultations have remained pretty stable. Legros was charging $250 in 1968, Joyce Jillson charges $300 in 1989 and Norvell charges $100 and up. (Imagine paying your doctor, dentist, therapist or car dealer what you paid for their services twenty years ago.)

But what has not changed at all is the pitch. The comprehensive services offered by George Cardinal Legros, Jillson and Norvell all promise, in varying degrees of hyperbole, but in one stroke: fore-knowledge, self-knowledge, social success, contentment, the realization of hidden potential, romance and the *summum bonum* before which even these great boons fade to insignificance: profit. (Norvell promises, somewhat redundantly, 'All the money, the love, the glamor, the success, the romance, the security, the joy, the happiness you should have'.)

In short, astrology will provide the client with the Open Sesame into the American Dream.

It scarcely matters that astrology cannot deliver such goods. Nothing else can either. As countries such as Sweden and the United States pretty well prove, profit and contentment are not necessary corollaries. Anyone who has spent time among the rich knows they are no happier than the rest of us. They just have the wherewithal to throw their weight about a bit. 'More' and 'better' are not synonyms – though the whole of the Church of Progress is based upon the assumption that they are. In any event, professional astrologers would not be in business for long if too many philosophical and psychological truths began creeping into their advertisements.

According to an English astrologer, P. I. H. Naylor, the two questions she is most commonly asked are: 'When am I going to get some more money?' and 'When is my husband/wife going to die?'. Put bluntly like that, these queries do not speak well of high spiritual aspirations prevailing among the astrologers' clientele. Yet closer analysis reveals that Mrs Naylor's clients are interested in obtaining no more than a higher standard of living and a greater degree of personal freedom; precisely the chief aims (along with status or prestige), held out to humanity at large by the Church of Progress. The *New Scientist* editorial

25

463

quoted earlier, seeks to persuade youngsters that a career in science is 'entertaining, important and rewarding' (i.e. diversion, prestige, money). True, there is no promise there of romance or winning the lottery, but maybe science might try that – given the waning interest in its wares. Norvell even guarantees his services or your money back; signed by a notary public. Imagine going through twelve years of astronomy to get your PhD. and then trying to get your money back once you discovered that it was not in fact entertaining, important or rewarding! At its worst, then, this level of astrology is no worse than the society that creates a demand for it; at best, where prediction becomes inextricably mingled with character analysis, it serves a purpose.

Counseling

Not all clients are interested only in money or the demise of spouses. Some come with legitimate questions. Some have a more or less accurate picture of themselves and their capabilities, or at least are willing to listen to someone able to provide such a picture. Good astrologers are often, by their nature, good psychologists, and a growing number these days have formal psychological training. Jungians and Gestalt psychologists in particular find astrology useful in their practices. A number of studies have been done looking into the nature and quality of astrological advice. Dr Geoffrey Dean, analyzing these, concluded that for the most part the advice was sound, humane and relatively inexpensive. 'In such cases, astrology, without needing to be true, acts as an organizing device for the otherwise unmanageable smorgasbord of human experience.' Another study by psychologists L. Sechrest and J. Bryan of eighteen mail-order astrological marriage-counselors found that the advice was realistic, clear, personal and friendly, though not particularly 'astrological'.

Astrology as Placebo?

Since astrological counseling provides the bread-and-butter for the vast majority of professional astrologers, the question imposes itself: is astrological practice at this level devoid of truth (as Dr Dean implies), and are its acknowledged therapeutic benefits simply the result of sound advice that would be just as sound if astrology weren't involved?

At the moment it is impossible to answer scientifically yes or no. Determining astrological veracity within the context of counseling has never been attempted systematically, and would be very difficult, though perhaps not impossible, to test objectively. Psychologists have been racking their brains for a century trying in vain to devise objective personality tests. They invariably confront three immovable stumbling blocks: (1) the human personality by its nature resists quantification, (2) human beings do not know themselves very well, (3) outsiders (e.g. psychologists) who do not necessarily know themselves any better than the rest of us are hardly in a position to make objective judgements on the basis of test results. Add astrology and it becomes an equation with four unknowns instead of three . . . Who is to judge the accuracy of an astrological reading? The astrologer? The astrologee? Or an 'impartial' outsider? It's next to impossible. About the only element open in principle to quantitative study is prediction, which everyone agrees is astrology's most problematic aspect.

Nonetheless, an astrological reading invariably entails prediction. If astrologers refused to make predictions, they'd lose most of their clients. We all want to be told we are geniuses, but also that we shall shortly meet a tall, dark, handsome stranger. In principle it should be possible to secure the co-operation of a group of astrologers and their clients. The astrologers might be asked to make their predictions as specific as possible (date of meeting tall, dark, handsome stranger, height of stranger, size shoes, financial status of stranger, outcome of meeting, and so on). The clients might be asked to keep careful track of the astrologers' predictions and the results could then be subjected to statistical analysis in some fashion. But in practice it is not that simple. Astrologers shy away from predicting the stranger's height and the precise date of the encounter; they argue that the horoscope was not designed to reveal information on this level – though they may well predict propitious and unpropitious times for romance, financial activity, creative endeavor, travel or domestic decisions. But there is enormous scope for ratiocination by all parties and on the verdict as to what constitutes accurate and inaccurate prediction; a problem that has historical antecedents (see pp. 118–19). An example: the specific, accurate (to the day) prediction of an assassination attempt on the president of the United States is a successful prediction that brooks no argument. On the other hand, the warning that 'dire events' attended the ides of November and December 1986 is difficult to assess. The fact that the Iran–Contra scandal broke then would not convince skeptics, or even impress eternal skeptics, in this case with good reason. They might argue that the nature of the world political situation is such that any given two-month period is bound to produce a surfeit of events that qualify as 'dire'.

On the personal level that normally prevails between astrologer and client, even prediction may be accurate sufficiently often and in important situations to at least not dismiss it. There have simply been too many correct, detailed, historically authenticated astrological predictions to ascribe it all to chance. J. B. S. Haldane (see p. 146) may not have been impressed by 'a few lucky hits' but, depending upon the nature and frequency of those hits, the jury might be.

As for the counseling aspect of astrology, with all the qualifying and complicating conditions acknowledged, we think there is good reason to believe that more than a placebo effect is involved, though we cannot yet substantiate this scientifically.

On the scientific/philosophical front the question boils down to the legitimacy of successive extrapolations.

Extrapolation 1: The Horoscope

We take it as a given now, amply proved by Gauquelin's statistics, that our personalities correspond in some testable, quantifiable way to the position of the planets at birth (ignoring for the moment, the zodiac, and all that remains unproved). It is not that the child is 'influenced' by that planetary configuration, but rather that he or she inescapably shares in the meaning of that moment.

For example, Saturn symbolizes those cosmic functions which may, under the proper circumstances and all being propitious, work out in the twentieth century in the ability and desire to become a scientist. When Saturn is on one of the angles in relation to the earth, at that moment it might be said that a 'scientific' note is being struck. The other planets are all, simultaneously, striking notes of their own. A celestial chord sounds. A child born at that moment takes its first breath and for the first time is an independent being. Whatever the nature of the individual 'soul' or personality may be, it will automatically be tuned to that chord and for the rest of its life, it will resonate when the heavens produce significant harmonics. The horoscope represents the score of that celestial chord. From the horoscope the astrologer must determine its meaning. This is the first extrapolation.

The meanings traditionally assigned to Mars, Venus, the moon, Jupiter and Saturn have been proven. Those of Mercury, the sun and the outer planets have not been. But since tradition has proven correct in every other instance, it is probably safe to assume that it is also correct regarding the sun and Mercury at least. It is also proven that the position of the planets has meaning in the broad sense – Mars on the angle significant for athletes, Mars 'fleeing' the angle significant for artists and writers, etc. From this it follows that the angular relationship between the planets (the aspects) *has* to have significance as well. And since these meanings are indelibly written into the human psyche, it is not so astonishing that people in the past were able to gain access to those meanings – even if we still don't know how they did it. (We don't know how the Chinese developed acupuncture, either. But they did, and the medical profession has finally acknowledged that acupuncture works, and therefore must be based upon physical realities still unknown to the West.) In principle, on the basis of these factors alone, astrological interpretation of the personality is plausible. There is nothing spooky, kooky or superstitious about it; it is no more implausible than making music out of an infinite combination of notes. But like music, a vast number of variables and imponderables are involved; the opportunities for bad astrology are as boundless as the opportunities for bad music. None the less, good music gets composed.

How accurate are astrological readings? That is a question difficult to answer and, as we argued above, next to impossible to approach scientifically. Our long personal experience has convinced us that they are often very accurate indeed. Opponents have tried to show the way in which astrological readings employ clever generalities to cover any and all situations ('You are highly creative, but you are also exacting and precise'). But astrologers do not always deal in generalities. Many former skeptics have come to accept astrology on the basis of personal readings where an astrologer zeroed in on specific information, information from the ex-skeptic's own past or present – family relationships, health matters, domestic relations, long-kept secrets that could not conceivably have been guessed, and that would have made the astrologer look ridiculous had the information been false. But there is no way to scientifically refute eternal skeptics on this point. It is always possible that we, those other converted skeptics, Kepler and the thousands of other convinced astrologers and their clients before us throughout the ages have all been deluding ourselves. It's possible. The very success of the Church of Progress proves the power of delusion to perpetuate itself. At least for a few centuries. So why not for a few millennia – suggesting in turn that gullibility must have a selective advantage, an intriguing probability that keen evolutionists might enjoy explaining away?

Finally, the only way to make up your mind on this question of astrological interpretation/counseling and even prediction is to test them personally. Consult a few professional astrologers. Give them as little information as possible about yourself and compare their readings. Go with specific questions and compare answers. Make sure you take notes, or tape the astrologer's predictions and see if they come to pass. Allow generously for your own gullibility factor, none of us are without it, but avoid eternal skepticism and try to be fair. Also bear in mind that astrology is more art than science, like medical diagnosis but more so. If you have anything subtle wrong with you, you might go to half a dozen doctors before one came up with the right diagnosis. This does not mean that medicine is a fraud, or that the doctors who were wrong were quacks. It means that the problem is complex. In another situation, a given doctor may be reliably tuned in to whatever it is that ails you, and yet be fighting a malpractice suit for treatment that went drastically wrong with some other patient. Finding a right astrologer is no more and no less scientific than finding the right doctor.*

Along with putting professional astrologers to the test, members of the jury might also take that daring, death-defying step no opponent of astrology has ever taken. Try interpreting charts for yourself. Computers now take all the effort out of chart computation; there is a variety of astrological software, basic how-to astrological texts are readily available (see the Bibliography) and classes in astrology are run everywhere. But remember, chart interpretation is more art than science. As with any art, there are those with great talent, those with less and those without. For the talented, that first brush with astrology often comes as a kind of revelation. You get the feeling that you have been given the key to a great storehouse of wisdom; to a mode of insight into the working of the cosmos and its relation to the human psyche that, mysteriously, you already understand and have always understood, but only now is it

---

* Serious astrological organizations have followed the lead of other professional bodies and require their participating astrologers to undergo rigorous training and pass difficult examinations before qualifying for a diploma. But, of course, these have no official recognition within the Church of Progress. Anyone can put out a shingle calling himself or herself an astrologer. So incompetence among astrologers is probably even more rife than it is among other professionals and of course there is no board of review or possibility of redress. But this is not really the fault of the serious astrologers; it is more a consequence of the obduracy of their opponents.

revealed to you through astrology. If you have little talent or no talent the experience will be very different. The *Tao Te Ching* puts it nicely:

> When the best student hears about the way (the Tao)
> he practices it assiduously;
> When the average student hears about the way
> It seems to him one moment there and gone the next;
> When the worst student hears about the way
> He laughs out loud.
> If he did not laugh
> It would be unworthy of being the way.*

Lao Tze, *Tao Te Ching*, tr. D. C. Lau
(Penguin Edition, 1963), p. 101 (verse 41)

If, on the basis of your own experience, you decide that there is something to astrological character-interpretation and counseling after all, you will not be able to shove this conviction down any unwilling throats, but then, perhaps, you may not feel the need to. You will also come to appreciate both the subtleties of character interpretation and temptations and the pitfalls of astrological prediction that follow.

Extrapolation 2: Astrological Prediction

The individual astrological reading is an interpretation of the significance of a particular planetary configuration. If it is, indeed, possible to derive accurate psychological information relating to the past or present from such a primary extrapolation, then in principle it should be possible to extend the process forward and, within limits, predict the future, since the position of the planets in the future can be predicted with perfect

---

* A different translation considerably alters the meaning of the last two lines: 'The foolish student hears of the Tao and laughs aloud. If there were no laughter, the Tao would not be what it is.' Lao Tzu, *Tao Te Ching*, tr. Gia-Fu Feng and Jane English (Alfred Knopf, 1975)

accuracy.* For example, let's say a champion boxer is born with Mars on the Ascendant (Gauquelin Zone 1). He has a title defense coming up in three months' time. An astrologer looking at the celestial line-up for that day finds the transitting Mars in conjunction with the radix Mars (Mars in its orbit relative to the earth has come round to the same spot it was on the boxer's day of birth), and there is a favorable aspect to Jupiter. The astrologer would interpret this as a propitious sign; the boxer will be experiencing a particularly 'martial' period; Mars is reinforcing his already strongly positioned Mars, while Jupiter, planet of success/renown, is smiling upon the enterprise. All else being equal, and, depending upon the chart of the opponent, the astrologer would not hesitate to predict a victory.

That, at any rate, is the principle involved. And in principle, there can be no logical objection to this second extrapolation: the configuration of the planets at birth has meaning – this is proven. The astrologer has had access to that meaning from time immemorial and in principle can delineate character on that basis. The ability to predict follows from a sufficiently accurate delineation of character. But that is of course the nub of the problem: how accurate are the delineations, and how do we judge objectively the degree of accuracy? Since our case neither stands nor falls upon the answer to those questions, we are happy to leave them open. But if we are correct in insisting that astrological interpretation has value, even in its present unsettled state, and that astrological prediction at least deserves consideration before it is jettisoned, the next question follows inescapably: what can we do about it?

---

* This is the basis of scientific prediction. If enough is known about two chemicals, then it is possible to predict with great accuracy what will happen when they are put together. The difference between astrological and scientific prediction lies in the number (and trustworthiness) of the variables involved. But the principle is essentially the same.

Philosophical Implications: Free Will or no Free Will?

This is a question sometimes raised by astrologers as well as by their opponents. The astrologers, convinced that astrological prediction is valid, are forced to confront the philosophical and quite practical dilemma that follows from that belief. If it is indeed possible to accurately predict the future, does this mean we are powerless to change that future if the prediction is dire? Opponents of course do not believe it possible to accurately predict the future through astrology. But a common objection to astrology (which we did not address earlier since it is purely a philosophical not a scientific objection) is that belief in astrology presupposes a lack of free will and the abdication of personal responsibility for one's own life. Amusingly enough, a closely related objection is raised by the Fundamentalist Christian Right (which rejects astrology for many of the same reasons, and with the same expression of *ex cathedra* outrage, as their sworn enemies, the Atheists, Rationalists, Materialists and Humanists). The Fundamentalists maintain that belief in astrology means a denial of the Will of God (which is effectively the Determinism of the Church of Progress except that it is God instead of Chance that turns the wheel of fortune and tells it when to stop).

This question of Free Will has plagued philosophers from the beginning of recorded history at least. Some devoted most of their lives to the many and thorny problems involved, and there is no room here to explore the subject thoroughly. On the other hand, many of the complexities and contradictions are illusory and disappear once the question is placed in its proper context, and for this, not that much space is required.

The usual astrological answer to the problem is: the stars incline but do not compel. But how to assess the relative strengths of inclination and compulsion? To what extent are we capable of acting against our own inclinations? The question becomes very real when important personal issues are at stake. Two astrological anecdotes illustrate what is involved.

> The advice of the best astrologer in the world is of no avail if you do not abide by it.

A woman once consulted me about herself. She had no particular problems, but just wanted to know what dangers lay in her map.

I found Jupiter badly affected by planets, place and house and I warned her never to go to law or to ride horses. (Jupiter rules both of these things.)

'Oh, but I love horses and I must ride!' she exclaimed. 'My life would be empty without horses.'

I repeated my warning. For a year she took my advice – and then, lulled by a false sense of security because nothing happened, she went riding. The horse bolted, involved her in an accident with a motor cyclist and both she and the motor cyclist were badly injured. The result was a court case which ended with her having to pay the damages. She then consulted me as to how to get out of it! There was nothing I could do. The warning had been given in time, the so called 'hammer blow' was written in her map. She could have avoided it by accepting the original advice given, but preferred not to do so.

She had freedom of will: the horse had not. Yet she *had* been warned! We can only advise. We cannot alter the course when things have happened.

Madeleine Montalban, *Prediction* Magazine, April 1968

A second anecdote is provided by Alan Leo, the English astrologer instrumental in reviving interest in astrology early in this century. Leo warned a client that financial troubles were imminent. To avert danger, the man transferred all his belongings into his wife's name. Three weeks later the wife ran off with the chauffeur.

Could this man have averted financial ruin? Was Miss Montalban's client 'free' to stay off horses and keep clear of lawsuits? No less important, to what extent were the astrologers actually *responsible* for initiating these events? Both these anecdotes would seem to be cases of accurate prediction, but both could also be called instances where the prophecy was self-fulfilling, and the astrological meddling only exacerbated or initiated possibilities hitherto dormant in the chart (or, eternal skeptics might argue, precipitating them through suggestion alone). Without having been warned, the horseback-riding lady would not have stopped riding for a year, and if she had been involved in an accident, it would not have been *that* accident. The man facing financial problems certainly would not have transferred his belongings to his wife. Whatever troubles may have arisen, they would not have involved his wife's running off with the chauffeur with all his money. And perhaps neither of these misfortunes would have occurred without the astrologer's advice setting the stage for them. Who can say?*

Free Will and Destiny

The problem of free will is inextricably bound to that of 'destiny' – a favorite among astrologers as well as dramatists. The seventeenth-century French astrologer Morin de Ville-franche wrote:

> the birthdates and the events in the lives of men are enchained by Providence in view of a necessary concourse of the communal realization of destiny, in such a way that he who is by birth destined, for example, to die by assassination does not fail to encounter his assassin, and that he who must be unhappily married will invariably seek out the woman who shall see to it that it is so.

It is interesting to test such a statement against concrete examples. John F. Kennedy, for instance, was warned by a dozen astrologers and clairvoyants of the dangers of assassination, and by some of the precise danger-period. But it is clear that,

---

* In contrast to these anecdotes, there are many others in which precognitive warnings (not necessarily via astrology, but also by way of dreams or psychics) alerted people to coming danger and they managed to avert it. *Fate* Magazine runs a column of these in each issue. What this means is that the warning served to put these people momentarily into a higher state of awareness or attention, and when the crisis occurred, because of the warning, they actually had a measure of free will at their disposal and were able to make use of it. But these anecdotes, though not that uncommon, are still exceptional. In the course of our 'normal' daily lives, free will is hypothetical, seldom actual.

even had he been impressed by the sincerity and number of these predictions, his position was such that he could not have heeded them, while his personality was such that he would not even take the customary precautions. As for unhappily married couples, they are not uncommon. Members of the jury may want to make a few selections from the files of their own experience and to test them against de Villefranche's eloquent but forbidding pronouncement.

But what of those who have spent a lifetime supposedly acquiring free will? What of the yogi, the saint and the Zen master? Are these men as bound to their destinies as the ordinary enslaved free citizen? Taking historical examples – Christ, Buddha, Socrates, etc. – it may appear that they are no freer than Miss Montalban's horse-loving lady. On the surface, their lives and destinies seem even more ineluctably predetermined. Even more so. Yet it is sometimes hard to avoid concluding that, gruesome and ignominious as the deaths of these great historical personages were, they were chosen deliberately, perhaps as ultimate tests of the state of their liberation from the cross of the flesh, and the coils of time?

We do not pretend to know. Moreover, it is impossible to judge the motives of people whose lives are lived on higher levels than our own. And no one knows whether or not the details of these stories are factual history or symbolism or both.

One possibility is that destiny is 'written' but the manner and, more important, the spirit in which we go to meet our destiny is not.

And what of those who have not had time to consider or act upon these timeless questions? What of children who die, and young men cut down in wars? We don't know. But if obliged to choose between conflicting opinions on the subject that correspond to nothing within our personal experience, we would tend to take that of those responsible for cathedrals above that of those responsible for the H-bomb and the electric toothbrush. And we would hazard that, in the dimensions of eternity, innocence goes uncondemned, while ignorance does not – in Hindu philosophy, *avidya*, willful ignorance, is the only sin, and it is interesting that the word 'sin' derives from a word meaning 'to miss the mark'.

But the knottier questions involved are seldom addressed. Most astrologers, as well as most modern philosophers, would take Miss Montalban's position: her horsewoman client was perfectly free to act upon her advice and avert the catastrophe. Jean-Paul Sartre, for example, claims that a waiter is a waiter because at some time he made the decision to become one. This is a position shared by Sartre's fellow existentialists.

The linguistic philosopher, Antony Flew, a Fellow of the *Skeptical Inquirer*, cites, as an example of free will in action, a couple who decide to get married, there being no external compulsion for them to do so. This example would meet with little opposition from Flew's particular philosophical school.

But both examples are belied by common, universal experience. Did Sartre imagine that this hypothetical waiter could have been a prize fighter? Or an existentialist philosopher? Or a neuro-surgeon? A multiplicity of demonstrable genetic and environmental factors cuts the waiter's choice down to waiting or some equivalent to which his pyschological bent and intellectual capacity – along with his aims or lack of them – constrain him.

Flew attempts to stave off similar objections to his own example. He argues that even if behavioral psychologists should prove that the couple, due to their emotional involvement, could not have refrained from marrying, still, according to common usage of the word 'free', this couple, acting without external compulsion, were acting freely and therefore free will exists.

But all this proves is that, in this context, the word 'free' is meaningless. Take the exact opposite example of Flew's happily married couple; the classic case of unrequited love. Is the forlorn lover 'free' to stop caring for his uncooperative beloved? There is no external force compelling him to suffer. Surely, if 'free will' is so readily available, our unhappy lover need only avail himself of it.

The 1968 *Time* Magazine feature on astrology concludes:

The good astrologer senses the mood of his client, perceives his problems and finds the most positive way of fitting them into the context of his horoscope. Then he looks ahead, shaping his predictions so that they amount to constructive counsel. The client might have been better advised to consult a psychiatrist, marriage counsellor, physician, lawyer or employment agency. But there are many troubled people who refuse to accept personal responsibility for their lives, insisting that some outer force is in control . . .

Yet in this same issue of *Time*, an article describing an Israeli/ Egypt flare-up contends: 'These warnings served chiefly to illustrate the fact that violence has a momentum of its own . . .'

Can *Time* have it both ways? If violence has a momentum of its own, then the acceptance or non-acceptance of personal responsibility is irrelevant. And has the author of the astrology feature himself succeeded in accepting personal responsibility for his own life? If so, perhaps he would do well to stop wasting his time denigrating astrology for *Time* and instead walk over the water to the Middle East to teach them the secret. For it is obvious that if large numbers of people would accept personal responsibility for their lives, violence would no longer have a momentum of its own.

In a talk on the BBC, Dr Stephen Rose, a biologist, declared: 'The ways to change men's minds permanently are two and only two: by the use of rational argument, and by changing the structure of society. The two triumphs of humanity are man's capacity for rational thought and discussion, and his capacity to modify society.' In other words, Dr Rose is counseling the use of free will.

But in all of history we can think of no single instance of a man's mind (to say nothing of men's minds) permanently changed through rational discussion. Never in history has the volume and intensity of rational discussion been greater than at the present moment, and it has been going on for several centuries. Yet never before has triumphant mankind been faced simultaneously with the Bomb, chemical and bacteriological warfare, Star Wars, gross and uncontrollable over-population, imminent famine throughout much of the Third World, irre- versible world-wide pollution and destruction of the ecosystem everywhere, ubiquitous racial strife and, of course, that violence that has a momentum of its own. Indeed, the present moment would seem to stand as apodictic proof of humanity's helplessness, of the futility of rational discussion, and of our shameful incapacity to do anything to 'modify society' beyond degrade it still further.*

Does this mean, then, that there is no free will after all? Do we exist in a fantastically complex, but pre-determined web of cause-and-effect?

The Determinist Argument

This view is not uncommon in science or in philosophy. 'Uncertainty' (a kind of random free will) may attend events on the quantum level (see Culver and Ianna, p. 158) but above that all is predetermined. Cosmologists win Nobel Prizes for developing theories designed to prove that everything in the universe was set in motion and predetermined in the Big Bang, an event supposedly lasting three seconds. (Of course, this means that the prize-winning theory itself was also prefigured in those spectacular three seconds.) Though uncommon, a very similar view is sometimes expressed by astrologers. Philip Barford, an astrologer, declares:

> If as astrologers we accept the overall implications of any doctrine of cosmic harmony, then we have also to admit the implication of what we regard as evidence. The solar system is a functional whole, regulated by and manifesting ideal relationships on every

---

* It is true, over the past few years, there has been a political thaw between the superpowers, a growing sense of the importance of the environment throughout much of the world, and at least a few signs that humanity is not quite ready to commit suicide without a measure of resistance. But this has nothing to do with 'rational discussion' or with Dr Rose's imaginary 'ability to modify society'. It is merely an expression of the universal desire to live, and possibly a sign that the numbers of the frightened are beginning to encroach upon the preserves of the greedy and the mindless.

plane to which consciousness can ascend. At any single instant in the life of this system, the cosmic mechanism is manifesting a pattern of structural relations entirely and absolutely determined by the initial 'spin' imparted to it at the instant of its ideal conception. Astrologers often like to compromise by stating that astrology simply indicates the prevailing influences and opportunities within which we have freedom to choose between alternatives. This is absolutely inconsistent with the basic astrological principle. Any choice made in the conviction of free will is a moment expressing a predetermined cosmic pattern. Pragmatically, it is impossible to believe in free will and remain an astrologer. Logically, the doctrine of free will is a myth. Our only freedom is the intellectual recognition of necessity [1]. If this conclusion seems unpalatable, one can always reject the notion of cosmic harmony [2], and with it, any attempt to predict future events or to read character on the map.

Astrological Journal, vol. IV, no. 3, p. 10

But it is not that Mr Barford's conclusion is unpalatable; it is that, despite his pontifical tone, he stands self-condemned. In the very paragraph denying us free will we are already given two opportunities to use it: first, we are told (1) that our only freedom is the intellectual recognition of pre-determination which is already free will; and then (2) we are given the alternative of rejecting the notion of cosmic harmony, which is also free will.

Barford's argument is based upon a bizarre cosmology that would have 'consciousness' bring the solar system into being, impart to it its 'spin' and then vanish, presumably to create other equally cheerless systems. To be consistent, if the solar system is held to be a manifestation of consciousness, then consciousness with its concomitant free will would seem bound to be an attribute of the system itself. Clearly, we are also at liberty to use our free will in rejecting Barford's Newtonian notion of Divine Mechanics.

Equally inconsistent are the views of the well-known geneticist, C. D. Darlington:

> In genetics all behaviour is genetically determined, but it is also
> environmentally determined . . . the division of determination into
> two systems, genotype (the genetic make-up of the individual) and
> the environment, entails as a corollary the successive interaction of
> those two systems and the introduction of one into the other. It is
> this interaction which gives us the illusion of free will . . . a choice
> seems so to us because in every fresh contingency it is a new
> reaction of genotype and environment.
>
> *Genetics and Man*, 1964, p. 346

Here, those two famous woodland deities, Genotype and Environment, impart that initial 'spin'. Darlington presumes that
both these 'systems', though dynamic, are closed. To save
beating about the philosophical bush, to destroy this contention
it is enough to cite the experiments proving that, as the yogis
have always maintained, people can gain control over even their
involuntary functions. These conclusions are solidly buttressed
by many experiments with biofeedback, all corroborating our
ability to control our bodily systems by willing them faster or
slower; and, as further proof, the medical profession now
concedes that a change in 'attitude' can mean the difference
between life and death in otherwise terminal diseases. This
means that our personal 'environment' can be altered through
the exercise of will. Environment is not a closed system. The
future is therefore unpredictable, not because of its complexity,
but because of its very nature. And free will is not an
illusion.

On the other hand, as we have pointed out, humanity's
'great triumph' which is, according to Dr Rose, the capacity
to modify society, is reduced to absurdity by every daily newspaper.

It would appear, then, that we have free will and that we do
not have it, a situation summed up pithily by Schopenhauer,
who declared, 'Man has free will, but not the will to use it.'
Since this is a paradox, the contemporary philosopher may
dismiss it as nonsense, but to the unrequited lover it makes
perfect sense.

Free Will – Viewed Philosophically and Psychologically

The paradox is only apparent, and vanishes once the unnatural strictures of logic are abandoned. It is not a question of yes-or-no; yes, we have it, or no, we don't have it. Professor Darlington, above, in maintaining the absence of free will, unwittingly supplies the key to its existence. According to him, the 'illusion of free will' is caused by the interaction of genotype and environment. But if free will is an 'illusion', 'interaction' is not.

Yet what is 'interaction'? Certainly it is not genotype. Nor is it environment. It is not material, a thing. Nor is it energy, acting upon something. Yet it cannot be dismissed, for no matter how impalpable, no matter how unsusceptible to measurement, without it neither genotype nor environment would have any meaning; and neither could change.

'Interaction' is the mysterious 'Third Force' that is a necessary party to every event upon every level of the universe. In Hans Jenny's experiments will was represented by 'frequency'; between lover and beloved it is 'desire'; between the sculptor and the block of wood it is 'inspiration'; it is the Holy Spirit in the Divine Trinity fundamental to all traditions.

Will (the Third Force in Gurdjieff's terminology) manifests itself in values, which are registered by the emotions but are undetectable by the senses, and therefore dismissed by the logician and Rationalist.

Nevertheless, the universe, and all that is within it, presents itself to the Rationalist just as it does to the mystic or the artist – as a hierarchy of values.

If a Rationalist trips over a foot-stool he may, in a fit of pique, hurl it against the wall. So if he trips over his young daugher, to be logically consistent, he should do the same to her. But unless he is a very quick-thinking, and deeply principled Rationalist, though just as piqued, he will almost certainly not do so. He may even momentarily forget that Darwin decreed evolution free from principles of higher and lower. What has happened? Value, that which cannot be measured, replicated in the laboratory, or predicted has entered the Rationalist's life . . . luckily for his daughter.

Our lives are organized upon scales of value, and we cannot escape from that fact. The Rationalist values reason. The logician extols logic because the exercise of this useful but prosaic faculty affords him the keenest pleasure he is capable of experiencing. Both may argue that all values, including their own, are subjective, 'merely emotive', but this is itself a value judgement, and we are under no obligation, logical or otherwise, to accept it; or even to waste our time by worrying over such logical distinctions. For if values are by definition non-sense, then logic is by definition worth-less.

Meanwhile, who is to say that truths provided by the emotions are less trustworthy than truths provided by the senses? Yes, it is impossible to 'prove' emotional truths and it is impossible to shove these truths down unwilling throats. But the instruments used to prove data of the senses are no more than extensions of the senses themselves, and so are tautologies: the senses simply corroborate themselves. Scientists then assume that this data corresponds to the real physical world, and these assumptions are buttressed by mathematics that is often based upon hypotheses which themselves have no observable relationship to 'reality' at all. As many physicists and philosophers have pointed out (corroborating the ancient mystics) this sense-derived view of reality is in fact subjective, peculiar to our particular human observational faculties. Other observational faculties would present an altogether different picture of even physical reality (see p. 219).

If this is the case with 'knowledge' derived from the senses, then it is possible to say with a clear conscience that we know – if, indeed, we know anything at all – that Bach's Fourth Brandenburg Concerto is objectively a better piece of music than 'The Star-Spangled Banner'; that Chartres is objectively a better building than the New York Trade Center; that St Francis was objectively a better man than Hitler and that humanity lives on an objectively higher level of consciousness than a cabbage, which in turn lives at a higher level of consciousness than a stone. These conclusions, based upon common emotional experience, can be said to be quite as objective in their own way as the 'hard' experience of the senses, which of course is not 'hard' at all.

Our emotions tell us that levels exist. And all traditions teach that humanity's special purpose in the cosmic hierarchy is to ascend from the level we are born at to another and higher level. But there is nothing automatic or fortuitous about this process. An individual man or woman must recognize that levels exist and that the possibility and the necessity exist to go from one level to another. Obviously, if the process is not automatic, then it must be willed. For it to be willed we must have free will to some extent or another or we could not even begin to try.

As a matter of practical experience, we can say honestly, all else being equal, that we are 'free' to go and buy a newspaper now or wait and buy one ten minutes from now. But as a matter of equally indubitable experience, the bigot is not 'free' to recognize the Jew and Black as his equals; the Rationalist can live in Chartres for a month and come out railing against religion and singing the praises of rational discussion; the unrequited lover is chained to his misery with bonds more secure than a galley slave's; the hot-head cannot keep his temper; the lazy man finds a hundred good reasons not to do morning exercises; and, as *Time* so rightly observes, violence has a momentum of its own.

The question 'Do we have free will or do we not?' cannot be answered 'yes' or 'no'. Rather, we may say that, as long as our emotions are not involved, we have it. But no sooner do our emotions become involved than we lose it. And since, as a matter of common experience, our emotions are involved in all but the most trivial of our thoughts and actions, in effect we have no free will. Our actual position is that of dogs in a park, distracted by every smell – what is called 'strong will' (the billionaire's drive to go on accumulating money, or the politician's willingness to suffer any indignity or humiliation as long as it leads to power) is rarely more than a bloodhound on a particularly fragrant trail. We are not born free. We are born in chains, live in chains, and die in chains unless we wake up to the situation and attempt to extricate ourselves.*

Yet if the free will question is so readily approachable, why is it that it is everywhere misunderstood? How, in the face of the overwhelming evidence to the contrary, can people maintain that by means of rational discussion men's minds can be altered and society modified?

Perhaps because this illusion is flattering, because it makes them feel educated and magnanimous, and, above all, because it is comforting. For the actual emotional recognition of our true individual lack of free will is a sobering, even devastating experience. (Philosophical determinists, Rationalists and others may verbally deny free will, but in their private lives they behave just as does everyone else – as though they possessed it.)

Literature and Free Will

The question of free will, confined to philosophy, is little more than mental gymnastics. But once we personally and individually confront the reality of our lack of free will and the consequences this has in the conduct of our lives, the question becomes both central and poignant.

It also becomes confusing. If we are honest we will be forced to admit that most of our 'decisions' did not involve real choice. The schools we went to, the professions we went into, the mates we married or divorced – mostly we could not have done otherwise without in some sense going against our particular personal grain, or without involving us in alternatives that were

---

* St Augustine maintained that free will existed only in so far as man was free to choose 'salvation'. This is not another way of stating the fallacious arguments of Barford and Flew. St Augustine is rightly recognizing our normal lack of free will and maintaining that it exists for us only in so far as we are willing to embark upon the spiritual path whose ultimate goal is 'salvation' – a word that has been, unfortunately, irreparably debased but that, in its original sense, meant the return to and the union with the spiritual source of all that is; in the Christian context, God.

in some way painful, or damaging to our self-image, or counter to what others expected of us. Even so, it is next to impossible to overcome the conviction that *some* element of real choice was involved and introspection rarely allows us to isolate it since it is also next to impossible to view our own lives with sufficient objectivity. So where then can we look for practical answers?

Modern philosophy touches upon nothing relevant to our lives. Psychology is not much better. Experiments with rats, dogs and monkeys may tell us something about rats, dogs, monkeys and also about the sensitivity and the morals of the human beings that perform these experiments, but they teach us little about ourselves. But there is one place where the dilemma posed by free will can be usefully examined with at least a degree of objectivity and dispassion: literature, particularly Western literature.

Without undue oversimplification it might be said that almost every major dramatic situation in Western literature – from *Oedipus Rex* to Shakespeare's plays to Kafka's novels – unwittingly dramatizes the human predicament regarding free will; what literature reveals is our inability to act except according to pattern in circumstances that require the inner freedom to act otherwise.

The oppressive and compelling power that dramatic literature exercises over us is good evidence of the measure of its truthfulness. If we actually had free will at our beck and call we should find the trials and tribulations of most of our tragic heroes silly. But as it is, if we have any literary discrimination at all, we are repelled by the cheap 'happy end', by 'romances' and by 'entertainment', which in effect attribute unlimited free will to heroes and heroines who have earned none. We accept as 'real' the plight of the protagonist ensnared in his own personality and unable to avert his destiny, or even to alter his reaction towards his destiny – which would be a first major step in altering it. And yet the possibility is there, no matter how remote. Though we may know from the onset that Lear will die, that the three sisters will never get to Moscow, that K. will be forever denied entrance into the castle, were the possibility absent there would be no tension; and our belief in the situation would be suspended. Tension in literature is created by the pull of opposing possibilities.

Our Western dramatic protagonists waste their energy trying to alter external situations more often than not brought about by flaws in their own characters. Secular literature is largely concerned with will-less people, whose tragedy is that they are incapable of seeing themselves as they are. And we respond because, like Pogo's famous 'enemy', they are us. If Othello could see himself as something of an ass, there would be no tragedy.

Western literature provides an accurate if depressing picture of our effective lack of free will. Without quite being forced to face up to our own inner contradictions we can watch their results play out in the lives of fictional characters and perhaps even learn from them – at least we can come to a clearer understanding of the dilemma. But secular literature does not provide us with the means of solving it. What is missing from practically all of Western literature is the understanding of 'level'. The acquisition of free will involves an inner transformation, an ascent from our natural will-less state to higher planes where degrees of freedom may be exercised. This is the domain of sacred literature.

Sacred literature dramatizes the struggle to acquire a measure of free will. But since this struggle, the only true drama, takes place within us and there are few if any external manifestations of it, sacred literature is couched in allegorical or symbolic terms (Christ's Temptation in the Wilderness, *The Bhagavad Gita*, *The Conference of the Birds*) . . .

There is not much valid modern sacred literature, and our reaction to the sacred literature of the past is usually colored by our Church of Progress schooling. There, if we read these works at all, we read them as historical documents. More often than not they seem dull, incoherent, and perfectly irrelevant to our modern daily lives. But once they are seen in their true light, as dramatizations of the quest to acquire free will, as chronicles of the stages of the transformation of the soul, then every nuance of the story acquires the most intense meaning. That meaning is inner and eternal, and for those who understand what is at stake, the battles of Arjuna, of Horus and Seth, the quest of Bardasanes for 'the pearl of great price' can be as vivid today as they were in the distant past.

Astrology, Free Will and 'Level'

The conviction that we *ought* to have free will is innate. The most zealous determinists and behaviorists behave as though they had it, just as does everyone else. The understanding that we do not have it is acquired only through bitter personal experience. Between the conviction that we ought to have it and the understanding that we do not have it lies the cerebral sandlot where philosophers like Antony Flew and astrologers like Philip Barford play at their childish games.

The ability to face the understanding that we do not have free will in any substantive sense is a precondition for embarking on the path of transformation. (Obviously, there is no point trying to acquire something we imagine we already possess.) The determination to realize the innate conviction that we could and should have free will represents a first step along that path. But both are possible only if we answer Yes to that fundamental philosophical question. Unless we believe that we are on this earth for a purpose, that we have specific spiritual possibilities, that we are not obliged to live out our lives at the mercy of our own emotional states (which in turn depend upon what other people think of us, upon the whims of fortune, upon the weather, the traffic, the line at the check-out counter, our mother-in-law, our bank balance and a hundred other factors all largely beyond our control), there is no point in embarking upon any of this inner work. But if we answer Yes to that question, then astrology may play an important, multi-faceted role in the quest. Let's look briefly at astrology's chief aspects in that light, in ascending order of consequence.

PREDICTION: The attraction of prediction (astrological or other) is nearly irresistible. As it stands it is probably a good thing that astrological prediction is as problematical as it is. If accurate, the good things will come to pass anyhow, but with no free will to speak of at our command, we are helpless to avert disasters, and may even bring them on by meddling with fate.

True, if astrological predictions really were substantially accurate *and* sufficiently specific, it might wake us up individually and collectively to our lack of free will – an experience that would prove salutary if sobering. On the other hand, even in our present condition, the right kind of warning under the right circumstances can certainly be useful. Most responsible astrologers avoid too much specificity – partly to avoid being wrong, partly to avoid the possibility of self-fulfilling prophecies, partly because the stars tend to presage trends, states or conditions rather than events. Forewarned is forearmed, and it is not altogether impossible to react constructively rather than blindly to accurately predicted difficult (or propitious) financial, domestic, romantic or physical times. But we leave open the question of the actual or possible accuracy of general predictions of this nature.

CHARACTER DELINEATION: No matter how accurate this may be, it is useless if all we are willing to hear is that we are geniuses. If we are to some degree realistic, then astrological counseling can serve a real purpose (as we have seen, even its critics acknowledge its value in that role). But if we embark seriously on the path to self-knowledge its value increases exponentially.

It is not that we can't get to know ourselves without astrology. After enough self-observation we will learn what our reaction will be when the stick is dropped. But, as we hope this book has convincingly demonstrated, there is an indisputable link between us and the heavens. The horoscope is the score of the particular and unique chord that is us. An interpretation by a skilled astrologer, or better yet, by the individual who has taken the trouble to acquire the skill to interpret his or her own chart, can be a profoundly rewarding and on-going experience.

There is something curiously satisfying about seeing both strengths and weaknesses prefigured in the stars. But what we do with this information depends entirely upon ourselves. Used wrongly, we simply justify our excesses and shortcomings. Used correctly, we may see – with a clarity difficult to acquire in any other way – the fundamental nature of the difficulties confronting us. This is what so many psychologists who use astrology in therapy have found. It seems easier to face those aspects of ourselves we would rather not acknowledge if we can see these unlovely traits corroborated by astrology. More important, if we understand what is involved in the process of inner awakening and transformation, the difficulties revealed by the chart become opportunities. The energy involved in a blazing temper need not manifest in destruction and estrangement – if it can be consciously channeled to constructive purposes. The stars reveal the qualities we are born with, and the difficulties with which we must contend. But because the stars are the embodiments of divine principles, and these principles have been recognized for thousands of years, the horoscope also contains, implicit within it, the inner nature of the individual transformational path or quest.

THE FAULT, DEAR BRUTUS: It is rare to find an anti-astrology tract that does not somewhere refer to the line from *Julius Caesar*: 'the fault, dear Brutus, is not in our stars, but in ourselves, that we are underlings.' By using this quote, Rationalists prove that they have read Shakespeare, or at least each other, and it lends specious credence to their belief that (despite the consistent use of astrological imagery and allusions throughout the body of his work) this greatest of Western secular writers did not believe in it either . . . not really. The point is actually moot, but few astrologers would disagree with Cassius in any case. Certainly, the fault that we are underlings is in ourselves. But the *kind* of underlings we are: *that* is in the stars. It is unlikely that Shakespeare would disapprove of that extrapolation of his thinking.

To accept the validity of an astrological reading of the

horoscope does not in any sense entail the refusal to accept responsibility for our lives. On the contrary, used correctly, the horoscope details the precise nature of those responsibilities. The horoscope is a map in four dimensions. It tells us what the heavens have bequeathed us by virtue of our moment of birth; the specific nature of the seed as it were. More important, it tells us what the heavens expect from us, since the nature of the seed necessarily implies its goal; its fruit. The sunflower seed will not become an oak tree, and the acorn will not become an orchid. Finally, and perhaps most important, for those interested in embarking upon this path, it may divulge the timing of the successive stages of transformation.

Initiatic Astrology in the Age of Aquarius

What the stars do *not* tell us is the extent of our desire to stop being underlings. That is to say, it is impossible to determine from the horoscope alone who may choose to acquire a measure of free will and who will not. (Qualities like tenacity, stubbornness, and a will to succeed may be detectable in the horoscope but are themselves no indication. Directed towards mundane goals these qualities will yield mundane rewards, and free will is not among these.) The ability to exercise free will is directly associated with the spiritual level achieved; the great masters, saints, yogis and shamans were in complete control of their emotional, intellectual and physical faculties. It is this, perhaps more than anything else, that distinguishes them from the rest of us. It follows that if the ability to exercise (or even acquire) free will cannot be deduced from the horoscope, then neither can the horoscope reveal the 'level' the individual was born at or has achieved.

Despite Darwin's famous disclaimer, we pay homage to the principle of level in innumerable mundane ways, and could barely function as human beings without it.

We would not say there was a difference of 'level' between one stone and another, or between one cabbage and another, or even between one dog and another. But who would say that the work of the skilled butcher takes place on the same 'level' as that of the skilled brain surgeon? Or that Escoffier's achievement was of the same order as Leonardo's? The potentiality to exist at different levels seems to be an exclusively human trait, shared by nothing else in nature as far as we can gather.

The reality of levels effectively underpins every judgement we make. In largely physical areas, level is easily determined. It takes little discernment to decide who is the strongest weight-lifter or the fastest sprinter, even though the quantitative differences between the leaders may be minute. But it is next to impossible to determine who is the most intelligent scientist or mathematician or the most accomplished and profound artist, composer or writer. Yet it is self-evident that there is a vast difference in level between best and worst in art and between the most and least intelligent in intellectual matters; a difference that is not simply quantitative. There are, as it were, orders or levels of intelligence and of understanding that defy quantification.

If we cannot create objective criteria for all that concerns 'level' in the normal course of daily life, it is hardly fair to expect astrology to produce them. And it does not. Though astrologers often try to apply hindsight to account for historically significant people, the truth is that they cannot do it on demand. Nothing in Hitler's horoscope would have revealed to an astrologer, in advance, that this man was to become an apotheosis of mediocrity, or that he would have the malignant power to infect an entire nation with his own pathological hatreds, fears and prejudices. Given Goethe's horoscope, the astrologer would predict an intelligent and imaginative man with a propensity for an impressive number of love affairs, but he would miss that one quality that makes Goethe worth reading today – genius.

But if level is not written into the horoscope, it is written into the individual. Astrologers might not be able to distinguish between mass murderers, average citizens, geniuses and saints on the basis of 'blind' horoscope readings. But astrology is no more a parlor game than microbiology, and on the practical, personal basis of normal astrological counseling, 'level' loses some of its mystery; indeed, within limits it imposes itself. An experienced professional astrologer can judge the level a client has attained and will counsel accordingly. A psychologist would do the same. The difference is that the astrologer has, as a starting reference point, the absolutely objective primary information provided by the horoscope; information unavailable from any other source and this is independent of any psychological self-portrait or history the client might furnish.

Thereafter, it is a matter of the accuracy of the reading and the willingness and/or ability of the client to act upon it. Understood in this light, and used in this fashion, astrology becomes the exact opposite of what its opponents imagine it to be: it is not an abdication of responsibility but its embrace. Without claiming that astrological character-delineation and counseling can be defended scientifically, we would say with some assurance that in the hands of a skilled practitioner it has considerable validity as an art. Though perhaps it does not advance knowledge of the 'real world out there' as Culver and Ianna call it; there can be no doubt that in the 'unreal' world inside, where people love and grieve and suffer and question it can, and often does, serve a very real function. But this is a matter for the jury to explore for themselves.

VI.

THE SUMMING UP

In developing our case for astrology, we explored five principal themes:

1) History. Drawing evidence from a number of sources, we challenged the reigning 'dreaming Chaldean' account of astrology's origins. Astrology was not initially a chaotic Babylonian superstition, subsequently rationalized or organized by the Greeks. Astrology is demonstrably much older, certainly predating Egypt. It is based upon the interplay of cosmic, Pythagorean numerological principles. Its original function was not as a dubious means of prediction, or even a method of character analysis. It was almost certainly initiatic; the efficacy of religious ceremonies and rituals was linked to the movements of the planets, and the positions of certain stars, in particular Sirius. We showed that while different systems of astrological practice prevail all over the world, the fundamental meanings ascribed to the planets are the same the world over, and probably refer back to that primordial astrology whose origins antedate recorded history.

2) Objections. We discussed all the major objections to astrology put forward by its opponents. We carefully distinguished between astrology's basic premise – that there is a correlation between events in the heavens and events on earth and that there is a correspondence between the position of planets at birth and the human personality – and astrology's practice as a means of predicting the future and analyzing character. We showed that *all* the objections pertaining to astrology's basic premise were unfounded. There is absolutely nothing in contemporary science that rules out astrology in principle. More-

over, there is a wealth of evidence proving the validity of astrology's premise.

Astrology as a practice was on much shakier ground, especially as a means for predicting the future. In particular, almost no scientific support has yet been found for the zodiac, the basis of practically all Westen astrological interpretation. Many tests have been designed, some by astrologers, seeking to establish the validity of the zodiac, and almost all have come up negative. At the same time, we argued that what astrology's opponents called disproof was mostly unproof. Astrology as a practice cannot be treated like geology or astronomy. An interpretive, or artistic, element is intrinsic to it. This does not mean astrological practice is false, or that it is a pseudoscience as its detractors claim; it means simply that it is not reducible to a hard science, any more than music is. Given the nature of the evidence so far compiled, it is still premature to say that astrology as a practice is invalid.

3) Evidence. We compiled, collated and discussed the formidable body of evidence supporting the astrological premise. This evidence comes from two sources:

i) Indirect evidence gathered from the various fields of science proving that correspondences exist between celestial and terrestrial events. Some of this evidence proves that both inorganic chemical reactions and living organisms are incredibly sensitive to minute fluctuations of the magnetic and electro-magnetic environment. Other experiments confirm the influence of the sun-spot cycle on a variety of earthly phenomena, and a number of researchers believe that the sun-spot cycle in turn might be keyed to the orbits of the planets. No one to date has been able to categorically prove that connection. Though most of this indirect evidence does not relate directly to astrology, it proves that the kind of correspondences claimed by astrologers are feasible *in principle* within the context of the scientifically validated physical world. A number of eminent scientists were quoted agreeing on this point.

ii) Direct evidence. This section was devoted mostly to the three decades of work by the French psychologist and statistician, Michel Gauquelin. In massive tests carried out in half a dozen countries, Gauquelin found that eminence in certain professions was related to the diurnal position of specific planets at birth. Never faulted in spite of repeated efforts by opponents; confirmed and validated by a number of independent authorities, Gauquelin's work effectively proves the validity of the oldest and most universal astrological belief: the meanings assigned to different planets and the personality types traditionally associated with those planets: Mars with athletes and soldiers, scientists with Saturn, writers with the moon, actors with Jupiter, among others. Gauquelin's work is Exhibit A in our defense. Until or unless discredited, Gauquelin's work alone proves the validity of the astrological premise; the correspondence between the position of the planets at the moment of birth and the human personality.

3a) We described a few provocative but not conclusive tests that appeared to validate astrological practice; the alleged ability of astrologers to delineate character on the basis of the horoscope alone. We also contended that many of the negative results to date may have been the result of tests too crudely tuned to isolate the astrological factors from the background noise. On the other hand, these negative tests made it clear that many astrological beliefs, in particular those related to the zodiacal signs, rising signs and aspects, were over-simplifications and had to be approached with new circumspection. The question of scientific validation remained open, but the astrologers had their work cut out for them if ever they hoped to establish it.

3b) Drawing upon the Cymatic work of Hans Jenny and the theories of the astronomer Dr Percy Seymour, we constructed a plausible scenario for astrology's *modus operandi*. We argued that the solar system was, above all, a true system whose interacting elements inescapably affected each other. Advances in modern science proved that the ancient Platonic concept of the 'Harmony of the Spheres' had to be taken lierally, not merely as a poetic image. Upon that understanding, the modern principle of Resonance provided the framework within which those proven astrological correspondences could be satisfactorily explained, at least in principle. This explanation in terms of Resonance routed the argument stubbornly reiterated by astrology's critics – that the magnitude of the forces 'exerted' by the planets was far too small to bring about those astrological correspondences. We showed that this argument was grounded solidly in the physics of the nineteenth century and was indefensible as science under any circumstances. Any lingering respectability that it might have had vanished altogether when astrology was studied within the context of an appropriate model: the concert hall rather than the hammer hitting the nail.

4) Heresy in the Church of Progress. We analyzed the campaign to discredit astrology by people calling themselves Rationalists (acting allegedly in the interests of truth on behalf of science). But the highly emotional nature of that opposition betrayed its true nature. Clearly something other than truth, reason or science was at stake. Upon close examination, Rationalism proved to be no more than a belief system in its own right, the credo of a debased religion largely devoted to proselytizing a gospel of negation – joyless, perverse, aimless, yet capable of retaining the allegiance of its adherents on psychological rather than intellectual, philosophical or scientific grounds. Proof of the validity of the astrological premise presupposes disproof of Rationalism, and the ultimate downfall of the Church of Progress, hence the intensity of the opposition.

5) Astrology as a practice. Though our defense is mainly concerned with astrology's premise, rather than its practice, its practice is what everyone is familiar with. So we looked briefly at the various aspects of contemporary astrological practice. Newspaper astrology was obviously devoid of value, but nobody ever really pretended otherwise. Astrological prediction was problematical at best, but there were too many recorded, spectacular, historical 'hits' to dismiss it altogether. On the other hand, astrological counseling, though more difficult to judge objectively, almost certainly served a useful function, particularly when allied to the less hidebound schools of psychological therapy. We touched upon the relationship between astrology and free will and level.

Conclusion

By looking at astrology in terms of level; by accepting its essential *qualitative* nature, and by looking closely into the demonstrable astrological content of ancient texts and myths, both the origins and the history of astrology present very different pictures from that officially endorsed by Establishment science.

At its most popular and debased level, there can be no doubt that astrology has been effectively superstition from the early Assyrian Empire to the present. But at the same time, it is also apparent that it has been astrology's Pythagorean and metaphysical basis that commended it to so many of the greatest minds of the past. We hope we have made that attraction clear and understandable.

Astrology on this level expresses the fundamental *order* and coherence of the universe. Astrology provided a *modus operandi* for studying the interchange between the solar system and fixed stars (those much-misunderstood 'gods' of the ancients) and humanity. Seen in this light, it may seem strange that modern scholarship, and in particular, modern science, should find astrology so absurd and abhorrent since it is committed in its entirety to the study of precisely that same order and coherence. For the universe is in every one of its manifestations and interchanges nothing but order and coherence – though that order and coherence is invariably the outcome or result of a fundamental drama in which the forces of order prevail over the forces of disorder. It is this drama that is the basis of so many of the Creation myths all over the world, in Egypt for example, expressed in the battles between Seth and Horus, and the Osirian cycle of death and rebirth.

But if disorder or randomness were the essential characteristic of our world, the norm as it were, and order merely an accident, there could be no science in any meaningful sense, since nothing would be measurable, repeatable or predictable – and measurability, repeatability and predictability are the cornerstones of the scientific method.

Yet, it is a fact that not a single one of astrology's many and vociferous foes addresses this aspect of astrology (astrology as a paradigm of cosmic order), while virtually every serious book that attempts to defend astrology within the framework of our modern understanding insists upon the existence, reality and validity of these metaphysical and Pythagorean principles.*

This impasse is probably beyond resolve. For it does not rest upon proof or disproof, the desire for objectivity, or even upon deliberate bad faith and stupidity on the part of astrology's opponents, though there is no shortage of either. It rests ultimately upon psychological factors, upon levels of understanding, and upon different – and diametrically opposed – ways of viewing the world.

Coda

Astrology studies the meaning of the cosmic moment, as it is revealed in the conjunctions and configurations of the planets against the symbolic background of the zodiac.

In this, astrology is an inquiry into the Third Force, or universal will. Just as Jenny's sound frequencies represented the will of the experimenter, and Mozart's music represents his genius or 'inspiration', which is directed will, so the magnetic and electro-magnetic frequencies produced by the planets represent the 'will' of the solar system. That we cannot perceive or measure this will is not surprising; we cannot perceive or measure our own. But we know we would have no music without it.

The birth chart (and doubtless the conception chart if it could ever be determined) represent the cosmic chords whose imprint we bear, or perhaps more accurately, whose imprint we *are*.

This brings us back full circle to that astrology of the

---

* The extreme science-oriented wing of astrology is an exception. Its proponents accept the scientific evidence as it stands but are as uncomprehending of the metaphysical implications as the skeptics.

ancients, in which the stars were equated with 'windows' or 'doors', and future financial windfalls and predicting the probable date of the demise of spouses were not paramount concerns. For the horoscope is also a map of potentiality.

The music of the spheres was understood, in all likelihood far better than it is now (since everything pertaining to the spiritual was understood better than it is now). And astrology not only served as a focus for acquiring self-knowledge. It also provided those on the path or way with objective celestially determined moments to perform rituals, ceremonies or meditative sessions that would open the way into the higher or divine principles symbolized by or embodied in the planets, fixed stars and probably the zodiac. This was why (according to Dr Charles Muses, see pp. 64–8) the Egyptians used the same glyph for the word 'star' as they did for 'window' or 'door' – the stars were 'openings'.

If we believe that the universe is a conscious creation and that humanity is on earth for a purpose, then whatever serves that purpose is practical (whatever does not serve that purpose is at best a waste of time, at worst, evil – that which does not further). Knowledge of that purpose is science; Sacred Science. There cannot be the slightest doubt that this science of order, purpose, meaning and the transformation of the carnal or material into the spiritual was what once prevailed on earth. For a civilization to be worthy of the name, it must be based upon a sacred science. Through the efforts of a number of brilliant scholars over the past couple of centuries, key elements of the lost sacred science have been rediscovered or reformulated. Astrology was one branch of this science. Our main concern in this book has been to convince the jury that the ancients initially responsible for the development of astrology, whoever they may have been, knew exactly what they were doing. Whatever reservations may attend the modern practice of astrology, its basic premise – that correlations exist between events in the heavens and events on earth, and that there is a correspondence between the position of the planets at birth and the human personality – has been demonstrated beyond any possible doubt. The validity of the basic premise of astrology presupposes a universe in which consciousness, meaning and order are written into the fabric of its creation – as all traditional religions and societies have always insisted. And in this universe, on this particular planet, humanity has been placed for a reason; with unique privileges and unique responsibilities. In ancient times, astrology was one of the sciences that provided insight into the divine forces responsible for creation. It also provided those who understood its laws with the guidelines for carrying out their pre-ordained responsibilities, that inner transformation of the carnal, material and merely rational beings they were by birth into the spiritual beings we all are by birthright. There is reason to believe that astrology may once again play that role in the civilization of the future.

The defense rests.

Appendix

186 Signers of the Anti-Astrology Manifesto, 'Objections to Astrology'

NOBEL PRIZE-WINNERS

Hans A. Bethe, *professor emeritus of physics, Cornell*

Sir Francis Crick, *Medical Research Council, Cambridge, Eng.*

Sir John Eccles, *distinguished professor of physiology and biophysics, SUNY at Buffalo*

Gerhard Herzberg, *distinguished research scientist, National Research Council of Canada*

Wassily Leontief, *professor of economics, Harvard University*

Konrad Lorenz, *univ. prof., Austrian Academy of Sciences*

André M. Lwoff, *honorary professor, Institut Pasteur, Paris*

Sir Peter Medawar, *Medical Research Council, Middlesex, Eng.*

Robert S. Milliken, *dist. prof. of chemistry, Univ. of Chicago*

Jacques Monod, *Institut Pasteur, Paris*

Linus C. Pauling, *professor of chemistry, Stanford University*

Edward M. Purcell, *Gerhard Gade univ. prof., Harvard Univ.*

Paul A. Samuelson, *professor of economics, MIT*

Julian Schwinger, *professor of physics, Univ. of Calif., Los Angeles*

Glenn T. Seaborg, *univ. professor, Univ. of Calif., Berkeley*

J. Tinbergen, *professor emeritus, Rotterdam, The Netherlands*

N. Tinbergen, *emer. professor of animal behavior, Oxford Univ.*

Harold C. Urey, *professor emeritus, Univ. of Calif., San Diego*

George Wald, *professor of biology, Harvard University*

George O. Abell, *chmn., Dept. of Astron., Univ. of Calif., Los Angeles*

Lawrence H. Adler, *professor, Univ. of Calif., Los Angeles*

Edoardo Amaldi, *prof. of physics, University of Rome*

Richard Berendzen, *dean Coll. of Arts and Sci., American Univ.*

William P. Bidelman, *professor, Case Western Reserve Univ.*

Jacob Bigeleisen, *professor, University of Rochester*

D. Scott Birney, *prof. of astronomy, Wellesley College*

Karl-Heinz Böhm, *professor, University of Washington*

Lyle B. Borst, *prof. of physics and astronomy, SUNY at Buffalo*

Peter B. Boyce, *staff astronomer, Lowell Observatory*

Harvey Brooks, *professor of technology and public policy, Harvard*

William Buscombe, *prof. of astronomy, Northwestern Univ.*

Eugene R. Capriotti, *prof. of astronomy, Ohio State Univ.*

H. E. Carter, *coord. of interdisciplinary programs, Univ. of Arizona*

J. W. Chamberlain, *prof. of astronomy, Rice University*

Von Del Chamberlain, *Smithsonian Institution*

S. Chandrasekhar, *prof. of astronomy, Univ. of Chicago*

Mark R. Chartrand III, *chmn., Hayden Planetarium*

Hong-Yee Chiu, *NASA*

Preston Cloud, *prof. of geology, Univ. of Calif., Santa Barbara*

Peter S. Conti, *prof. of astrophysics, Univ. of Colorado*

Allan F. Cook II, *astrophysicist, Smithsonian Observatory*

Alan Cottrell, *master, Jesus College, Cambridge, England*

Bryce Crawford, Jr., *prof. of chemisty, Univ. of Minnesota*

David D. Cudaback, *research astronomer, Univ. of Calif., Berkeley*

A. Dalgarno, *prof. of astronomy, Harvard*

Hallowell Davis, *Central Inst. for the Deaf, Univ. City, Mo.*

Morris S. Davis, *prof. of astronomy, Univ. of No. Carolina*

Peter van de Kamp, *director emeritus, Sproul Observatory*

A. H. Delsemme, *prof. of astrophysics, Univ. of Toledo*

Robert H. Dicke, *Albert Einstein prof. of science, Princeton*

Bertram Donn, *head, Astrochemical Branch, Goddard Space Center, NASA*

Paul Doty, *prof. of biochemistry, Harvard*

Frank D. Drake, *dir. Natl. Astron. and Ionosphere Ctr., Cornell*

Lee A. DuBridge, *pres. emeritus, Calif. Inst. of Technology*

Harold Edgerton, *professor, MIT*

H. K. Eichhorn-von Wurmb, *chmn., Dept. of Astron., Univ. of South Florida*

R. M. Emberson, *dir. Tech. Services Inst. of Electrical and Electronics Engineers*

Howard W. Emmons, *prof. of mechanical engineering, Harvard*

Eugene E. Epstein, *staff scientist, The Aerospace Corp.*

Henry Eyring, *distinguished prof. of chemistry, Univ. of Utah*

Charles A. Federer, Jr., *president, Sky Pub. Corp.*

Robert Fleischer, *Astronomy Section, National Science Foundation*

Henry F. Fliegel, *technical staff, Jet Propulsion Laboratory*

William A. Fowler, *institute prof. of physics, Calif. Inst. of Tech.*

Fred A. Franklin, *astronomer, Smithsonian Astrophysical Observatory*

Laurence W. Fredrick, *prof. of astronomy, Univ. of Virginia*

Tom Gehrels, *Lunar and Planetary Lab., Univ. of Arizona*

Riccardo Giacconi, *Center for Astrophysics, Cambridge, Mass.*

Owen Gingerich, *prof. of astronomy, Harvard*

Thomas Gold, *professor, Cornell*

Leo Goldberg, *director, Kitt Peak National Observatory*

Maurice Goldhaber, *Brookhaven National Laboratory*

Mark A. Gordon, *Natl. Radio Astronomy Observatory*

Jesse L. Greenstein, *prof. of astrophysics, Calif. Inst. of Tech.*

Kenneth Greisen, *prof. of physics, Cornell*

Howard D. Greyber, *consultant, Potomac, Md.*

Herbert Gursky, *astrophysicist, Smithsonian Institution*

John P. Hagen, *chmn., Dept. of Astronomy, Penn. State Univ.*

Philip Handler, *president, National Academy of Sciences*

William K. Hartmann, *Planetary Science Inst., Tucson, Arizona*

Leland J. Haworth, *spec. assist. to the pres., Associated Univs.*

Carl Heiles, *prof. of astronomy, Univ. of Calif., Berkeley*

A. Heiser, *director, Dyer Observatory, Vanderbilt University*

H. L. Helfer, *prof. of astronomy, Univ. of Rochester*

George H. Herbig, *astronomer, Lick Observatory, Univ. of Calif.*

Arthur A. Hoag, *astronomer, Kitt Peak Natl. Observatory*

Paul W. Hodge, *prof. of astronomy, Univ. of Washington*

Dorrit Hoffleit, *director, Maria Mitchell Observatory*

William E. Howard III, *Natl. Radio Astronomy Observatory*

Nancy Houk, *Dept. of Astronomy, Univ. of Michigan*

Fred Hoyle, *fellow, St. John's College, Cambridge Univ.*

Icko Iben, Jr., *chmn., Dept. of Astronomy, Univ. of Illinois*

John T. Jefferies, *director, Inst. of Astronomy, Univ. of Hawaii*

Frank C. Jettner, *Dept. of Astronomy, SUNY at Albany*

J. R. Jokipii, *prof. of planetary sciences, Univ. of Arizona*

Kenneth Kellermann, *Nat. Radio Astronomy Observatory*

Joost H. Kiewiet de Jonge, *assoc. prof. of astron., Univ. of Pittsburgh*

Ivan R. King, *prof. of astron., Univ. of Calif., Berkeley*

Rudolph Kompfner, *professor emeritus, Stanford University*

William S. Kovach, *staff scientist, General Dynamics/Convair*

M. R. Kundu, *prof. of astronomy, Univ. of Maryland*

Lewis Larmore, *dir. of tech., Office of Naval Research*

Kam-Ching Leung, *dir., Behlen Observatory, Univ. of Nebraska*

I. M. Levitt, *dir. emer., Fels Planetarium of Franklin Institute*

C. C. Lin, *professor, MIT*

Albert P. Linnell, *professor, Michigan State Univ.*

M. Stanley Livingston, *Dept. of Physics, MIT*

Frank J. Low, *research prof., Univ. of Arizona*

Willem J. Luyten, *Univ. of Minnesota*

Richard E. McCrosky, *Smithsonian Astrophysical Observatory*

W. D. McElroy, *Univ. of Calif., San Diego*

Carl S. Marvel, *prof. of chemistry, Univ. of Arizona*

Margaret W. Mayall, *consul., Am. Assoc. of Variable Star Obser.*

Nicholas U. Mayall, *former dir., Kitt Peak Natl. Observatory*

Donald H. Menzel, *former director, Harvard College Observatory*

Alfred H. Mikesell, *Kitt Peak Natl. Observatory*

Freeman D. Miller, *prof. of astronomy, Univ. of Michigan*

Alan T. Moffet, *prof. of radio astron., Calif. Inst. of Technology*

Delo E. Mook, *assist. prof. of physics and astronomy, Dartmouth*

Marston Morse, *prof. emer., Inst. for Adv. Study, Princeton*

G. F. W. Mulders, *former head, Astron. Section, NSF*

Guido Münch, *prof. of astronomy, Calif. Inst. of Technology*

Edward P. Ney, *regents prof. of astronomy, Univ. of Minn.*

J. Neyman, *director, statistical lab., Univ. of Calif., Berkeley*

C. R. O'Dell, *project scientist, Large Space Telescope, NASA*

John A. O'Keefe, *Goddard Space Flight Center, NASA*

J. H. Oort, *dir., University Observatory, Leiden, Netherlands*

Tobias C. Owen, *prof. of astronomy, SUNY at Stony Brook*

Eugene N. Parker, *prof. of physics and astron., Univ. of Chicago*

Arno A. Penzias, *Bell Laboratories*

A. Keith Pierce, *solar astronomer, Kitt Peak Natl. Observatory*

Daniel M. Popper, *professor of astronomy, UCLA*

Frank Press, *prof. of geophysics, MIT*

R. M. Price, *radio spectrum manager, Natl. Science Foundation*

William M. Protheroe, *prof. of astronomy, Ohio State University*

John D. G. Rather, *Dept. of Astronomy, Univ. of Calif., Irvine*

Robert S. Richardson, *former assoc. dir., Griffith Observatory*

A. Marguerite Risley, *prof. emer., Randolph-Macon College*

Franklin E. Roach, *astronomer, Honolulu, Hawaii*

Walter Orr Roberts, *Aspen Inst. for Humanistic Studies*

William W. Roberts, Jr., *associate prof., Univ. of Virginia*

R. N. Robertson, *Australian National Univ.*

James P. Rodman, *prof. of astronomy, Mt. Union College*

Bruno Rossi, *prof. emeritus, MIT*

E. E. Salpeter, *professor, Cornell University*

Getrude Scharff-Goldhaber, *physicist, Brookhaven Natl. Lab.*

John D. Schopp, *prof. of astronomy, San Diego State University*

Julian J. Schreur, *prof. of astronomy, Valdosta State College*

E. L. Scott, *professor, University of California, Berkeley*

Frederick Seitz, *president, The Rockefeller Unversity*

C. D. Shane, *Lick Observatory*

Alan H. Shapley, *U.S. Dept. of Commerce, NOAA*

Frank H. Shu, *assoc. prof. of astronomy, Univ. of Calif., Berkeley*

Bancroft W. Sitterly, *prof. of physics emer., American Univ.*

Charlotte M. Sitterly, *Washington, D.C.*

B. F. Skinner, *prof. emeritus, Harvard*

Harlan J. Smith, *dir., McDonald Observ., Univ. of Texas, Austin*

Sabatino Sofia, *staff scientist, NASA*

František Šorm, *professor, Institute of Organic Chemistry, Prague, Czech.*

G. Ledyard Stebbins, *prof. emeritus, Univ. of Calif.*

C. Bruce Stephenson, *prof. of astronomy, Case Western Reserve*

Walter H. Stockmayer, *prof. of chemistry, Dartmouth*

Marshall H. Stone, *professor, University of Massachusetts*

N. Wyman Storer, *prof. emeritus of astronomy, Univ. of Kansas*

Hans E. Suess, *prof. of geochemistry, Univ. of Calif., San Diego*

T. L. Swihart, *prof. of astronomy, Univ. of Arizona*

Appendix

Pol Swings, *Institut d'Astrophysique, Esneux, Belgium*

J. Szentágothai, *Semmelweis Univ. Med. School, Budapest*

Joseph H. Taylor, Jr., *assoc. prof. of astronomy, Univ. of Mass.*

Frederick E. Terman, *vice-pres. and provost emeritus, Stanford*

Yervant Terzian, *assoc. prof. of space science, Cornell*

Patrick Thaddeus, *Inst. for Space Studies, New York, N.Y.*

Kip S. Thorne, *prof. of theor. physics, Calif. Inst. of Technology*

Charles R. Tolbert, *McCormick Observ., Charlottesville, Va.*

Alar Toomre, *prof. of applied mathematics, MIT*

Merle A. Tuve, *Carnegie Institution of Washington*

S. Vasilevskis, *emer. prof. of astronomy, Univ. of Calif., Santa Cruz*

Maurice B. Visscher, *emer. prof. of physiology, Univ. of Minn.*

Joan Vorpahl, *Aerospace Corp., Los Angeles*

Campbell M. Wade, *Natl. Radio Astronomy Observatory*

N. E. Wagman, *emer. dir., Allegheny Observatory, Univ. of Pittsb.*

George Wallerstein, *prof. of astronomy, Univ. of Washington*

Fred L. Whipple, *Phillips astronomer, Harvard*

Hassler Whitney, *professor, Inst. for Advanced Study, Princeton*

Adolf N. Witt, *prof. of astronomy, Univ. of Toledo*

Frank Bradshaw Wood, *prof. of astronomy, University of Florida*

Charles E. Worley, *astronomer, U.S. Naval Observatory*

Jeffries Wyman, *Instituto Regina Elena, Rome*

Chi Yuan, *assoc. prof. of physics, CCNY*

Bibliography

Historical books which openly or implicitly uphold the accepted scholarly view of astrology:

Berthelot, R., *La Pensée d'Asie et l'astrobiologie*, Paris, 1938

Bok, Bart J. and Jerome, Lawrence E., *Objections to Astrology*, Prometheus Books, Buffalo, NY, 1976

Culver, R. B. and Ianna, P. A., *The Gemini Syndrome: A Scientific Evaluation of Astrology*, Prometheus Books, Buffalo, NY, 1984

Cumont, Franz, *Astrology and Religion Among the Greeks and Romans*, Dover, 1912

Edwards, I. E. S., *The Pyramids of Egypt,* Penguin Books, 1961

Eisler, Robert, *The Royal Art of Astrology*, Herbert Joseph, 1946. (See Eisler's bibliography for a complete list of the scholarly works on the history of astrology)

Graubard, Mark, *Astrology's Demise and its Bearing on the Decline and Death of Beliefs*, Osiris, 1958

Koestler, A., *The Sleepwalkers*, Hutchinson, 1968

Neugebauer, O., *The Exact Sciences in Antiquity*, Brown University Press, 1957; and van Hoesen, *Greek Horoscopes*, American Philosophical Society, vol. 48, 1959

Ronan, C., *Changing Views of the Universe*, Eyre and Spottiswoode, 1966

Thompson, R. C. (ed.), *The Reports of the Magicians and Astrologers of Nineveh and Babylon*, Luzac, 1900

Historical books which openly (or inadvertently) support the traditional view of astrology:

Antoniadi, E. M., *L'Astronomie Égyptienne*, Paris, 1934

Bibliography

Campbell, Joseph, *The Hero with a Thousand Faces*, World Publishing Co., 1968

deGrazia, A. (ed.), *The Velikovsky Affair*, Sidgwick and Jackson, 1966

Ghalioungui, P., *Magic and Medical Science in Ancient Egypt*, Hodder and Stoughton, 1963

Guenon, R., *The Reign of Quantity*, Luzac, 1946

Hodson, F. R. (ed.), *The Place of Astronomy in the Ancient World*, A Joint Symposium of the Royal Society and the British Academy, Oxford University Press, 1974

Irwin, R. A., *The Problem of Ezekiel*, Chicago, 1943

Musaios (Dr Charles Muses), *The Lion Path: Or You Can Take It With You*, Golden Scepter (US), 1985

Plato, *The Timaeus*

Plotinus, *The Enneads*

Schmidt, Wilhelm, *Beginnings of Religion*, Methuen, 1933

Schwaller de Lubicz, Isha, *Her-Bak, Her-Bak, Disciple*, Hodder and Stoughton, London, 1954 (US, Inner Traditions International)

Schwaller de Lubicz, R. A., *Le Temple de l'homme* (3 vols.), Dervy Livres, Paris; *Sacred Science, The Temple in Man, The Egyptian Miracle*, Inner Traditions International (US), 1982

Tomaschek, R., *Tradition und Fortschritt in Klassischen Astrologie*, Ebertin Verlag

Velikovsky, I., *Worlds in Collision*, 1950, *Ages in Chaos*, 1953, *Earth in Upheaval*, Doubleday (US), 1956

Books relating to astrology's Pythagorean principles and symbolism:

Bell, E. T., *The Magic of Numbers*, McGraw-Hill, 1946

Bennett, J. G., *The Dramatic Universe*, Hodder and Stoughton, 1956

Collin, Rodney, *The Theory of Celestial Influence*, Stuart and Watkins, 1955

Fulcanelli, *Le Mystère des cathédrales*, Neville Spearman, 1971

Ghyka, Matila, *The Geometry of Art and Life*, Sheed, 1958; *Essai sur le rythme*, Gallimard, 1938; *Le Nombre d'or*, Gallimard, 1931

Harré, Rom, *The Anticipation of Nature*, Hutchinson, 1965 (for a critique of the 'Neo-Pythagoreanism' of Eddington, etc.)

Hauschka, R., *The Nature of Substance*, Stuart and Watkins, 1966

Iamblichus (attributed), *The Theology of Arithmetic*, tr. Robin Waterfield, Phanes Press, 1988 (US)

Jenny, Hans, *Cymatics*, Basilius Press, Basel, 1966

Kepler, J., *Prodromus Dissertationum Cosmographicarum seu Mysterium Cosmographicum* (Kepler's early work in which he believed he had found the relationship between the perfect solids and the orbits and velocities of the planets), translated from the Latin by R. A. Schwaller de Lubicz in *The Egyptian Miracle*

Kramrish, Stella, *The Hindu Temple*, Univ. of Calcutta, 1946

Lawlor, Robert, *Sacred Geometry*, Thames and Hudson (UK), Crossroad (US), 1982

McClain, Ernest, *The Pythagorean Plato; The Myth of Invariance*, Nicolas Hays (US), 1976

Michell, J., *The Dimensions of Paradise*, Harper and Row (US), 1988

Ouspensky, P. D., *In Search of the Miraculous*, 1950; *A New Model of the Universe*, Routledge and Kegan Paul, 1931

Pettigrew, J. B., *Design in Nature*, Longman, 1908

Senard, M., *Le Zodiaque*, Lausanne, 1948

Thompson, D'Arcy Wentworth, *On Growth and Form*, Cambridge, 1917

West, John Anthony, *Serpent in the Sky: The High Wisdom of Ancient Egypt*, Julian Press, 1987 (US)

Whyte, L. L. (ed.), *Aspects of Form*, Lund Humphries, 1951

Young, Arthur M., *The Reflexive Universe, The Geometry of Meaning*, Delacorte (US)

Books on the techniques of astrology:

Carter, C. E. O., *The Principles of Astrology*, Theosophical Publishing House, 5th ed., 1963; *Astrological Aspects; an Encyclopaedia of Psychological Astrology*, Theosophical Publishing House, 1963

Davidson, Ronald C., *Astrology*, Arco Handbooks (a particularly lucid, concise and reasonably priced manual)

Ptolemy, C., *Tetrabiblos*, translated from the Greek paraphrase by Proclus by J. M. Ashmand, 1822; Foulsham edition, 1917

Bibliography

Books pertaining to the evidence for astrology:

Dean, Geoffrey and Mather, Arthur, *Recent Advances in Natal Astrology: A Critical Review*, Analogic (Australia), 1977

Dewey and Dakin, *Cycles: The Science of Prediction*, Holt, 1950

Eysenck, H. J. and Nias, D. K., *Astrology: Science or Superstition?*, Maurice Temple Smith (UK), 1982

Fyfe, A., *Moon and Plant*, Society for Cancer Research, 1968

Gauquelin, M., *Cosmic Influences on Human Behavior*, Garnstone (UK), 1973; *Birthtimes*, Hill and Wang (US), 1983 (in UK), *The Truth About Astrology*); *Written in the Stars*, Aquarian Press, 1988. (See Gauquelin's bibliographies for extensive lists of scientific works establishing celestial–terrestrial correlations)

Huntington, E., *Mainsprings of Civilization*, J. Wiley, 1945

Piccardi, G., *The Chemical Basis of Medical Climatology*, C. T. Thomas, 1962

Seymour, Percy, *Astrology: The Evidence of Science*, Lennard Publishing (UK), 1988

Books pertaining in one way or another to the dispute variously described as 'The Two Cultures' or as 'Science vs. Religion', but which may perhaps be regarded more precisely as 'Materialism vs. Tradition'. The materialistic point of view:

Ayer, A. J., *Language, Truth and Logic*, Gollancz, 1936; *The Problem of Knowledge*, Macmillan, 1956

Calvin, John, *Institutes of the Christian Religion*, 1540

Darlington, C. D., *Genetics and Man*, Allen and Unwin, 1964

Darwin, Charles, *The Origin of Species*, 1859

Haldane, J. B. S., *Science and Life: Essays of a Rationalist*, Barrie and Rockliffe, 1968

Hitler, A., *Mein Kampf*, 1925

Lenin, V. I., *Imperialism*, 1917

Locke, John, *Essay Concerning Human Understanding*, 1690

Medawar, P. B., *The Future of Man*, Methuen, 1960; *The Art of the Soluble*, Methuen, 1967

Milton, John, *Paradise Lost*, 1667

Monod, Jacques, *Chance and Necessity*, Penguin, 1971

Ogden, C. K. and Richards, I. A., *The Meaning of Meaning*, Routledge and Kegan Paul, 1956

Russell, Bertrand, *Why I am Not a Christian*, Watts, 1927; *Mysticism and Logic* (Philosophical Essays), Longman, 1910; *Autobiography*, vol. I, Allen and Unwin, 1967

Ryle, G., *The Concept of Mind*, Hutchinson, 1949

Sartre, J. P., *Being and Nothingness*, 1949; *Existentialism and Humanism*, Methuen, 1948

Swift, Jonathan, *Gulliver's Travels*, 1726

Ziman, John, *Public Knowledge: The Social Dimension of Science*, Cambridge, 1966

Books opposing materialism and/or supporting tradition, the 'New Physics' and anti-Darwinian evolution:

Abercrombie, L. Johnson, *The Anatomy of Judgement*, Faber, 1965

Augustine, St, *Confessions*; *The City of God*, Penguin, 1972

Barzun, J., *Science: The Glorious Entertainment*, Secker and Warburg (UK), 1969

Bennett, J. G., *The Crisis in Human Affairs*, Hodder and Stoughton (UK), 1948

Bodley, John H., *Victims of Progress*, Benjamin Cummings, 1982

Bohm, David, *Wholeness and the Implicate Order*, Ark (UK), 1983; and F. David Peat, *Science, Order and Creativity*, Bantam (US), 1987

Briggs, John P. and Peat, F. David, *Looking Glass Universe*, Simon and Schuster (US), 1984

Capra, Fritjof, *The Tao of Physics*, Wildwood (UK), 1975

Davies, Paul, *The Cosmic Blueprint*; *Superforce: The Search for a Grand Unified Theory of Nature*; *God and the New Physics*, Simon & Schuster (US)

Eckhart, Meister, translated by C. de B. Evans, Stuart and Watkins (UK), 1963

Gleick, James, *Chaos: Making a New Science*, Viking (US), 1987

Grene, Marjorie, *The Knower and the Known*, Faber, 1966

Griffin, David Ray (ed.), *The Re-enchantment of Science: Postmodern Proposals*, SUNY Press (US), 1987

Hardy, Alister, *The Living Stream*; *The Divine Flame*, Collins (UK), 1965

Bibliography

Heller, Erich, *The Disinherited Mind*, Meridian (US), 1959

Hudson, Liam, *Contrary Imagination*, Methuen (UK), 1966

Huxley, Aldous, *The Perennial Philosophy*, Collins (UK), 1958

Jahn, Robert G. and Dunne, Brenda J., *Margins of Reality: The Role of Consciousness in the Physical World*, Harcourt, Brace, Jovanovitch (NY), 1987

James, William, *The Varieties of Religious Experience*, Macmillan (US), 1961

Kafka, Franz, *The Trial*; *The Castle*

Kierkegaard, Søren, *Journals*

Koestler, A. (ed.), *Beyond Reductionism*, Hutchinson (UK), 1969

Lovelock, James, *Gaia*, Oxford University Press, 1987

Nicoll, Maurice, *Living Time*, Vincent Stuart, 1951

Polkinghorne, John, *Science and Creation: The Search for Understanding*, New Science Library, Shambhala (US)

Russell, E. S., *The Directiveness of Organic Activity*, University Press, Cambridge, 1945

Schroedinger, I., *What is Life?*, Cambridge, 1962

Sheldrake, Rupert, *A New Science of Life: the Hypothesis of Formative Causation*, Tarcher (US), 1981; *The Presence of the Past, Morphic Resonance and the Habits of Nature*, Times Books (US), 1988

Tricker, R. A. R., *The Assessment of Speculative Science*, Mills and Boon (UK), 1965

von Uexkull, J., *Theoretical Biology*, 1926

Wald, George, *Synthesis of Science and Religion: Critical Essays and Dialogues*, Bhaktivedanta Institute, 1988

Weber, Renée (ed.), *Dialogues with Scientists and Sages*, Routledge and Kegan Paul (UK), 1986

Whitehead, A. N., *Adventure of Ideas*, Cambridge, 1933

Zukav, Gary, *The Dancing Wu-Li Masters*, William Morrow, 1978

Indexes

Index

Names Index

Names Index

ARKANA – NEW-AGE BOOKS FOR MIND, BODY AND SPIRIT

A selection of titles

With over 200 titles currently in print, Arkana is the leading name in quality new-age books for mind, body and spirit. Arkana encompasses the spirituality of both East and West, ancient and new, in fiction and non-fiction. A vast range of interests is covered, including Psychology and Transformation, Health, Science and Mysticism, Women's Spirituality and Astrology.

If you would like a catalogue of Arkana books, please write to:

Arkana Marketing Department
Penguin Books Ltd
27 Wright's Lane
London W8 5TZ

ARKANA – NEW-AGE BOOKS FOR MIND, BODY AND SPIRIT

A selection of titles

The Revised Waite's Compendium of Natal Astrology
Alan Candlish

This completely revised edition retains the basic structure of Waite's classic work while making major improvements to accuracy and readability.

Aromatherapy for Everyone   Robert Tisserand

The therapeutic value of essential oils was recognized as far back as Ancient Egyptian times. Today there is an upsurge in the use of these fragrant and medicinal oils to soothe and heal both mind and body. Here is a comprehensive guide to every aspect of aromatherapy by the man whose name is synonymous with its practice and teaching.

Tao Te Ching   The Richard Wilhelm Edition

Encompassing philosophical speculation and mystical reflection, the *Tao Te Ching* has been translated more often than any other book except the Bible, and more analysed than any other Chinese classic. Richard Wilhelm's acclaimed 1910 translation is here made available in English.

The Book of the Dead   E. A. Wallis Budge

Intended to give the deceased immortality, the Ancient Egyptian *Book of the Dead* was a vital piece of 'luggage' on the soul's journey to the other world, providing for every need: victory over enemies, the procurement of friendship and – ultimately – entry into the kingdom of Osiris.

Yoga: Immortality and Freedom   Mircea Eliade

Eliade's excellent volume explores the tradition of yoga with exceptional directness and detail.

'One of the most important and exhaustive single-volume studies of the major ascetic techniques of India and their history yet to appear in English' – *San Francisco Chronicle*

ARKANA – NEW-AGE BOOKS FOR MIND, BODY AND SPIRIT

CONTEMPORARY ASTROLOGY – A NEW SERIES IN ARKANA

Series Editor: Howard Sasportas

The ancient science of astrology, founded on the correlation between celestial movements and terrestrial events, recognizes the universe as an indivisible whole in which all parts are interconnected. Mirroring this perception of the unity of life, modern physics has revealed the web of relationship underlying everything in existence. Despite the inevitable backlash as old paradigms expire, we are now entering an age where scientific explanations and models of the cosmos are in accord with basic astrological principles and beliefs. In such a climate, astrology is poised to once again emerge as a serious tool for a greater understanding of our true nature. In readable books written by experts, Arkana's *Contemporary Astrology* series offers all the insight and practical wisdom of the newest vanguard of astrological thought.

Titles already published or in preparation

The Gods of Change: Pain, Crisis and the Transits of Uranus, Neptune and Pluto Howard Sasportas

A Handbook of Medical Astrology Jane Ridder-Patrick

Character and Fate: The Psychology of the Birthchart Katharine Merlin

Chiron and the Healing Journey: An Astrological and Psychological Perspective Melanie Reinhart

Working With Astrology Michael Harding and Charles Harvey

Saturn: A New Look at an Old Devil Liz Greene

The Karmic Journey Judy Hall

Saturn In Transit Erin Sullivan